ILLUMINATED PIXELS

THE WHY, WHAT, AND HOW OF DIGITAL LIGHTING

Virginia Bowman Wissler

Course Technology PTR

A part of Cengage Learning

COURSE TECHNOLOGY
CENGAGE Learning·

Australia, Brazil, Japan, Korea, Mexico, Singapore, Spain, United Kingdom, United States

COURSE TECHNOLOGY
CENGAGE Learning·

**Illuminated Pixels: The Why, What, and
How of Digital Lighting**
Virginia Bowman Wissler

**Publisher and General Manager,
Course Technology PTR:**
Stacy L. Hiquet

Associate Director of Marketing:
Sarah Panella

Manager of Editorial Services:
Heather Talbot

Senior Marketing Manager:
Mark Hughes

Executive Editor:
Kevin Harreld

Project Editor:
Cathleen D. Small and Kim V. Benbow

Technical Reviewer:
MacDuff Knox

Copy Editor:
Caroline Roop

Interior Layout Tech:
Bill Hartman

Cover Designer:
Luke Fletcher

Indexer:
Valerie Haynes Perry

Proofreader:
Cathleen D. Small

For product information and technology assistance, contact us at
Cengage Learning Customer & Sales Support, 1-800-354-9706.

For permission to use material from this text or product,
submit all requests online at **cengage.com/permissions**.
Further permissions questions can be emailed to
permissionrequest@cengage.com.

All trademarks are the property of their respective owners.

All images © Cengage Learning unless otherwise noted.

Library of Congress Control Number: 2011926537

ISBN-13: 978-1-4354-5635-8

ISBN-10: 1-4354-5635-1

Course Technology, a part of Cengage Learning
20 Channel Center Street
Boston, MA 02210
USA

Cengage Learning is a leading provider of customized learning solutions
with office locations around the globe, including Singapore, the United
Kingdom, Australia, Mexico, Brazil, and Japan. Locate your local office at:
international.cengage.com/region.

Cengage Learning products are represented in Canada by Nelson
Education, Ltd.

For your lifelong learning solutions, visit **courseptr.com**.

Visit our corporate website at **cengage.com**.

Printed in Canada
1 2 3 4 5 6 7 14 13 12

*To my husband, John, and my two
lovely children, Preston and Tyler*

Acknowledgments

A well-known African proverb says, "It takes a village to raise a child." I can tell you that no large project, even a seemingly solo one such as authoring a book, ever comes to fruition without the help and support of many other people. I'd like to thank the many, many people who made this book possible. First, I'd like to thank my husband for his support in writing this book, which took several years to complete.

Several other people helped to make this book a reality. First is the team at Course Technology PTR: my acquisitions editor, Kevin Harreld, who worked with me on the timeline for the book and many other requests; the editors, Cathleen Small, Kim Benbow, and Caroline Roop; the layout artist, Bill Hartman, who had the patience of Job in working with me on the layout; and Mark Hughes and Luke Fletcher, who assisted with the cover, along with my husband, John Wissler, who designed it. In addition, Michael Ford, CG supervisor at Sony Pictures Imageworks and editor of the *Inspired* series of books, lined me up with the publisher. Without Mike, the book may have remained in the land of good intentions and unfinished projects.

I'd like to thank my interviewees: Rob Bredow, who, even though he is a very busy man, granted not one but two interviews and a review of the book; Mohit Kallianpur, who gave special insight into the lighting pipeline at Disney; Andrew Whitehurst, who responded to a ping through LinkedIn; and both Quentin Frost and Michael Kennedy, who I've known for many years and whose work and talent I respect. I'd like to thank my technical editor, MacDuff "Duffy" Knox, who I also have known for many years. Having Duffy look over the material to spot any errors was vastly reassuring.

I'd like to acknowledge Sande Scoredos. Sande was my former boss and the Executive Director of Training and Artist Development at Imageworks before she passed away in 2010. She gave me my first break into training and was unfailingly supportive of my abilities as a teacher. Those who knew Sande know she was a dynamo of a lady, and she is sorely missed.

I'd like to thank my students at SCAD-Atlanta, many of whom gave the book early review and feedback (an enthusiastic test audience) and who generously donated images for the book. Links to contributor sites can be found on the companion website, www.illuminated-pixels.com.

A special thanks to my friends in the industry who fielded my questions, helping to make sure the book was as accurate and up to date as possible. Along this line, I want to give a big thanks to the many people who have shared their knowledge and insight with me over the years. Most of what I learned was on the job, and much of the information presented in this book was gathered along the way from coworkers who were generous with their time and experience. I owe a tremendous debt to these people, and this debt of gratitude is my key motivator for teaching—I cannot repay these people, but I consider sharing knowledge with others "paying it forward" rather than paying it back.

About the Author

Virginia Bowman Wissler has more than a decade of experience in the 3D animation and visual effects fields, working first at Square LA (the gaming company that created the well-known *Final Fantasy* series) and later for seven years at Sony Pictures Imageworks, first as a Technical Director and later as Digital Instructor. Her experience as a Senior Technical Director on *Star Trek: Insurrection*, *Stuart Little*, *Hollow Man*, *Cast Away*, and *2012* and as Lead Technical Director on *Stuart Little 2* and *Matrix Reloaded* has given her years of hands-on experience making the highest-quality 3D imagery, working with and learning from the best in the industry. She later trained artists on films such as *The Polar Express*, *Monster House*, *Superman Returns*, *The Chronicles of Narnia*, and the Academy Award–winning *Spider-Man 2*. As a trainer, she developed her skills at writing course content and presenting information in a clear, well-organized, and interesting manner.

Virginia is presently a Professor of Visual Effects at Savannah College of Art and Design (SCAD), Atlanta campus. *3D World* rated SCAD as one of the top three digital media schools in the world, frequently placing students in major film-production houses, such as Pixar, Industrial Light & Magic, Rhythm & Hues, and Sony Pictures Imageworks. Virginia includes many of the concepts found in *Illuminated Pixels* as part of the lighting courses she teaches at SCAD, allowing her to further refine the clarity, presentation, and pertinence of the material. She is familiar with presenting material to a wide variety of skill and experience levels, covering topics from general concepts to specific techniques.

About the Technical Editor

MacDuff Knox was born and raised in Canada. He has a background in stage lighting, acting, and computer consulting. After a number of years in Toronto working as an actor, he changed careers and found a job as a visual effects artist at Rhythm & Hues Studios in Los Angeles. He worked for several years at R&H, primarily on commercials, and then moved to Sony Pictures Imageworks, where he spent the next 10 years working on visual effects films, such as *Stuart Little*, *Harry Potter and the Sorcerer's Stone*, *The Polar Express*, and *Beowulf*. He later moved into the animation world as a Senior Technical Director at Disney Feature Animation, where he continues to work, contributing to films such as *Tangled* and *Wreck-It Ralph*. His complete filmography can be found at http://www.imdb.com/name/nm0461649/.

Contents

Part I
Foundations (Introduction to the "How")

Chapter 2
Shadows...**41**

Part II
The Goals of Lighting (the "Why")

Chapter 5
Goal 3: Directing the Eye 117

Chapter 6
Goals 4–6: Creating the Illusion of Dimension 133

Chapter 7
Goals 7–10: Providing Cohesiveness and Visual Interest 157

Part III
The Properties of Light (the "What")

Chapter 8
Light Placement 179

Chapter 11
Light Color...227

Part IV
Technique (More "How")

Chapter 12
Three-Point Lighting and Beyond 253

Chapter 13
Camera Essentials 291

Chapter 16
Global Illumination 369

Chapter 17
Image-Based Lighting and More..401

Chapter 18
Multi-Pass Rendering **429**

Part V
Interviews (with the Pros)

Introduction

"We are affected and defined by light. Light is the most important tool we have to work with, not only as cinematographers, but as people."

—Laszlo Kovacs, Cinematographer

ABOUT THE BOOK

The premise of this book is that great lighting comes from an understanding of three basic components. Each of these areas is important, much like a three-legged stool. We all know what happens if one of the legs of a three-legged stool is wobbly or short. These three areas are:

1. The aesthetics of the image
2. The physics of light
3. Appropriate technique

I coin these three areas the why, what, and how of lighting, respectively. (Catchy, isn't it?)

"Why" is the question *"Why are you lighting?"* and refers to the aesthetic intent of your lights, defined by 10 goals of lighting discussed in the book. These goals of lighting underlie great cinematography, photography, and even paintings. *Illuminated Pixels* shows the importance of these foundational principles to the modern digital lighter, giving concrete examples of how these principles are used in digital lighting today.

"What" asks the question *"What are the physical properties of light that you are trying to imitate?"* Without knowledge of real lights, you may inadvertently create illumination that appears odd or unnatural. The book discusses the properties of light not just in a theoretical sense, but with further discussion of the digital tools that re-create them.

"How" asks the question *"How will you accomplish this?"* It is the last question to ask, and it refers to the specific technique you will use. The mention of appropriate technique is important because you will want to know a variety of techniques and their pros and cons, and pick which one is best suited for the task at hand. Technique is, after all, going to get the job done, and mastering it is an essential skill for any accomplished digital artist.

***Illuminated Pixels* offers a balanced look at all the components that make up great lighting.** By discussing first concept and then how concept is applied through specific techniques, each of these important areas—artistry, real-world physics, and computer technology—is integrated in a practical, useful way, giving the reader real tools and knowledge needed to master the art of digital lighting.

WHY THIS BOOK WAS WRITTEN

The number-one reason why this book was written is because there is a need for it. Although literally dozens of books and DVDs cover 3D animation, only a tiny number address digital lighting. This gap is remarkable considering that no 3D image comes to completion without the necessary steps of lighting, shading, and rendering. Tossing in a few lights just to see things is easy, but making it look good—or in some cases photoreal—well, that is another matter entirely. In fact, it turns out to be rather difficult to do. As Sharon Calahan, Director of Photography at Pixar, eloquently puts it, "It is not enough to simply illuminate the scene."

Mastering digital lighting takes some know-how and experience, and it helps immensely to have training or reference material. I wanted to make another book available so that people had more choice in material on the subject. I also believe that much of the existing material focuses too heavily on technique. Too often the aesthetics of lighting and understanding the physics of light are given only a cursory nod, if mentioned at all. This is not at all to say that learning technique is a bad thing. In fact, knowing technique is essential to great lighting, and this book will cover a great deal of technique. You must know more than just technique, however, to produce great imagery. Knowing technique alone doesn't make you a great lighter; it makes you a great technician. To create compelling imagery, you need a foundation in all three areas: the aesthetic (the realm of imagination), the physical (the realm of the real), and the technical (the realm of the computer).

Illuminated Pixels presents many digital-lighting practices and techniques that are difficult to learn outside of the studio setting in which they are developed. Often the people who are developing the latest techniques do not have the time to pass that knowledge on to anyone other than their coworkers, and then it's back to work! Because of this, many great approaches to lighting are unknown or even unavailable to artists not working in a professional studio. Sometimes these studios use tools that either are not available in common software (known as "off-the-shelf" software) or are poorly documented. This book seeks to bridge that gap, presenting techniques that are the standard fare used by advanced lighters, along with discussion and instruction that may not be commonly available. Many special thanks to friends and associates in the CG image-making community who were generous with their time and energy, offering suggestions and feedback. Without them, the book would not be as current and comprehensive.

The inspiration for this book came many years ago with a short series of classes I taught at Sony Pictures Imageworks, entitled "Lighting Concepts." The course, consisting of eight one-hour lectures, was originally designed to teach core concepts of digital lighting to non-lighters. Thus, it presented the material in a "from the ground up" fashion. The series ended up being attended by many experienced lighters as well and was adapted to contain information of interest to these advanced artists. Although this book is greatly expanded from its humble beginning, the premise remains the same—to have appeal and interest to novice and experienced digital lighters alike. *Illuminated Pixels* can be used as a course book for beginners, as well as a reference book for those more experienced.

The goals of the book are:

◆ To teach the fundamentals that underlie great lighting

◆ To serve as a reference book for experienced digital lighters

◆ To offer tips and techniques not readily available to those outside of a studio environment

HOW TO USE THIS BOOK

The book is organized into four main Parts, which correspond roughly to the why, what, and how, and concludes with an interviews section.

- **Part I** contains foundational material, covers basic technique, and is a must-read for new lighters. More experienced lighters may also want to skim over these chapters. The topics are covered in depth and may contain a surprising amount of useful information.
- **Part II** covers in detail the goals of lighting. I am such a believer in the importance of these goals that I think everyone should read these chapters. Advanced lighters can read them for enjoyment and as a reminder.
- **Part III** looks at the physics of real lights and goes into a fair amount of depth. The properties are related to digital lighting.
- **Part IV** continues with techniques, from intermediate to advanced, picking up for the most part where the chapters in Part I leave off.
- **Part V** contains industry interviews, covering topics from workflow to industry trends. Those curious about the industry, including what it is like and how to break in, can find out from the people who know.

Because the book contains such a wide variety of information and goes from beginning to advanced, it is laid out to make skimming and referencing easy. Each chapter has an introduction with its main topics outlined. Read this to get an idea of whether you want to read the chapter. Each chapter introduction also has a mini table of contents so you can quickly find the section that interests you.

Within each chapter, skimming is made easy because important sentences at the start of key paragraphs are bolded. You can actually read the chapter by just reading the bolded sentences (try it out, you'll see), stopping at portions that interest you for more in-depth reading. Additionally, summary boxes throughout the chapter contain important points, something like the chapter's CliffsNotes. The end of each chapter also has a brief outline of key points to remember.

The book has a companion website, www.illuminated-pixels.com. The website will be constantly evolving with examples, tips, links to other interesting sites, and a forum for discussion. Although the book is not software-specific, the sample scenes by necessity do use specific software. In many cases, these scenes are offered up simply to be explored. You can learn a great deal just by looking at other people's scene files. Other times, the website may contain instructions for how to use certain tools, especially if the tool is not well documented elsewhere. The website also contains additional related material that didn't make it into the book, such as information on cameras, materials, and compositing techniques. These topics are important to know, but not everything can be in one book, after all. If you find it useful, be sure to check back for updates and new information.

As you read the book and look at the website, you may have suggestions on how to improve them, or other examples and techniques you wish to share with the digital lighting community. All suggestions are welcome.

Illuminated Pixels **presents topics more or less from beginning to advanced throughout the course of the book.** I say "more or less" because some topics are delved into in great detail right away. The book begins with some technique—the "how of lighting"—because if pure concept is taught first and students don't have a way to apply it or relate it specifically to their subject, then much of the discussion is lost. For this reason, the chapters in Part I will get you started in the fundamentals of digital lighting. These chapters will give you a technical foundation with which to apply the concepts taught in later chapters. Specifically, after reading these chapters (and some of your own software-specific documentation), you will be able to do the exercises found at the end of later chapters, if you so choose.

Because the topics found in Part I are foundational, don't be fooled into thinking you must have read it all before or that it is all simple. Even on a basic subject, such as light types, Chapter 1 presents tips on usage that aren't commonly found in other training material. Chapter 2, covering shadows, goes into a great deal of detail with the idea that it is better to begin with good habits than to break bad ones later. (If Chapter 2 gets too beefy for newer lighters, just read the first half of it.) I hope even more experienced lighters will find choice tidbits in Part I and that beginning lighters will find useful and clear instruction on how to get started.

PART I

FOUNDATIONS
(INTRODUCTION TO THE "HOW")

"You must always continue to be a student, to continue to learn."
—Vittorio Storaro, Cinematographer

Figure 1.1 *Toy Story* was the first full 3D film ever made. At the time of this render, technology had many limitations, yet talented artists were still able to create imagery that holds up by today's standards.

Chapter 1
First Things First

"Begin at the beginning," the King said, very gravely, "and

go on till you come to the end, then stop."

—*Alice in Wonderland*
by Lewis Carroll, Victorian author and poet

This chapter covers a variety of 3D concepts that the digital lighter should learn first, including light types, rendering, and simple lighting techniques. While these concepts should be learned early on, not all of them are "basic." Material in this chapter is primarily geared to a beginning to intermediate user and can be used as a reference by an advanced user. Many of the concepts and techniques in this chapter take practice to master; therefore, the information may take some time to sink in, so start with the easier topics that make sense, practice as many of the good workflow techniques as you can, and re-read sections as needed. You will likely refer to this chapter many times. If you have some experience with lighting, on the other hand, the chapter may fill in gaps and answer some questions you may have had.

1.1 GETTING STARTED

This section describes an easy setup and workflow for placing lights that is smooth and will allow you to concentrate on how you want the scene to look. This section is introductory. If you have experience with using 3D packages and lighting, then you may want to skip it. If you are somewhat new to 3D or lighting in 3D, then I'd recommend reading on. The workflow presented here is by no means a rule. If you are an experienced lighter, you no doubt have a workflow in place. If not, give these suggestions a try and feel free to adopt any of those that will work for you.

1.1.1 Setup for Placing Lights

When placing lights in your scene, a few workflow techniques will help you preview your lights, so you can see roughly how they will affect the scene before you even render. This will make the task of placing them faster and more efficient.

Most 3D animation packages default to having four panels that view the scene: the three orthographic views of top, side, and front and one perspective view. All four views preview a wireframe of your objects. While good for many tasks, this default setup is, in fact, often not the most ideal for lighting.

A variation of the default four-panel setup that is useful for lighting has at least two perspective views open, sometimes more. One perspective view is set to render the scene. We'll call this camera the "rendercam." This camera should be carefully composed to view the scene from the desired position, and it may be animated. You will not want to move this camera. It is a good idea to lock it so you don't accidentally move it. If you are working on a group project in which the animation is finished, the rendercam will already be created and keyed along with any animation in the scene and provided to you along with the animation. If starting from scratch or working on your own project, you will want to create a separate render camera from the beginning. Be sure to name this rendering camera something descriptive rather than leaving a default name like "perspective" or "persp2." Naming the camera will keep you from having to guess or hunt and peck through cameras to find which one is intended to render the scene. Make sure your rendering camera is set before you begin lighting.

Since the rendering camera will be fixed, you will need another free-floating camera that can be moved about the scene. Moving this other camera will not interfere with your render camera's position and framing. Use this additional perspective camera to see the relationship of objects to one another, to the main render camera, and to the lights. I often use the default perspective camera for this purpose.

Depending on what kind of light you are adding, you will likely have other views open as well. These may be any of the orthographic views and a view looking through the light you are currently positioning. Yes, in almost all packages you can look through most lights as if they were a camera, but more on that in the next section. A modified four-panel setup for lighting may be as follows: (1) one panel having a free-floating perspective camera, (2) another camera looking through the camera that will render the scene, (3) the third panel being a view from the light you are currently positioning if this light is a spotlight or directional light, and (4) any other view of your choice (Figure 1.2).

Figure 1.2 Sample layout for setting up lights.

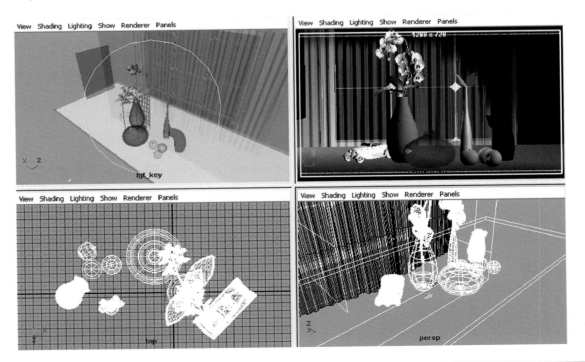

1.1.2 INTRODUCTION TO THE VIRTUAL 3D CAMERA

The 3D camera is a virtual representation of a real camera. Like a real camera, the scene is captured from the point of view of the 3D camera. The virtual 3D camera has many settings that imitate the behavior of a real camera. Some of these are found in the camera itself; others are found in overall render options. Chapter 13, "Cameras and Film," continues with an in-depth look at cameras. Here we touch upon a few basics that will help you get started lighting.

Before you begin lighting, you will want to establish how the camera will view the scene. How a scene is lit is determined in part by what you actually see. Most of the wonderfully lit scenes you see in film look great from the exact angle of the camera, but heaven forbid they are viewed from any other position! Once you have placed objects in your scene, you will want to adjust the rendering camera for proper framing and composition. *Framing* refers to where the borders of your image lie, while *composition* is created by the placement and spatial relationships of the objects within the frame.

Obviously, placement of the camera will hugely determine how the objects in view are composed. The art of camera placement and motion has been well refined for decades by the cinematographer. For the most part, when just starting out you will simply move the camera around until you like what you see, often tweaking the positions of objects and animation as you go. Later on, a study of common camera moves and positions will help to refine your skills with the camera.

The width and height of the final image will affect how objects are framed. The ratio of width to height is known as the *aspect ratio*. Deciding on the width and height of your renders is an important creative decision if you have the luxury of having any size you desire. When working on a film, the exact width and height is generally decided by someone else. If the animation is your own, you can choose the format that you feel will best show the action or objects in your animation. You should decide on format very early on, as it will affect how all the objects and the camera itself are positioned. The aspect ratio is a global setting—in most software packages, whatever aspect ratio you decide will affect all the cameras in the scene.

A bit of setup to the rendering camera's panel will make the task of placing lights vastly easier. First, set the render camera's panel to preview the scene in shaded rather than wireframe mode (Figure 1.3). Next, and even more importantly, set it to *preview the actual lights in the scene* (Figure 1.4). With this setup you will be able to see how the lights will illuminate the scene before you even render. This is certainly a rough approximation, but it's better than no approximation. Many packages even preview shadow placement. When you are deciding on the placement of your lights, keep an eye constantly on the rendercam's shaded, lit panel.

TIP

If you are placing a light that has a low intensity and is difficult to see in the interactive shaded mode, temporarily turn up the intensity of this light and maybe even give it a bright color like cyan in order to better preview it. Once the light is placed, readjust its color and intensity back to its original level.

Figure 1.3 (Left) Wireframe preview gives little information as to how the scene will look once it is rendered.

Figure 1.4 (Right) Previewing with shaded, lit mode, with the camera's border displayed, gives a much better idea of how the scene will look.

 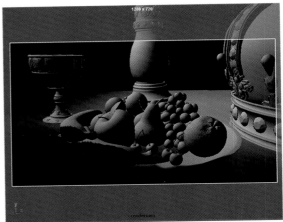

Displaying the borders of the rendering area in the rendercam's panel will also help when composing and lighting the image. The width and height of the panel are generally different than the width and height of the rendered image. I like to know exactly what is going to be in my render, and displaying the borders helps me to know exactly what is in frame and what isn't. This feature is available in most packages. It's generally an option in the camera itself and may be called something like "display resolution" or "show camera reticle."

PANEL SETUP FOR THE RENDER CAMERA:
- ✓ Use shaded mode.
- ✓ Display the effects of the lights.
- ✓ Display the borders of the rendering area.

And remember: While positioning almost any light, keep an eye on the shaded render camera's panel.

1.2 BASIC COMPUTER-GENERATED LIGHT TYPES

Almost every package has six basic light types: point light, spotlight, directional light, area light, ambient light, and volume light. You will want to be familiar with each of these light types. Most artists with even a small introduction to 3D lighting have learned about at least some CG (computer-generated) light types in order to add lights to their scenes. The topic of light types is deceptively simple, however. It's very common for new and intermediate lighters to use the various light types incorrectly, either using a light not well suited for the situation or not using it to its full advantage. This section not only defines the various light types, but even more importantly discusses situations for which the light type is best suited and tips on usage. Both beginning and intermediate users will likely find useful information here. This section ends with a comparison chart.

Two other light types that are increasingly common are *environment lights* and *light-emitting geometry*. Being more advanced in usage, these lights are covered in Chapter 16, "Global Illumination," and Chapter 17, "Image-Based Lighting and More."

1.2.1 POINT LIGHT

Point lights cast rays outward radially in all directions from an infinitely small central source. The digital point light source has zero dimensions (0D); it has no width, or depth, or height. Since the origin of the light rays is infinitely small, the light rays produced are perfectly radial, emanating outward like the spokes from a wheel with no criss-crossing or intersecting (Figure 1.5). Point lights cast illumination in all directions (Figure 1.6 and Figure 1.7). For this reason, the rotation of the light is irrelevant. Only the location in space determines how the light will shine into the scene.

Point lights imitate light sources that shine radially in all directions, like a star or a bare bulb. However, *not all lights that shine radially in all directions in the real world are best imitated by the CG point light.* For example, even though the sun is a star, it's imitated best by a directional light rather than a point light, and a bulb that resides in a shaded lamp or wall sconce is better imitated with one or two spotlights rather than a point light (for why, read the section in this chapter that discusses each type of light).

Point lights are often overused by new lighters. There is a tendency to simply plop point lights into the scene and to turn on their shadows. However, unless you need light radiating in all directions, you don't need a point light. For example, if illumination is needed only on one side of the light (for example, a light that is placed over the scene), then a point light isn't the best option; a spotlight is a better choice (Figures 1.8 and 1.9). Why *not* just use a point light? Unless light is needed in all directions, casting it in all directions results in unwanted render calculations. This is especially true when shadows are turned on.

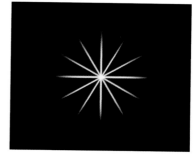

Figure 1.5 Point light.

Figure 1.6 A render using a point light illustrating light and shadows in all directions.

Figure 1.7 This abstract image uses a point light to illuminate behind the gold bars. (*Image by Luke Heathcock.*)

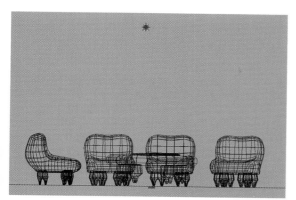

Figure 1.8 In this scene, a point light isn't the best choice, as light isn't needed in all directions.

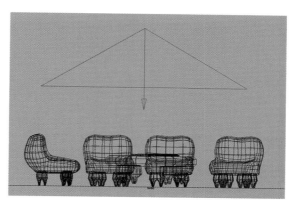

Figure 1.9 A spotlight is the better choice for this scene.

Figure 1.10 Image of a hotspot created by a point light.

When using point lights, you will want to eliminate unwanted shadow calculations. If a point light has shadows turned on, it will by default calculate shadows in all directions. In some cases, light is needed in all directions but the shadows are only needed in one or a few directions. Point lights can turn shadow calculations off in certain directions with some types of shadows. When possible, it's good to turn off unnecessary calculations to speed up render times. How to optimize point light shadows is covered in the next chapter, Section 2.5.2, "Optimizing Mapped Shadows."

Point lights are prone to creating hot centers of illumination, called *hotspots*, on surfaces to which they are very near. Hotspots (Figure 1.10) crop up especially if the light has attenuation (decreases in intensity with distance). A simple and obvious fix is to move the point light away from the surface a bit.

WHEN AND HOW TO USE POINT LIGHTS

When Is Using a Point Light a Good Choice?

✓ When you need to see light cast radially in *all directions* in the scene.

For other lighting situations, you can generally substitute another light type like a spotlight or directional light.

Tips for Using Point Lights:

- If shadows aren't needed in all directions, turn off unnecessary shadow calculations (Section 2.5.2) if possible.
- Watch for and eliminate hotspots.
- In many cases, a point source can be imitated with a spotlight or spotlights instead.

1.2.2 DIRECTIONAL LIGHT

***Directional* (sometimes called *linear* or *distant*) lights cast parallel rays in a specified direction throughout the entire scene.** The rays are perfectly parallel and never intersect (Figure 1.11). By default, the illumination from a directional light will cover the entire scene, regardless of the light's position. (See Figures 1.12 and 1.13 for examples of directional light.) The icon of the light could even be underneath the subjects being lit. Only the rotation of the light is important.

The distinctive features of the directional light are:

◆ The light rays are perfectly parallel
◆ The light floods the entire scene

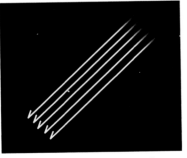

Figure 1.11 Directional light.

Figure 1.12 Render showing the parallel light and shadows from a directional light.

Figure 1.13 Directional lights can be good choices for clear sunlight as illustrated in this image by Bryce Stine.

Directional lights are sometimes called "distant lights" because they imitate light that is coming from very far away. When a light source is extremely far away, the rays finally reaching the subject are near parallel (see Figure 1.14). Rays pointing in other directions than directly at the subject have scattered off long before reaching the subject. While the rays aren't in fact perfectly parallel, they are so close that for all intents and purposes we can consider them so. A real-world example of a distant light is the sun. While the sun is spherical in nature and massive like an area light, the light reaching the earth comes from so far away that the rays reaching us look parallel. A directional light can be a good choice to imitate light that is distant and uniform, such as sunlight on a clear day.

Directional lights are also well suited to the task of flooding the scene with a low level of illumination to brighten shadow areas. Light that brightens ("fills in") the shadows is known as *fill light*. Directional lights can make good fill lights, especially if they don't need shadows. Another situation that is a good candidate for a directional light is if you want to provide fast preliminary lighting. Directional lights can quickly light a scene because they are easy to place (only rotation is important), and they can illuminate the entire scene.

Directional lights can be problematic with some shadow types, such as depth-mapped shadows (discussed in Chapter 2, "Shadows"). When you need more shadow control, a spotlight may be a better option for you.

Because a directional light casts parallel rays, its illumination will be constant across any given plane. In some cases this may be desired, and in other cases this may be too uniform and bland. In contrast, illumination from a source such as a point or spotlight will vary across planar surfaces, due to the changing angle of the radial rays. Figures 1.15 through 1.18 illustrate the visual differences between parallel and radial rays.

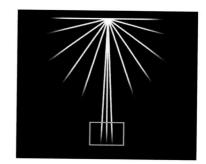

Figure 1.14 Lights that are very far away contribute near-parallel rays.

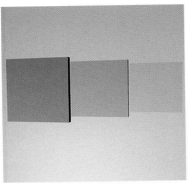

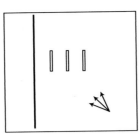

Figure 1.16 Side view diagram of Figure 1.15.

Figure 1.15 A scene of planar primitives lit with one point light placed in the front and center. All geometry has the same lambert shader, and the light has no attenuation. The cubes closest to the point light darken due to the light striking them at a more glancing angle.

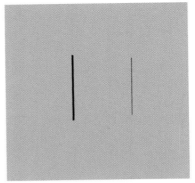

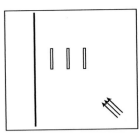

Figure 1.18 Side view diagram of Figure 1.17.

Figure 1.17 Shows the same scene, rendered from the same view, but lit with a directional light instead of a radial light. Since all front faces of the cubes are parallel and the light rays are parallel, the light intensity doesn't vary across the surfaces of the planes.

WHEN AND HOW TO USE DIRECTIONAL LIGHTS

When Is Using a Directional Light a Good Choice?

✓ When the light you are imitating is very far and...

✓ You have a large area of your scene to flood with light, or...

✓ You need a shadow-less fill that covers a large area, or...

✓ You want to quickly add light to a scene for preview purposes.

Directional lights work well when you wish to flood the entire scene with light from a certain direction.

Tips for Using Directional Lights:

• In some cases directional lights don't work well with depth-mapped shadows.

• Keep in mind the illumination from a directional light is very uniform, which may or may not be desired.

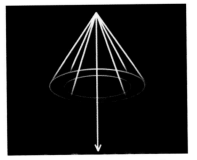

Figure 1.19 Spotlight.

1.2.3 SPOTLIGHT

Like point lights, spotlights also cast radial rays from an infinitely small point (0D) (Figure 1.19). The difference between a point light and a spotlight is that the illumination of the spotlight is confined within a conical area. The center of this cone is oriented down an axis representing the spotlight's direction. This axis is the z-axis of the light. Similar to point lights, spotlights contribute perfectly hard light due to the fact their source has no dimension. Position, rotation, and cone angle are all important in defining the effect of the spotlight (see Figures 1.20 and 1.21).

Figure 1.20 (Left) A render of a spotlight showing confined illumination and radial rays.

Figure 1.21 (Right) This scene uses a spotlight as the primary light source. (*Image by Leandro Ibraim.*)

The cone angle of a spotlight is most often defined in degrees. For example, 180 degrees is a perfect hemisphere (1/2 sphere) of light. In addition to the primary cone angle, a second cone angle is used to create both an inner and outer cone. The area between the cone angles is known as the *penumbra* (Figure 1.22). Within the inner cone, the intensity of the light is at 100%, while outside the outer cone the intensity is at 0%. In between the intensity interpolates (runs a gradient between the two values) smoothly. Depending on the light shader, the user may set the inner and outer angles independently or the penumbra angle and either the inner or outer cone. Spotlight shaders often have an additional parameter that focuses the intensity of the light on the very center of the spotlight. In this case, the illumination within the inner cone isn't uniform but rather is brightest in the very center, along the z-axis of the light. Depending on the light shader, this parameter may be called different names such as "dropoff" or "beam distribution." It typically takes somewhat high numbers such as five or greater to see much of an effect. You may need to increase the light's intensity or broaden the cone angle when setting this parameter.

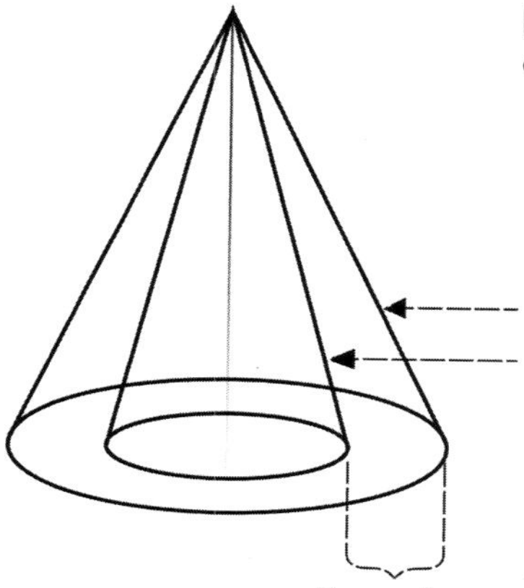

Figure 1.22 Diagram showing cone angle and penumbra.

Outer cone
Inner cone

Penumbra

Spotlights look unrealistic with no penumbra set (Figure 1.23). Be sure to give the edge of the spotlight, if you see it, some softness by setting the penumbra to a value other than zero (Figure 1.24). The use of both dropoff and penumbra together will create a smooth gradient from the center to edges of the spotlight (Figure 1.25).

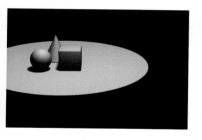

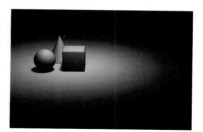

Figure 1.23 (Left) A spotlight with no penumbra set.

Figure 1.24 (Center) A spotlight with a penumbra set.

Figure 1.25 (Right) A spotlight with both penumbra and dropoff.

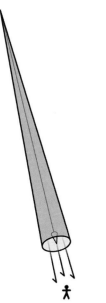

Figure 1.26 A faraway spotlight with a narrow cone angle can imitate a directional light.

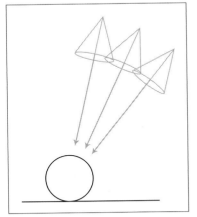

Figure 1.27 Multiple spotlights imitating a single area light.

Spotlights have the advantage of being highly controllable. Their illumination can be both aimed in a particular direction and confined to a certain volume. In addition, the shadows cast by spotlights can be carefully managed. (Chapter 2, "Shadows," covers shadow management in detail.) Because of these advantages, spotlights are commonly used in animation production. Spotlights imitate real-world lights that have their light confined to a cone, such as beams from a car light, flashlight, and stage spotlights. However, spotlights can be used for many types of lights that aren't spotlights in real life, often replacing other light types such as point and directional lights.

A spotlight can be used to imitate a directional light by simply pulling the spotlight far back from its subject. And I mean *far*. Remember that directional lights are imitating lights that are far away, and that is exactly what you are doing with the spotlight when you pull it far from the subject. The farther the light is from the source, the more parallel are the rays reaching the subject (Figure 1.26). The advantage of using a spotlight to imitate a distant light rather than a directional light is that the illumination of the spotlight can be confined to a limited area, and the shadows from a spotlight can be controlled more easily. Be sure to reduce the cone angle to just where you need light.

Multiple spotlights can also imitate area lights if you place them in a row or grid (see Figure 1.27). The advantage of this technique is that it typically has a shorter render time than an area light. The disadvantage is there are more lights to manage. This technique is used less often now that faster machines have made the use of area lights more feasible, but it's still handy to know. Since this technique requires more management of lights, discussion of it is saved for Chapter 15, "Tricks of the Trade."

When previewing a spotlight in the interactive viewer, it is sometimes helpful to scale the icon of the light so that it's large enough to clearly see how the cone angle covers the scene. Scaling the icon usually has no effect on the light's illumination, though occasionally it may, so keep that in mind.

WHEN AND HOW TO USE SPOTLIGHTS

When Is Using a Spotlight a Good Choice?

✓ When you are imitating a cone of hard light, or...

✓ You want to confine your light calculations to a finite area (which is often).

Tips for Using Spotlights:

- To imitate a linear light, pull the spotlight back to a great distance from the subject.
- To imitate an area light, use several spotlights around the subject.
- It helps to scale the light in order to preview the area contained inside the cone.

1.2.4 Area Light

Area lights cast light outward from a user-defined geometric shape (Figure 1.28). In most software packages, this shape is a 2D plane. A true area light will cast illumination as if there are many, many small lights along the area's surface. For this reason, the computation time required can be extremely long. Area lights emit scattered and intersecting rays (Figure 1.29). Position, rotation, and geometric description (both scale and shape) are all important considerations when placing an area light.

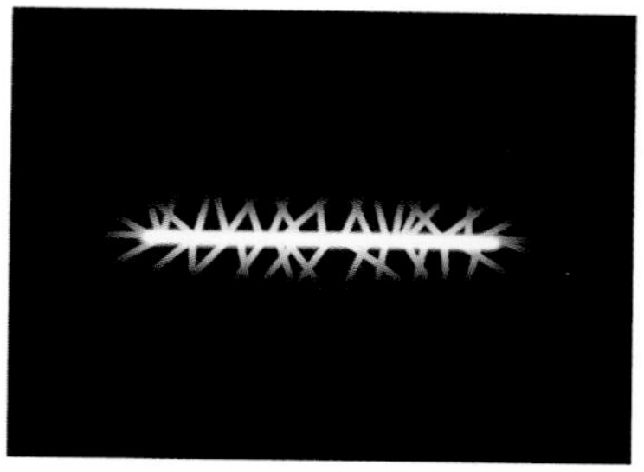

Area lights imitate all sources of diffused and scattered light. Scattered light is known as *soft light*. Soft light typically comes from large light sources (Figures 1.30 and 1.31). Soft light also may be created by bouncing light off a large matte surface or passing it through a diffuser like a sheer cloth (Figure 1.31), practices commonly employed by photographers. Soft light is discussed extensively in Chapter 10, "Property 3: Light Diffusion," but at this point it is important to know that soft light has a unique appearance.

The three distinct visual characteristics of soft light are:

1. Shadows cast by soft light are blurred and indistinct.
2. Specular highlights, when visible, are large and often less bright than highlights from non-soft light sources.
3. The light from a soft light source will tend to "wrap around" more than one half of the objects it illuminates, transitioning gradually from lit to unlit areas (Figures 1.35 and Figure 1.36).

Area lights are unique in that they are the only basic light type to provide all three of these visual characteristics.

The larger the area light, the more it will display its distinctive qualities. Conversely, the smaller and/or farther away the area light is, the less it will display these qualities.

Figure 1.28 Area light.

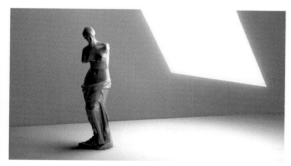

Figure 1.29 A render using an area light as the primary light source. Notice the indistinct shadow and large highlight.

Figure 1.30 Fluorescent bulbs are long tubes, emitting scattered light.

Figure 1.31 Photographers often create soft light with diffusers and reflectors.

Figure 1.32 (Left) Small area light.

Figure 1.33 (Center) Medium area light.

Figure 1.34 (Right) Large area light.

Figure 1.35 (Left) The illumination from a small area light doesn't "wrap around" the subject significantly and transitions abruptly from lit to unlit areas much like the illumination from a spot, point, or directional light.

Figure 1.36 (Right) A large area light illuminates more of the subject, as the light wraps past half hemisphere. Notice how much more of the statue is receiving light in this figure as compared to Figure 1.35 and how the transition from lit to unlit areas is more gradual.

Figures 1.32 through 1.34 show the effects of scaling the area light upon highlight size, shadow softness, and light wrap. Figure 1.32 has the smallest area light, while Figure 1.34 has the largest area light. The intensity of the area light has been adjusted to maintain a roughly equal luminance in the three images. Notice the highlight becomes dimmer as it becomes larger.

Theoretically, a large digital area light will have more points of light placed along it than a small area light. This results in longer render times and brighter illumination. However, now is a good time to mention that different software packages calculate area lights in different ways. Not all digital area lights are "true" area lights. Since a true area light is very time-consuming to calculate, many applications perform various optimizations that speed up the render of the light, usually at the cost of accuracy. For example, the area light in Maya's software renderer correctly calculates the soft shadow and large highlight, but it doesn't correctly calculate light wrap. Additionally, depending on the software, the area light may or may not become brighter and take longer to render with increasing scale. A bit of experimentation with the package of your choice will let you know how your area light will respond.

Before using an area light, consider whether the light you are imitating is a soft light. Does the light emit from a tube or an area? Has it passed through a diffuser (like a lampshade or curtain), or has it bounced off another object? Does your light need soft shadows, large highlights, and gradual terminators? If so, then an area light may be a good choice for you. Also consider how much render time you are willing to deal with. The studio or project you are working on will generally have guidelines in this area. Some projects may make extensive use of area lights, other projects may cheat their look by faster means such as tricks in the shaders, and still other projects may use environment lights or emissive geometry instead. The tradeoff is generally quality and/or ease of use versus render time.

Area lights can be a bit trickier to use than the other light types mentioned. A few tips will help you to use them most effectively.

First, you will want to find out how your area light handles light intensity. As noted, some area lights change in intensity with scale, while others don't. Additionally, some area lights attenuate (decrease intensity) with distance, while others don't. You will need to see how your area light behaves in order to use it, or you may be mystified when your area light completely blows out the scene with too much light or, conversely, doesn't seem to be casting any light at all.

Secondly, when using an area light, you will want to pay special attention to its size and distance from the subject. If your area light is very small and/or far away, then it's going to lose much of its soft-light look and may have little advantage over another light type, such as a spotlight or directional light. The farther your area light is from the subject, the larger you will need to scale it in order to obtain the same soft-light look. In cases where a larger area light means a longer render time, it's important to keep the area as near (and thus as small) as is feasible (Figures 1.37 and 1.38).

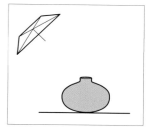

Figure 1.37 Large and near—good scale and placement of this area light in order to achieve soft light.

NOTE

Some lighters (and projects for that matter) use area lights liberally, even using small/faraway area lights to imitate hard lights, like the sun. Other lighters will keep their use of area lights to a minimum in order to keep render times as low as possible.

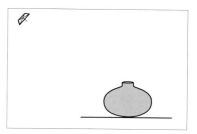

Figure 1.38 Small and far—an area light this small and far away will cast relatively hard light and could be replaced by a point or spotlight.

Finally, check to see if your area light is casting light from one or both sides. Most area lights have the option to cast light from either one or both sides of the plane. This feature helps to optimize the light, since often you only need illumination from one. If this feature is available, be sure to use it. Also, if this feature is available and turned on by default, be sure you know which side is emitting the light in order to avoid frustration.

WHEN AND HOW TO USE AREA LIGHTS

When is Using an Area Light a Good Choice?

✓ When imitating a soft light source.

Tips for Using Area Lights:

- Pay careful attention to how your software handles intensity for area lights.
- Cast light from only one side of planar area lights whenever possible.
- Be aware that a small, faraway area light will have little soft-light advantage.
- If low render time is the top priority, use sparingly.

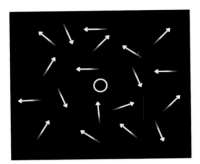

Figure 1.39 Ambient light.

Figure 1.40 Extremely scattered light produces an evenly lit, nearly shadowless image. The light seems to come from everywhere and nowhere, with no particular directionality.

1.2.5 AMBIENT

Ambient is a type of CG light that uniformly illuminates a surface (Figure 1.39). In contrast to other lights that cast light outward from the light source, the illumination from an ambient light comes from no particular direction. This means that moving, rotating, or scaling the light will have no effect on its illumination, nor will changing the surface orientation make any difference.

CG ambient light is meant to imitate light that is 100% uniformly scattered throughout the environment, and thus reaches the surface from essentially all directions. A real-world example is the illumination found in a shadowed area on an overcast day. In this case the light has been completely scattered by atmospheric and weather conditions. Indoor environments with artificial sources also have ambient light caused by the reflection of light off the many surfaces in the room, bouncing enough times so that its direction becomes unclear. Real-world ambient light has little to no sense of directionality and produces almost no shadow (Figure 1.40).

NOTE
The term "ambient light" has a different meaning for photographers than for digital artists. Digital artists use the term "ambient" to describe uniformly scattered light. Photographers, on the other hand, use the term to mean *any existing light* not added by the photographer for the purpose of taking pictures, including both scattered and direct light, as in this photograph of cows.

CG ambient light is a cheat: The light isn't actually bounced around the scene or diffused within an atmosphere. The problem with CG ambient light is that it isn't a very good cheat. The surfaces are lit *too* uniformly, with no shaping or shadowing at all, a situation that doesn't occur in life and doesn't look correct. CG ambient light causes objects to lose their sense of volume, appearing flat and two-dimensional, as in Figure 1.41.

When and how to use CG ambient light depends on what techniques are employed when using the light. The old rule of thumb regarding ambient light has been simple: Do not use it, due to its lack of realism. However, *this is not true*! Read on to see why.

Ambient light can be successfully used when combined with an ambient shadow. You may have heard that ambient light doesn't have a shadow, but indeed *it does*. I noted real-world ambient light is *nearly* shadowless, but it does have one. In life, all light shadows. The shadow from fully scattered light has a very different appearance than other shadows, however. Like the light creating it, the shadow from ambient light falls in no particular direction. Instead, shadows occur where objects are in close proximity to each other.

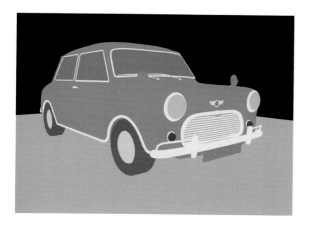

Figure 1.41 (Left) CG render of a car lit with one ambient light only. The 3D model looks like a flat drawing of shapes with little sense of volume.

Figure 1.42 (Right) CG render of a car lit with one ambient light combined with an occlusion shadow. Notice the return of a sense of volume and the detail in areas like the hubcaps and front grate.

Figure 1.43 (Left) This scene is lit by only two lights: a directional light and an ambient light. The ambient light in this scene is flat and unrealistic.

Figure 1.44 (Right) The same scene with the same two lights, only now the ambient light is shadowed with occlusion. The result is much improved and could be a useful, if simple, lighting design.

One digital technique that will calculate the type of shadow produced by ambient light is known as *ambient occlusion*. How to add and use ambient occlusion is covered in detail in Chapter 16, "Global Illumination"; here we examine only how it affects a scene visually. The rule "do not use ambient" came from the days before occlusion. Ambient light with an occlusion shadow produces a much more realistic result and can often be used to good effect. Compare Figure 1.41 to 1.42 and Figure 1.43 to 1.44 for examples.

Without occlusion shadow techniques, ambient light should generally be used only at very low intensities, if at all. A very low-level ambient may be used to lighten the darkest areas of your scene, in combination with other fill lights. Too much ambient light without ambient occlusion will indeed look flat and unrealistic and should be avoided. One exception to this rule is if you just need quick lighting to "see things" and somewhat poorer quality is okay, such as with preliminary lighting or pre-visualization. Often when lighting a scene or doing a demo in which I simply need to be able to see everything quickly, I will toss in an ambient light along with a directional light. With a few mouse clicks, I have a simple lighting setup that allows me to see the basic action of the scene.

Maya's ambient light has a parameter called "ambient shade" that makes the ambient light behave *unlike a true ambient*. If the "ambient shade" parameter is set to 1, the light will behave entirely like a shadowless point light. The default setting for ambient shade is .45, which can be confusing to new lighters as it gives the light a decidedly non-ambient directionality. Set ambient shade to 0 to make the light behave like a true ambient.

WHEN AND HOW TO USE AMBIENT LIGHTS

When Is Using an Ambient Light a Good Choice?

✓ When you are imitating fully scattered indirect illumination (however, see the following Tips).

✓ When you need to prevent the scene from "going to black."

✓ When you need to quickly see into the shadow areas for preview purposes.

Tips for Using Ambient Light:

• Without occlusion, use ambient rarely and, if so, at low intensities.

• With occlusion, higher intensities are fine.

• Be on the lookout for having your scene look too flat or unrealistic.

1.2.6 VOLUME LIGHT

Volume lights confine their illumination within a specified volumetric shape. Typically the illumination within this volume may be ambient, radial, or directional. The volume light shapes are preset and are generally available in primitive shapes: sphere, cone, cylinder, and box (Figure 1.45). Size, position, rotation, and shape are all important in determining where the volume light will shine. While specifics vary from package to package, most volume lights have some or all of these common controls:

◆ Selecting the shape of the volume light, usually choosing from box, sphere, cone, and cylinder.

◆ Transforming (move, rotate, scale) the area light.

◆ Changing the type of light inside, choices typically being radial, linear, and ambient.

◆ Specifying the axis and/or direction along this axis of the volume light that the light shines along for cone, box, and cylinder shapes.

◆ If using radial light, specifying whether the light shines outward or inward. (The light can shine inward to the center rather than radiating outward.)

◆ Specifying the intensity and even color of light along the axis of the light and/or from center to edges of the volume.

Volume lights do not imitate any particular type of real-world light. Rather, they are simply a tool for giving you additional controls as to *where* the light will affect the scene—namely, inside the area of the volume light. When and how to use them can vary quite a bit, depending on what you want them to do.

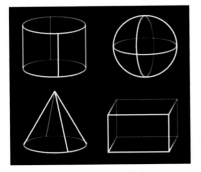

Figure 1.45 Volume lights.

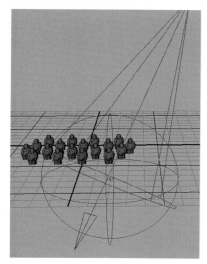

Figure 1.46 Scene file showing the volume and spotlight used in Figure 1.47.

Figure 1.47 This scene uses two lights—a spotlight and a volume light. The spotlight casts direct illumination and creates the shadow, while the volume light contains ambient illumination (with occlusion), confining the ambient to just around the Buddha statuettes.

Volume lights can be used in all sorts of interesting and useful ways, all of them cheats. You will want to have a fair understanding of what the lights are trying to do before using a volume light to create the look you are after. A rule of thumb in general is *the more artificial the endeavor, the more important it becomes that the lighter understands the effect being cheated so as to avoid having the lighting look incorrect* (see Rule #7 later in this chapter in the sidebar "Seven Rules for Good Lighting Technique").

To give you some ideas, here are a few fun cheats and tricks involving volume lights:

- Use a volume light to cast light in specified shapes.
- Use a volume light to confine directional light to a specified area rather than throughout the entire scene.
- A volume light containing ambient light can also be used to increase the ambient in only certain areas of the scene, rather than throughout the entire scene. This could be used to enhance an area that has brighter direct light and, therefore, would have correspondingly brighter scattered light as well (Figures 1.46 and 1.47).
- One way to cheat the look of a soft or core shadow is to use a volume light set to shine as ambient light and set it to a negative intensity (which removes light rather than adds it). This creates a contact shadow without the high render time associated with ambient occlusion. This cheat can be good for static (nonmoving) objects (Figures 1.48 and 1.49).
- Volume lights can be used to gain very precise control over how the light attenuates (decreases in intensity with distance).

Figure 1.48 A simple spotlight with a cast shadow.

Figure 1.49 A volume light with a negative intensity was used to create a core shadow under the vase.

WHEN AND HOW TO USE VOLUME LIGHTS

When Is Using a Volume Light a Good Choice?

✓ When you want to confine the light's effects to a specified area.

Tip for Using a Volume Light:

- Be sure you fully understand the effect you are cheating.

1.2.7 SECTION SUMMARY: COMPARISON OF BASIC LIGHT TYPES

This section summarizes the basic light types, comparing when to use each one, the kind of real-world light imitated, the visual differences, and some tips on usage.

A Visual Comparison of the Basic Light Types

Figure 1.50
Point light.

Figure 1.51
Directional light.

Figure 1.52
Spotlight.

Figure 1.53
Area light.

Figure 1.54
Ambient light.

Figure 1.55
Volume light.

Table 1.1 Comparison Chart for Basic Light Types

Light Type	Characteristics	Light Imitated	When to Use	Tips on Usage
Point	0D. Radiates outward in all directions. Position important. Perfectly hard light.	Small light sources. Example: bare bulb.	When you need to see light cast radially in all directions. When you need shadows cast in all directions.	Turn off unnecessary shadow calculations. Watch for hotspots. Can often be imitated with a spotlight instead.
Directional	0D. Casts parallel rays (in one direction). Uniform throughout the scene. Rotation important. Perfectly hard light.	Distant light. Example: sun.	When the light you are imitating is very far. When you have a large area of your scene to flood with light.	Can be hard to control the shadows; often best with ray-traced shadows rather than depth-mapped shadows. May be replaced by a faraway spotlight.
Spot	0D. Radiates from a central point in the area of a cone. Position, rotation, and cone angle important. Hard light.	Spotlights. Examples: search light, flashlight, car headlight. Can imitate other lights as well.	When you want to imitate a cone of light. When you want to confine your light calculations to a finite area.	Has easily controlled depth-map shadows. Can be used to imitate a distant light, area light, or point light source. Scale the light in order to preview it better.
Area	Typically a 2D plane. Casts light from all parts of an area. Computationally expensive. Soft light.	Large and near light sources. Diffused light. Diffusely reflected light. Examples: tube lighting, softbox.	When you need soft light and you have the time to render it, or when you cannot or choose not to cheat the look of it by other means.	Use area lights sparingly to keep render times low. A larger area light—blurrier shadow, larger highlight, brighter illumination (sometimes), and longer render times.
Ambient	Dimensionless. Shines on the surface from all directions evenly. Directionless. Perfectly soft light.	Fully and uniformly scattered light. Example: skylight on a cloudy day.	When imitating indirect illumination.	Without occlusion, use rarely and at low intensities. With occlusion, higher intensities are fine. Use material ambient parameter carefully.
Volume	3D. Illumination confined within a geometric shape. Hard or perfectly soft (ambient) light.	Has no real-world counterpart.	When you want to confine the light to a specified area. Volume lights can be used for a variety of cheats.	Know what you are trying to achieve when cheating a look to avoid a fake-looking scene.

1.3 SIMPLE LIGHTING TECHNIQUES

In this section a few basic lighting techniques and general workflow tips will be covered, since it helps to have good practices and a few tricks under your sleeve right away. These techniques are easy to use. If you have some experience lighting, you probably have already used them and may want to skip this section, though if you suspect you may have accumulated any bad habits over time, you may want to read on.

1.3.1 TIPS FOR INTERACTIVE PLACEMENT OF LIGHTS

The workflow for placing lights varies depending on the kind of light you are positioning. Many new digital lighters use the tools with which they are familiar, rotating and translating to move the light while looking at it in the default views. Depending on the light type this may or may not be the most efficient approach. This section covers a few approaches suited to the different light types.

One of the easiest ways to place a *spotlight* **is to look through it as if it were a camera,** and then move it in the same exact way you would move a camera (usually some combination of mouse clicks and hotkeys). This method has the advantage of being fast. To aim the spotlight at your subject, simply frame your subject in the light's view. (In Maya select the subject, then hit "f" while looking through the light.) Then back the light away from the subject and tumble about to change the light angle upon the scene (Figure 1.56).

One caveat about this method: When moving lights by looking through the lights, it's very easy to place the lights too close to the subject. When looking through the light, the natural tendency is to frame the subject in the view. However, the result is that the light is likely right on top of the subject. To help correct for this, be sure to use other views to confirm that your light is the right distance from the subject, and as noted, use the shaded rendercam's view.

Another technique good for spotlights and directional lights is to use the center-and-interest manipulators. The center-and-interest manipulator is more commonly used with cameras, but it works just as well with lights that have a central axis. Just position the interest roughly at the same place as the subject and use the center to move the light itself, while checking the position in the orthographic views (Figure 1.57).

Directional lights can be placed anywhere in the scene and just rotated to adjust their angle of illumination. For this reason, you can position a directional light with only one panel open, which is the shaded rendercam panel. Just keep an eye on the preview of the scene lighting in this panel while *rotating* the directional light.

Point lights and area lights are best placed while keeping an eye on their position in the three orthographic views, the shaded rendercam view, and possibly a perspective view. The best way to position the point light is to translate using the top, front, and side panels (or conversely a few perspective views), all the while keeping an eye on the shaded rendercam window as you move the light to see roughly the effects of its illumination.

Ambient lights can be placed anywhere in the scene, provided they are truly ambient. They don't need to be positioned or rotated—just drop them in.

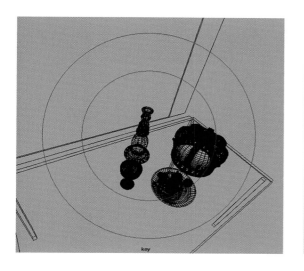

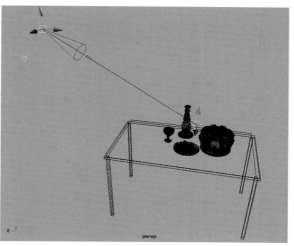

Figure 1.56 (Left) The view through a spotlight. Circles represent the inner and outer cone angles.

Figure 1.57 (Right) A spotlight being moved with the center-and-interest manipulator. The interest can be easily positioned at the subject.

1.3.2 LIGHT LINKING

A simple technique that is worth mentioning early on is that of *light linking*. Light linking is the practice of making your digital lights shine on some surfaces and not on others. The steps to do this vary from software to software, but this is a very common feature and often used. The light may be told to shine on a surface or surfaces only (inclusive light linking), or a light may be told to shine on anything *but* that surface or surfaces (exclusive light linking).

Obviously, light linking is completely fake and is something that only an artist in the digital world can do. For the purpose of creating an artistic image, however, it's very useful and artists rely on it often. Cinematographers and photographers would love to have this feature—a similar effect can be achieved in real life but with much greater effort. That being said, because the effect is a cheat, you will want to make sure that if you have chosen to light-link something, your images still look correct.

Light linking can be used if you want to add more light to just one or a few objects in a group (see Figure 1.60 for an example) to draw attention to that subject, to provide more shaping, to add more fill, to brighten a dark subject, or for any number of reasons. Conversely, you may want to remove a light from one object but still have this light affect everything else in the scene.

A common application of light linking is to create special lights for certain subjects that have modified settings. For example, imagine a scene that is lit by only one light. This primary light is called the *key light*. In our imaginary scene, the key light looks great on all objects… except for one. What do you do? You don't want to change the key because it looks good overall, but one object would look better if the key were positioned slightly differently. A possible solution here is to create two key lights. Light-link the first key to shine on all *except* the offending object (exclusive linking), and light-link the second key to shine on *only* this same object (inclusive linking). You can then adjust this second key to better illuminate the odd object without changing the rest of the scene.

SEVEN RULES FOR GOOD LIGHTING TECHNIQUE

While digital lighting has many suggestions and few rules, I consider these suggestions to be essential enough to call "rules for good lighting technique," no matter whether you have one day of experience or twenty years.

1 Do not place lights too close.

A common mistake is to place lights too close to the subject. When lights are too close to the subject(s), their illumination may be inaccurate, or you may need even more lights than you would otherwise, making the whole setup difficult to control. This can happen to even experienced lighters. I recall a shot in the film *Stuart Little* in which I was helping to debug some problems in which the intensity of the lights seemed to be fluctuating oddly, even though there was no animation on the lights. The shot was a close-up of Stuart (a digital mouse) talking. As he spoke, his head moved slightly in the frame. It turned out the lights were placed so close to the subject that even this small movement had the character moving in and out of the illumination. Mystery solved—the lights were much too close.

2 Do not use too many lights.

Another common mistake is the use of too many lights, which increase render time and become difficult to manage. It's easy to become overwhelmed by the lights in the scene and suddenly have lights that you aren't sure what they do. These lights can produce effects that you don't want them to, and suddenly the lighting of the scene is slipping out of your control. We've all been there at one time or another. The solution is to back up, find out what each light is doing (see Rule #4: *Get Back on Track When Needed*), and eliminate any unnecessary lights. For example, don't have two lights shining in basically the same area when one will do, or have a light that points off into space somehow ("How'd that get there?") or is far too close to its subject and is thus only illuminating a small area, or have lights shining around the corner that you don't even see, and so on.

3 Know what each light is doing.

This brings me to another rule of lighting—short and sweet, but possibly the most important one: *Always know what each of your lights and its shadow is doing*. I recall a cinematography class I took years ago, and the instructor, also a cinematographer, said, "If you don't know what a light is doing, don't add it!" In some cases you may be working on a large collaborative project, perhaps with a full environment of lights that you didn't set up. If at all possible, it's still a good idea to determine what these inherited set lights are doing in order to optimize and control your shot. I have found without exception that the better I understood the lighting of a shot I inherited, the better I could use the lighting to get out of it what I wanted. In any case, if the scene is just too big and time really doesn't permit, you still would of course need to know exactly what any light *you add or edit* is doing.

4 Get back on track when needed.

If you lose track of what your lights are doing, these tips can help you get back on track. One helpful method is to view the scene with just the light in question. Many software packages have the option of previewing interactively with just the selected light(s). This is very helpful. You also can render with just the light in question, called *light soloing*. This may be the best or only way to track down a problem or reestablish what each light is doing if you have become lost, ultimately saving you time in the end.

5 Name things descriptively.

It is best to name your lights descriptively. If you're working alone, this will help you to keep track of the purpose of each light (remembering what "spotlight7" does is harder than what "fill_screen_left" does) without having to pick the light and see which one it is. Practicing naming your lights is a good habit to start from the beginning. It may appear to be time consuming, but naming lights takes only a second. When working on a team, naming lights in the scene becomes essential so that team members can understand one another's files without spending a half day trying to figure it out. Since, at some point, each of us is likely to work on a team and need to hand off files, getting into good habits right away is the best. The habit of a sloppy scene can be a hard one to break, to the frustration of your co-workers (and your boss) later on.

6 Only add complexity as needed.

Too often students of lighting learn a technique that adds complexity, and because it is done professionally, they think that is the way to do things in general. Not true! Complexity is added professionally only when it's needed. But what constitutes "needing it"?

- It gives you extra controls you need to enhance the image.

- It saves time in the long run.

If added complexity doesn't specifically give you some sort of advantage, then don't do it. Never add complexity "just because." Complexity comes at a price, which is that the scene takes longer to set up and is more difficult to manage. Experienced lighters are also prone to adding complexity too soon, which results in a slower-than-it-needs-to-be workflow. A good rule of thumb is "keep it simple" (believe me, it gets complicated soon enough!).

7 The bigger the "cheat," the more knowledge you need.

The more artificial the endeavor, the more important it becomes that the lighter understand the effect being cheated so as to avoid having the scene look weird or wrong. I know of no exceptions to this (other than luck or having someone else set it all up for you). Inside the computer the laws of physics don't apply. We can choose to imitate these physical laws closely or deviate from them dramatically. The ability to do things that aren't possible in the real world is a big creative advantage, but it also means an artist has, as the saying goes, "enough rope to hang himself." The solution is to keep a careful eye on the aesthetics of the scene, arm yourself with the knowledge of how things operate in the real world, and understand your tools. Hey, isn't that the "why, what, and how" of lighting again?

The scene now has two key lights, but it still maintains the appearance of having only one light. This technique is used often (see Figures 1.58 and 1.59 for examples). When using this technique, it's very important that the two lights are not too different from each other. You want the two lights to still appear as only one light; if they are too different from one another, the lighting will look implausible and therefore artificial and inaccurate.

Light linking adds complexity to your scene. While learning how to light-link is easy, proper use of light linking can become tricky, especially in a big scene with lots of linking going on. In the latter case, managing such a scene is no longer introductory, it's advanced. It is very, very important (oops, here comes one of those "rules of lighting") to . . . *only add complexity as needed.*

Use light linking:

◆ To exclude light only from certain surfaces.

◆ To add light only to certain surfaces.

◆ To exchange one light for another in order to make an object or group of objects receive unique light settings.

Figure 1.58 A simple scene lit with a single key light.

Figure 1.59 This scene has two keys, both light-linked so they appear like a single light. The first key shines on everything *except for* the short vase, while the second key shines *only* on the short vase. The second key has been moved to reposition the highlight and gain more shaping on the short vase.

Figure 1.60 In this example, additional light is linked and exclusive to the tall vases, helping to define and separate them from the background.

1.3.3 SPECULAR- AND DIFFUSE-ONLY LIGHTS

Another simple technique that can be useful early on is the practice of making lights specular only or diffuse only. To understand this, you need only a very basic understanding of how surfaces are represented digitally. A lit surface has a broad illumination covering any areas that are facing the light. This broad illumination is known as the *diffuse illumination*. If the surface is smooth or glossy you will also see a small bright shiny area on the surface, known as the *specular highlight*. Each light added will contribute to the diffuse illumination as well as add another specular highlight on any glossy surfaces (Figure 1.61).

In CG, a light can be made to contribute to the specular or the diffuse component if desired, rather than both. In most light shaders, this is a simple check box. Look for it in your lights and you will likely find it. Uncheck the box for specular or diffuse and see what happens. This technique is super easy to use and unlike light linking, it's difficult to run into trouble with it. If you check "specular only" and you don't really want that, it's going to be very obvious very quickly.

Making a light nonspecular is useful when you don't want a specular highlight from a particular light because the highlight is distracting. Is this a complete cheat far removed from reality? Actually, no. In life, some types of light don't contribute much in the way of a specular highlight. A full discussion on this is in Chapter 10, "Light Diffusion." For now, if you have a highlight that is distracting or unwanted, it's good to know that you can simply turn it off (Figures 1.62 and 1.63).

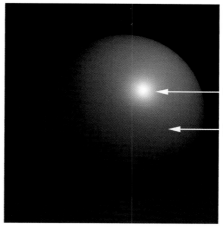

Figure 1.61 A render showing diffuse and specular illumination.

Specular

Diffuse

Figure 1.62 (Left) All lights contribute to specular highlights in this image. This gives the toy elephant an unwanted metallic feel.

Figure 1.63 (Right) In this render, specular highlights have been turned off from all but the primary light source.

Conversely, you can make a light contribute *only* specular by turning off its diffuse contribution. This is useful when you want to carefully place a highlight somewhere for aesthetic reasons (Figures 1.64 and 1.65). Another application of this technique is to combine a specular-only light with a diffuse-only light, allowing you to control the specular and diffuse independently.

Figure 1.64 (Left) This render of vases has an additional specular-only light shining on the middle vase.

Figure 1.65 (Right) The original render without the specular-only light for comparison.

1.4 RENDER BASICS

render (v.)
1. to represent in a drawing or painting.
2. to perform an interpretation of (a musical piece, for example).
3. to cause to become; make.
4. to express in another language or form; translate.
5. *computer science:* to convert (graphics) from a file into visual form.

The term "render" has many meanings, a few of which are listed above. A rendering can be a translation of something, as in "a rendering of the Old English text." In the arts, the term "render" means to represent in a drawing or painting. Thus *rendering* is an appropriate term for the stage in the CG process where all of the geometry, lights, materials, and scene descriptions are converted from a 3D scene file to a 2D image.

Rendering is done by the computer, and the artist provides a number of settings that determine exactly how it is done. For the artist who is new to lighting, these settings can be daunting. Where to begin? Which ones should be adjusted first, or at all? This section takes a look at some of the basics of rendering, looking at rendering methods from an artist's point of view and discussing those render settings with which you will need to be familiar first.

1.4.1 BRIEF OVERVIEW OF RENDERING ALGORITHMS

An *algorithm* is a step-by-step procedure for solving a problem, and *render algorithms* are the various means by which the computer can perform the task of rendering. With the first image you render, a decision is made as to which algorithm gets used. If you haven't chosen it specifically, then the software will use a default, effectively choosing it for you. Since each algorithm has different looks and capabilities, the default may or may not work for you.

Three common methods of rendering are:

◆ Scanline rendering
◆ Ray tracing
◆ Global illumination

Each method provides its own advantages and disadvantages. This section provides a brief overview of the most common algorithms used, highlighting the benefits and drawbacks of each from the artist's point of view. This section does *not* look at the computer science behind the technique. For a more in-depth look at algorithms, refer to Chapter 14, "Rendering for the Artist," and Chapter 16, "Global Illumination.'

Introduction to Scanline Rendering

In most software packages, the default rendering algorithm used is something called *scanline rendering.* **The largest advantage of scanline rendering is that it's fast.** Because of its speed, scanline rendering and similar methods have traditionally been used in animation production in which many frames need to be rendered and speed is a large concern. As computers have become faster over the years, however, scanline rendering has been increasingly supplemented or even replaced by other, more computationally expensive rendering algorithms.

The primary disadvantage of scanline rendering is that it's less realistic than other methods. It doesn't calculate "real" reflections. In other words, if you have one object sitting next to another reflective object, the first object will not appear in the reflective surface. Additionally, scanline renders don't calculate for the refraction of transparent objects. *Refraction* is the bending of light as it passes through a transparent surface, distorting the view of what is behind. Without refraction, transparent objects can be disappointingly flat and unrealistic-looking. Another distinctive feature of scanline renders is that often the only shadow available is a type known as a *depth-mapped shadow.* Depth-mapped shadows don't blur realistically with distance nor do they account for the transparency of a surface.

Even with these many limitations, don't be fooled into thinking that scanline renders are doomed to be of poor quality, which is a common misconception among new lighters. High-quality images can be created with this rendering method. However, to do so relies more heavily on the skill of the digital artist and less on the renderer itself. A skilled lighter can fill in the gaps left by scanline rendering. It may surprise you to find that most feature films before 2002 used scanline methods almost exclusively with little to no ray tracing and no global illumination whatsoever.

Today scanline rendering is often combined with other, more computationally expensive render methods. These other methods fill in the gaps left by scanline's capabilities. Much time can be saved by having the bulk of the rendering done with scanline. This type of compromise makes efficient use of the best of many different algorithms and is an approach frequently used by studios today.

Introduction to Ray Tracing

Ray tracing is another common algorithm found in most packages. Ray tracing has a more realistic look than scanline rendering (Figure 1.66). It will calculate the reflections of one object into another as well as refractions for transparent surfaces. Additionally, ray tracing has a unique way of calculating shadows that is more realistic; they blur increasingly with distance and account for surface properties such as transparency (for example, accurate shadows from stained-glass windows).

The drawback is that ray tracing is much slower than scanline rendering. All those realistic calculations take more time. They also need memory; ray tracing requires much more memory to process a scene, which can be a problem when rendering scenes with complex geometry and many textures. An average computer may not be able to ray trace a very complex scene at all, as it may "hang" (pause) indefinitely if it runs out of memory.

Introduction to Global Illumination

Increasingly common are global illumination methods. Global illumination (GI) isn't a single algorithm, but rather it describes a group of algorithms, all which share a common feature. They all calculate some form of *indirect light*. Indirect light is any light that reaches a surface after bouncing off another surface (also called *bounce light* or *diffusely reflected light*) or after being scattered by the environment (Figures 1.67 through 1.69). In both scanline and ray tracing, indirect light must be added by the artist. Accurate calculation of indirect light by the renderer can greatly add to the realism of a scene, and can be a big timesaver to the artist.

Figure 1.66 Ray-traced reflections are an integral part of Lighting McQueen's look, as evidenced by this frame from *Cars 2*. (© 2011, Disney/Pixar. All rights reserved.)

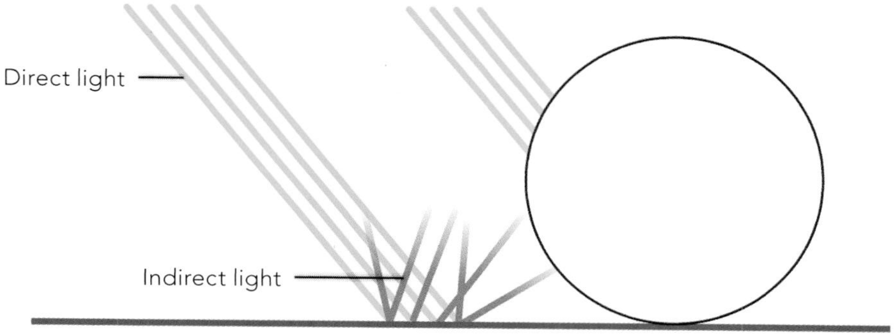

Figure 1.67 Diagram showing both direct and indirect light.

Figure 1.68 (Left) A render showing direct light only.

Figure 1.69 (Right) A render with both direct and indirect light.

NOTE

While traditional ray tracing does not include the calculation of indirect light, ray tracing can be extended to include reflected light, a method known as *ray-traced global illumination*.

Some global illumination methods also calculate *caustics*, which are patterns of light that become focused upon reflection or refraction. We are familiar with caustics as the patterns of moving light seen at the bottom of a pool or in the center of a bottle's shadow (Figure 1.70).

The primary advantage of using global illumination is greatly increased realism, primarily from the calculation of indirect light. Recall the old cheat for indirect light is with a CG ambient light, which was disappointingly flat without occlusion, or the addition of many lights by the artist, which can be hard to manage and requires more skill from the artist. With global illumination, indirect light is calculated by the renderer. In many cases, global illumination methods produce pleasing images more easily, as there is less need for fakes and special techniques (Figure 1.71).

Figure 1.70 A photograph of caustics, seen in the bright spots in the center of the shadows.

Table 1.2 Comparison of Ray Tracing, Scanline, and Global Illumination Methods

	Scanline	Ray Trace	Global Illumination
Advantages	Very fast. Can deal with very complex scenes.	Real reflections. Refractions. Shadows blur with distance. Shadows account for material properties (i.e., stained-glass shadows).	Calculates both direct and indirect light. Realistic ambient light and shadows. Caustics (some methods).
Disadvantages	No real reflection. No refractions. Shadows blur uniformly. Shadows don't account for material properties. Calculates direct light only.	Slow. May have trouble dealing with very complex scenes. Calculates direct light only.	Very slow. May have trouble dealing with very complex scenes.

Figure 1.71 *Cloudy with a Chance of Meatballs* was rendered with full global illumination. (© 2009 Sony Pictures Animation Inc. All rights reserved. Courtesy of Sony Pictures Animation.)

The cost of global illumination is, of course, greatly increased render time. Global illumination methods take longer to render than ray-traced scenes, and many, many times longer than scanline renders. Like ray tracing, they require more memory. For this reason, while global illumination methods have been around for a very long time, they were initially almost never used in animation production. Because the processing speed and power of the computer has grown, however, global illumination methods have become more feasible and are finding increasingly widespread use (Figure 1.71).

Selecting a Rendering Algorithm

When choosing your rendering algorithm, you should consider which features you want along with which disadvantages you can live with. On a large production the rendering algorithm (or algorithms as the case may be) is considered carefully. What kind of time schedule do you have? What are the skills and abilities of you and the others on your team? The algorithm used will have far-reaching repercussions and will affect everything from the techniques employed—and thus the skill sets needed by the artists who employ them—to what software and hardware are needed. Also consider what your render is for: Are you just learning, or is this a professional job? When simply rendering for personal enrichment, you have a good opportunity to explore what the different rendering methods can do and experience their limitations.

Selecting the render method may be with a pull-down menu, a check box, or a combination of both. Your software will have documentation covering this. Once you decide what you need your renderer to do and select the appropriate option, a number of additional settings become available that are specific to that algorithm. There may be just a few settings or a rather daunting list. In order to use a particular algorithm, you'll need to know about its associated settings.

The algorithm that is the easiest to use when just getting started is scanline rendering, because it has the least number of special settings. Generally, when using this method you primarily need to pay special attention to the file output and quality-control settings, and these are covered in the next subsection (Section 1.4.2). From there, you can graduate to ray tracing and incorporating ray-traced shadows. If you are new to lighting and shading, you may be better off practicing with scenes *without* ray-traced reflective or transparent surfaces at first. In short order, these material properties can be added, but that way there is no confusion about strange artifacts when you are first learning the basics.

Many students are eager to learn global illumination methods first. I generally recommend, however, that serious students of lighting learn global illumination *last*. While the number of animation projects using global illumination methods increases every year, GI is far from the exclusive render method used in animation production. Many studios combine global illumination methods with more traditional methods to gain the best of both worlds. A lighter who hasn't mastered lighting both with and without global illumination may find himself at a disadvantage. By learning to light first without global illumination, you increase your skills and avoid having GI become a crutch. For those who must find out about it now (and I know you are out there), refer to Chapter 16, "Global Illumination."

1.4.2 Introduction to Render Settings

In order to make a start on rendering your images, you will want to understand some common parameters that define how the image will be rendered. These parameters are simply called *render settings* or *render globals* because they are global to the scene and not specific to a particular object or material. Your 3D software will generally have one dialog box where many different render globals can be set. This dialog box can be rather intimidating to the new user, who may be unsure what in the world all these settings do and which ones he should be using. Generally, the majority of these setting can be left with the defaults until you have a reason to change them. This section will look at the settings you may want to change right away.

Output Settings

A variety of settings refer to file output, such as file size, name, numbering, and image format. These settings determine the characteristics of the image file itself. They are, for the most part, self-explanatory but are discussed briefly here.

File Size

One of the first things you will want to determine is file size. In fact, determining the ratio of width to height (the aspect ratio), is one of the very first things you will want to do, even before animating or placing the camera. The aspect ratio of an animation is typically decided at the storyboard phase, as it affects framing and composition, which in turn affect animation, modeling, and lighting.

When dealing with digital images, file sizes are generally described in terms of pixels wide by pixels high. A default file size in many applications is often 640x480 (640 pixels wide by 480 pixels high). This size has a 4:3 aspect ratio derived from the video resolution of older television sets and many computer monitors. A more modern aspect ratio is 16:9, which on an HD television is a resolution of 1280x720 or 1920x1080.

How many pixels do you need? It depends on the size in inches desired and how many pixels per inch will be displayed/printed. When viewing on a monitor that displays 72 pixels per inch, a 640x480 pixel image will be 8.9x6.7 inches. Not so bad. But for film that is displayed on a massive theater screen, a much higher resolution is desired. Images for film are about 2,000 pixels wide (known as "2k"). Images for print also need to be much larger. Printed images appear at 300 dpi (dots per inch, or rather pixels per inch as far as your digital file is concerned). A 640x480 file would print 2.1x1.6 inches, which is very small indeed. To decide on your file size, consider the intended output for your images (video, film, or print), as well as the aspect ratio (the width to height relationship) that you need.

File Name

It is best to name your images something descriptive and logical. A good practice is to relate the name of the rendered sequence to the name of the digital file that created the sequence, to help keep track of which scene created which render. In other words, if your scene file is named "my_ scene_v1.mb," then a frame rendered from this scene may be called "my_ scene_v1.0001.tif." Assuming, of course, that your scene is only outputting one render at a time. If you want to vary it, try adding a modifier at the end but still relating the base name, such as an output render called "my _scene_v1_bty.0001.tif." You can come up with your own naming convention but (1) make it logical and (2) stick to it.

TIP

It is also a good practice to version up your scene file with each important render (such as any render you have shown to a boss or client). Doing this will prevent you from overwriting a scene file that you may need later (for example, if your supervisor decides to go back to a render that you showed him last week).

File Numbering

You have a few options as to how a series of images is numbered. The numbers may be unpadded, which means they have no zeros preceding them. An unpadded sequence could have names like this:

image.1.tif, image.2.tif, image.3.tif . . . image.9.tif, image.10.tif, image.11.tif, and so on.

Padded numbering has zeros in front of the frame count so there is always the same number of digits. Padded numbers with four places are called *four padded*; five places are called *five padded*, and so forth. A four-padded sequence looks like this:

image.0001.tif, image.0002.tif . . . image.0099.tif, image.0100.tif, image.0101.tif, and so on.

Padded numbers often sort better when listing, and some applications prefer this format. When padding sequence numbers, you will want to decide how many places to pad. A three-padded sequence would not be enough if the frames exceeded 999, for example. You will want to keep the amount of padding consistent throughout the production. Four-padding is usually enough.

File Format

File format refers to the type of file, such as a TIF or JPEG. Each file format has advantages and disadvantages. Not all file formats can be easily viewed, and some are intrinsically larger than others. A full discussion of the many file formats is beyond the scope of this book, but a few common formats are worth noting.

A common file format is JPEG. JPEG files can be read and viewed by almost any application. JPEG files also compress their images, making them smaller. This is good news if you wish to email an image or post it on the Internet but bad news if you want your image to maintain all of its glorious detail. JPEG compression is "lossy," which means it loses data upon compression. A loss of data often introduces artifacts. The greater the compression of the file, the greater the artifact will be. If I work with JPEGs, I always save them at the highest quality. I never use JPEGs if I want my image to retain all of its quality, and it isn't a good format for delivery of final work.

Another common file type is a TIF file. TIF files have the advantage of being compressed (or not) and offer lossless compression with LZW compression. In addition, TIF files may contain more data per pixel. TIF files aren't widely supported by web browsers but are a common format for photographs and image editing, as they can store data in RGB and CMYK channels.

A high-end 3D format is *OpenEXR* (or just EXR for short, extension .exr) developed by Industrial Light & Magic and released as open source in 2003. EXR can store much more information per pixel and offers both lossy and lossless compression. It can store an arbitrary number of channels, which means it can hold additional passes all in one file. For example, it can store both the left- and right-eye images for 3D stereo in a single file. The EXR format is preferred by many studios because of its extended capabilities.

Quality Settings

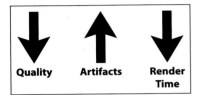

Figure 1.72 Low quality means many artifacts but low render times. Lower quality is good for early test renders.

Most applications have a section in the render settings to control the overall image *quality*. By "quality" I do not mean a pretty or well-composed image, but rather how smooth and artifact-free the render is. *Artifacts* are small (and sometimes not-so-small) inaccuracies in the final render. You will want to know something about quality settings even with your first render in order to set the level of quality you want.

3D applications generally have quality presets such as "low, medium, and high" or "draft, intermediate, production" or the like. If the quality level is set to "low" or the equivalent, the image likely renders quickly but with artifacts and may be missing some features. When the overall quality is "high" or the equivalent, your image will render smoothly but will take much longer to render.

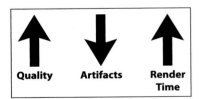

Figure 1.73 As quality increases so does render time. High quality is needed for final renders.

Most applications default to low-quality settings. Why? Because the software creators assume your initial renders will be test renders. For test renders, you don't need high-quality images. Even with small artifacts, you can get a general idea of how things look, which is all you need at first. Low-quality settings render very fast, and *at first speed is more important than detail* (Figure 1.72). You will want to raise the quality setting of the render as you refine the lighting of the scene, however, and you'll certainly need high-quality settings by the time you finish (Figure 1.73). Using the settings in this way is an efficient workflow.

Render-quality settings eliminate problems with *aliasing*. The most common artifact from aliasing is the formation of jagged edges along pixels of very different color or value, known informally as *jaggies* or *stair-stepping* (see Figure 1.74). If you see jaggies all throughout your image, you will need to increase the render-quality setting (Figure 1.75).

Take a look at your software's documentation to find where to change the overall quality while you work. Depending on the software and rendering algorithm used, render-quality settings may also control other features, such as ray-traced reflections and refractions, motion blur, and the like. These features are discussed in later chapters.

Figure 1.74 (Left) An image showing aliasing problems.

Figure 1.75 (Right) The same image rendered with higher-quality settings.

THE RENDER-QUALITY RULES OF THUMB

- Use low quality for fast test renders.
- Use high quality for final renders.

Work with the quality settings as you do test renders to gain more speed when you need it.

Always remember to reset the quality to high for final renders.

1.5 CHAPTER CONCLUSION

This chapter has provided a solid foundation for 3D lighting, as well as provided some basic techniques. Important details sometimes omitted from technical manuals were added—for example, while any manual will have an introduction to light types, not all give pointers on when each type should be used. Introductory topics, such a workflow for placing lights, have been covered in detail. Because a bit of technique is fun and useful early on, easy-to-use and common techniques have been presented here as well. Finally, good lighting habits have been encouraged along with the very first foray into the 3D scene, such as those found in the side-bar "Seven Rules for Good Lighting Technique." Between this chapter and the next chapter on shadows, you will have a solid beginning-to-intermediate technical knowledge that will allow you to complete the hands-on exercises found throughout the book and that will be built upon in later discussions of technique.

1.5.1 Important Points

◆ It's helpful when lighting to lock off the rendering camera and create another perspective camera for viewing the scene from any angle.

◆ Shade the view of your rendering camera to preview light placement.

◆ Camera placement and aspect ratio are important to framing and composition.

◆ Point lights should be used only when you need light in all directions.

◆ Directional lights cast parallel rays that fill the entire scene.

◆ Directional lights imitate faraway light sources.

◆ Directional lights are also good for low-level, shadowless fills.

◆ The illumination and shadows from a spotlight can be carefully controlled.

◆ Spotlights can be used to imitate many other light types.

◆ Area lights generate realistic soft light.

◆ The larger the area light, the softer the light; when area lights are small and far away, they lose much of their soft-light look.

◆ Area lights take a long time to render, so use only when needed.

◆ Ambient light is a cheat to imitate fully scattered, directionless light.

◆ Ambient light by default will flatten a scene and doesn't look very realistic.

◆ Ambient light is much more realistic when combined with occlusion.

◆ Volume lights can be used for many interesting cheats, but know what you are doing when you use them.

◆ Light linking is a common and useful practice, but it can be overused.

◆ It can be helpful to turn off the specular or diffuse contribution from a light to achieve a particular look.

◆ The most common rendering methods (algorithms) are scanline, ray tracing, and global illumination.

◆ Scanline renders are fast and less realistic.

◆ Many techniques are available to improve the appearance of scanline renders.

◆ Ray-traced renders have the advantage of generating real reflection, refractions, and realistic shadows, but they take much longer to render.

◆ Global illumination calculates real reflected light and caustics, but it renders very slowly.

◆ Due to increasing processing speed, global illumination methods are increasingly used in animation productions.

◆ A basic knowledge of render settings is needed with the first image you render.

◆ Keeping renders efficient and optimized is an important part of lighting well.

◆ To have the fastest render, keep the quality settings as low as possible while still achieving the look you need.

1.5.2 TERMS

perspective camera
render camera
aspect ratio
point light
directional/distant light
spotlight
cone angle
outer and inner cones
penumbra
area light
soft light

terminator
ambient light
direct light
indirect light
volume light
light linking
specular component
diffuse component
specular- and diffuse-only
  lights
algorithm

scanline
ray tracing
global illumination
reflected light
caustics
render globals
output settings
padded numbering
render-quality settings
artifacts
aliasing

1.5.3 EXERCISES

1. Create a still life and light it with a variety of CG light types. Be sure to use each light type in an appropriate fashion—don't throw in a smorgasbord of lights just to have them. For example, try an area light as a bounce light, a spotlight as an overhead light in a room, a point light coming from a candle, or a directional light representing sun or moonlight.

2. Light a scene with an area light as the primary light source. Be sure to consider what kind of scene would *need* an area light first. Become familiar with the settings of the area light in your software, and how it looks. Remember: Don't let your area light be too small and far away, or you will lose its advantage!

3. Determine the default quality settings in the software package of your choice. Practice changing these settings and notice the difference in both render time and final image quality. Save out some of your renders, specifying your render resolution, file type, and file name.

Figure 2.1 Shadows play an important role in setting the mood, directing the eye, and telling the story in this still from *Notorious*, directed by Alfred Hitchcock (1946, courtesy of Everett Collection).

Chapter 2
Shadows

"Where there is much light, the shadow is deep."

— *Johann Wolfgang von Goethe,*
German Playwright, Poet, Novelist, and Dramatist (1749–1832)

How to add shadows to 3D renders is one of the first things most digital artists learn. Without shadows, your images will simply not look very realistic. While turning shadows on is easy, getting the best use out of them is harder. Often the shadows look disappointingly CG or perplexing errors pop up, problems that cannot be eliminated without a bit more knowledge.

Fully mastering the use of shadows is a skill that takes time and practice. Knowing how to use shadows well involves a fair amount of knowledge, such as knowing which shadow type to use in certain situations, knowing the best settings for the parameters associated with shadows, knowing how to speed up your shadow renders, and general problem solving ("debugging"). In addition to these technical concerns, one must consider the artistic impact of shadows as well.

This chapter provides an in-depth look at shadows and how to best use their parameters. The focus of this chapter is how to use shadows effectively so that renders are optimized, artifacts are eliminated, and your shadows have the best possible look with standard techniques.

2.1 BEFORE TECHNIQUE

Before diving into the technique of digital shadows, we should take some time to consider how shadows look in the real world as well as at their use artistically.

2.1.1 TYPES OF SHADOWS

---

shadow (n.):
1. A dark figure or image cast on the ground or some surface by a body intercepting light;
2. Shade or comparative darkness, as in an area.
Rembrandt's figures often emerge gradually from the shadows.

Not all shadows are the same. A study of real-world shadows will reveal that they can be blurry or crisp, dark or light, directional or directionless, large or small (Figures 2.3 and 2.4). It is essential that the digital lighter studies how shadows look in life, so he can re-create them accurately in 3D. The appearance of real-world shadow depends on the nature of the light casting the shadow and the other lights in the scene. Shadows can be categorized according to their appearance and the kind of light causing them.

Figure 2.2 Cast shadow.

The *cast shadow* comes to mind when one thinks of "shadow" (Figure 2.2). This type of shadow happens when one body intercepts light from another body or from other parts of the same surface. Cast shadows result from light that has a particular direction to it, and the shadow likewise falls in a particular direction. Digital lights rarely cast shadows by default, but rather cast shadows need to be "turned on" and calculated with a particular rendering algorithm.

Figure 2.3 In life, shadows may be dark and crisp...

Figure 2.4 ...or blurry and indistinct.

Figure 2.5 Contact shadow.

A *contact shadow* is the soft, blurry, indistinct shadow created when two surfaces are close to one another (Figure 2.5). Contact shadows fall in no particular direction, as they are the shadows formed by fully scattered light throughout the environment.

The presence of contact shadows in your digital image will enhance its realism. Contact shadows create a darker core within a cast shadow and help to ground objects to each other. Combining both cast and contact CG shadows produces a more realistic result than just a cast shadow alone (Figure 2.6).

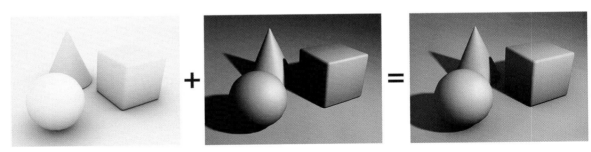

Figure 2.6 Cast and contact together.

The *shadow side* (Figure 2.7) of an object is the side facing away from the light and therefore is in darkness (i.e., "the shadow side of the moon"). Unlike cast and contact shadows, you don't have to do anything to get this type of shadow; it is part of the diffuse calculation and happens automatically. The shadow side should not be neglected when lighting digitally, however. Integrating the appearance of the shadow side with the appearance of cast and contact shadows is an important consideration for the image as a whole (Figure 2.8). A common error is to have the shadow sides of objects either too dark or too light relative to the cast shadows in the scene.

Figure 2.7 Shadow side.

Figure 2.8 The darkness of the shadow sides of these objects has been lit to blend with the density of the cast shadows.

The phrase *"in the shadows"* is an artistic meaning of the word "shadow," and refers to any portion of the image not well illuminated. In computer-generated imagery, these areas aren't usually referred to as "shadow," yet they are an important aesthetic consideration for the image overall. In Figure 2.9, the far spheres lie in the penumbra of the spotlight and are "in the shadows." In Figure 2.14, the character emerges from the shadows of the house.

Figure 2.9 "In the shadows."

2.1.2 SHADOW SIZE

Shadow size is determined by several factors, those being the angle of the light, the size of the light, and the distance of the light relative to both the shadow-casting and shadow-receiving surfaces.

The most important factor in shadow size is the relative *angle* of light to the shadow-casting and shadow-receiving objects. For example, if light rays are perpendicular to the shadow-receiving surface, the shadow will be relatively small (Figure 2.10). If the light is at an extreme angle to the shadow-receiving surface, the shadow will stretch out and be large. This is why shadows later in the day stretch out and become longer (Figure 2.11). When you think about it, this fact is rather obvious. When you want your shadow to stretch out and be large, work with the angle of illumination.

Another factor that influences the size of the shadow is the *size of the light*. The size of the light will affect both the blurriness and the size of the shadow. In life, a *larger* light produces a *smaller* shadow, all other factors being equal. The rule of thumb here is that if the light source is smaller than the shadow-casting object, then the shadow will be larger than the subject. On the other hand, if the light source is larger than the shadow-casting object, then the shadow will be smaller than the object. (See Figures 2.12 and 2.13 for illustration.)

A shadow can be divided into two zones—the *shadow core*, in which light is 100% occluded, and the *shadow penumbra*, the area in which light is partly occluded. In the area of the penumbra, the shadow is light and blurry.

Some lighters consider the shadow from a large light to be larger than that of a small light, because they include the penumbra in the total shadow volume. In life, however, the density of a shadow fades rapidly with distance from the core, and in the outer regions of the penumbra the density is so small as to be negligible. This is to say, in plainer terms, that the shadow core is mostly what we *see* of a shadow. In life, when the shadow core is smaller, the shadow itself looks smaller.

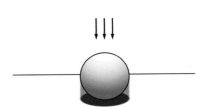

Figure 2.10 This light is perpendicular to the receiving plane, creating a relatively small shadow.

Figure 2.11 When light is at an angle to the receiving plane, the shadow stretches out and becomes longer.

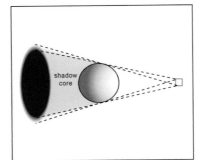

Figure 2.12 When the light source is *smaller* than the subject, then the shadow is *larger*.

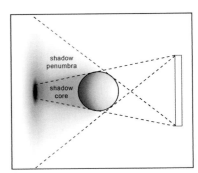

Figure 2.13 When the light source is *larger* than the subject, then the (core) shadow is *smaller*.

The final factor affecting shadow size is *distance*. Some believe the closer a light is to the subject, the larger its shadow will be. However, this is only true if certain conditions are met, but, generally speaking, isn't accurate. How the shadow responds to distance again relates to the size of the light. If the light is smaller than the shadow-casting object, then moving the light closer will enlarge the shadow. On the other hand, if the light is larger than the shadow-casting object, then moving the light closer will shrink the shadow. To throw another piece of wood on the fire, it's not just the distance to the light that matters. The distance of the shadow-receiving object from the shadow-casting object matters as well. When the light is smaller than the sub-ject, its shadow grows larger and larger with distance; when the light is larger than its subject, its core shadow grows smaller and smaller with distance. (Refer to Figures 2.12 and 2.13 again for illustration.)

Phew, that sounds confusing. But really there are just two important points made in this section. First, the best approach in determining shadow size is to move the light around and see what happens. Also, in terms of real-world light, the shadow *core* has the greatest visual impact and determines our perception of the size of the shadow.

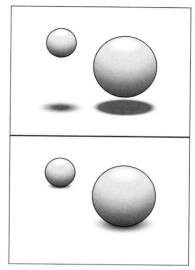

Figure 2.15 Shadows play an important role in defining spatial relationships.

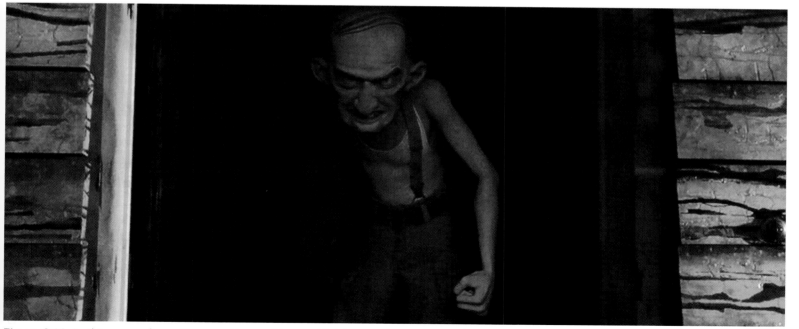

Figure 2.14 In this scene from *Monster House*, Horace Nebbercracker emerges from the shadows of his house. (© 2006 Columbia Pictures Industries, Inc. and GH One LLC. All rights reserved, courtesy of Columbia Pictures.)

2.1.3 THE ART OF SHADOWS

Shadows are an important visual element in an image. Shadows help to set the mood and define the visual style of a piece (Figure 2.1). The placement of shadows can direct the viewer's attention, literally pointing to some objects while hiding others. Shadows reveal more than they hide. They reveal the position and quality of the light casting them and the spatial relationship of objects to each other (Figure 2.15). The way shadows lay across a surface will help reveal form. How the shadow looks reveals the nature of the surface—for example, if the object is transparent or not. In some cases shadows reveal objects that are off-screen (Figure 2.16). Shadows can simply add visual interest. For the digital lighter, shadows are an important part of adding realism.

Figure 2.16 In this classic shot from *Nosferatu: A Symphony of Horror* (1922), the shadow reveals elements off-screen (in this case Nosferatu—a.k.a. Dracula—himself) while setting the mood.

2.2 SHADOW BASICS

While mastering shadows can take some time, the bare essentials generally can be learned quickly. This section provides an overview of the most fundamental use of digital shadows—which ones to use, how to turn them on, and a few basic settings. Artists new to digital lighting will find this section to include a manageable amount of information in order to get started.

Figure 2.17 and Figure 2.18 illustrate clearly the visual differences between depth-mapped and ray-traced shadows. Notice how the ray-traced shadows account for surface transparency and blur more with increased distance from the shadow-casting object.

2.2.1 DEPTH-MAPPED AND RAY-TRACED SHADOWS

Most applications provide two basic types of digital shadow methods: depth-mapped shadows and ray-traced shadows. These methods are very different from each other in how they are generated, how they look, and some of the parameters associated with them. Each method has advantages and disadvantages. Section 2.3, "Shadow Generation," looks in detail at how shadows are calculated; in this section, we will look only at each method's advantages and disadvantages in order to help you decide which shadow is the best to use in a particular situation.

Depth-mapped shadows render fast. This is their one main advantage. And when I say "fast," I mean smoking fast. In addition to the shadow calculation itself being quick, the shadow data can be saved and reused (as a separate file or "map," thus the name) without having to recalculate it, making the final render even faster. The big disadvantage to depth-mapped shadows is that they aren't very realistic-looking (Figure 2.17). They don't account for surface properties such as transparency, which means that the depth-mapped shadow is always uniformly opaque. They also blur uniformly with distance, unlike real shadows. Depth-mapped shadows also don't motion blur (Figure 2.19). In many animations this will not be noticeable, but in scenes with extreme blur, the shadows will look incorrect.

Ray-traced shadows, on the other hand, are much more realistic looking. They account for surface properties such as transparency and color (Figure 2.18). They blur realistically with distance. Ray-traced shadows motion blur (Figure 2.20). This additional beauty comes at a cost—they take much longer to render. They also cannot be pre-calculated, which means they

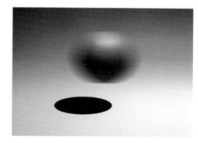

Figure 2.19 Motion blur with a depth-mapped shadow.

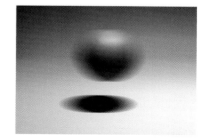

Figure 2.20 Motion blur with a ray-traced shadow.

are recalculated with each and every render. Ray-traced shadows require much more memory, which means the computer can slow down or even stop altogether when handling very complex scenes that may exceed the amount of memory available.

ADVANTAGES AND DISADVANTAGES OF DEPTH-MAPPED AND RAY-TRACED SHADOWS

Depth-Mapped Shadows

Advantages

- ✓ Very fast render time
- ✓ Able to be saved and reused
- ✓ Low memory requirements

Disadvantages

- Do not blur more with increasing distance
- Do not account for surface transparency
- Do not motion blur

Ray-Traced Shadows

Advantages

- ✓ Blur realistically with distance
- ✓ Account for surface transparency
- ✓ Motion blur

Disadvantages

- Slow render time
- Must be recalculated after each render
- Have high memory requirements

When should you use a ray-traced shadow? Ray-traced shadows have always enjoyed a certain amount of popularity because they generally yield good results. In the past, however, animation and visual effects productions largely avoided using ray-traced shadows due to their high render times. For example, Sony Imageworks *Spider-Man 2*, which won an Oscar for visual effects in 2004, used depth-mapped shadows almost exclusively. With the increasing power of the computer, however, ray-traced shadows have become more popular. For example, Imagework's newer films, like *Alice* (2010) and *G-Force* (2010), used ray-traced shadows exclusively. Many studios, however, still make extensive use of depth-mapped shadows and their more technologically advanced companion, *deep shadows* (see Section 2.3.3, "Introduction to Deep Shadows," and 15.2.1 "Using Deep Shadows") due to the fact that these shadow types can be pre-calculated.

The general rule of thumb is to only take on additional render time if it gives you a distinct advantage, or if it's an established workflow for the project you are on. For example, if you had worked on *Green Lantern* (2011), then bombs away on the ray-traced shadows. If you had worked on *Toy Story 3* (2010), however, then mapped shadows would have been the order of the day. Often projects that are opting for a more photo-realistic look will use ray-traced shadows while stylized animations will use mapped shadows.

Use ray-traced shadows if:

◆ Using ray-traced shadows is an established workflow of the project you are on, *or*

◆ The shadow is prominent or plays an important visual role, *and*

◆ It needs to blur realistically with distance, *and/or*

◆ It needs to show surface transparency, *and*

◆ You have no other more efficient means of achieving these looks.

In cases where a depth-mapped shadow will do just as well as a ray-traced shadow, then consider using the depth-mapped shadow. For example, if the shadow is small and far away or overall blurry and indistinct, then a depth-mapped shadow may be just fine. If you have the option for deep shadows, you can use these in place of ray-traced shadows without sacrificing any of the visual quality. You will experience the greatest savings in render time if you don't use even one ray-traced shadow.

MAKING THE MOST OF DEPTH-MAPPED SHADOWS

Since ray-traced shadows are much more realistic-looking than depth-mapped shadows, you may wonder if depth-mapped shadows are used much. You may be surprised to find out that depth-mapped shadows are used extensively by many feature-film studios that have very high quality standards and in projects that require even a photo-realistic look. For example, the Oscar-winning visual effects film *Avatar* (2009) used depth-mapped shadows extensively because of the significant speed advantage. How were these shadows used so successfully?

A much more realistic look can be achieved from depth-mapped shadows with some know-how and special techniques (Figures 2.21 to 2.23). Sadly, many techniques that are the staple fare of the production artist are unavailable and entirely unknown to the average user. In this chapter we will only look at methods commonly available and at least relatively easy to use. Chapter 15, "Tricks of the Trade," will cover advanced shadow techniques.

While ray-traced shadows are used much more often than they used to be, depth-mapped shadows remain a viable way to reduce render time, so knowing how to use them effectively should be part of every lighter's arsenal of tricks.

Figure 2.21 Depth-mapped render. We'll use the render time of this as our base (100%).

Figure 2.22 Ray-traced shadow. Render time was five times that of the depth-mapped image (500%).

Figure 2.23 Depth-mapped "with love." Using some special tricks, the look of these depth-mapped shadows is significantly improved. Render time was 50% more than when using default depth map (150%) but still far less than that of the ray-traced render.

2.2.2 ADDING SHADOWS

CG lights, by default, provide no shadow. To have a shadow, the light must have its shadows "turned on." Here we will simply look at ways to add depth-mapped or ray-traced shadows. Obviously the exact method will vary depending on the software. A tutorial or two in your software's documentation will cover the specifics.

Adding depth-mapped shadows usually requires only a simple "on" switch in the light. Some applications have lights in which the artist must input the name of a shadow file in order to activate depth-mapped shadows. This method is used (and preferred) by advanced lighters in order to gain more control; it isn't commonly available in your standard software. To start with, it's reasonable to say that typically you simply do one thing—check depth-mapped shadows "on" in a particular light, and there they are.

By default, these shadows are hard-edged, completely dark, and often may have jagged edges around the borders of the shadow, unofficially called *jaggies*. The jagged edges are a common artifact of depth-mapped shadows (Figure 2.24). To get rid of them, one solution is to increase the shadow size or *shadow resolution* (Figure 2.25). This parameter will be found in the light somewhere near the option to turn the depth-mapped shadow on. Increasing the blur of a mapped shadow will also eliminate jagged edges (Figure 2.26).

Figure 2.24 D-map 256 squared.

NOTE
Increasing shadow resolution is the "brute force" way of getting rid of shadow jaggies. More sophisticated and optimized methods are covered in Section 2.4, "Shadow Parameters."

While depth-mapped shadows can be rendered with most any rendering algorithm, in order to use ray-traced shadows your software needs to be rendering with the ray-tracing algorithm. Ray-traced shadows often need to be set in two places: (1) turn ray-traced shadows on in each light, and (2) activate ray tracing globally, usually in the render settings.

2.2.3 INTRODUCTION TO SHADOW BLUR

The first setting you will likely want to adjust when using shadows is the *blurriness* of the shadow. *Blur* refers to the softness of the shadow. This parameter may have other names, such as "width," "softness," "light radius," or "filter size." Whatever the name, hunt this parameter down and use it. Digital shadows are by default perfectly hard-edged. Since shadows in life are never perfectly hard-edged, *you should always add at least a tiny bit of blur to avoid a telltale CG look to your shadows.*

Figure 2.25 D-map 2048 squared.

TIP
When using depth-mapped shadows, adjust the blur to your liking before increasing the shadow resolution to eliminate jaggies. The shadow blur may smooth out the jagged edges, and you may not need a higher shadow resolution after all. Compare Figures 2.24 and 2.26.

Figure 2.26 D-map 256 squared and blurred.

How blur is calculated is very different for depth-mapped shadows than ray-traced shadows. This means the same numerical value for blur will have different results depending on whether you are using a depth-mapped or ray-traced shadow. Other factors weigh in as well; a blur setting that is good for a particular light in a particular scene may not work in a different light or different scene. Be prepared at first to try different values and to test how much blur this actually gives for your situation.

How much blur is the right amount? Believe it or not, there are some definite guidelines for this. Tips on deciding how much blur to add are covered in Section 2.4.1, "Shadow Blur." Without delving too deeply at this point, you should first *consider how blurry the shadow would be in life*, and also of course use your artistic judgment.

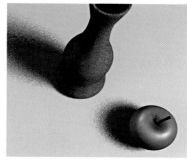

Figure 2.27 Too few shadow samples.

When blurring ray-traced shadows, you will need to adjust the number of *shadow samples* in order to avoid artifacts. You may notice that when you initially blur a ray-traced shadow, the edges of the shadow don't transition in a smooth gradient, but instead speckle with tiny light and dark patches (Figure 2.27). To smooth the shadow edge of a ray-traced shadow, you will need to increase a setting called "shadow samples" or "shadow rays." This parameter is found in each light usually near the parameter for blurring your ray-traced shadow. In many applications, it defaults to only 1. Raise this number in tiny amounts, test rendering each time, until the objectionable speckles disappear (Figure 2.28). Since increasing shadow samples increases the render time, use only the smallest number needed to eliminate artifacts.

Figure 2.28 More shadow samples and a longer render time.

TIP

When adjusting quality settings such as shadow samples, make sure your global render settings are at a high enough quality as well. Remember that low-quality global settings act as a sort of quality cap, which can make the high-quality settings in the lights ineffective. You don't want to keep cranking up your shadow samples in all of your lights only to find you were rendering on "draft" or "low" as your global quality setting and that was the problem, not the individual lights. Oops!

2.3 SHADOW GENERATION

A variety of algorithms are used to create shadows. As noted, the two most common methods of shadow generation are depth-mapped shadows (Figure 2.29) and ray-traced shadows. Being most common, these are discussed in detail here. Also important and often used are *deep shadows* and *ambient-occlusion shadows*. A full discussion of these more advanced methods will be saved for later chapters. (Deep shadows are discussed further in Chapter 15, "Tricks of the Trade," while ambient occlusion is discussed extensively in Chapter 16, "Global Illumination.")

2.3.1 DEPTH-MAPPED SHADOWS

Depth-mapped shadows are calculated by rendering a file from the view of the light, as if the light was a camera (Figure 2.29). During the render of the shadow map, a single ray per pixel is cast into the scene. The ray stops when it hits an object, and the direction and distance it traveled is recorded in that pixel. This records just how far away surfaces are from the light (Figure 2.30). No surface attributes (such as transparency and color) are recorded.

Figure 2.29 Preview of a depth-mapped shadow file.

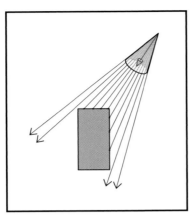

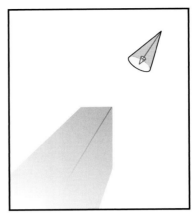

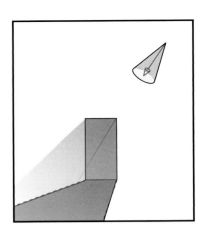

Figure 2.30 (Left) Rays are cast from the position of the light to generate the depth map.

Figure 2.31 (Center) It may be helpful to consider this map to be describing a shadow volume that occupies 3D space.

Figure 2.32 (Right) When the scene is rendered, anything behind or intersecting this volume is in darkness.

Figure 2.33 Pin art.

If you have a viewing utility that will open shadow maps, the information stored in the map can be viewed as a grayscale image (Figure 2.29). Don't be misled into thinking that it *is* a grayscale image, however. Many people describe depth maps as containing only distance information, but it may be useful to think of the data as a three-dimensional shadow volume instead (Figure 2.31). You can visualize this by considering how a push-pin box records a volume when an object is pushed into it, due to the distance each pin travels (Figure 2.33). Similar to the push-pin shape, only the front of the "shadow volume" is described and not the back. As far as the light is concerned, this volume goes on forever in the areas behind the surfaces it "sees." When the scene is rendered, the depth map file is called by the shadowing light. If the surface being rendered falls within the shadow volume described by the map, then the surface is considered in shadow; if it doesn't, it is illuminated (Figure 2.32).

For most lights, one depth map per shadow-casting light is generated. In the case of the spotlight, the cone angle of the spotlight is by default the angle of view of the camera rendering the depth map. Directional lights render orthographic shadows that generally encompass every shadow-casting object in the scene. Each point light renders a total of six depth maps, one down each positive and negative axis of the point light.

2.3.2 RAY-TRACED SHADOWS

Ray-traced shadows are calculated with a ray-tracing algorithm. This method of shadow generation is very different from depth-mapped shadows. At render time a ray or rays are shot from each pixel in the image plane into the scene, and upon hitting a surface the rays split, becoming more rays, one headed toward each light in the scene. If the ray is intercepted by an object before reaching the light, then the renderer calculates the surface to be in shadow (Figure 2.34). The renderer also accounts for the material settings on the intercepting body (such as transparency) and colors the shadow accordingly. When ray tracing, all of the objects and textures in the scene are stored in memory with even one ray-traced shadow, which makes for very high memory requirements for complex scenes. Also, each light that has ray-traced shadows adds to the calculations and increases render time.

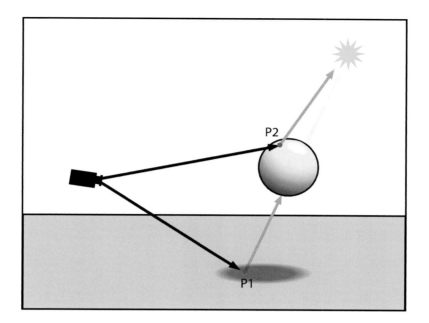

Figure 2.34 Diagram of how a ray-traced shadow is calculated. Point P1 is calculated as being shadowed because the ray from the point to a light is intercepted by a surface, while point P2 is not intercepted and therefore is not in shadow.

2.3.3 INTRODUCTION TO DEEP SHADOWS

***Deep shadows* are a special type of shadow map that have extended capabilities** (Figure 2.35). Deep shadows store more information per pixel than a regular depth map and combine some of the advantages of regular depth-mapped shadows with ray-traced shadows.

Deep shadows can:

◆ Be pre-calculated and re-used.

◆ Render semi-transparent shadows accurately.

◆ Render shadows for volumetric effects like clouds, smoke, and motion blur.

Because deep shadows store more information, they take longer to render and have a larger file size. Deep shadows are covered in detail Chapter 15, "Tricks of the Trade."

2.3.4 INTRODUCTION TO AMBIENT OCCLUSION

***Ambient occlusion* imitates the shadow produced by uniformly scattered light.** Digital artists call fully scattered light "ambient" and use the ambient light type as one way to imitate it. Ambient light is generally considered "shadowless" light, but this isn't exactly true. In life, all light shadows. Ambient light doesn't produce a cast shadow; it does, however, produce a contact shadow (Figure 2.5). Digital ambient, likewise, can be shadowed, and the technique to do so is ambient occlusion. Being somewhat more advanced in usage, generating and using occlusion is covered in detail in Chapter 16, "Global Illumination."

Figure 2.35 Deep shadows.

2.4 SHADOW PARAMETERS

Understanding how to use shadow parameters is critical to getting the best look from your shadows. Many of these parameters were introduced in Section 2.2. In this section, we take a deeper look at how to find the optimum settings for each.

Going forward, it will be important for you to fully understand the following shadow parameters:

◆ Shadow blur

◆ Shadow density/color

◆ Shadow samples

◆ Bias

◆ Shadow resolution

2.4.1 SHADOW BLUR

In life, *shadow blur* is related to the size of the light. The larger the light source, the more blurred the shadow becomes (Figures 2.36 through 2.38). Diffused light also creates soft shadows. Diffused light has passed through a medium that has scattered the light, such as a curtain or lampshade. Both large light sources and diffused lights are sources of *soft light. Soft light creates soft shadows.*

Figure 2.36 (Left) Shadow blur from a small light source.

Figure 2.37 (Center) Shadow blur from a medium light source.

Figure 2.38 (Right) Shadow blur from a large light source.

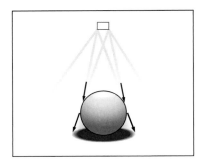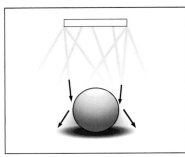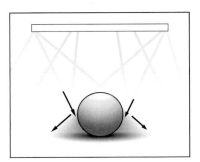

CG light types such as point lights, spotlights, and directional lights have no volume; they are 0 dimensional. For most CG lights, blurring the shadow doesn't involve scaling the light but rather is done through a parameter in the light. As noted, this parameter goes by many names, such as "width," "light radius," or "filter size," but here we will simply say "blur." Of the basic CG light types, the *area light* is the only one that realistically blurs its shadows based on the scale of the light and does so for ray-traced shadows only. If using a point light, spotlight, or directional light, you will need to manually input the amount of shadow blur that matches the scale or diffusion of the light it is imitating. **Here are some guidelines on how much shadow blur to use:**

◆ If your light source is large and near, add a significant amount of blur.

◆ If your light source is diffused, add a significant amount of blur.

◆ If you light source is small and/or very far away, add just a small amount of blur.

◆ If your shadow is to be crisp, add just a tiny amount of blur to soften hard edges.

Depending on whether the shadow is depth-mapped or ray traced, the blur will have different results and different optimum settings. Finding the optimum settings for your scene may take a bit of experimentation. As noted, depth-mapped shadows blur uniformly, while ray-traced shadows blur increasingly with distance.

Figures 2.39 and 2.40 show how ray-traced shadows realistically calculate blur; the amount of blur increases as the distance between the sphere and ground increases. Figures 2.41 and 2.42 illustrate the uniform blur of the CG depth-mapped shadow; the amount of blur remains constant at all distances.

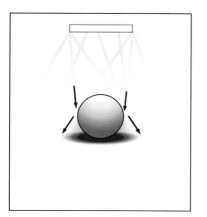

Figure 2.39 Diagram of a ray-traced shadow when the shadow-receiving object is *near to* the shadow-casting object. Notice the minimal amount of shadow blur.

Figure 2.40 Diagram of a ray-traced shadow when the shadow-receiving object is *far from* the shadow-casting object. Notice the increased amount of shadow blur.

Figure 2.41 Diagram of a depth-mapped shadow when the shadow-receiving object is *near to* the shadow-casting object.

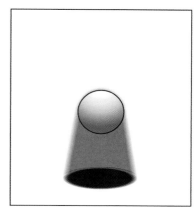

Figure 2.42 Diagram of a depth-mapped shadow when the shadow-receiving object is *far from* the shadow-casting object. Notice the amount of shadow blur remains unchanged from Figure 2.41.

The units of blur for a depth-mapped shadow may be in *absolute pixels* or based on a *percentage* of the depth-mapped file. If the blur is in *absolute pixels*, then changing shadow resolution means readjusting the blur setting. For example, a 10-pixel blur will have a much greater effect on a 256-square map than it will on a 2048-square map. As you increase the size of the map, you will need to increase the blur setting in order to get the same effect. A larger map will have less blur.

Many artists prefer a blur based on a *percentage* of the depth map instead. Blur calculated as a percentage of the map will remain the same even if the size of the depth map is changed: A 5% blur on a 256 (a 12-pixel blur) looks the same as a 5% blur on a 2048-square map (a 102-pixel blur). The advantage of calculating shadow blur as a percentage of the map is that you don't have to adjust any blur settings when you go from a low-resolution shadow map to a high-resolution one.

Ray-traced shadow blur is based on a theoretical size of the light in world units. Ray-traced shadows blur as if the light actually has volume. This means that scenes that are very large will need larger blur settings than small-scale scenes in order to achieve the same effect. Calculating ray-traced shadow blur in world units also means that if your light is farther away from the shadow-receiving objects, then a larger blur setting will be needed to achieve the same result as when the light is close. This scale is "theoretical" in that the light doesn't actually have any dimension; only the shadow is affected—the specular and diffuse contribution from the light remains unchanged.

A COMPARISON OF SHADOW BLUR FOR RAY-TRACED AND DEPTH-MAPPED SHADOWS

Ray-Traced

- Blurs increasingly with distance.
- Increasing blur increases render time.
- Blur is calculated in world units.

Depth-Mapped

- Blurs uniformly with distance.
- Increasing blur usually doesn't significantly increase render time.
- Blur is based on the size of the depth-map file.

Figure 2.43 Ray-traced shadow.

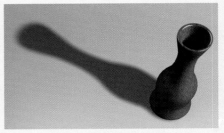

Figure 2.44 Depth-mapped shadow.

2.4.2 SHADOW DENSITY AND COLOR

Another shadow parameter you may want to adjust is the *density* or *color* of the shadow. The *density* of a shadow refers to the darkness of the shadow. By default, a digital shadow will occlude light 100%, which is to say that it will occlude all the light. The darkness of a digital shadow can be lifted, however. In many lights, a *shadow color* parameter will change both the density and the color of the shadow. If the shadow color is black, then the shadow is fully opaque. If the shadow color is gray, the shadow will be less dense and will allow some illumination from the light to pass through. If the shadow color is white, no shadow will be visible (though it will still be calculated, so this isn't a way to turn shadows "off"). If the shadow color is a color, the shadow will be both lightened and tinted that color. Tinting the shadow in this manner will colorize it uniformly throughout. Some lights have separate controls for shadow color and density.

In life, fully opaque objects occlude light 100%; lightening your digital shadows is a "cheat." However, contrary to some opinions, just because it is a cheat doesn't mean you need to avoid it. CG rendering is full of unrealistic cheats that we use regularly, such as light linking or not turning a shadow on at all. A closer look at life will reveal why lightening the shadow density can, indeed, be useful.

In life, most shadows are naturally lightened by the presence of scattered environment light. Unless you are rendering with global illumination, your scene will not have this scattered light. If naturally occurring scattered light isn't present and you want your shadows to be lighter, then you will need to do this yourself. One way to lighten the shadows is to add additional light sources that shine into the shadow areas, known as *fill lights*. Another way is to lighten the density or color parameter of the shadow as we've been discussing.

Close observation will also reveal that as shadows become softer, they typically also become less dense as more scattered light wraps around to fill them in. In many cases, the digital lighter can imitate this by *decreasing shadow density as he increases shadow blur*. Figures 2.45 through 2.47 show the relationship of shadow density to shadow blur.

Figure 2.45 (Left) A fully dense (black), very crisp shadow.

Figure 2.46 (Center) The density of this shadow has been reduced and the blur increased.

Figure 2.47 (Right) This shadow is even more blurry and lightened. It also is tinted a slight warm color.

Whether or not you should lighten shadows is almost like a religious preference amongst experienced lighters. Some say "no way!" while others use this technique often with good results. Obviously, I'm in the latter category. One advantage of lifting the shadow density is that no additional lights are needed; another is that it is relatively easy to do. But the bottom line is that if your efforts to modify the shadow density give you poor results or don't suit your lighting style, and you can achieve a similar result with other methods, then by all means use other methods.

Keep in mind that since it is a cheat, you will want to be careful so that your scene continues to look realistic. In particular, when working with shadow color or density, *you will need to make sure that the shadow density integrates with the shadow sides of your objects* (Figure 2.48 and 2.49). Fill lights are still needed to do this task. (Chapter 12, "Three-Point Lighting and More," covers how to use and place fill light.)

Figure 2.48 (Left) The shadow side in this render is too dark relative to the cast shadow.

Figure 2.49 (Right) The shadow side in this image is integrated better with the cast shadow.

Figure 2.50 Deep-blue shadows in *Monsters, Inc.* help to create the rich look of the environments (© 2001, Disney/Pixar).

Adding color to your shadows can be an artistic choice and can dictate the color of the scattered light in the scene. For example, in day scenes the shadows may take on a blue cast (Figure 2.50). On white surfaces, slightly tinted shadows can keep your whites from looking dull (compare Figure 2.52 and 2.53). Lightening and colorizing depth-mapped shadows can also be a way to indicate transparency for surfaces with uniformly colored transparency (Figure 2.51).

Figure 2.51 Colored depth-mapped shadow.

Figure 2.52 Digital shadows can look dull on white surfaces.

Figure 2.53 Slightly tinting the shadow is a subtle way to increase visual interest.

2.4.3 SHADOW SAMPLES

Shadow samples **is a parameter that controls how many times the renderer samples each pixel to see whether the surface is in shadow.** Shadow samples is a quality setting. The higher the number of samples, the higher the shadow quality and the longer the render takes. As with any quality setting, you definitely don't just want to set this to a high number and call it a day. Rather, you should test to identify the lowest possible number of shadow samples you can have while still maintaining an image with acceptable quality. The artifact caused by too low of samples is a speckling in the shadow, particularly along any edges that have been blurred. Higher blur usually requires a higher sample rate, especially with ray-traced shadows. The need for higher samples is the main reason why larger blur with ray-traced shadows takes longer to render.

NOTE

When working on digital elements that will have grain added, a tiny (*very tiny*) bit of speckling will be masked by the grain. In this case, it may not be worth the extra sampling (and render time) needed to make the shadow immaculately smooth.

2.4.4 BIAS

The *bias* parameter will move the shadow away from the light. This is a pure cheat, having no physical counterpart. This cheat is designed to compensate for limitations in the way digital shadows are calculated, and it is present simply to account for artifacts. Digital shadows are calculated to begin at the place where the surface exists and continue onward away from the light. To understand this, it is again helpful to consider the shadow as a volume. The problem occurs when the renderer cannot accurately determine whether the shadow is in front of the surface or vice versa. Similar to when you have two surfaces in the exact spot in your scene, bits of one will show in front and then the other in a very odd way. The solution for this is to move the shadow away from the shadow-casting surface, so the object is clearly in front of its shadow. The bias parameter does this when it pushes the shadow away from the light.

Self-shadowing artifacts or simply *self-shadowing* for short refers to when a surface shadows itself incorrectly. *Bias is used to correct for self-shadowing artifacts.*

Depth-mapped and ray-traced shadows have different needs for bias. When using ray-traced shadows, "just a dab will do." If you see any self-shadowing artifacts, then add a small amount of bias (like .001 or less), and you can generally call it a day. Bias is a much larger issue when it comes to depth-mapped shadows. Depth-mapped shadows are prone to self-shadowing artifacts related to bias. Section 2.6, "Gallery of Shadow Problems and Solutions," has many examples of what incorrect bias settings may look like.

How much bias a depth shadow needs depends on several factors and may require little attention or quite a bit from the lighter to avoid artifacts. In addition to not enough bias causing artifacts, *too much* bias can also cause problems. If a shadow is biased too much, it will separate from the shadow-casting object (see Figures 2.70 and 2.72 in Section 2.6). A lighter needs to be very careful when adjusting the bias parameter to make sure he isn't introducing new problems.

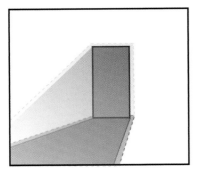

Figure 2.54 When a depth-mapped shadow is blurred, it expands out in front of the surface.

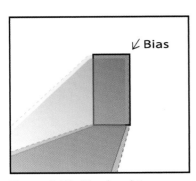

Figure 2.55 Shadow bias pushes the depth shadow back so the surface is in front of the shadow.

TIP

A good rule of thumb when adding shadows is to *test-render the scene both before and after adding each shadow*, saving the render so you can toggle back and forth to be very clear on what each shadow has done and to check for artifacts and any unwanted self-shadowing that may be otherwise hard to catch. I cannot stress enough how important this workflow is in order to catch and eliminate errors, especially when working with the bias parameter.

How much a depth shadow is blurred will impact the amount of bias needed. In general, increasing the blur increases the bias needed. When you consider that the depth map blurs uniformly, this is explained. When a depth shadow is blurred, it enlarges the area the shadow covers (Figure 2.54). Think of a two-dimensional blur of a white-and-black shape: The blurred area goes both outside and inside the original shape. When the depth shadow blurs it will expand to be in front of the objects as well and darken the subject incorrectly. This, too, is a self-shadowing artifact, one that is harder to catch unless you are paying attention. To correct for this, you will want to increase the bias (Figure 2.55). Simply brightening the light isn't a good solution, as this will also brighten objects that do *not* have self-shadowing artifacts, causing some objects to be brighter than others in an incorrect manner. It also causes the intensity setting in the light to be misleading, since the light may need a much higher setting than it would otherwise.

Because of self-shadowing artifacts and the fact that one can only bias a shadow so far before it begins to separate, in some cases you can only blur a depth-mapped shadow a certain amount before running into problems. Again, careful testing is needed to determine this point.

The scale of the scene will also affect how much bias is needed. The units for bias are typically in world units, so a large-scale scene may need larger bias settings for its shadows. How the depth map is created will affect whether the bias settings will need to be adjusted.

Mid-distance depth maps are a type of depth map that helps account for problems with self-shadowing with less need to adjust the bias setting. Mid-distance maps don't start the shadow at the same place the surface starts, but rather they begin the shadow between the first and second surfaces that the depth rays hit, which is generally the middle of the object (Figure 2.56). If only one surface is intersected, such as a ground plane with nothing behind it, then this single surface isn't included in the shadow.

Beginning the shadow somewhere *inside* the object eliminates the vast majority of self-shadowing artifacts without the need to use the bias parameter. However, mid-distance maps aren't a cure-all, and there are situations where they don't solve self-shadowing problems. Thin objects with two sides (such as a plate or board) aren't helped much by mid-distance maps. Self-shadowing artifacts may show up at corners and edges when mid-distance maps are used.

Depth-mapped shadows can be calculated using methods known as mid-distance, min-distance, or max-distance. Min-distance maps are the ones initially described in Section 2.3.1, "Depth-Mapped Shadows," while mid-distance maps have been discussed here. In addition to these, max-distance depth maps are calculated from the second surface the depth ray hits, or typically the back side of an object. Max-distance shadows are especially prone to artifacts and are rarely used.

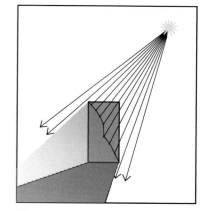

Figure 2.56 Diagram of a mid-distance shadow. The depth shadow is determined by averaging the distance of the front side with the back side, resulting in the shadow volume beginning somewhere in the middle of the object.

TIP

Choosing which type of depth map to create is typically an option found somewhere in the light or render globals, when available. In Maya, mid-distance maps are the default and may be switched to min-distance by unchecking the Use Mid Dist option in the light.

2.4.5 SHADOW RESOLUTION

One of the first things to decide when using a depth-mapped shadow is what size the shadow map will be. Shadow maps have a pixel resolution in x and y (width and height). Shadow files are square, however, so only one resolution needs to be set, and this size is used for the both x and y of the image. How big should a depth-map file be? Several factors influence the size needed. Many people decide this initially by trial and error, but a few relationships apply that can give you a better idea and a good starting point.

One factor influencing the size needed is how big the shadow will be in the final image. When determining the size of the shadow in the final image, consider how big the final image is and also how much of this image the shadow occupies. For example, if a final image is approximately 2,000 pixels across and a shadow prominently occupies a third of this, then the shadow file should be at least 2000/3, or about 700 pixels. A good starting point for the shadow resolution may be 1,024 squared.

Another factor influencing the shadow resolution is the softness of the shadow. The greater the blur, the smaller the shadow resolution needed. The blur will smooth out any jagged edges. It's a good idea to determine how much blur you need and then be prepared to readjust your shadow size. Don't render a shadow larger than you need for your scene.

Be aware that some programs require multiples of two for shadow maps: 256; 512; 1,024; 2,046; 4,096; 8,192. A 1024x1024 map is called "1k squared" or "1k" for short. If your shadow is over 4,096 ("4k"), then rethink your strategy and refer to Section 2.5.2, "Optimizing Mapped Shadows," and if needed look at Chapter 15, "Tricks of the Trade," for additional ways to optimize it.

WHAT TO CONSIDER WHEN DETERMINING THE SIZE OF THE DEPTH MAP
- The size of the final render
- The screen area the shadow occupies and its prominence
- The amount of blur on the shadow
- How optimized the depth map is (see Section 2.5.2)

2.5 SHADOW WORKFLOW AND EFFICIENCY TIPS

In this section, we will cover practical usage of shadows.

2.5.1 SETTING OBJECTS' SHADOW ATTRIBUTES

When optimizing a scene for the most efficient render, you will want to turn off unneeded calculations. Modifying the render attributes per surface is part of this task. *Render attributes* are settings that control how specific surfaces are rendered. One attribute you will want to turn on or off is *whether the object is shadow-casting or not*. If the object doesn't *cast* a shadow, turn off shadow-casting calculations. Casting a shadow isn't the same as receiving a shadow. A ground plane, for example, should always have shadow-casting turned off. The ground plane only receives shadows; it doesn't itself cast shadows on any other object. Including the ground plane in shadow calculations is a common mistake. Turning off calculations for objects that don't need to cast shadows improves render time and helps eliminate artifacts.

2.5.2 OPTIMIZING MAPPED SHADOWS

"Optimizing" a mapped shadow means setting up the map so that the shadow-casting objects fill as much of the area as possible within the map (compare Figures 2.57 and 2.58). Doing this allows you to render a smaller map since there are fewer blank areas and thus fewer wasted pixels. This is a necessary first step because it's only when the shadow is optimized that you will be able to choose the best resolution for your shadow.

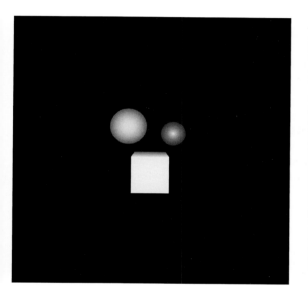
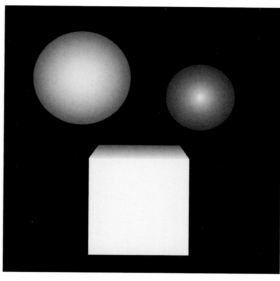

Figure 2.57 (Left) Non-optimized shadow map.

Figure 2.58 (Right) Optimized shadow map.

NOTE

While this subsection focuses on depth-mapped shadows, these techniques work the same on deep shadow maps as well.

Consider the example in the previous section, in which a shadow filled about 1/3 of a 2,000-pixel-wide final render, occupying about 700 pixels of screen space. Now here's where optimizing the depth map makes the difference. If the shadowing object fills the frame of the depth map, then a 1k map should do the job. But if your object takes up a mere tenth of your map, you need a map ten times this size to get the same effective resolution, at least 10k square!

NOTE

Realize that a 1k map is 1000x1000 pixels for a total of one million pixels (rounding the numbers here for easy math). A 10k map is 10,000x10,000, which is 1,000,000,000—one billion pixels! This is not 10 times larger but 100 times larger, with a much longer render time and larger file size.

Unfortunately, many off-the-shelf software packages (software available to the home user) have very limited tools for generating and optimizing depth-mapped shadows. The shadows can be optimized, but doing so requires some gymnastics on the part of the lighter to get past the limitations of the software. The lack of easy-to-use tools is one reason why many lighters simply abandon depth-mapped shadows and turn on the ray-traced shadows button. This is unfortunate. Most production houses, on the other hand, have methods and tools available to greatly optimize their depth-mapped shadows, allowing for much better results.

When optimizing point light depth shadows, you should turn shadows off in unwanted directions. By default, point lights render a total of six depth maps per light per frame. These depth maps are from cameras pointing away from the point light in six directions, corresponding to the six faces of a cube. Shadows are rendered one for each positive and negative axis of the light: There is a shadow rendered in the positive y-axis, the negative y-axis, the positive x-axis, the negative x-axis, the positive z-axis, and the negative z-axis. When shadows aren't needed in all directions, rendering them means wasted calculations and wasted render time. You can optimize your point light shadows by turning off shadow calculations in the directions they aren't needed. Most packages have simple check-box options for this.

When working with distant lights, you should turn off the shadow-casting attribute of any object not casting a shadow. You will want to do this anyway, but with distant lights this is especially important. A distant light illuminates the entire scene, and by default the depth shadow will encompass every single shadow-casting object. With a large scene you may need an extremely high-resolution shadow in order to get enough detail in your shadow. For this reason, directional lights are often not a good choice if you need detailed depth maps. Turning shadow casting off for unwanted objects means the depth map will frame fewer objects. This helps if the objects are close together, but isn't much help if they are spaced far apart. For example, don't allow a gigantic ground plane to be included in a depth map.

Most packages will allow you to limit the scale of the distant light's depth map and center it around the light's icon in the scene, but it can be hard to determine exactly what is in this area. In general, controlling depth-mapped shadows with distant lights can be tricky.

Spotlights are the easiest to control when using depth-mapped shadows. For this reason they are used often in animation productions. The depth map defaults to rendering the area inside the cone of the spotlight (Figure 2.59). You can easily see what will be rendered in the depth shadow by looking through the spotlight. What you see in the cone is what will be in the depth map. If you see just a few tiny shadow-casting objects and lots of shadow-receiving area or blank area, then you know your shadow map will likewise have much blank, wasted area and need optimizing.

A simple way to optimize the depth map of a spotlight is to frame the subjects to be just within the cone of light, which generally involves narrowing the cone angle (Figure 2.60). While narrowing the cone angle is generally suggested as a way to optimize your spotlight's depth map, in practice this advice is only moderately helpful. Be aware that the narrowness of the cone angle isn't what optimizes the shadow; but rather the framing of the objects so they lie just within the cone of light. What if a narrow cone angle isn't what you want for the illumination of your scene?

Another option generally available is to set the angle used by the depth map camera to something *different* from the spotlight's cone angle. Obviously, you would want to use a *smaller* angle of view for the depth camera than the light's cone angle (Figure 2.61). A good way to find the smallest possible angle to use and still contain all of the shadow-casting elements is to look through the light and reduce the light's cone until it just encompasses the shadow-casting elements. Write this number down. Reset your spotlight cone to where you need it for illumination, and set the depth render angle to be the smaller number you have written down. This method is rather crude and has limitations, but unfortunately that is about as fancy as many packages get.

TIP

In all cases when you optimize the mapped shadow, be sure to test frames throughout the animation. You don't want your character accidentally walking out of his shadow.

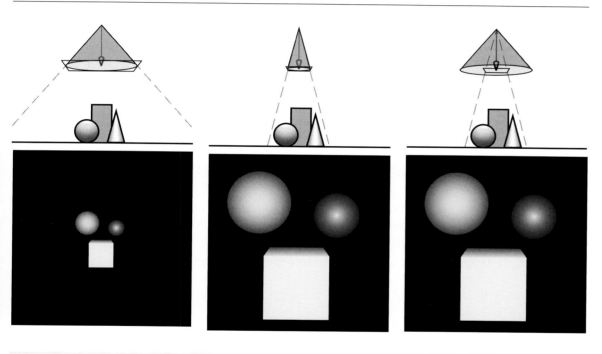

Figure 2.59 (Left) Diagram of a non-optimized, wide spotlight cone angle and what the shadow map would look like.

Figure 2.60 (Center) Diagram narrowing the spotlight cone angle and what the shadow would look like.

Figure 2.61 (Right) Diagram of a narrow optimized shadow camera angle of view with a wide spotlight cone angle and what the shadow map would look like.

HOW TO OPTIMIZE SHADOW MAPS:

✓ Make sure the subject fills the map, with as little blank area as possible.
✓ Check how much the subject fills the frame by looking through the light.
✓ If necessary (and if an available option), narrow the shadow camera field of view to less than the cone angle of the light.
✓ If necessary (and if an available option), create a special shadow camera to best optimize the map (see Section 15.2.2, "Advanced Mapped Shadow Techniques").
✓ And remember, only render the shadow as large as it needs to be.

2.5.3 Tips on Adding Shadows and Troubleshooting

Here is a list of things to keep in mind when generating shadows. Some of these tips have been said before but bear repeating; others are new.

- ✓ The number one rule of shadows: Always know what shadow goes to what light and what each shadow is doing.
- ✓ Save and reuse your depth maps once the positions of lights and objects are set.
- ✓ Optimize all depth maps.
- ✓ Turn off shadows in unwanted directions for point lights.
- ✓ Turn off shadow-casting attributes for objects that don't cast shadows.
- ✓ Keep quality settings as low as possible while maintaining sufficiently good results.
- ✓ Check shadow-pass renders the first time before using to avoid future problems or mysteries (if you have a viewer to do so).
- ✓ Render a before and after when adding shadows to catch any problems so that you can be sure you know what the shadow is doing.
- ✓ Add shadows one at a time.
- ✓ To troubleshoot, render with just the light in question ("light solo").
- ✓ Keep a careful eye on bias when blurring a depth-mapped shadow.
- ✓ For the lowest render times, use depth-mapped shadows only. The first ray-traced shadow added to the scene adds the most time.
- ✓ To keep render time down, use ray-traced shadows only when needed—for "real" shadow transparency and realistic blurring with distance.
- ✓ If ray-tracing, keep shadow samples (rays) and bounces as low as possible to keep render time down.
- ✓ Be aware that when adding shadows you may need to change your lights' intensity and position. For this reason, it's a good idea not to wait too late to add them.
- ✓ Render only one map for unmoving objects and reuse it for all frames.

2.6 GALLERY OF SHADOW PROBLEMS AND SOLUTIONS

Digital shadows are prone to artifacts. In addition, a number of common shadow problems are the result of user error. Here are images of the artifacts and errors you might encounter, along with solutions to the problems presented. While some of these problems have been discussed before, this section includes all of them and is intended to be a useful gallery of images that can be used as a quick reference.

IMAGE GALLERY OF PROBLEMS AND SOLUTIONS

If you have problems with the shadows in your scene, you can skim through this section for what the problem—and solution—might be. Common artifacts and errors are shown on the left, fixes are on the right.

 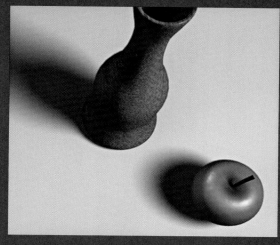

Figure 2.62 (Left)
Render with artifact.

Figure 2.63 (Right)
Corrected render.

Problem: Speckles along the blurred edges of the shadow.

Solution: Shadow samples are too low. Raise shadow samples. Raising shadow samples increases render time, so the correct number of samples is the lowest possible number needed to eliminate artifacts.

Figure 2.64 (Left)
Render with user error.

Figure 2.65 (Right)
Corrected render.

Problem: Ray-traced shadows aren't showing up in reflected objects or behind transparent objects. Areas of reflection appear "glowy."

Solution: Ray-traced shadow bounces are too low. Make sure that the shadow bounces are set to 2 or higher. Keep this number as low as possible to keep render time down.

IMAGE GALLERY OF PROBLEMS AND SOLUTIONS (CONTINUED)

Figure 2.66 (Left)
Render with artifact.

Figure 2.67 (Right)
Corrected render.

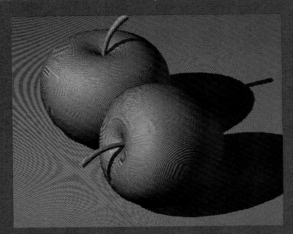 

Problem: Surface has weird speckles or patterns on the front of it.

Solution: This artifact is typical of a shadow with zero blur and zero bias on a ray-traced or min-distance map. To fix, add a very small amount of bias.

NOTE
Figure 2.66 also incorrectly includes the ground plane in the shadow calculations.

Figure 2.68 (Left)
Render with artifact.

Figure 2.69 (Right)
Corrected render.

Problem: Jagged edges around shadow.

Solutions: The resolution of the depth map is too low and/or isn't optimized. (1) Optimize the depth map; (2) if the map is optimized, increase the resolution of the depth-map.

IMAGE GALLERY OF PROBLEMS AND SOLUTIONS (CONTINUED)

Figure 2.70 (Left) Render with artifact.

Figure 2.71 (Right) Corrected render.

Problem: Shadow seems oddly cut off under geometry.

Solution: This artifact usually appears with too much blur and bias on a mid-distance map. Reduce bias and possibly blur. Try a min-distance map as a possibility.

Figure 2.72 (Left) Render with artifact.

Figure 2.73 (Right) Corrected render.

Problem: Shadow is separating from the geometry and/or has disappeared in places.

Solution: Reduce bias.

IMAGE GALLERY OF PROBLEMS AND SOLUTIONS (CONTINUED)

Figure 2.74 (Left)
Render with artifact.

Figure 2.75 (Right)
Corrected render.

Problem: Front faces of geometry have strange soft shadows or overall darkening.

Solution: Too low of bias for the blur setting. Increase bias; may need to decrease blur.

Figure 2.76 (Left)
Render with artifact.

Figure 2.77 (Right)
Corrected render.

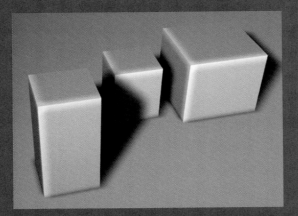 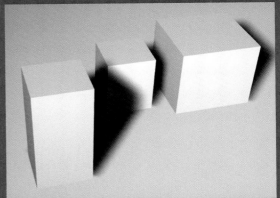

Problem: Surface is too dark; corners and edges look light or dark.

Solution: This artifact is from too low of bias on a blurred min-distance map. Increase bias; may need to decrease blur.

NOTE
Figure 2.76 also incorrectly includes the ground plane in the shadow calculations.

IMAGE GALLERY OF PROBLEMS AND SOLUTIONS (CONTINUED)

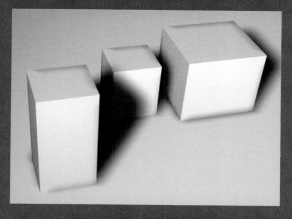 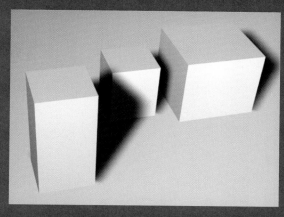

Figure 2.78 (Left) Image with self-shadowing artifact.

Figure 2.79 (Right) Corrected render.

Problem: Object darkens strangely along bottom edges where it meets another surface and at corners.

Solution: This artifact is from too low of bias on a blurred mid-distance map.

Increase bias; may need to decrease blur.

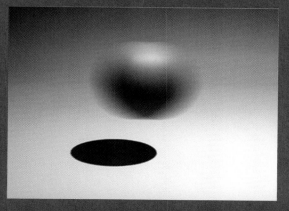 

Figure 2.80 (Left) Image with shadow limitations.

Figure 2.81 (Right) Corrected render.

Problem: Shadow doesn't motion blur correctly.

Solution: Depth-mapped shadows don't motion blur. Switch to ray-traced or deep shadows.

IMAGE GALLERY OF PROBLEMS AND SOLUTIONS (CONTINUED)

Figure 2.82 (Left)
Image with user error.

Figure 2.83 (Right)
Corrected image.

Problem: Cast shadow and shadow side don't match.

Solution: Typically add fill to shadow side only; possibly darken shadow.

Figure 2.84 (Left)
Image with shadow
limitations.

Figure 2.85 (Top right)
Corrected image A.

Figure 2.86 (Bottom right)
Corrected image B.

Problem: Surface seems to float (happens typically with a very blurred depth shadow).

Solution: Add a contact shadow using other techniques such as occlusion (Figure 2.85). Switch to a ray-traced shadow (Figure 2.86).

IMAGE GALLERY OF PROBLEMS AND SOLUTIONS (CONTINUED)

Figure 2.87 (Left)
Image with shadow limitations.

Figure 2.88 (Right)
Corrected image.

Problem: Shadow needs to lighten with distance but doesn't.

Solution: Fill in distant shadow with other light; lighten shadow overall and create a dark shadow core with contact shadow techniques.

Figure 2.89 (Left)
Image with user error.

Figure 2.90 (Right)
Corrected image.

Problem: Shadow is perfectly hard.

Solution: Even for a crisp shadow, add a very small amount of blur to keep it from looking CG.

2.7 CHAPTER CONCLUSION

This chapter has established a solid foundation for understanding and using digital shadows, focusing on the common shadow types of ray-traced and depth-mapped shadows. We have gone into a great deal of detail right away on this subject, with the idea that it's better to learn good habits early than to eliminate bad habits later. Hopefully this chapter will serve as a useful reference for the setup and debugging of shadows and provide a basis for learning advanced shadow techniques.

2.7.1 IMPORTANT POINTS

- Having an in-depth knowledge of shadows is necessary to create the best image.
- When crafting shadows, an artist should consider not only cast shadows but also the shadow side, contact shadows, and areas "in the shadows."
- The two most common types of digital shadows are depth-mapped and ray-traced shadows.
- Depth-mapped shadows are fast but less realistic-looking.
- Ray-traced shadows blur realistically with distance and consider surface properties such as transparency.
- Due to their longer render times, ray-traced shadows should be used only when their distinct visual advantage is necessary and/or you have the time to render them.
- A better look can be obtained out of depth-mapped shadows with some know-how.
- The most common shadow parameters adjusted are shadow blur and color/density.
- In life, soft light creates soft shadows.
- An increase in shadow blur and a decrease in shadow density often go hand in hand.
- When working with shadow density or color, be sure to carefully match the cast shadow and shadow sides of your objects.
- Be sure to optimize your depth-map shadows (objects filling the frame).
- Increasing depth-map resolution increases render time—use the smallest map possible.
- When creating ray-traced shadows, shadow samples/rays may need to be increased.
- Increasing shadow rays increases render time; use only the lowest number needed.
- Depth-map units are typically in pixels or a percentage of the map size.
- Ray-traced shadow units are typically in world units, setting a theoretical size of the light.
- Bias will push the shadow away from the light and is used to correct for self-shadowing artifacts.
- Incorrectly set bias can result in a number of artifacts, so use this parameter carefully.

2.7.2 Terms

cast shadow

contact shadow

shadow side

"in the shadows"

shadow core

shadow penumbra

depth-mapped shadow

ray-traced shadow

deep shadows

ambient occlusion

shadow blur

shadow density

shadow samples

shadow bias

min-distance map

mid-distance map

max-distance map

2.7.3 Exercises

1. Create a simple scene with a ground shape, a few primitive shapes, and a shadow-casting light. Play around with the relative orientation of the light to the ground plane and of the shadow-casting objects to the light and the ground plane. Create three images: (1) an image where the shadows are long and play a prominent visual role; (2) an image in which the shadows are as small as possible; and (3) an image in which the shadows are hidden from view.

2. Create two still-life scenes that have shadowing light(s). Use shadows to help set the mood and direct the eye in these scenes. Use both ray-traced and depth-mapped shadows. (You may have only one shadow type in each scene or mix them up—just be sure you use each shadow to its best advantage!)

3. Take some photographs of real-world shadows. Experiment with photographing items under a bare bulb versus diffused light. (You can make your own diffuser at home with a curtain or lamp shade.) Try photographing a simple item like a fire hydrant under full sun versus a cloudy sky. Compare the shadows in the photographs. In what ways are they different?

Before you light any scene, consider *why* you are lighting. And it is not, my friends, just to "see stuff." When lighting, you must consider the purpose of your lights. The "why" of lighting relates to the aesthetic intent of the image and is one of the three components that make up great lighting. The answer to the question "Why am I lighting?" determines the choices you make in your lighting. When you have an idea of what your lights are supposed to be doing, then you will know the best placement and attributes needed to achieve this.

The primary purpose of lighting is to help tell the story. As an old adage (and pop singer Rod Stewart) says, every picture tells a story (doesn't it?). It is obvious that an image that is part of a narrative tells a story. An image doesn't have to be part of a narrative to have a story, however. In a more general sense, the story of an image is the reason it was created in the first place. Whether the image is for advertising, feature film, or a fine-art piece, you will want to make sure your lighting complements and furthers this reason. The lighting in a scene may have several objectives, all subservient to the overall purpose or story of the image. In any given image, the lighting may satisfy one, many, or all of these goals. When approaching the lighting of a scene, consider carefully the purpose or story-point of the image and how each goal of lighting relates to this intention. How these goals are broken out is not a rule; different people have outlined these objectives in different ways. Some sort of categorization, however, is necessary for discussion and analysis.

This book defines 10 goals of lighting:

1. Establish setting
2. Enhance mood
3. Direct the eye
4. Create the illusion of depth
5. Create the illusion of volume
6. Reveal substance
7. Maintain continuity
8. Integrate elements
9. Set visual style
10. Create visual interest

NOTE

I'd like to give credit to Sharon Calahan, the lighting designer for films such as Pixar's *Toy Story*. Early in my career, I had the pleasure of hearing and being inspired by her talk about the objectives of lighting at a 1996 SIGGRAPH lecture, "Pixel Cinematography." For further reading, see her chapter "Storytelling through Lighting, a Computer Graphics Perspective" in *Advanced RenderMan*. Other than her treatment on the subject, I have never seen or heard any other in-depth treatment of the goals of lighting for digital artists. Seeing a need for more discussion on this essential topic, it is my pleasure to humbly adapt and expand on her work here.

The goals of lighting form the basis of excellent lighting. A study of the great painters, photographers, and cinematographers—the Masters of Light long before digital imagery came into being—show that they had an understanding not only of technique, but also of the artistry of their craft, and they used it to powerfully sculpt the audience's reactions. The most effective lighting comes from understanding the underlying principles.

The chapters in Part II discuss each of the goals in detail and give examples of how to use your lights to accomplish the goal. I am such a believer in the importance of this subject that I recommend that everyone, from beginning to advanced, take the time to read the chapters in Part II.

PART II

THE GOALS OF LIGHTING
(THE "WHY")

"I believe that the best cameraman is one who recognizes the source, the story, as the basis of his work."
—James Wong Howe, Cinematographer

Figure 3.1 *Nocturne, Railway Crossing, Chicago* by Fredrick Childe Hassam (ca. 1893, at the Museum of Fine Art, Boston).

Chapter 3
Goal 1: Establishing Setting

"For my part I know nothing with any certainty, but

the sight of the stars makes me dream."

—Vincent van Gogh, 19th century Impressionist painter

One of the most fundamental goals of lighting is to orient the audience as to the *setting* of the story. The setting is the time and place in which a situation or event exists. Is the scene outdoors or inside? Is it fireside or in an office? Is the time night, midday, or sunset? Each of these times and places would have very different lighting. Setting also involves the weather. Is the day foggy or clear? Is it raining? Everything about the light will vary depending on the setting, such as its color, position, intensity, and softness.

Various times and locations have lighting that is unique to each of them. When creating setting, you should stay near to the real properties of light at those times and places. A certain amount of artistic interpretation is fine, however. Depending on how much realism is desired, you may deviate little or a lot. Also, even in a strictly realistic representation the artist has a fair amount of leeway, since both the appearance of things and our perception of them does in fact vary somewhat.

To create digital lighting for environments, you need to understand what the light does naturally. You will want to know how light appears at different times, weather conditions, and places. This chapter covers the first goal of lighting: establishing setting. We begin with setting not because it's the most important, but rather because it's a logical early consideration when starting to light a scene.

3.1 TIME OF DAY

Different times of day have very characteristic lighting (Figure 3.2). We can immediately tell the time of day by the light that is present—its color, intensity, and angle.

A determining factor in the color of sunlight throughout the day is the location of the sun on the horizon. When the sun is low on the horizon, the rays reaching the Earth have passed through much atmosphere before reaching us. When the sun is directly overhead, the rays pass through a much smaller distance of atmosphere (see Figure 3.3). How much distance the sun's rays have passed through the atmosphere will affect the color of the light reaching the Earth. Atmosphere scatters the sun's rays, and it scatters the smaller wavelengths of blue light more than the larger wavelengths of red light. This means the lower the sun is on the horizon, the more the direct light is tinted red and the scattered light is tinted blue.

Figure 3.2 A time-of-day series representing sunset to night (Paul Tillery).

Figure 3.4 Dawn.

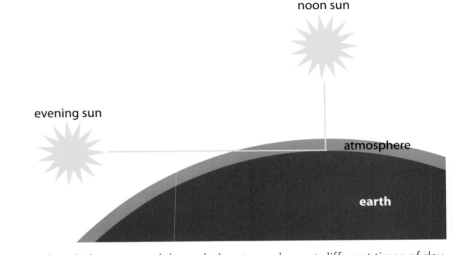

Figure 3.3 Diagram illustrating how light rays travel through the atmosphere at different times of day.

At *sunrise and early morning* **the sun is low on the horizon, and the direct light is red-toned while the scattered light is very blue-toned** (Figures 3.3 and 3.4). In most respects, sunrise closely resembles sunset, and in fact, in many photographs it's difficult to tell the two apart. Toned-down, slightly bluer versions of sunset colors, such as pale blues, purples, pinks, and pale oranges and yellows, will give the best impression. Dawn is a quiet and cool time, when the world is still waking, and the sun is just beginning to warm the day. Mist is also often associated with morning. Mist is a diffuser, and it softens the light (Figure 3.5).

Midday **sun is coming down from overhead and has strong contrasts.** At high noon (12:00 p.m.) the sun is directly above. However, angles coming in at 30 degrees or so top-down to the subject will still read as midday and are often more pleasing than light from directly overhead. Natural lighting at high noon is typically harsh (Figure 3.6). Stage lighting usually modifies it by adding additional illumination to fill in the shadows (Figure 3.7).

Figure 3.6 Midday in *Rango* (©2011 Paramount Pictures. All rights reserved. Courtesy of Everett Collection). The bright direct light and strong shadows give the feeling of desert heat.

Figure 3.7 Often the contrast of midday is lessened for artistic reasons, especially in close-ups of characters where high contrast may be objectionable.

At midday, direct light is near white with the shadows being slightly more blue. How exactly you represent midday light can vary: You may lean a bit more toward cool or a bit more toward warm; you may have more or less contrast for artistic reasons. In some stylized full CG productions, the shadows may be interpreted as highly blue. The important point to remember is that the direct light at midday appears slightly warmer than the indirect light. I say "appears" because in your scene, you may find the colors of your lights more vibrant than you would expect. Which brings me to another point: A daylight rendition that uses no color in the lights will look disappointingly lifeless. Notice the subtle but important color shifts in the following examples (Figures 3.8 through 3.10).

A few ways you may interpret the colors of light at midday:

◆ White direct light, blue-toned; dark shadows.

◆ Pale yellow direct light; shadows neutral and dark.

◆ Slightly yellow-tinted direct light; slightly blue-tinted shadows (splitting the color difference).

◆ Pale yellow direct light; very blue-toned shadows (an artistic interpretation).

◆ More or less contrast.

Figure 3.8 (Left) Warmer with higher contrast for a feeling of harshness or heat.

Figure 3.9 (Center) Cool shadows, neutral direct light.

Figure 3.10 (Right) Very saturated shadows as an artistic interpretation.

During the *late day/early evening* the direct light is warming up and contrast is less. The direct light is less intense. Shadows are lighter, more blue, and, of course, longer than at midday. Photographers call this time the "golden hour" due to the color of the direct light and its pleasing appearance (Figures 3.11 and 3.12). The light is changing rapidly at this time of day, so the golden hour (which isn't actually an hour) is fleeting.

Figure 3.11 The "golden hour"—just before sunset.

Figure 3.12 Very late afternoon in *Surf's Up*, approaching the "golden hour" (©2007 Sony Pictures Animation Inc. All rights reserved. Courtesy of Sony Pictures Animation).

At *sunset* the sun is slipping just over the horizon. The direct light is red/gold while the indirect light is a deep blue. We are all familiar with the many colors of sunset. Sunsets are associated with rich reds, gold, and purples. Late sunsets may have deep, long shadows. An image with reds, gold, and dark-reddish or bluish shadows will read as sunset if the light is coming from the horizon (Figure 3.13 and 3.14). Sunsets tend to be more dramatically colored than sunrises.

Figure 3.13 Though dawn and sunset actually often look alike, bolder colors and reds give the impression of sunset rather than sunrise.

Figure 3.14 A photograph of sunset.

***Night* is lit only by moonlight (Figure 3.15) or artificial light sources.** The scattered light that remains when the sun has set is true blue. Pale true blue is the most physically accurate color for night, but it can often look a bit purplish to us. Night is generally represented with an overall blue light, the hue being anything from true blue to cyan (Figure 3.16). A typical way to represent night is with blue fill light and a white backlight. When the moon is present, it may contribute clear white light or very slightly tinted blue or yellow. The moon is often the motivation for the backlight or a dim direct light. Artificial light sources such as street lamps appear a rich gold, orange, or yellow at night. If the moon or artificial lights aren't present, the scene may be lit with blues only.

Figure 3.15 Night, lit by a dim moon.

Figure 3.16 Night can be represented in shades from blue to cyan. These images use low-level blue fill and the moon as a strong white rim light.

Various representations of night, each using three light sources: a lamp, the moon, and dark-blue skylight (Figures 3.17 through 3.19):

Figure 3.17 (Left) An artificial lamp is the key; a dim moon and deep blue skylight provide fill.

Figure 3.18 (Center) Pale moonlight is a low-level key here; the lamp provides a rim; dark blue skylight is the fill.

Figure 3.19 (Right) A bright moon provides a rim; the lamp is the key; dark blue skylight is the fill.

TIME-OF-DAY SUMMARY

Here is a brief summary of the lighting for different times of day.

Morning:

- Warm red/gold/pink direct light.
- Blue-toned indirect lighting.
- May include mist, which softens light quality.
- Like sunset but cooler time of day; cooler colors "feel" more like morning.

Midday:

- High contrast—in film/video this contrast is usually reduced with set lighting.
- Strong overhead lighting.
- Crisp, dark shadows.
- Direct illumination can be represented as white, cool (slightly blue), or warm (slightly yellow-orange).
- Indirect illumination is cooler (more blue) than direct illumination.

Early Evening ("Golden Hour"):

- Warm red/gold direct light.
- Blue indirect light.
- Pleasing time of day.

Sunset:

- Vivid red-gold direct light.
- Deep blue shadows.
- Often associated with reds.

Night:

- Low-level blue indirect light.
- Moonlight is cool/white.
- Often replicated in movies using blue indirect light and a white backlight.

Figure 3.20 Time-of-day lineup from left to right: dawn, midday, "golden hour," sunset, night.

3.2 WEATHER

Weather will also greatly influence the lighting of the scene.

Overcast days **are blue-toned or grayish in comparison to clear days.** Clouds act as large diffusing agents, scattering all rays of light. The light of an overcast day is more uniform with little differentiation between shadow and non-shadow. Shadows are mostly in the form of contact shadows (occlusion). The light is very, very soft and can look flat and bland. It is best portrayed in grays or very pale tints of blue. Overcast days make for good portraits if you are using a real camera and just using natural light, due to the soft quality of the light.

Fog, smog, and mist **all have particles suspended in the air that (1) obstruct distant views and (2) soften the light.** These particles, while tiny, are visible. When objects are very distant, many particles are between the viewer and the distant objects, and what you see are the particles themselves. In CG, obscuring fog is known simply as *atmosphere*. Atmosphere will reduce contrast, reduce textural detail, and typically desaturate the scene (Figure 3.21). Colors of distant objects will tend to the color of the atmosphere, which typically is grayish, blue, brown, or gold, depending on the scene. Fog, smog, and mist will soften and diffuse light, similar to overcast days.

Figure 3.21 A gray, misty day in *Beowulf* (©2007 Paramount Pictures. All rights reserved. Courtesy of Everett Collection).

Rain and ***snow*** **have additional qualities unique to them**. When rain and snow are in the air (in other words, when it's raining or snowing), they diffuse light and add atmosphere. Water makes surfaces darker and more reflective. Rainy environments are typically depicted as uniformly blue or gray-blue (Figure 3.22). On *clear snowy days* the white snow acts as a giant reflector, bouncing much light back into the environment, making the scene bright and the shadows lifted (Figure 3.23). Photographs aren't always the best reference for clear snowy scenes, as the limitations of the film can make the shadows look much darker than they are in life, detracting from a "snowy feel." When representing snowy days, it is often best to keep the shadows light and bluish.

Figure 3.22 (Left) A photograph of a rainy day—overall gray and misty.

Figure 3.23 (Right) A photograph of snow and ice—light and bright, with clear blue shadows.

3.3 LOCATION

Different locations have different types of light associated with them. Depending on location, the light will vary in color, position, intensity, and quality. Environment lighting is a well-thought-out task in digital production. You need to consider the various sources of light appearing in the environment, how those sources look in life, and any artistic interpretations to be placed on them. Each environment will have a unique interpretation, but generalities can be made that give environments recognizable characteristics. While the possible environments are endless, here are a few that are common or interesting.

Indoor lighting **is usually lit with bulbs using a tungsten filament, which has a warm orange color**. Even though indoor light is in reality a very warm color, when lighting a fully indoor scene the color may be balanced to be white or closer to white, or leave the lights yellow or orange tinted for artistic reasons (Figure 3.26).

Firelight and candlelight are also warm in color, usually a deep orange (Figure 3.24). An artistic interpretation of fire is to make the light more yellow near the source, turning to red farther away.

Figure 3.24 Warm firelight contrasts with cool night skylight in this evening scene from *Surf's Up* (©2007 Sony Pictures Animation Inc. All rights reserved. Courtesy of Sony Pictures Animation).

***Fluorescent light* takes on a greenish cast in comparison to other light sources** (see Figure 3.25). Fluorescent lighting doesn't emit color continuously along the spectrum, as other light sources do. Rather, it emits light that spikes in the green wavelength. The green cast of fluorescent light is usually considered unpleasant, and it is often neutralized with the use of filters in real photography.

***Mixed lighting* refers to scenes with a variety of light colors,** typically a mix of indoor or artificial light and outdoor or natural light (Figure 3.27). Indoor lighting and outdoor lighting have very different looks to them: indoor lights are typically tungsten bulbs, which are much warmer than daylight. In photographs the difference between the orange indoor and blue outdoor light is very apparent. It isn't uncommon to minimize this difference if it's distracting, but never so much so that the colors of indoor and outdoor light are the same.

Figure 3.25 This image from *Monsters, Inc.* accurately captures fluorescent light as greenish and unappealing (©2001 Disney/Pixar).

Figure 3.26 A tungsten bulb (*Open Season*, ©2006 Sony Pictures Animation Inc. All rights reserved. Courtesy of Sony Pictures Animation).

Forest **light is dappled and overall green (Figure 3.30).** The areas of direct sunlight may be white, pale blue, or pale yellow, and the diffused indirect light will be green. Direct light should be broken up into spots, and the areas of diffused green light should have indistinct and fuzzy shadows. Unlike the green of a fluorescent light, the gold-green of a forest is generally considered pleasant.

Figure 3.27 This photograph captures mixed lighting, with both warm interior light and cool outdoor light.

Underwater **scenes have their own distinct look (Figure 3.28).** Water quickly filters out all wavelengths other than blue. Red is the first to go, followed by yellow. In shallower waters you will see more colors. The water itself quickly tints and obscures faraway objects. Freshwater lakes and streams are murkier brownish-green, while oceans are clear cyan to blue. In shallower depths, sunlight will form undulating, caustic patterns. In addition to the lighting, animations of seaweed waving and small particles floating in the water greatly enhance the underwater impression.

Cities at night **are lit with a multitude of artificial light sources, with a wide variety of creative interpretations (Figure 3.29).** A typical scene that comes to mind is a dark-blue street lit with pools of warm light from streetlamps. Perhaps additional warm lights are illuminating sidewalks from shop windows, adding a bit more gaiety to the scene. A different approach is to use many multicolored lights, coming from advertising and building lights. Another approach that is a departure from the typical "blue for night" stereotype is to light a night city almost entirely in warm tones, coming from many orange and yellow artificial light sources.

Figure 3.28 Underwater scene (image by Vivi Qin).

Figure 3.29 A photograph of Hong Kong at night.

Figure 3.30 A forest scene, using warmer, dappled direct light with greenish fill (image by Ross Cantrell).

3.4 SETTING AND STORY

Setting is closely tied to story. In addition to the fact that the story is obviously occurring somewhere, the choice of setting should reflect the mood and action of that moment. During battle, a thunderstorm rages; when our hero is wounded and all may be lost, the skies are gray and still. When we discover that he is actually okay, the clouds part, and the sun breaks through. Perhaps such a close relationship may seem too obvious, but in fact this type of parallel is used often, especially in animated features. Watch the early classic animated films such as *Bambi* (1942) to see how the setting reflects and enhances the story, at times even shaping the characters and driving the plot. Consider the colorful and joyous spring season into which Bambi is born (Figure 3.31) contrasted with the cold and snowy winter day when he loses his mother (Figure 3.32).

When considering setting, keep in mind not only the lighting but also the mood evoked by the setting and how they both fit in with the story you are telling. The next chapter, "Goal 2: Creating Mood," takes a closer look at mood and story.

Figure 3.31 Spring is the time for beginnings, with flowers and lush growth setting off the arrival of Bambi and his new friendship with the baby skunk, Flower (©Disney. All rights reserved).

Figure 3.32 The scene is made empty and desolate by the obscuring snowfall when Bambi finds his mother is gone and follows his father, a strong and distant figure (©Disney. All rights reserved).

3.5 CHAPTER CONCLUSION

Helping to establish the setting is one of the fundamental goals of lighting. In this chapter we've seen how certain times of day, weather conditions, and locations have properties of light that are characteristic of them. We've also seen how even though these settings can be identified in part by their lighting, that a large amount of creative interpretation is possible when replicating them. However, it is a rare instance when our lighting isn't based at least in part on a real-world counterpart. Often when first approaching a scene, we should consider: What would real light be doing in this setting, and how can I best imitate this? By understanding how real light looks in certain settings, we have a solid basis on which to formulate our lighting design.

3.5.1 IMPORTANT POINTS

- Lighting plays an important role in establishing a story's setting.
- When creating lighting that represents a certain setting, it's important to understand what real-world light would look like in this environment.
- The lower the sun is upon the horizon, the more red the direct light is from it.
- Shadows are more blue-toned than the sun's direct light.
- Night is often represented by cyan to true-blue lighting.
- Days have diffused light due to fog, snow, and rain; they are often more consistent (grayish) in color, or overall tinted blue.
- Indoor light is warmer in general than outdoor light. Tungsten light is orange.
- Fluorescent light is green.
- The digital lighter should not feel limited by formulas when lighting environments, as a certain amount of artistic interpretation is acceptable. How much depends on the style of the piece.

3.5.2 TERMS

setting   "golden hour"
tungsten   mixed lighting

3.5.3 EXERCISES

1. Using your digital camera or a friend's, play around with the white-balance setting. Try taking some photographs indoors but set the white point to day exterior. Try taking some photos outdoors with the white point set to interior. Wait until dusk and take pictures with both natural and artificial light sources in the image. What do the colors look like? If you have any fluorescent lighting, take a photograph of that too. Print out or save your images and be prepared to discuss them.

2. Choose a day when the weather is clear. Set an object outside in the morning in a sunny location. Photograph it in the morning, then again at noon, sunset, and dusk. Analyze the color of the direct light and shadows in the pictures.

3. Set up a simple 3D interior scene. Light the interior scene with both artificial and natural light sources.

4. Set up a simple 3D exterior scene. Light the scene for three times of day: high noon (midday), sunset, and night. Change nothing but the lighting.

Figure 4.1 Lighting sets the tone in this memorable scene from *Apocalypse Now* (Francis Ford Coppola, Director; Vittorio Storaro, Cinematographer) (©1979 United Artists. Courtesy of Everett Collection).

Chapter 4
Goal 2: Creating Mood

"It is difficult to articulate the subtleties in cinema, because there aren't words or metaphors which describe many of the emotions you are attempting to evoke."

—Conrad Hall, present-day Cinematographer

The lighting of a scene sets an emotional tone. As much as music can evoke instinctive reactions, so can different types of lighting. These reactions are subconscious and, for the most part, universal. Whether the lighting is bright and the colors of the objects revealed, high or low contrast, or monochromatic, all influence the mood of an image. Lighting plays a critical role in creating mood and ambience; it closely relates to the story and purpose of a piece.

This chapter takes an in-depth look at *goal two of lighting: creating mood.* Creating mood involves many subtleties, and like a musical score, it should have a consistent flavor for an entire narrative, yet at the same time vary from scene to scene to enhance the storyline at that particular moment.

4.1 VISUAL TENSION

Images may have greater or lesser degrees of visual tension. An image may have balance and unity or be unbalanced and chaotic. It may be restful to the eye or full of movement. It may have a harmonious color scheme or be full of contrasts in color and value. All of these attributes will add up to create the level of visual tension in an image.

Visual tension leads to emotional tension. The visual tension in our images should be designed to parallel the story. As the action becomes more dramatic, the visual tension should increase; as the action becomes more peaceful, the visual tension should decrease. Thus, as image crafters, we partake in bringing the audience emotionally into the story being told.

4.1.1 CONTRAST

"Contrast is what makes photography interesting."

—Conrad Hall, Cinematographer

One of the greatest visual contributors to the mood of an image is the level of *contrast* in the image. The term *contrast* has several meanings, a few of which are listed below. Contrast, in all of its forms, creates tension.

contrast

1. to set in opposition in order to show or emphasize differences;
2. the use of opposing elements, such as colors, forms, or lines, in proximity to produce an intensified effect in a work of art.
3. the difference in brightness between the light and dark areas of a picture, such as a photograph or video image.

Visual contrast creates visual tension. In reference to imagery, the term *contrast* usually refers to the range of values found in the image—in other words, the *overall contrast range*. Images may be categorized as being either high contrast or low contrast. High-contrast images have a large range of values, all the way from black to white. Low-contrast images, on the other hand, have a limited range of values, such as using only mid-grays. High-contrast images have more visual tension, while low-contrast images have less visual tension.

High-contrast images are often used to add drama. Renaissance painters often put even simple still lifes in high contrast to give the subject presence. Having a full range of values may even in some cases make an image more visually interesting. Combining high contrast with a dominance of dark values will create an oppressive, isolated, sad or scary feel (Figures 4.2 and 4.3). Primitive man had an instinctive fear and caution of the dark, for dangers can be lurking where one cannot see. Dramas typically use high-contrast lighting. Horror films use high contrast with a dominance of dark values.

Figure 4.2 (Left) High-contrast lighting and an odd up-light on the face of the bust create an eerie mood in this still life (Damien Wisdom).

Figure 4.3 (Right) Taking a tip from the film noir genre, this environment uses shadows, low light angles, and contrast to create a feeling of mystery (Geoffrey Crowell).

Low-contrast images **have less visual tension and often seem safe, cheerful, or in some cases even stagnant** (see Figures 4.4 through 4.6). Scenes with even illumination and few shadows usually create a comfortable and predictable feeling. Comedies and sitcoms, for example, are typically well illuminated with few shadows, as are newscasts and children's cartoons.

Figure 4.4 (Left) Low-contrast lighting is perfect for this playful character (Leandro Ibraim).

Figure 4.5 (Right) Limiting both color and contrast enhances a peaceful feel in the still life of fruit (Andrea Sipl).

Figure 4.6 Overall bright lighting and lively colors are well suited to this image from the comedic short *Drag'N'Fly* (SCAD-Atlanta students; lighting artist Bianca Gee).

Contrast is more than just the range of values in an image, however. Another definition of contrast is the juxtaposition of any type of dissimilar elements. We may have dissimilar values, colors, shapes (rounded vs. angular), horizontal and vertical lines, or moving vs. nonmoving objects. For example, lines in parallel have no juxtaposition contrast and little visual tension (Figure 4.7). Dissimilar orientation of lines and objects, on the other hand, will create greater visual tension (Figures 4.8 and 4.9). The key to this type of contrast is that the elements be significantly different and that they be placed next to or near each other.

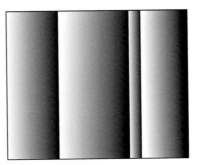

Figure 4.7 (Left) A gradient from black to white has a full contrast range but lacks visual tension.

Figure 4.8 (Center) Juxtaposing black and white areas creates more visual tension.

Figure 4.9 (Right) Contrasts in both value and shape increase the visual tension even more.

Lighting establishes the contrast level of a scene. Lighters control the contrast of a scene by adjusting the intensity of their lights, making some areas brighter and others darker. Contrast can be reduced by brightening shadows so these areas are not significantly darker than areas under direct illumination. Lighting plays a direct role in juxtaposing contrasts in value by illuminating objects so that bright edges appear next to dark ones. The hardness or softness of the light affects mood as well. Dark, crisp shadows and harsh transitions (as with hard light) lend themselves to stark moods. On the other hand, light, blurry shadows and gradual transitions (as with soft light) lend themselves to gentle images and softer subjects. In general, hard light produces more contrast and more visual tension, while soft light produces less contrast and less visual tension. (For more on soft and hard light, see Chapter 10, "Light Diffusion.")

4.1.2 HIDING AND REVEALING ELEMENTS

Choosing which elements to hide or reveal is a powerful storytelling tool. When tonal values are used to conceal areas the audience wants to see, mystery, suspense, or anxiety is produced. Often the "bad guy" is introduced in silhouette. Perhaps a person's eyes, which are naturally the focal point in a face, are concealed (Figure 4.12). Other times we may clearly reveal an element previously hidden. Figures 4.10 and 4.11 show how lighting can affect the mood, even on the simplest of subjects.

In *The Godfather* (directed by Francis Ford Coppola; cinematographer Gordon Willis), the Mafia leader Don Corleone was characteristically lit in a manner to hide his eyes and thus hide his thoughts, making him inscrutable (see Figure 8.1 in Chapter 8, "Light Position"). During his final moments, however, additional light reveals his eyes and softens his features, leaving him seeming exposed and vulnerable. Lighter values can also conceal, such as using a white mist in the classic horror film *The Fog* (1980), or as in *Sin City* (2005), where the cannibalistic Kevin likewise had his eyes hidden, in this case by glasses that were always a graphic white.

One of my all-time favorite scenes is from the great film *Apocalypse Now*. Based on a novel by Joseph Conrad called *Heart of Darkness*, the film follows a young captain who is seeking out a Green Beret who has disappeared into the deepest jungles of Cambodia during the Vietnam War. The Green Beret, named Kurtz, is suspected to have gone insane and has established himself as a god among a violent native tribe. When late in the film we finally reach Kurtz, he is shrouded by darkness. Light slowly reveals the long anticipated and enigmatic character. At first, all we can see are his hands, brightly lit and symbolically washing in a bowl. Next, a thin line of illumination outlines the back of his shaved head. Finally, he leans slowly into the light and his face appears out of the darkness.

Figure 4.10 A simple subject, lit without contrast or tension.

Figure 4.11 A simple subject lit to convey a sense of mystery.

An important principle in lighting is, **What is *not* lit is as important as what *is* lit.** Don't believe that when lighting you have to show everything. As modern-day cinematographer Sven Nykvist has said: "Nothing can ruin the atmosphere as easily as too much light."

4.1.3 THE UNEXPECTED AND CHAOTIC

Elements that are unexpected or chaotic create visual tension. When it comes to lighting, this can be any unusual light. Placement affects mood most noticeably when the light placement is odd or unexpected. For example, an upward-pointing light on a person's face is so unnatural that it's often used to represent villains or to create a disturbing feeling. Or a light may flash on and off, as in the case of a lightning storm or a strobe. An interior light that flickers is likely to create an uncomfortable feeling as well, especially if the room suddenly goes completely dark. In *Apocalypse Now*, the varying colors of fireworks going off during a battle scene enhance the feeling of chaos and madness. In *Toy Story 3*, in the scene where the toys are facing possible destruction in the trash compactor, revolving spotlights heighten the sense of danger and urgency. Figure 4.13 shows a student short about a monkey trying to disable a self-destruct button, in which a flashing red siren increases story tension.

Figure 4.12 Hiding what the audience wishes to see creates tension.

Figure 4.13 The short *Monkey Business* (Chris Palmer) uses a flashing warning light to enhance the urgency of the monkey's dilemma.

4.2 COLOR AND EMOTION

> "Mere colour, unspoiled by meaning, and unallied with definite
>
> form, can speak to the soul in a thousand different ways"
>
> —Oscar Wilde

Different colors and combinations of color evoke emotional responses. Throughout the history of man, color has been linked to symbolism and emotion. Linking color with emotion is part of our everyday language: A person may be "green with envy," so mad they "see red," or they "feel blue." Evidence of color symbolism occurred as early as 200,000 years ago in primitive cave paintings where red, the color of blood, is believed to have symbolized life (Figure 4.14). A brief look at any culture will reveal color linked to powerful symbols, intended to conjure specific emotional reactions.

Figure 4.14 Paleolithic rock painting of equines in the Lascaux caves of southwestern France, 17,000 B.C.

4.2.1 COLOR ASSOCIATIONS

Commonly held symbols or moods linked to certain colors are known as *color associations.* For example, many of us have heard that red and saturated yellow conjure a feeling of excitement, while greens and blues tend to be calming. Color associations are often considered in advertising and other fields. Prisons have been painted pink to reduce aggression; rooms painted blue to soothe captive animals; restaurants painted red to stimulate appetite. Yet the study of how colors affect our moods and actions, known as *color psychology*, engenders some controversy. Some believe in its validity, while others view it with skepticism. The Kansas City pink prison cells were determined to be more annoying than effective and were returned to their original gray.

Here is a list of some of the common (Western) color associations as well as a few reactions to certain colors you may have not considered.

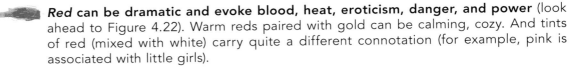

Red **can be dramatic and evoke blood, heat, eroticism, danger, and power** (look ahead to Figure 4.22). Warm reds paired with gold can be calming, cozy. And tints of red (mixed with white) carry quite a different connotation (for example, pink is associated with little girls).

Orange **is often considered stimulating**. Most people either strongly like or dislike bold orange. Yet most people also find warmly tinted light to be cozy and pleasant (Figure 4.15), such as firelight or a sunset. So while green is said to calm and orange to stimulate, when it comes to light, most of us find an orangish light more pleasant and relaxing than a greenish light.

Figure 4.15 In *Ratatouille* a warm gold light envelopes Remy as he looks upon the bounty of food (©2007 Disney/Pixar).

Yellow is typically thought of as a happy color, especially pure yellow and tints of yellow. Yellow is the color of daisies and sunflowers. Yet darker shades of yellow can have an unpleasant dingy quality about them and be dull. Pure yellow is the most luminous of the hues, but it can be overwhelming when highly saturated. Pale yellows, on the other hand, have a delicate quality.

Green is a color associated with growth and nature, bringing to mind health and relaxation. Many pastoral images are rich in greens. When applied to flesh tones, however, green light can generate the opposite feeling—that of uneasiness and unhealthiness.

Cyan is a bright, energetic color. Originally termed "cyan-blue," it's blue's more vibrant cousin, found between blue and green on the color wheel. Like green, cyan light can be pastoral or have an unpleasant quality. Cyan-tinted light can be used to give a cadaverous feeling to skin (Figure 4.16).

Figure 4.16 Harry Potter's nemesis, Voldemort, is most often depicted in cyan-blue light, which renders his skin cold and cadaverous. (Still from *Harry Potter and the Deathly Hallows*, ©2010 Warner Brothers and Ent. Harry Potter publishing rights. Courtesy of Everett Collection.)

- **Blue** **is often associated with peace and tranquility.** It's most people's favorite color, yet it can also be depressing, cold, and even menacing. Villains in movies are often portrayed in blue light. Blue light is typical for implying outdoor night.

- **Purple** **is mysterious color.** In ancient times, purple became associated with royalty as purple dye was very expensive to produce. Purple is also often associated with creativity, magic, wisdom, and spiritualism (Figure 4.17). It is the favorite color of many artists.

Figure 4.17 In *Avatar*, purple is the color of intimacy, connection, and spirituality. Here Neytiri and Jake make a bond with the "tree of voices" and choose each other as partners (©2009 TM & 20th Century Fox. Courtesy of Everett Collection).

While useful, a list of common color associations is also general and oversimplified. It does not take into account variations in saturation and value, how colors change in combination with other colors, or cultural context. The color associations discussed so far are Western in thought. Other cultures have other connotations. For example, in Western culture white represents purity and innocence, while in Eastern cultures white is associated with death and is typically worn at funerals. For Catholicism, red is the color of both the pope's robe (power) and the devil's skin (danger, evil); yet in India, a bride's wedding dress is red.

Almost universally, red is perceived as stimulating and blue as calming. These colors have actual physical effects on us. Red has been shown to stimulate the central nervous system, increase breathing, raise the heartbeat, and increase appetite. Blue, on the other hand, calms the nervous system and reduces the heartbeat and blood pressure. However, while red is proven to be invigorating, how this is interpreted depends on culture and context—from bride to pope to the devil.

How color affects us depends on context. While it is clear that we respond to color, how we do so depends on many factors: other colors, the story point, the pose and gesture of characters, our preconceived notions, even the culture in which we live. In practice, the emotional effects of color cannot easily be categorized.

The best way to understand the use of color is to look at its effects in a wide variety of images. As the saying goes, a picture is really worth a thousand words. Also, experiment with color yourself and always keep in mind the bigger picture, which is the context in which you are using the color.

4.2.2 COLOR COMBINATIONS

The impact of a color image comes from the combination of all the colors; no color can be analyzed completely independently of its neighbors. The possibilities are endless, but few generalities are discussed here.

Complementary **palettes (colors opposite each other on the color wheel) provide contrast of color and are higher in visual tension.** When complementary colors are placed next to each other, each intensifies the apparent saturation of the other, an effect known as *simultaneous contrast*. A complementary palette is often visually interesting. Dabs of a complementary color can be used to enliven an otherwise analogous and restful color scheme. Complementary color schemes can also be discordant if the areas of contrasting color are large, saturated, and of equal weight. In this case each area competes for attention with neither color dominating, creating an uncomfortable level of tension (Figure 4.18). It's a bit like cooking—a little garlic adds flavor; too much garlic overwhelms the senses.

Combinations of many bright, saturated colors tend to have a happy, upbeat feel. Think of the colors often associated with children's toys and playrooms. When combined with low-contrast lighting, a combination of a variety of clear primary and secondary colors will lend itself to a lighthearted mood (Figure 4.19).

Figure 4.18 Van Gogh explored the effects of simultaneous contrast in his painting with saturated hues, often with the intention of creating a jarring effect. Of his painting *Night Café in Arles* (ca. 1888, Yale University Art Gallery), he said. "I have tried to express the terrible passions of humanity by means of red and green."

Figure 4.19 In August Macke's *Fashion Window*, vibrant blocks of pure color convey the impression of a sunny, happy, yet ordinary day (ca. 1913, Westfalisches Landesmuseum fur Kunst und Kulturgeschichte, Munster).

Monochromatic (using variations of one color) or analogous (using colors adjacent on the color wheel) palettes lack color contrast and are lower in visual tension. They may be used to evoke moods of peace or serenity (Figure 4.20). Very limited palettes may even contribute to moods of stagnation, listlessness, or depression (Figure 4.21).

A color scheme may also be limited by way of desaturation. Highly desaturated images can evoke moods of oppression and lifelessness. Consider the effect of limiting color contrast combined with high value contrast.

Figure 4.20 (Left) In the painting "The Hair is Braided" (1882, at the National Museum of Art, Architecture and Design, Norway) by Christian Krohg, a limited analogous palette compliments the serene and quiet subject.

Figure 4.21 (Right) A limited palette with dark, desaturated reds contributes to the somber and even frightening mood in Egon Schiele's "Selbstseher or Death and Man" (ca. 1911, at the Leopold Museum in Vienna).

4.2.3 Using Color Symbolically

Color can be used symbolically throughout a story. When a color is used symbolically, it is repeatedly combined with certain characters, environments, situations, or concepts. Soon into the story, we begin to associate the appearance of this color with the desired element, usually without realizing it. As Bruce Block succinctly puts it in *The Visual Story*, "If every murder in a story occurs in blue light, the audience will expect a murder whenever blue light is presented to them." This storytelling technique helps establish and maintain the character and presence of elements in the story.

Each story is unique and can carve out its own associations; the only rule when using color in this manner is to be consistent throughout the entire story. Previously held color associations are easy to replace, if only for the duration of the story. A little known fact is that our reactions to color are easily manipulated, affected by associations as recent as a few minutes ago. Many visual stories take advantage of this when they use color symbolically.

One of the greatest uses of color in film to date was in *The Last Emperor* (1987), which told the story of Pu Yi, China's last emperor. Cinematographer Vittorio Storaro explained, "It was possible, I thought, to register in images the road backward in time, that psychoanalytic road through the various colors of different wavelengths that make up the entire chromatic spectrum of visible energy. Just as white light could represent the end of his life journey, so Pu Yi's various ages could be represented by the various 'ages of the colors.'" The film begins with the color red, which is the color of beginnings and Communist China. Yellow is the color of the Emperor, the sun, and to Storaro, consciousness. Yellow dominates the moment of Pu Yi's coronation, at age three. Later, green represents knowledge of the outside world, as Pu Yi's English tutor is first seen riding a green bicycle. Other colors represent other eras of Pu Yi's life, while a more balanced spectrum represents his old age.

In *American Beauty* (1999), cinematographer Conrad Hall uses the color red as a central motif of the film. It represents a primal life force, one often contained or lying just beneath the surface of ordinary suburban lives. In the film, red is first seen when Carolyn, a repressed and driven housewife, is pruning vibrant red roses. Later it bursts forth in Lester's fantasies about Angela, where she lays on a bed of rose petals (Figure 4.22), and finally in the splatter of blood that marks the end of the film.

Figure 4.22 In *American Beauty* (1999), the color red represents vital life force and sexuality (©DreamWorks. Courtesy of Everett Collection).

4.3 REVEALING ACTION, AMBIENCE, AND CHARACTER

During the course of an animation or film, each scene is unique. Each scene holds a new plot twist, moves the story forward in a unique way. Likewise, the lighting will vary from shot to shot depending on environment, character, and the action taking place.

Any change in the action can motivate a change in the lighting. Light is a visual score, enhancing our emotional response to the story taking place. If the story changes in mood, then the lighting should change, too. A story that is lit the same all the way through without variety often appears flat and boring, even if the lighting is beautiful!

When lighting an environment, also take into account its *ambience* as it relates to the story. *Ambience* is the general atmosphere of an environment. Lighting an environment to reflect its mood is a powerful statement. When designing the lighting for an environment, ask yourself what happens in this setting. What are its inhabitants like? Is the setting a happy place (lighthearted) or dangerous ("dark and dangerous"); is it dull and boring (bland in color and action) or magical? Lighting for mood is not incompatible with the goal of a realistic setting. Remember that physically accurate lighting can be heavily interpreted (read: changed!) to enhance mood. Depending on the needs of the narrative, the lighting can lean more toward strict realism or away from it. Also, the setting (and thus what kinds of light would naturally appear) should be carefully chosen. (See Chapter 3 for more on setting.)

Similarly, a great amount of character is brought out by lighting. Male characters tend to be lit for personality, for example with grazing lights to bring out rugged features (Figure 4.25). Female characters are often lit for beauty, with soft frontal lights that minimize facial lines (Figure 4.26). Villains are often lit with harsh light, or bright top-down lights that emphasize the brows and hide the eyes, or even more menacingly, with up-lighting (Figure 4.27). Even a loved and familiar face can turn villainous with the right lighting. Characters may be lit in a consistent manner throughout a piece to help enhance the perception of their personality. On the other hand, the lighting may change suddenly or gradually to reflect a change in their emotional or spiritual state.

Figure 4.23 In this short, the purple neon enhances the less-than-pleasant quality of this theater (Paul Tillery).

Figure 4.24 Outdoors, the gray day, barren and colorless concrete, and deep shadows tell the audience this theater is not ideal (Paul Tillery).

Figure 4.25 Grazing light that pulls out every well-worn wrinkle leads us to imagine a character as interesting as the features.

Figure 4.26 This woman has been lit for beauty—a soft frontal fill flatters her face and minimizes imperfections while the sun halos her hair.

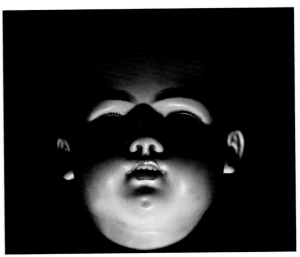

Figure 4.27 Up-lighting makes even this benign subject appear spooky.

In animation production, the color and lighting of a film is developed with a *color script*. Each frame in the color script need not be an elaborate work of art, but rather it must establish appropriate look and feel (Figure 4.28). The color script relates color and light to mood and story, rather than focusing on detailed modeling or illustration. The color script is closely followed by the lighting department.

For many, designing the lighting to reflect the mood of the story is the most creative and exciting part. If you are designing the lighting, first consider the overall mood or style of the piece. Then for each scene, ask yourself what the dominant mood is and where that mood is coming from. Is a change in plot most important? Is illustrating the ambience of the place most important? Or is the current emotional state of the character the focus of the story? Then consider what ways the lighting might enhance this.

Figure 4.28 Selected frames from the color script for *Up* (©2009 Disney/Pixar) by Lou Romano illustrate how light and color return to Carl's world when the balloons lift him from his lonely life.

CASE STUDY: USE OF LIGHTING IN *TOY STORY 3*

Toy Story 3 (Director of Photography for Lighting, Kim White; Art Direction by Daisuke "Dice" Tsutsumi) is an excellent example of how lighting may be used to further the story.

An early sequence in the film shows a video of Andy playing with his toys when he was young (Figure 4.29). Audiences will recall similar scenes from the first two films, and the environment and lighting are familiar. Warm light streams in from the window; blue walls are adorned with stars. In this sequence, saturation is amplified, making these memories seem even more nostalgic. Next, the film cuts to Andy's room as it appears at the time of *Toy Story 3*. In contrast to the memories, we see now that Andy has grown up. His room is recognizable but different—the childish decorations are replaced by those of a teen, and the toys have been put away. The colors and light are different in Andy's room as well. The room has a bluer light and the colors are less saturated, all reenforcing the feeling that the golden years are past (Figure 4.30). Life is indeed less happy for the toys now, as they no longer have a place in grown-up Andy's world. They are stored in a chest and forgotten.

Through a series of events, Woody and the gang are donated accidentally to Sunnyside Daycare, which they first perceive as the ideal location—toys here are never outgrown, as they always have new children to play with them. The daycare is represented in warm and colorful tones. The rooms are bright and well-lit. The overall feeling generated by this color and light scheme is cheerful and happy.

With the first play session, the gang realizes that this location is *not* ideal—they have been taken to the toddler room. Toys in this room are soon broken and thrown away. An overhead view of the chaos is gray and cold. The location is the same, but now the mood and thus the lighting are very different. When night falls, the toys are locked into crates, and the transformation is complete. The lighting is now high-contrast and overall dark. The shadow of window panes on the floor reenforces the impression of bars, and the toys, dimly lit, peer out from cell-like crates. Sunnyside has become a prison.

Our perception of the leader of the daycare toys, Lotso (short for Lots'O'Huggin), also changes. At first appearing benevolent and cuddly, the strawberry-scented bear soon reveals his darker side as a cruel gang leader. Lighting on him and his cohorts changes to match our new perception, in some cases leading the way. When Buzz becomes suspicious and begins snooping around, he finds Lotso's gang playing poker in the vending machine. The sickly green light foreshadows his next discovery— that these toys are not so nice after all. In many scenes after this, Lotso appears backlit and in partial shadow.

While the other toys are at Sunnyside, Woody is having adventures of his own. Leaving the gang, he is discovered and taken home by the little girl Bonnie. Bonnie consistently appears under dappled light (Figure 4.31), giving her the aura of a peaceful and safe haven. Bonnie's lighting is an example of linking a lighting style to a character; in every scene with Bonnie, the light is dappled—even when dappled light doesn't necessarily make sense, such as inside her room.

The climactic finale in the trash compactor also clearly uses lighting to enhance the audience's response. Upon arrival, the time of day is night, and the dump is lit by the unappealing yellow-green lights that are associated with danger throughout the film. As Woody and the other friends are almost sucked down into the blazing inferno, they are enveloped by red-orange light. Once rescued, the time of day is dawn, with its warm direct light and promise of new beginnings.

This case study gives but a few examples. A further study of *Toy Story 3* will reveal how in each scene the lighting is carefully crafted to enhance character, place, and action.

Figure 4.29 Andy's room as a child is warm and inviting (©2010 Disney/Pixar).

Figure 4.30 Andy's room as a teenager has cooler and less saturated colors (©2010 Disney/Pixar).

Figure 4.31 Bonnie, in dappled light (©2010 Disney/Pixar).

LIGHTING FOR MOOD: QUESTIONS TO ASK YOURSELF

- What is happening in the story at that time?
- What is the dominant mood of the scene and where is that mood coming from?
- Is a change in plot most important?
- Is illustrating the ambience of the place most important?
- Is the current emotional state of the character the focus of the story?
- What is the overall feeling of the story—happy, sad, scary, comedic, etc.?
- What elements should be revealed? What elements would benefit from being hidden?
- What kinds of things happen in the setting?
- What are its inhabitants like?
- What feelings would this setting elicit if you were there?
- What are the personality and spiritual state of the character(s) in the scene?
- Is bringing out the character's personality important to the story?
- Should the character be lit for beauty?
- Do any of the characters usually receive a particular lighting approach that you should follow?
- Is there any symbolic use of color that would enhance this scene?

4.4 CHAPTER CONCLUSION

Lighting and its associated task, shading, play an essential role in the creation of the mood of an image, a sequence, or an entire story. All the properties of light contribute to our emotional response to certain lighting conditions. Foremost is the overall tonal range, as determined by the ratio of brights to darks. Additional color schemes can be selected and reused, using cultural associations or creating your own. Finally, light quality and position can also be manipulated to help establish a certain mood and further the narrative.

By applying the principles discussed, lighting can be used to:

◆ Create the overall mood of an entire piece
◆ Parallel the story to enhance the action
◆ Reveal the character of people
◆ Establish the ambience of places

4.4.1 IMPORTANT POINTS

◆ The overall purpose of lighting is to help tell the story. All other objectives are subservient to this purpose.
◆ One of the main goals of lighting is to enhance mood.
◆ The range of values in an image will influence its emotional tone—overall dark and high-contrast values create visual tension, while overall light and low-contrast values have less visual tension.
◆ Visual contrast creates visual tension, and visual tension creates emotional tension.
◆ The visual tension should pace with the storyline tension to enhance it.
◆ Hiding what the audience wishes to see creates tension and suspense.
◆ What is *not lit* is as important as what *is lit*.
◆ Color will influence the mood of an image, but its effect varies greatly depending on context and past associations.
◆ Color associations are easily formed and broken.
◆ Color is often used symbolically.
◆ Lighting an environment to reflect its unique mood is a powerful storytelling statement.
◆ Characters are often lit to enhance the impression of their personality, mental, or spiritual state.
◆ Lighting should parallel the story to enhance the audience's emotional response to it.

4.4.2 TERMS

lighting design   color association   color script
contrast   color psychology
simultaneous contrast   ambiance

4.4.3 EXERCISES

1. Gather a variety of images that use light to convey a particular mood. Identify in each image the specific properties of light that contribute to the mood of the image.

2. Pretend you are working for an advertising agency. Set up and light two scenes: The first is an advertisement for a children's toy store; the next is for a promotional piece for the opening of a new nightclub.

3. Take a trip to your local gallery. Sitting before an image that especially moves you, analyze what techniques the artist used to convey the feeling of the piece. Write a paragraph about it.

4. Choose a familiar short story (or use your own if you have one in mind). Any of *Aesop's Fables* make great short stories if you are having trouble thinking of one. Create your own color script limited to about five frames, choosing important story moments to illustrate. Don't worry about making great drawings or frame-able paintings; concentrate instead on using color, light, and contrast to capture the mood at each story point.

5. Rent and watch a classic or modern film with great cinematography (suggestions: *Citizen Kane, The Godfather, Apocalypse Now, Amélie, Vertigo, Blade Runner, 2001: A Space Odyssey, Pan's Labyrinth, Ben Hur*). Pay careful attention to the contrast levels, color schemes, light direction and placement and how they change from scene to scene to reflect the storyline. Write about what you observe.

Figure 5.1 Central placement and a bright beam of light draw our attention to the girl Lyra in this still from *The Golden Compass*. (©2007 New Line Cinema. Courtesy of Everett Collection. Digital bears by London-based visual effects studio, Framestore.)

Chapter 5
Goal 3: Directing the Eye

"Art is not what you see, but what you make others see."

—Edgar Degas, 19th-Century Impressionist Painter

Another goal of lighting is to direct the audience's attention. Directing the viewer's eye is essential to visual storytelling. When the audience looks at what is pertinent, the story is clear and compelling. If the audience is confused or distracted, they can be taken out of the story. In a visual narrative, any given shot is held for only a fleeting amount of time. Where the audience is supposed to be looking needs to be clear, or the moment will be lost. As Sharon Calahan puts it in the *Advanced RenderMan* book, "the storytelling effectiveness of a shot often depends on how well, and how quickly, the viewer's eye is led to the key story elements."

In order to focus attention, one must have a good understanding of what attracts the eye. Many people have an intuitive grasp of these attractors, but further study will improve even the most talented artist. For some, an objective study of composition and what attracts the eye will reveal weaknesses in their lighting design, resulting in an improved image once a careful analysis is made. For the most effective lighting, it is essential to light a scene with what attracts the eye in mind.

This chapter examines *the third goal of lighting: directing the eye.* We look in detail at the many ways in which lighting and shading can be used to capture and maintain a viewer's attention. Understanding this will ensure that you enhance, rather than distract from, the intended focus of a shot.

5.1 COMPOSITION

composition (n.)
The spatial property resulting from the arrangement of parts in relation to each other and to the whole

The purpose of composition is to give a structure to our images and to direct the eye. Composition "tells the audience where to look, what to look at, and in what order" (Blain Brown, *Cinematography: Theory and Practice*).

***Compositional elements* are the basic building blocks of an image** and generally include tone, line, shape, color, texture, and movement. This section is not a full treatment on the subject of composition; for that, many excellent art books are available. Rather, this section takes

Figure 5.2 Tone.

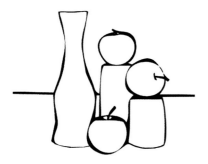

Figure 5.3 Line.

a brief look at the compositional elements. By studying the compositional elements, we can better understand the image as a whole.

- ◆ *Tone* **refers the light and dark shades of an image.** Tone and lighting go hand in hand. Light, by its very nature, creates tonal changes as it wraps around surfaces and fades with distance (Figure 5.2).

- ◆ **A** *line* **is a "path" throughout an image.** In math, lines are straight ("the shortest distance between two points"), but when it comes to art, lines can be straight or curving (Figure 5.3).

   Lines can be continuous, interrupted, or even implied. *Continuous lines* are uninterrupted lines, either curving or straight (Figure 5.4). They can be formed by elongated shapes and also by the boundaries or edges of objects, known as *contour lines*. Folds and creases in objects can also form lines, such the vertical line formed in the corner of a room. *Interrupted lines*, or *broken* lines, are lines that start and stop intermittently. When viewing an interrupted line, our mind fills in the gaps to form one continuous line (Figure 5.5). *Implied lines* don't appear at all, but we perceive them as being there (Figure 5.6). Our minds will connect the dots between a series of similar elements and thus deduce the line. Even the line of sight of a character will form an implied line.

- ◆ *Shape*, **in its simplest sense, is an enclosed contour line that forms a discrete object.** The essential part of the shape is 2D. The primary shapes are geometric: triangle, circle, and square. These primary shapes form compositional primitives. In addition to the geometric primitives, shapes can be organic, with random, often curving contour lines. Due to the mind's tendency to group and categorize, we seek to simplify more complex forms and collections of forms into one of these basic shapes. Thus complex visual arrangements can be organized and structured into more simple themes (Figure 5.7).

- ◆ *Color* **is the unique spectral hue of something.** Every artist should be well versed in the definition and use of color. Color, like tone, has a strong effect in mood. Color choice and combinations of colors are important for creating pleasing aesthetics. Colors have "weight," which is the propensity to attract our attention (Figure 5.8).

- ◆ *Texture* **refers to surface detail, either tactile or visual.** This detail may originate from the bumpiness of the surface, as with carpet shag, or from a color pattern, such as wallpaper. Visually, the end result is the same: the surface appears broken up as opposed to uniform. Texture may indicate surface quality, such as smooth or rough. Texture may be of regular patterns or be random; it may be organic or geometric (Figure 5.9).

Figure 5.4 (Left) Continuous line.

Figure 5.5 (Center) Interrupted line.

Figure 5.6 (Right) Repeated similar elements form an implied line.

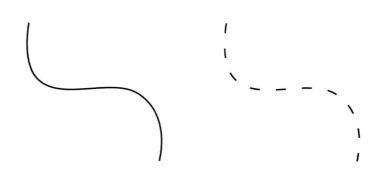

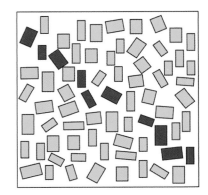

- ◆ *Movement* **has two meanings when it comes to visual imagery.** When we speak of motion in animation or film, we mean the physical motion of something through space, or the movement of the viewer's eye throughout an image. In this regard, even still frames have movement.

Some or all of these elements are present in all images, whether we are aware of them or not. They can be arranged to lead a viewer's eye past some elements while coming to rest on others.

5.2 VISUAL ATTRACTORS

Our eye is led through an image by specific visual attractors, due to the perceptual principles just outlined. Because our reactions to these visual elements are universal, the topics covered in the following sections should be familiar, but perhaps you haven't given them much thought. When creating your scene, keep these topics in mind so that you can be assured you are directing the viewer's attention where you want.

5.2.1 PRINCIPLES OF VISUAL ORGANIZATION

Our brain receives a huge amount of incoming data. To interpret all of the incoming stimuli, the brain simplifies, groups, and prioritizes the information. Without this process, the information would be overwhelming, like shopping at a mall during the holidays.

How the brain organizes incoming data is known as *perceptual organization*. A branch of psychology that studied perceptual organization was Gestaltism, which originated in Germany in the early 1900s. The Gestaltists defined a number of principles that describe how we group visual data.

These principles explain why we'll focus on some areas and not others.

- ◆ *Principle of proximity:* We group objects that are close to each other in space, even if these objects are radically different in size, color, form, etc. (Figure 5.10).
- ◆ *Principle of similarity*: Our mind will likewise group objects that have similar properties, such as similar shape, size, texture, color, or value. The items don't have to be identical, only similar (Figure 5.11).

Figure 5.10 (Left) Principle of proximity.

Figure 5.11 (Center) Principle of similarity.

Figure 5.12 (Right) Principle of continuity.

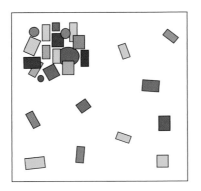 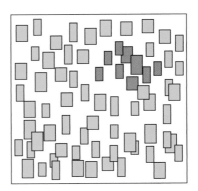 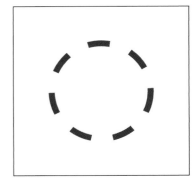

- ◆ *Principle of common fate*: Elements moving in the same direction or manner are also perceived as a grouping.
- ◆ *Principle of continuity*: The mind prefers continuous figures. If there are gaps in a shape, for example, we will intuitively fill in the gaps to create a continuous or enclosed form (Figure 5.12).
- ◆ *The law of figure and ground*: The mind will attempt to organize reality into the simplest forms possible. When presented with an image, the eye will attempt to discern a figure, picking one out of even a minimum of clues (Figure 5.13). Once a figure is identified, it will receive more attention. If a figure is difficult to discern, your eye will tend to move restlessly over the image.

Figure 5.13 What do you see in this image? The component parts are a variety of irregular and initially random-seeming blotches, but after a moment, the dots come together and the subject of the image emerges. Once a cohesive pattern is deduced, you will continue to see it from here on out.

5.2.2 The Role of Lines

Lines are especially important in directing the eye and developing the structure of an image. Lines cause our attention to move from one place to another. They can serve as connectors between elements and as pointers to other elements. Lines can also serve as boundaries that stop the eye from traveling farther and build frames and dividers around other objects. When objects are framed by lines, we tend to focus on the object. When the eye is drawn along a line, it will tend to keep moving in that direction until stopped by another visual element. Straight lines are more emphatic in their directionality, while curving lines cause the eye to move in a softer, more meandering manner over an image. Recall that repeated similar elements will also serve to lead our eye; according to the Principle of Similarity, we see these elements as a single unit, and according to the Principle of Continuity, we connect them to form an implied line.

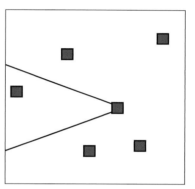

Figure 5.14 Converging lines literally point to the apex of their convergence.

Figure 5.15 Strong diagonal lines formed by the angel's and Abraham's arms form converging lines that point to Isaac's face in Caravaggio's "Sacrifice of Isaac" (ca. 1603, Uffizi Gallery, Florence).

The picture frame itself is a boundary of horizontal and vertical lines, of which the viewer is subconsciously aware at all times. All the elements within the screen relate to its edges. Whether an object is within the frame, partially within the frame, off-screen, or centered strongly determines mood and story, and if or in what way the eye is attracted.

Lines can be used to subdivide the picture plane, creating a frame within the frame. This can be used to create a different aspect ratio than that of the screen, to separate some objects from others, to create groupings, and to draw attention to certain elements.

THE VISUAL FUNCTIONS OF LINES:
- Lead the eye by connecting similar objects.
- Lead the eye by pointing to other elements.
- Stop the eye by serving as a boundary.
- Create frames and sub-frames within the image that emphasize certain objects.

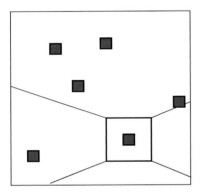

Figure 5.16 Framing an object will give it special emphasis.

Figure 5.17 (Right) Mary and child are given special emphasis through framing, which separates them from the many other figures in the painting "Adoration of the Magi" by Botticelli (ca. 1475, Uffizi Gallery, Florence).

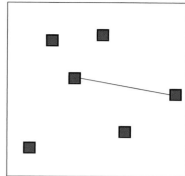

Figure 5.18 Lines connect.

Figure 5.19 (Left) An example of a line of sight. The viewer looks back and forth between the gem and the thief, connected by an implied line of sight (models and lighting by Jarel Kingsberry).

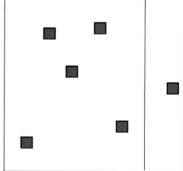

Figure 5.20 Lines can separate objects from each other.

Figure 5.21 (Left) The wall forms a line dividing the image, separating the thief and the gem in different sub-frames (models and lighting by Jarel Kingsberry).

5.2.3 Object on a Field

An *object on a field* is a special case of figure/ground in which an element stands out from the others and its environment, attracting extra attention to itself. Shapes are given special emphasis when they appear on a field. A "field" can be a blank or uniformly textured area. An object on a blank field is an object in isolation, which is an extremely strong visual attractor (Figures 5.22 and 5.23). If there is only one element, there's nothing else to look at.

An object doesn't need to be the only thing in the image to be isolated, however. It can be isolated simply by being separated from its fellows. The other objects are grouped together by the Principle of Proximity, leaving the separated object alone, drawing attention (Figures 5.24 and 5.25).

Additionally, a field doesn't have to be blank. Our minds will create a "field" from groupings of similar elements, according the Principle of Similarity. For example, if a circle is placed in a "field" of squares, then we will look at the circle. This holds true when the object is sufficiently different in any way from its surroundings (Figures 5.26 and 5.27). This difference can be in shape, size, color, orientation, and so on. In this case, isolation occurs when the *contrast* of one element stands out against the *cohesion* of all the others.

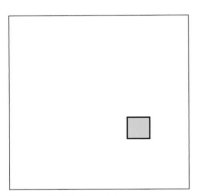

Figure 5.22 An object on a blank field.

Figure 5.23 (Right) Naturally, we look at a lone object in isolation.

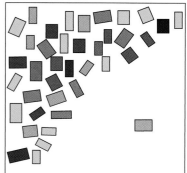

Figure 5.24 An object in isolation.

Figure 5.25 (Left) In this scene, the cow that is separated from the herd catches our attention.

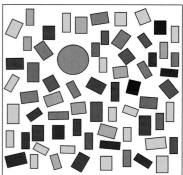

Figure 5.26 The many rectangles group together to form a field, while the circle stands out as the figure.

Figure 5.27 (Left) Our gaze is naturally drawn to the yellow sphere, as it is different from its fellows.

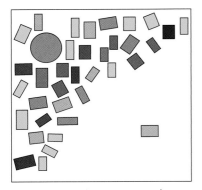

Figure 5.28 Our eye travels between the red circle and the isolated rectangle, both two strong attractors.

The eye tends to rest on an object on a field unless other elements pull it away. If there is only one figure or a dominant figure, it becomes the *focal point*, an area that draws our attention. Images have more than one element vying for our attention. When this happens, the eye moves back and forth between visual attractors, creating compositional movement (Figure 5.28).

5.2.4 MOVEMENT

Physical movement **is the strongest visual attractor.** When an object moves, our eye will immediately be drawn to it. Motion is relative, in that we look at the unique item. For example, we'll look at one still object among moving ones. Also, if all items are moving at a certain speed except for one, then we will again look at the unique object. According to the Principle of Common Fate, the similarly moving elements form a field upon which the differently moving object stands out.

Lighting can be used to enhance the perception of movement. When an object travels in and out of light or through lights of different properties, then our perception of its motion is enhanced. Varying the lighting also creates a more visually interesting animation. Compare Figures 5.29 and 5.30 to see how lighting can enhance the sense of motion even in a series of still frames.

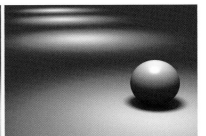

Figure 5.29 Traveling in and out of pools of light enhances the sensation of motion and creates visual interest.

Figure 5.30 The even illumination in this series of images makes the motion of the ball less apparent. Is the ball traveling toward the viewer, or is the viewer moving toward the ball? Without lighting cues, the movement is unclear.

5.2.5 OTHER ATTRACTORS

Especially important to lighters, the eye is drawn to *bright areas* of an image. An obvious way lighting can be used to focus attention is simply to put the object under brighter light. This technique is simple, effective, and used often (Figure 5.31).

Figure 5.31 This simple example illustrates how lighting can be used to isolate a subject.

Areas of *contrast* in general attract the eye. Be on the lookout for areas of high contrast and note whether these areas are where you wish your viewer to be looking. If not, you may want to make your values in this area more similar. Discussed in Section 4.1.1, "Contrast," elements can contrast in almost any way, such as tone, color, shape, size, and texture. While all types of contrast will tend to attract the eye, sharp, sudden contrasts in value are particularly attention-getting. Be on the lookout for contrasts created by shadows, especially multiple shadows, as they can be distracting if they compete with the subject for attention.

***Position* can be a large factor in focusing our gaze**. A centrally located object will draw and, more importantly, *hold* attention. For this reason, when the point of interest is centered, the image can become stagnant, as the eye moves to center and then stops. Some art books will tell you to avoid this, but it is a matter of intent (see Figures 5.1 and 5.33 for examples). If you want the viewer's gaze to be riveted or perhaps to convey a sense of stagnation, then perhaps a centrally located focal point is just the composition needed.

The *scale* of objects also affects their visual weight. Larger elements attract our attention, all other things being equal. The visual weight of scale, however, can be easily overridden by other visual cues.

***Saturated colors* similarly attract the eye**. The more saturated a color is, all other things being equal, the more it attracts the eye. This is especially true for a single saturated color amidst many desaturated ones (Figure 5.32). Since brighter, more saturated colors draw more attention, it takes less of an area of them to visually balance out a region of a darker, less saturated color. By adjusting the size, you can offset the visual pull of the color with the effect of scale. Saturation is a weak visual attractor.

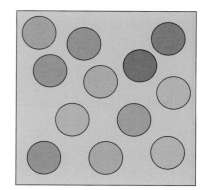

Figure 5.32 The effect of saturation: Which circle do you look at most?

Finally, *lens focus* will also direct the eye. When one portion of the image is clear and the others blurry, we'll naturally direct our gaze to the clear area. This can be used to eliminate a distracting background or to move our focus from one element to another. A *rack focus* is when focal distance of the lens changes dramatically during a shot, forcing our gaze from one element to another. Chapter 13, "Camera Essentials," discusses lens focus in detail with examples.

Figure 5.33 This poor little fellow from *Ice Age 2: The Meltdown* couldn't be more the center of attention—he is centrally located, different from all the others, pointed to by the lines made by the piranhas' mouths and gazes, placed high in the frame, slightly separated from the fish (in the center of a circular clearing similar to a bull's-eye), and placed over the brightest area of the background! (©2006 20th Century Fox. Courtesy of Everett Collection. Created at Blue Sky Studios.)

SIX TIPS FOR HOW TO KEEP THE FOCUS OF A SHOT, OR AVOID "SORE THUMBS"

A "sore thumb" is something within the shot that keeps attracting attention, but it's not the intended focus of the shot. While lighting and shading, it's very easy to accidentally create distracting elements. Here are six tips on how to avoid that happening.

1 **Look for distracting elements.** It sounds obvious, but the best thing a technical director can do to eliminate distracting elements is to watch for them. A list, either mental or written, can be extremely helpful with this. When you're armed with a list of what attracts the eye, it becomes easier to spot these elements in your images. Such a list appears in the summary of this chapter, or you can devise your own.

2 **Get a "fresh eye."** Often we overlook distracting elements in our work simply because we have been looking at the shot too long and may be focusing on other areas. In these situations, getting a "fresh eye" is extremely helpful. The following are a few tricks for getting a fresh eye:

- *Step away from your work for a while.* Take a break, go get a cup of coffee, or get some fresh air.
- *Flip the image.* Horizontal positioning maintains our orientation, while vertical positioning abstracts the image to check for value, color, and composition in general.
- *Squint at the image.* This is an old artist's trick to reduce an image to tonal values. Try it. It works!
- *Get additional input.* Someone else's view is literally a fresh eye. No matter how good you are, feedback on your work is critical. It's built into production in the form of daily reviews by supervisors. Feedback helps to catch errors and keeps an aesthetic continuity throughout the project.

3 **Modify lighting per subject, as needed.** Often certain objects need special lighting to help balance the scene. The illumination of lights can be made to shine exclusively or inclusively on certain objects, a technique known as *light linking*.

4 **Modify surface material properties.** Sometimes a surface that was developed in one scene looks very different in another scene. The material may suddenly attract undue attention to itself in some manner, such as "popping" in luminance in an unexpected way. The duties of the lighter include modifying the object's surface attributes so the subject best fits onto the shot and the final image is balanced.

5 **Eliminate technical errors.** In addition to modifying both light and surface material properties, distracting technical errors must be eliminated. They are the mark of an inexperienced lighter or low quality standards. Throughout this book, common artifacts and their fixes are identified.

6 **Adjust the shot in the composite.** Much work with your image can still be done in the composite. Areas of the image can be isolated and color-corrected. Often lighters render *passes*, which are renders containing only a subset of the final image, such as the character separate from the background, and then a render of the background without the character. These passes are then combined in the final composite. Each pass can then be manipulated more easily. Rendering in passes is discussed in Chapter 18, "Multi-Pass Rendering."

5.3 CHAPTER CONCLUSION

When creating an image that is part of a story, and especially in an animation where each image is on the screen only for a fraction of a second, the viewer's attention must be directed to the desired area quickly. This chapter has covered important principles of what attracts the eye. By understanding these principles, you can better evaluate your images in order to make sure they support the story and don't contain unwanted distractions.

In summary, the following sidebar provides a list of visual attractors to look for when evaluating your scene.

LIST OF VISUAL ATTRACTORS

- Motion
- Object on a field
- Leading lines
- Contrast
- Luminance
- Sub-frames
- Position
- Scale
- Lens focus
- Saturation

5.3.1 IMPORTANT POINTS

- An understanding of composition is important in order to effectively direct the viewer's eye throughout an image or shot.
- The elements of composition are line, shape, tone, color, and movement.
- Lines can be continuous, broken, or implied.
- When lighting a scene, the digital lighter must be careful to direct the viewer's eye in a way that complements the purpose of the image, as it is easy to inadvertently distract the viewer.
- The Gestaltist psychologists developed several principles that define how we organize visual information.

- Fundamental to human perception is the discernment of figure and ground.
- Due to how the human brain works, our attention is drawn to certain elements in certain situations.
- Elements that are isolated, bright, saturated, large, and centrally framed all attract the eye.
- Lines move the eye through an image and also can create frames around certain elements.

5.3.2 TERMS

composition	shape	visual organization
line	compositional primitives	Gestaltism
contour line	tone	figure and ground
broken line	color	visual attractors
implied line	movement	

5.3.3 EXERCISES

1. Take a trip to your local art gallery. Select a few paintings and analyze the composition. What compositional principles are being used? How are these principles organizing the elements of composition (line, tone, color, etc)? What basic shapes can you make out? Are these shapes positive or negative? Where does your eye move in the image?

2. Create a simple still life that includes many objects on a table. By using composition, framing, and lighting, create three to four images, each with a different focal point. Use a different means with each image to direct the eye. Feel free to rearrange the objects on the table and move the camera.

3. Film review: Find samples from film of composition enhancing the story.

Figure 6.1 The creation of deep space in *Blade Runner* (©1982 Warner Brothers. Courtesy of Everett Collection).

Chapter 6
Goals 4–6: Creating the Illusion of Dimension

"Photography deals exquisitely with appearances, but nothing is what it appears to be."

—Duane Michals, 20th-Century Photographer

We tend to think of photographs as being accurate representations of the world, and likewise, that renders of a three-dimensional scene are also accurate representations. The fact is, however, that a great deal of information is lost when a 3D environment, be it real or virtual, is captured in an image. While the world has width, height, and depth, an image has only two dimensions: width and height. It doesn't matter if the final output is a television, movie screen, or printed image. A picture has no depth: It is in actuality only a flat surface.

The impression of three dimensionality in a two-dimensional image is an *illusion* in which lighting and camerawork play a large role. This illusion is an essential part of making film, video, and animation. Many times the objective is to enhance a sense of 3D where there was none before; other times the objective is to flatten the image. In either case, the principles involved are the same, just applied differently.

This chapter discusses Goals 4 through 6: creating the illusion of depth, creating the illusion of volume, and revealing substance.

6.1 GOAL 4: CREATING DEPTH

The real world occupies *space*; it has height, width, and depth—it is three-dimensional.

Depth **is the sensation of the world occupying space going back away from the viewer**. In the digital 3D scene, the dimension of depth is typically along the z-axis of the camera, which is the axis that is down the center of the camera's view. When a three-dimensional scene is rendered to form an image, it loses the dimension of depth. An image doesn't have depth or a z-axis. An image exists only in width and height labeled x and y, respectively.

NOTE

Flattening the 3D world into x and y resolution of the final image is known as *rasterizing*, the same term that applies to converting vector drawings or fonts into resolution-dependent pixel information.

Unlike the real world, which is always perceived as three dimensional, an image can be made to portray great depth or conversely to show little to no depth. When an image has no illusion of depth, and all of the elements seem compressed into a single plane, it is known as having *flat space* (Figure 6.2). Conversely, an image that portrays a large distance between the viewer and background objects is said to have *deep space* (Figure 6.3). The creation of the sensation of depth is not an either/or proposition: An image may fall somewhere in between, having a sense of some space but not a great deal, known as *limited space*. If the impression of depth is unclear or confusing, then the image has *ambiguous space*.

Figure 6.2 Flat space in a medieval illustration.

Figure 6.3 Deep space in *Palazzo Ducale* by 18th-century painter Canaletto (ca. 1755, at the Galleria Degli Uffizi, Florence, Italy).

Manipulating the sensation of depth in an image has been done for centuries, beginning with painters and practiced today by photographers, cinematographers, and digital lighters alike. Ancient art typically occupied flat space. For medieval artists, a realistic representation of depth wasn't a goal, resulting in images with flat, limited, or ambiguous depth. Beginning with the Renaissance painters, artists began exploring various means of portraying a more realistic representation of depth using techniques such as linear perspective, atmospheric perspective, and foreshortening (see the following sidebar, "Dimension and the Artists of the Renaissance"). Modern images run the gamut from flat graphic styles to realistic representations. Photographs, film, video, and 3D renders naturally capture the sensation of depth, though just how much is under the control of the artist as we explore later in this chapter. The sensation of space affects the mood and the relationships of objects in the scene and can be manipulated for creative or storytelling purposes.

DIMENSION AND THE ARTISTS OF THE RENAISSANCE

The Renaissance (French for "rebirth") was a cultural movement in Europe that began after the Middle Ages, beginning in the mid-14th century and lasting through the 17th century. The period was marked by a renewed interest in all things Greek (classicism), the arts, and literature, and saw the birth of modern science—generally a good time to be had for artists and scholars.

Prior to the Renaissance, during the medieval period, artists weren't particularly concerned with realistic impressions of depth and form. The medieval artist was more concerned with religious symbolism. Relative size, for example, may have occasionally been used to indicate depth but was readily discarded in favor of using size to indicate the importance of a subject instead. Artists of the Renaissance broke free of stylized Byzantine paintings of the medieval period and sought to create more realistic representations of life. They developed a number of techniques to more accurately depict depth and give the impression of real volume to their subjects.

During the Renaissance, systems for *linear perspective* (Figure 6.4) and *atmospheric perspective* (Figure 6.5) were developed by painters. Leonardo da Vinci's *Mona Lisa* is without a doubt the most famous example of early use of atmospheric perspective. Related to linear perspective is *foreshortening*, in which objects appear compressed when viewed with their length laid along our line of sight (Figure 6.6). Renaissance artists also developed a technique called *chiaroscuro*, which uses strong contrasts in light and dark to convey a sense of volume (Figure 6.6).

Not all Renaissance artists used all these techniques. Especially in the early Renaissance, mixed depth cues were common. For example, Hieronymous Bosch (1450–1561) usually used atmospheric perspective to create the sensation of distant landscape, but at the same time often painted near and far figures similar sizes, which flattens space (Figure 6.7).

Figure 6.4 Careful use of linear perspective accurately portrays distance in *Salvage of the Corpse of St. Mark* by Jacopo Tintoretto (ca. 1548, at the Gallerie dell'Accademia, Venice).

Figure 6.5 *Child with St. Anne* by Leonardo da Vinci (ca. 1501, at the Louvre, Paris) demonstrates use of atmospheric perspective.

Figure 6.6 Caravaggio's *Supper in Emmaus* (ca. 1601, at National Gallery, London) is an example of foreshortening and of use of strong lighting contrast (chiaroscuro) to show form.

Figure 6.7 In Hieronymous Bosch's last painting, *Christ Carrying the Cross*, all the figures seem pressed together to a single depth, creating flat space (ca. 1516, Museum voor Schone Kunsten, Ghent, Belgium).

The space of the image is commonly divided into planes, most typically foreground, mid-ground, and background planes. Obviously space is not really limited to these zones, but dividing the space into planes helps us to organize it. Each plane can then be considered when structuring the image.

CITIZEN KANE AND DEEP SPACE

It would be impossible to speak of image space without a mention of *Citizen Kane* (Figure 6.8). Considered by some to be the greatest film ever made, *Citizen Kane* was filmed in 1941 by director Orson Welles and cinematographer Gregg Toland. Welles and Toland explored the perception of space in the film, pushing boundaries both technically and artistically. *Citizen Kane* popularized a technique known as *deep focus*. Not to be confused with deep space, deep focus is the portrayal of deep space while maintaining all layers in clear focus. Recent advancements in camera lenses made deep focus possible. Prior to this, deep space was more typically combined with a limited focus range, in which only one or a few planes of the image were clear. *Citizen Kane* used deep focus and manipulation of space as a storytelling tool to portray the relationships of characters to each other and their world. Deep focus exaggerates the sensation of space, as the eye travels from near to far objects within the image rather than being forced to look at only one plane. Gregg Toland believed that deep focus was more natural to what our eyes perceive in life.

Figure 6.8 Deep focus in *Citizen Kane* (1941, courtesy of Everett Collection).

6.1.1 Depth Cues

***Depth cues* are the visual features that give us the sensation of depth.** Some of these are lost when a 3D scene is rendered to a 2D image, others remain. The perception of space is achieved through the manipulation of depth cues. In general, *the more depth cues an image has, the greater the sensation of depth; conversely, the fewer depth cues an image has, the flatter it will seem.*

When a scene is flattened from 3D to 2D, it loses two important depth cues:

◆ Stereoscopy
◆ Ocular focusing

A number of depth cues remain when a scene is flattened to 2D, however. Almost all of these cues involve camera, lights, and staging and are, therefore, under the influence of the cinematographer on a live-action set. Likewise, many of these depth cues are under the influence of the digital technical director as well.

The following are depth cues that may remain in a 2D image:

◆ Atmospheric perspective
◆ Change in value or color
◆ Light and shadow placement
◆ Camera focus
◆ Linear perspective
◆ Size consistency
◆ Relative height
◆ Overlapping forms
◆ Motion parallax

This section looks at the various depth cues, examining how they influence our perception of space.

Stereoscopy

Since your left and right eyes are offset by a few inches, each eye receives a slightly different view of the world. *Stereoscopy* refers to the perception of depth due to differing images sent to the brain from each eye. It is an amazing ability of the brain to take two images and stitch them into a single 3D perception of the world, obtaining depth information from the differences in what each eye sees.

NOTE

As an interesting side note, most predator species have forward-facing eyes that allow for binocular vision and a good sense of distance when swooping down on prey. Prey species, on the other hand, have eyes placed on either side of their head. Each eye sees a different part of the world with little overlap, resulting in poor depth perception but an excellent all-around view to watch out for predators.

3D (STEREOSCOPIC) MOVIES

Stereo imagery is far from new. As early as the mid-1800s, photographers were exploring 3D imagery by taking two photographs, offset from each other by about eye distance, and then using special viewers to present one photo to each eye for a 3D view. While much has changed, the basic technique for creating stereo imagery remains the same. Modern 3D films recapture the depth cue of stereoscopy by rendering two versions of every scene (Figure 6.9), offset in space by about the width of your eyes. The two images are combined into one (Figure 6.10) and then separated again at the time of viewing with special glasses (Figure 6.11).

3D movies first became popular in the 1950s, after which they fell out of favor for several decades. In the past several years, however, audiences have seen a revival in the popularity of the 3D feature film. 3D stereo films now appear alongside their non-3D counterparts, especially in the case of full-feature CG animations (such as *Shrek 3*, *How to Train Your Dragon*, and more) and visual-effects films (such as *Avatar*). Animation production studios now commonly make two versions of their films—one for regular viewing and the other for 3D viewing.

The digital artists making the 3D stereo version may be a different team than those on the original. The artists on the stereo version take the files that made the normal-view film and re-create the same renders for the second eye. This task is more technical than artistic and may seem less exciting to some.

While 3D films recapture stereoscopic cues, they lack ocular focusing cues (both images are flat and at the same distance from the viewer), which is why the 3D films can sometimes be disorienting and may not quite capture fully a "real" sense of depth.

TIP

A stereoscopic artist position can be an excellent way to begin your career as a digital artist as well as provide an opportunity to learn the techniques of experienced artists.

Figure 6.9 Left- and right-eye stereo image (David Warner).

Figure 6.10 Left and right eye combined using the color channels, viewable with red/cyan stereoscopic glasses.

Figure 6.11 Back in the 1950s, the glasses were red and blue (left). Now glasses for 3D films have polarized lenses that retain full color in each eye (right).

Ocular Focusing (Ocular Accommodation)

Ocular accommodation **refers to how our eyes change focus when we look at near and then far objects.** When we look at objects at different distances from each other, tiny muscles in the eye change the shape of our lens and bring the objects of our attention into clear focus, allowing other distances to appear blurry. In contrast, the eye doesn't need to change focus as it looks at "near" versus "far" objects in a picture—all the objects exist at the same depth—that of the picture plane.

Atmospheric Perspective

Atmospheric perspective **forms many visual cues that indicate depth.** Atmospheric perspective is also known as *aerial perspective*. "Aerial" means "of the air" and refers to how the atmosphere lightens and dilutes the appearance of things as distance increases (Figure 6.12).

Due to atmosphere, distant objects:

➤ Are less saturated,

➤ Are lower in contrast,

➤ Tend toward the color of the atmosphere itself (usually blue or gray), and

➤ Are lower in detail (known as aerial or textural diffusion).

Figure 6.12 An example of atmospheric depth from *Harry Potter and the Prisoner of Azkaban*. This scene further frames the subject with dark foliage, a technique known as *repoussoir* that was often used by 18th-century romantic landscape painters. (©2004 Warner Brothers. Courtesy of Everett Collection.)

In fact, even without atmospheric perspective per se, these qualities suggest objects in the distance. For example, *saturated* and *high-contrast areas* in general tend to move forward in an image, while desaturated and low-contrast areas recede. Each of these effects, taken separately, provides a weak depth cue. Taken together, they are a powerful indicator of depth.

Atmospheric perspective, often called simply "atmosphere," is frequently used in feature film. Even a small amount of atmospheric haze added to an image can help create a greater sensation of depth.

TIP

Textural diffusion is of special concern for digital artists. When creating an environment, it is a good idea to limit detail in distant areas in terms of both textures and models, since generally this detail cannot be seen anyway. Limiting distant detail serves the practical purpose of saving both production and render time.

Figure 6.13 A gradient showing depth.

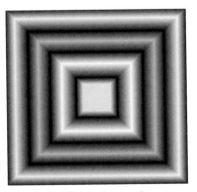

Figure 6.14 Random value changes lack depth.

Change in Value or Color

Varying the lighting **in foreground, midground, and background planes will help to separate areas of the environment into different distances from the viewer.** Sometimes this aspect of creating depth is overlooked in CG images where continuity between elements is a bigger concern.

Gradual transitions give the greatest sensation of depth. The values can go from lighter to darker, or vice versa. If distant areas are darker, the result is as if looking into a darkened cave or tunnel (Figure 6.13). When distant areas are lighter, it gives a feeling of atmosphere (Figure 6.12). In a darkened theater, the impression of depth can be enhanced the most by making the distant areas lighter, creating a gradient that is darkest in the theater itself, to the dark edges of the screen, to the lighter (and more distant) center of the screen.

Use of color can also help the sensation of depth. Saturated and warm hues tend to attract the eye and proceed forward, while desaturated and cool colors tend to recede (Figure 6.1).

Shadow and Light Placement

Where and how the *light and shadows* **fall is a strong visual cue for the shape and depth of things.** Shadows tell us the spatial relationships between objects and can help indicate the size and position of elements in a scene (Figures 6.15 and 6.16). Additionally, our brains are so used to interpreting the main light in environment as coming from above that this can influence our perception of form (Figures 6.17 and 6.18). Finally, *the use of backlights* also creates depth. Backlights (also known as rim lights) are positioned in such a way as to create a thin line of illumination on the foreground objects, helping to separate foreground from background and thus creating limited depth (Figure 6.20).

A number of depth cues involve the camera and arrangement of objects in the scene. How elements are placed and framed is known as *mis-en-scene*, or literally "placing on stage."

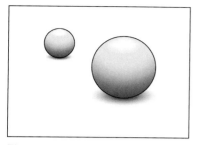

Figure 6.15 An image of two balls, approximately the same size but one near and the other far.

Figure 6.16 Due to shadow, in this image we see two balls at the same depth, one small and the other large.

Figure 6.17 A diagram of dents and bulges. Do you see two bulges and four dents?

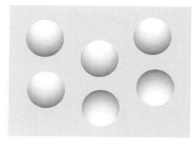

Figure 6.18 When the diagram from Figure 6.17 is flipped, we don't see the light from below but rather invert the dents and bulges so now there are four bulges and two dents.

Camera Focus

By adjusting the depth of field of a camera, various distances from the camera can be made to be blurry while other areas remain clear. In addition to directing our attention toward crisp areas, defocusing helps create a sensation of limited depth. Blurry areas appear to be some distance away from clear areas. The sensation of depth is limited, however, since all the objects out of focus blur together, creating a sense of only two planes: foreground and background (Figure 6.20).

Figure 6.19 The use of converging lines and repeated shapes creates a sensation of deep space.

Figure 6.20 A backlit foreground and defocused background create a picture with limited space.

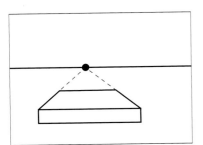

Figure 6.21 One-point perspective.

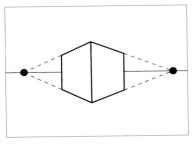

Figure 6.22 Two-point perspective.

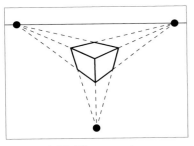

Figure 6.23 Three-point perspective.

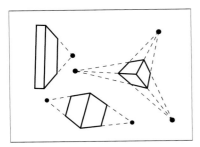

Figure 6.24 Multi-point perspective.

Linear Perspective

***Linear perspective* is the use of converging lines to create the illusion of depth.** In linear perspective, parallel lines (lines that are equally spaced along their entire length) viewed in 3D appear to converge on a single point known as a *vanishing point* (Figures 6.19 and 6.21 through 6.24). Every set of parallel lines has its own vanishing points making an infinite number of vanishing points possible, but one-point perspective, two-point perspective, and three-point perspective are the most common.

While draftsmen and painters must painstakingly re-create linear perspective, digital artists and photographers can capture this depth cue "for free." When photographing or rendering a scene, parallel lines will naturally converge just as they do when we view a scene in life. However, by manipulating the camera a photographer or digital artist can exaggerate or minimize the convergence of lines. The wider the angle of view, the faster lines will converge, exaggerating this cue. Conversely, an orthographic camera will not have any linear perspective whatsoever.

Relative Height

Another cue for depth is the *relative height* of objects in the scene in terms of their placement in the picture plane. Objects that are placed higher in view will tend to be seen as farther away. The reason for this is that objects that are farther away generally *are* higher up in our view, if they are sitting on approximately the same ground plane as us (which is true most of the time). This cue reads the best if combined with other depth cues (Figure 6.25).

Figure 6.25 Oriental art traditionally used height in the picture plane rather than perspective to represent distance from the viewer, as demonstrated in this Chinese illustration.

Relative Size

The farther away an object is, the smaller it appears, a fact that our brain uses to help determine the distances of things. The depth cue of *relative size* works best when the object (and its size) is familiar and/or with the same shape placed at various distances, such as a street scene full of cars and people. Repeated shapes can be actual objects, patterns of texture, or even pools of light.

A wide-angle lens will exaggerate the size difference of near versus far objects. Conversely, a narrow-angle lens will minimize size difference, and with an orthographic camera the objects will not diminish in size with distance at all.

TIP

Be careful of manipulating the actual scale of objects in your scene in order to create depth, because doing so may create a scene that looks odd or off. A better route is to work with the camera's angle of view/focal length.

Figure 6.26 (Left) An average street scene.

Figure 6.27 (Right) When one of the men in the distance is cut and pasted to the same level as the foreground people, the true difference in scale becomes apparent. He looks tiny!

Our brain uses other depth cues, such as converging lines and relative height, to determine whether the object is far or actually tiny. When an object is small but placed high in frame, it's seen as distant (Figure 6.26). Placed lower in frame, it seems smaller (Figure 6.27). The size we "expect" to see is also determined by converging lines. If converging lines indicate that an object should be smaller due to distance, and it's not, our brains will interpret the object as larger than it actually is, an optical illusion known as the Ponzo effect (Figure 6.28).

Figure 6.28 The Ponzo effect.

Overlapping Forms

A simple way to get one object to read as being nearer than another is to place it in front of the other. *Overlapping forms* produces a sensation of depth (Figure 6.29). On its own, overlapping forms is a rather weak indicator of depth and produces limited space or still results in flat space. Combined with other depth cues, however, it helps enhance the sensation of depth.

Figure 6.29 Overlapping forms create limited depth in this still life (Luke Heathcock).

Motion Parallax

Motion parallax occurs when objects near to us appear to move past more quickly than objects in the distance, even though their speeds and trajectories are the same. The motion referred to is relative: The objects can be moving and the viewer stationary, such as a herd of cattle running by, or the viewer can be moving and the objects stationary, as when one drives by a grove of trees. In either case, the farther the object, the slower the apparent motion. Pigeons, which have eyes placed on each side of their head and lack stereoscopic vision, take advantage of this depth cue when they bob their heads up and down. Try it—close one eye and bob your head up and down and you'll see what I mean. Now you know what those pigeons are doing.

Traditional 2D animation has long used this depth cue. Typically elements in the environment are placed on different planes (foreground, midground, and background planes) and panned by at different speeds to create a sensation of depth. A beautiful and classic example of this technique can be seen in the opening sequence of Walt Disney's *Bambi*.

As with linear perspective and size consistency, the focal length of the camera will affect how much motion parallax you see. When the focal length is long and the angle of view narrow, faraway objects will move by more quickly, similar to the speed of near objects. The wider the angle of view, the greater the difference between near and far objects' speeds.

6.1.2 Creating Flat Space

Creating flat space that portrays little to no depth is easy: You simply remove or reverse the depth cues we have been discussing. A narrow angle of view/long focal length will go a long way when flattening a scene. It will minimize parallax, size consistency, and the appearance of converging lines. Try to avoid physically translating the camera, instead rotating it or working with the lens to change what is in view: pan and tilt (which involve rotating the camera) instead of track; zoom instead of dolly to magnify the scene. Objects should be placed so that they don't overlap and oriented preferably so that they face you head-on, reducing the number of converging parallel lines. The background can be highly defocused to create limited space consisting of foreground and background only. Don't add any atmospheric haze—make everything equally clear in view regardless of distance, making sure distant objects retain high contrast and detail. Light everything the same throughout.

Figure 6.30 The right panel of *The Four Holy Men* (ca. 1526, Alte Pinakothek, Munich) by Albrecht Dürer uses variation in tone to create a sense of volume in the drapery.

VISUAL CUES FOR MANIPULATING SPACE

Methods for creating deep space:

- Use atmosphere.
- Vary lighting in near and far planes.
- Change value, contrast, color, and/or saturation.
- Use desaturated, less contrasting, and cooler colors in the distance.
- Defocus near or far elements.
- Use linear perspective.
- Use parallax.
- Move in and out of space with camera, such as dolly and track.
- Use a wider angle to exaggerate linear perspective, relative size, and parallax.
- Overlap objects.
- Use positioning in the picture plane—higher objects seem farther away.

Methods for creating flat space:

- Keep objects the same size on-screen, or even make far objects larger.
- Keep texture the same size, or even make far textures larger.
- Remove converging lines and vanishing points.
- Avoid translating the camera: Use pan and tilt instead of tracking; use zooms instead of dolly.
- Avoid overlapping objects.
- Limit contrast and color separation.

In general, to create deep space, use as many depth cues as possible. To create flat space, eliminate or reverse depth cues.

6.2 GOAL 5: SCULPTING VOLUME

Sculpting volume refers to maintaining a sense of an object's physical presence, of its form and the space it occupies in three dimensions. Lighting plays a large role in defining or obscuring the volume of a subject. In fact, lighting is one of the primary means by which this goal is accomplished. Every lighting artist, be they a technical director, photographer, or cinematographer, needs to have a solid understanding of how to use their lights to control the perception of volume. Lighting with this goal in mind is sometimes called *sculpting with light*.

We deduce the shape of an object by interpreting how light varies in brightness across its surface (Figure 6.30). Our brains are highly tuned to variations in tone, determining from it the position of the light as well as the orientation of the surface toward or away from the light.

We all know that the lit side of a solid object is the side facing the light. These variations in tone are the primary way in which we tell the volume of something. Simply put, we see bulges, bumps, and the mass of things because they catch the light. It stands to reason that if variations in tone due to light give us a sense of volume, the more variations in tone we have, the more of a sense of volume we will achieve. And this is indeed the case.

When an object is lit in such a way as to maximize the variations in light intensity across it, the sense of the volume of that surface is enhanced. Conversely, when an object is lit with uniform intensity over all areas of its surface, then our perception of the object's 3D volume is minimized. Uniform illumination generally occurs when the object is lit evenly from all directions, as in the case of ambient light (see Figure 6.31). Another type of "uniform illumination" is when the surface is not receiving any light at all, in which case all areas of the surface go to black due to lack of light (Figure 6.32). Okay, that sounds pretty obvious (of course, you cannot see the form of an unlit object), but bear with me on this one. This simple fact means that to show *maximum* shaping of form, *all* areas of the surface need to have variation in tone due to illumination (Figure 6.33). Not that you have to have or want maximum shaping. But if you do want it, now you know how to get it.

Figure 6.31 (Left) A render of a little girl model with a CG ambient light imitates pure uniform illumination—no shaping.

Figure 6.32 (Center) This may be rather obvious but... no illumination means no shaping.

Figure 6.33 (Right) The little girl lit to show form, with varying illumination across all parts of the surface.

SIMPLE RULE FOR SCULPTING WITH LIGHT

When there is variation in tone (due to illumination), then volume is revealed. When there is consistency of tone (due to illumination), then volume is obscured.

6.2.1 CONSIDERING THE INCIDENT ANGLE

The angle at which light strikes a surface is known as the *incident angle* (Figure 6.34). How the incident angle affects luminance really is quite simple: *If the light rays are perpendicular to the surface, the plane will be at maximum brightness. Conversely, the more grazing the angle, the darker the surface will be* (Figures 6.34 and 6.35).

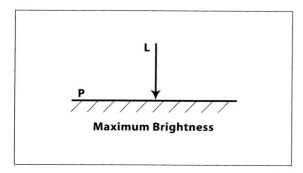

Maximum Brightness

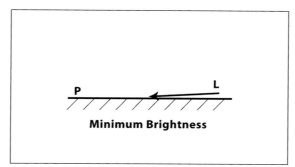

Minimum Brightness

Figure 6.34 (Left) If the light strikes the surface at a 90-degree angle, its illumination will be brightest.

Figure 6.35 (Right) If light strikes the surface at an angle, its illumination will be less.

You may think, Of course surfaces darken as they turn from light! Our knowledge of this is intuitive. When lighting, however, we will want to bring the light's incident angle to our *conscious awareness*. Keeping in mind the incident angle will allow us to better understand and predict how our lights will act, helping us to place our lights so they strike the surfaces we desire with the intensities we desire. In other words, it gives us control over our lights.

Sounds rather tech-y, this business of "considering the incident angle." If you're newer to lighting, you may wonder exactly how to get started. When deciding on where to place your lights to achieve the result you want and to get the most from each light, it is very helpful to consider your scene in terms of *planes* and *angles*.

First, consider your scene in terms of *planes*. The planes are the planes of the surface. Every surface, even if it is curved, can be broken down into surface planes. For example, even a complex curving form like human anatomy can be simplified into the planes that comprise it (Figure 6.36). Illustrators train themselves to see the underlying shapes so as to better capture the volume of their subjects. So, too, as lighters can we train ourselves to imagine the planes that make up even complex surfaces.

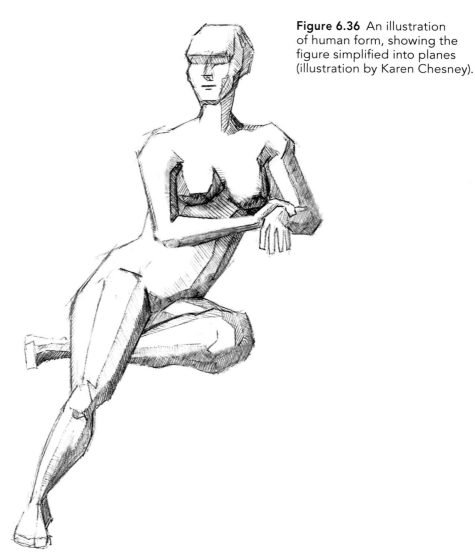

Figure 6.36 An illustration of human form, showing the figure simplified into planes (illustration by Karen Chesney).

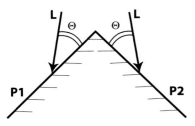

Figure 6.37 Planes P1 and P2 will have the same brightness. No shaping of form.

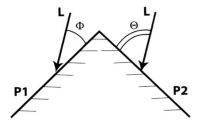

Figure 6.38 Plane P2 will be brighter than plane P1 and will show shaping of form.

Next, consider your scene in terms of *angles*. These angles are the incident angles. Again, the incident angle is the angle formed between the light ray and the surface plane. A light doesn't have just one incident angle, but rather, every ray of light striking the surface has an incident angle at the point it strikes, which is why it's useful to mentally simplify the surface into planes (Figure 6.37).

You can then consider if one plane is oriented more toward the light than another (and thus will be brighter), or know if a plane is at maximum brightness because it's perpendicular to the light ray, or know when it will receive no illumination because it's turned away from the light. Be aware that *the same angle of incidence equals the same intensity of illumination for any given surface, even if those surfaces are oriented differently in space.* When it comes to lighting, it's the angle of a surface to the light that is important, not its orientation in world space (Figures 6.37 and 6.38).

Initially, this type of visualization may seem awkward. Eventually, however, analysis of your image will become second nature, and you will be able to predict roughly what your lights will do before you place them. In the beginning, the best way to develop a sense of this is simply to practice.

6.2.2 LIGHTING A CUBE, "PLANE" AND SIMPLE

A simple exercise I recommend to anyone who is learning the skill of lighting is to light a cube, keeping in mind the concept of planes and angles. Such a simple shape clearly demonstrates how one can light a subject to achieve maximum shaping. This exercise is covered in cinematographer John Alton's book, *Painting with Light*, as well as photographer Ansel Adams's book, *The Negative*.

Position the cube and camera so that as many sides of the cube are seen as is possible. The more sides you can see, the greater the sense of volume you will be able to achieve. If you see only one side, looking directly at the cube, the image is flattened. Two sides are somewhat better, allowing for linear perspective, and three is best. It's not possible to see more than three sides of the cube, so that is the most dimensional view of the subject (Figure 6.39).

Lighting for volume is similar in principle. Maximum shaping is achieved when each plane of the subject has a different level of luminance. Try this and you will see. When all sides have the same level of flat luminance, there is no shaping whatsoever. If one of the three visible sides of the cube has a different level of luminance, some shaping is achieved. When each visible side is of a different brightness, the cube has maximum shaping (Figure 6.40).

Figure 6.39 The more sides of the cube you see, the greater your sense of its volume.

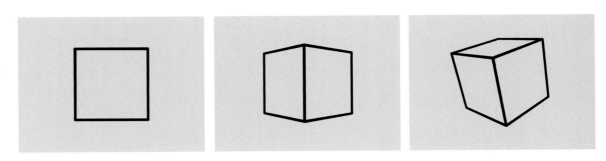

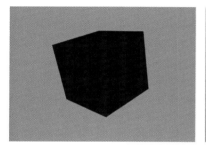  

Figure 6.40 Your sense of the cube's volume is greatest when each plane has a different level of luminance.

6.2.3 Light Position and Sculpting Form

A few generalities can be made about where to position your light(s) to most enhance the sense of volume. These generalities come from traditional photography and cinema. This section looks at light placement in regard to shaping, as well as a few special concerns for digital lighters.

Three basic light positions can be evaluated in terms of their effect on revealing form:

- ◆ Side light
- ◆ Front light
- ◆ Back light

Sidelight

Sidelight brings out form. Light coming in from the side of an object creates a large variation in tones across the surface, lightening and darkening as it goes over contours and curves. This range of tones reveals volume. Be aware that if a sidelight is pointing directly to the side or a bit from the back, then a large portion of the object will be in darkness. If it's in darkness, it's not being shaped. To shape the rest of the subject you will need another light on the shadow side, or you will need to reposition the sidelight so that it's slightly frontal (Figures 6.41 through 6.43).

Figure 6.41 (Left) A sidelight angled from the back leaves much of the subject in darkness and only one half of the face. (We deduce the rest due to symmetry.)

Figure 6.42 (Center) A sidelight angled from the front covers more of the subject for maximum shaping from *one* light.

Figure 6.43 (Right) Adding a sidelight on the opposite side shapes the whole figure.

Your object will have the most shaping if you use sidelights on both sides of the object. This is not to say that the lights need to or should be of equal intensity; rather, that even on the shadowed side of the object, a low-level light can be placed to model the surface in relative darkness, continuing to define form. This technique has been used by traditional artists for years, resulting in what some illustrators term a "core shadow" at the center of the object. Core shadow or not, continuing the techniques for shaping even in the darker areas results in maximum sculpting of form (Figure 6.44).

Figure 6.44 A beautifully lit scene from *Avatar*. Notice the sidelights on either side of the face and the tonal range from white to near black. (©2009 TM and 20th Century Fox. Courtesy of Everett Collection.)

Hard grazing sidelights pull out texture. When light reaches a surface not just from the side, but at an extreme grazing angle, it will enhance the visibility of tiny bumps and pits in a surface (compare Figures 6.45 and 6.46). Depending on the subject or scene, this may be desired—or not. You may like the rugged appearance of wall stucco for visual interest, but definitely not want to show every pit in your female model's face. Real-world lighters often use light angle to control the appearance of bumpiness. Of course, digital artists have an easier way of controlling the appearance of bumps. Generally, every material has a simple slider that allows you to raise or lower the bumpiness of a surface. In the vast majority of cases, adjusting a material parameter is how a digital artist will alter the appearance of the surface texture. However, in some situations changing the bump or displacement intensity overall isn't the best choice. The nice thing about using a light is that it will affect *only the areas illuminated by that light* rather than the whole surface, which can come in handy.

Figure 6.45 (Left) Grazing light (incident angle to back plane about 5 degrees), intensity 1.6.

Figure 6.46 (Right) More frontal sidelight (incident angle to back plane about 60 degrees), intensity .6. Same texture settings as Figure 6.45.

Frontal Light

Soft frontal light obscures form. A *frontal light* is placed at roughly the same position as the camera, pointing at the scene at about the same angle as the camera's view. Frontal light flattens form because the visible portion of the subject is well illuminated while the darker areas are along the sides and back of the subject and hidden from view. This results in less tonal range being visible. Less tonal range means less shaping. Frontal lights also minimize the appearance of surface bumpiness.

A common misconception here is that *any* frontal light flattens form, and they all do so equally well. Not true. *Soft* frontal light hides volume best. Soft light is very scattered and reaches the surface from many directions, evening out tones and texture. *Hard* frontal lights, on the other hand, still show a fair amount of shape, especially if the surface is at all shiny. With a hard bright frontal light, more tonal range is visible and the outer edges of the subject become dark in an odd fashion (Figure 6.47). Photographer Ansel Adams calls this a "dark halo" in his book *The Negative*. This type of look is often unappealing, and in many cases it's best to avoid a strong hard frontal light. In short, it's not only the direction of the light but also the softness or hardness of the light (known as *diffusion*) that affects the perception of form. For a digital frontal light to effectively flatten form, the light *must* be very soft (Figure 6.48).

Figure 6.47 (Left) A typical CG frontal light. Notice how you can clearly see the shape. Hmmm, not doing such a good job of obscuring form…

Figure 6.48 (Right) A soft frontal light. Notice how the volume is much more difficult to make out. *This* is the flattening frontal light the photographers are talking about!

An important point here is that generalities, while mostly true, don't always hold true. As demonstrated in these examples, a hard frontal light will actually reveal *more* volume than a back-angled sidelight! So *never let a formula dominate your own observation.* Formulas are useful guidelines, but should never replace your own critical evaluation of your scene.

Backlight

Light from the back defines the silhouette. A backlight does *not* define the volume of the object. It does, however, emphasize its *outline*, thus separating the subject from its background (Figure 6.20). For more on the rim light, see Chapter 12, "Three-Point Lighting and Beyond."

PRINCIPLES FOR SHAPING OBJECTS WITH LIGHT
- Frontal light flattens shape and texture.
- Side light brings out shape.
- Hard, grazing light brings out surface texture.
- Ambient and soft light obscures shape and texture.
- Rim lighting separates elements from the background.

6.2.4 Using Pattern to Reveal Form

In addition to light position and quality, patterns on the surfaces of objects are visual cues as to their volume. These patterns can be made by some property of the surface, such as patterns in the color of the material, like a checkered tablecloth or polka-dotted vase. Or they can be details of the physical model, such as folds in a cloth or grooves in wood. They can also be patterns as a result of light and shadow, such as striped shadows from a Venetian blind (Figure 6.49).

Patterns on an object naturally follow the contours of the surface. How these patterns turn and lay, spread out or squeeze together are all clues our brains use to determine the underlying form. Patterns that are regular and repeating give us the most information about shape, because they are easiest for our brains to decipher (Figure 6.50). Irregular and random patterns, on the other hand, can make contours more difficult to discern (Figure 6.51).

Figure 6.49 (Left) The regular shadow pattern on this model enhances rather than obscures the perception of form.

Figure 6.50 (Center) The form of the statue is discernable because of the regular pattern.

Figure 6.51 (Right) This stochastic pattern makes the form difficult to make out.

6.3 GOAL 6: REVEALING SUBSTANCE

Lighting also can be very important in revealing an object's substance. For example, is it made of glass or metal or wood? All of these surfaces have lighting approaches that may vary in order to best reveal the qualities of the substance as well as make it visually appealing. Those new to lighting may not initially realize that many materials require unique lighting approaches in order to gain the best look from them. Experienced lighters and those experienced with traditional photography may find this a more familiar concept.

Learning special techniques for various kinds of materials is something that takes time and a bit of expertise. Because of this, we will only look at this goal in a general way.

Figure 6.52 The materials in this still life received special attention and technique to obtain an appropriate look (Leadro Ibraim).

Standard lighting techniques usually apply to materials that have a significant diffuse component. Materials that don't have much of a diffuse component, on the other hand, may require special techniques to gain the best look. Materials that need special treatment are often those with reflective or semi-transparent/translucent properties. For details on lighting reflective and transparent surfaces, see Section 14.3, "Ray-Traced Reflections and Refractions."

Modified lighting is often required for these types of objects:

- Glass
- Fur
- Clouds/nebula
- Mirrored surfaces
- Very dark surfaces
- Very shiny surfaces
- Skin
- Wax
- Cloth
- And more…

Depending on the scene and the materials in the scene, the goal of revealing substance may weigh in a great deal or not at all. If the object is especially large in frame and/or important to the story, then it will generally receive special attention.

6.4 CHAPTER CONCLUSION

This chapter covered two important goals of lighting related to the dimensionality of the scene: creating depth and creating volume. Every image can portray either flat space or deep space, depending on how many depth cues are included. Knowing what these depth cues are allows you to gain the level of depth you want for your scene. Likewise, every 3D scene deals with the challenge of portraying volume. Usually the goal is to enhance the sensation of volume. The primary means to enhance the perception of volume is with well-placed lights. In every scene you need to ask yourself how much depth and shaping is needed, and what your lights are doing (or need to do) in order to accomplish this goal.

Additionally, this chapter looked briefly at lighting for various material properties. Consider whether any materials in your scene need extra attention in order to have the best or most realistic look. Objects such as glass, metal, water, clouds, skin, food, and cloth often need special treatment.

6.4.1 IMPORTANT POINTS

- ◆ Lighting plays an essential role in enhancing the three dimensionality of a scene.
- ◆ Depth refers to how much space away from a viewer a scene seems to occupy.
- ◆ The more depth cues an image has, the greater the sensation of depth it will portray.
- ◆ Flat images are created by removing or reversing depth cues.
- ◆ How light plays across a surface is one of the primary indicators of its volume.
- ◆ To achieve maximum shaping, tone should be varied across all the planes of the object.
- ◆ Light from the sidelight brings out volume.
- ◆ Grazing lights bring out texture
- ◆ Soft frontal light flattens volume.
- ◆ In most cases, digital frontal light doesn't flatten very well.
- ◆ Many materials require custom lighting in order to achieve the best look.

6.4.2 TERMS

space	depth cues	parallax
depth	stereoscopic cues	linear perspective
rasterizing	atmospheric perspective	relative height
deep space	textural diffusion	relative size
shallow space	rim light	incident angle
limited space	mis-en-scene	

6.4.3 EXERCISES

1. Sketch two scenes, one with deep space and the other with flat space.
2. Set up two 3D scenes. In one, maximize the sense of depth within the scene. Try to use as many depth cues as you can, including lighting, mis-en-scene, and lens work. In the second scene, modify the first scene to create flat or limited space.
3. Light a single cube, obtaining maximum shaping from only one light.
4. Set up a scene with a cube on a ground plane and in front of a background wall. Light the scene with two lights on the cube and one light on the background (three total lights). Notice how for this simple scene you can control the luminance of all of the planes with only three lights. Light the scene in a variety of ways to demonstrate this.
5. Set up a simple still life, and light it to obtain maximum shaping from the subjects. Be sure to include objects with curved surfaces (not just cubes for this exercise). Experiment with multiple sidelights, frontal lights, backlights, and grazing lights.
6. Create and light a simple still life very flatly, with only minimal discernment of form. You can use CG ambient light, but it cannot be your only light.

Figure 7.1 *Rango* was the first full CG film created by the visual effects studio Industrial Light & Magic. Drawing upon ILM's decades of live-action experience, the lighting and shading of the film maintains a photorealistic visual style. (©2011 Paramount Pictures. Courtesy of Everett Collection.)

Chapter 7
Goals 7–10: Providing Cohesiveness and Visual Interest

"Change must always be balanced with some degree of consistency."

—Ron D. Burton, present-day businessman

Projects involving 3D animation typically involve many people and can take weeks, **months, or even years to create.** While occasionally we see an animation project created entirely by only one person, usually even smaller projects involve a handful of people and take several weeks to create. A very large project like a feature film will take hundreds of people and up to a few years to produce. Different portions of a large project are created at different times, often out of order. Different sections of animation are done by different people, even at different studios, in different parts of the world, and using different tools. Digital elements are integrated into real-world elements ("live action") sometimes long after the live action has been filmed.

When there is this much going on in terms of people and time, maintaining cohesion between elements is an important task. All these elements need to come together to form one entity in which the gaps in time and the many different people involved are not noticeable. The final piece requires a sense of unity. Maintaining cohesion doesn't have to be that hard, however. It just means you need to pay attention. By keeping in mind a few guidelines, you should be able to maintain a sense of unity. Without attention to cohesion, however, you are absolutely sure to run into problems. Cohesion requires careful checking, and it also requires planning. This chapter covers some things to keep in mind when creating a single animation project by outlining Goals 7 through 9 of lighting. The chapter then concludes with a discussion of Goal 10: creating visual interest.

7.1 GOAL 7: MAINTAINING CONTINUITY

Maintaining continuity is the seventh goal of lighting. *Continuity* **refers to the consistency of elements** *over time.* When various elements are created for a visual narrative, such as characters, props, places, and even events, these things should appear to have a cohesive entity over their duration in the narrative. This is not to say that they cannot change over time (something has to change for the story to move forward), but rather that there are no jarring and unexpected discrepancies that make no sense to the viewer, which are out of place and without a purpose.

7.1.1 COMPONENTS OF FILM NARRATIVE

When discussing continuity, it's helpful to understand some of the components that make up a cinematic narrative. The two basic components are the *shot* and the *sequence*.

The fundamental component of film narrative is the *shot*. A shot refers to a continuous filming of the camera. A shot is created when the camera is turned on, records uninterrupted, and then is turned off, an action known as a *camera take*. When a film goes from one shot to the next, it is said to *cut* from shot to shot. The term comes from the physical cutting of the film, which was how early editing was done as well as the phrase yelled by the director to end a take: "Cut!!" The concept of the shot is the same for 3D animation—the final animation shot appears as one continuous render from one camera (even if getting there took many renders from many cameras).

Shots are combined to form *sequences*. A sequence is a group of consecutive shots that form a block of storytelling. All of these shots should relate to each other as a unified event. For example, a sequence may be a series of shots of two characters dialoguing in a kitchen. The camera may cut back and forth between the characters and off to something else in the room. All of these shots are the "kitchen sequence." A break in location or time (such as if the characters move outside or the story has suddenly shifted to later in the day) marks the beginning of a new sequence. Most simply put, a sequence is a group of related, uninterrupted shots.

7.1.2 THE CONTINUITY STYLE

Many conventions for maintaining continuity began with early Hollywood cinema and have been adopted as an international standard in commercial film and television. This group of strategies and techniques for maintaining consistency is known as the *continuity style* or *continuity editing*. The goal of the continuity style is to create a smooth flow from shot to shot, so that the editing doesn't draw any attention to itself, allowing the viewer to remain immersed in the story. Foremost among these conventions are various rules about camera cuts. While these rules involve the camera and not lighting, every technical director and animator should be familiar with them because of their importance to visual storytelling. *Film Directing Shot by Shot*, by Steven D. Katz, is an excellent reference for more on the subject.

7.1.3 LIGHT AND CONTINUITY

When maintaining continuity between shots, the lighting should not change unexpectedly and without motivation from shot to shot. The important phrase here is "without motivation." If the setting changes, the lighting clearly can change. Likewise, if the mood changes, and the lighting changes in a manner to complement the mood, then the audience will not notice or be distracted, but rather the change in lighting will enhance their emotional response. For example, imagine a young girl picking flowers in a field. The light is warm-toned and sunny, and the overall feel is happy. A subtle change occurs—the lighting becomes cooler, a bit dimmer, with more contrast. The result is that we sense something is amiss, but we don't know what it is yet. Next we hear a rustling in the bushes, and we see a wild boar approaching the girl. Here the change in lighting is enhancing the story.

If, on the other hand, the lighting changes without motivation, perhaps even accidentally on the part of the artist, then this change is likely to seem odd and out of place and be distracting. Once again, like all of the goals of lighting, we see that continuity is subservient to storytelling.

The Lighting Ratio

One of the most important factors in maintaining light continuity is the *lighting ratio*. The *lighting ratio* is the ratio of how much light is falling on the scene from the brightest to the darkest areas. If the subject is a face, for example, it is the difference in luminance between the lit side and the shadow side of the face.

Lighting ratio = Brightest illumination : Darkest illumination

The luminance in the darkest areas is always expressed with the number 1 in the ratio. For example, the lighting ratio will look something like this: 8:1, 4:1, 3:1, and so forth. These numbers do not refer to the exact intensities of the lights, only their relative brightness. 8:1 means the brightest areas are receiving eight times more light than the shadow areas; 4:1 means the bright areas are receiving four times more light, etc. When using three-point lighting, the lighting ratio is also known as the key:fill ratio. The lighting ratio measures the level of contrast in the scene due to illumination; the greater the difference between the two numbers in the ratio, the greater the contrast (see Figures 7.2 through 7.4).

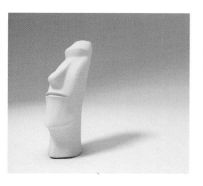  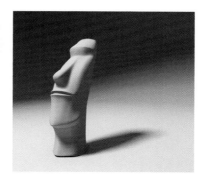

Figure 7.2 (Left) Lighting ratio of 2:1.

Figure 7.3 (Center) Lighting ratio of 4:1.

Figure 7.4 (Right) Lighting ratio of 10:1.

To maintain continuity, the lighting ratio needs to remain the same between shots. The actually intensities of the lights may change, however. It is the relationship of the brights to darks that needs to remain the same.

As a general rule, however, the lighting ratio may be changed when cutting from a far shot to a close-up. Close-up shots are most typically of characters' faces and often require a lower lighting ratio in order to look good. A lower lighting ratio means lighter shadows. On faces, strong shadows are often objectionable. It's perfectly all right to have a wide shot of two characters with a high lighting ratio and then cut to a close-up with a lower lighting ratio in order to keep the actors' faces looking good. In fact, this is done all of the time in cinema, and people don't notice at all.

Figure 7.5 (Left) Far shots may have higher contrast.

Figure 7.6 (Right) Close up, the contrast may be lessened.

Other Light Properties and Continuity

In addition to intensity, all aspects of your lights should be considered when maintaining light continuity. Here's a brief look at the other properties of light: color, position, and quality.

Lighting *color* likewise shouldn't change suddenly without reason. In particular, the overall color of light, known as *color temperature*, shouldn't change suddenly. If consecutive shots are jumping around in color and contrast, this is going to look odd to the audience. Unless, of course, there is a motivation for it (Figures 7.7 and 7.8).

Unexplained and obvious changes in lighting *direction* will generally confuse the audience as well. For example, if your main character is lit primarily on one side of the face in one shot and in the next shot is lit from the other side of the face, this is going to be a problem, as it implies the character has turned around. To be devil's advocate for a moment, however, the viewer won't notice if light direction does change a small amount, or sometimes even a larger amount in a surprising number of situations. For example, characters that are backlit by moonlight can remain backlit by moonlight no matter in what direction the camera faces them, and the audience won't notice, even though this would require the moon to be moving, which clearly can't be happening. However, unless (until) you know when you can get away with cheating the position of your lights, it's best to keep your light direction consistent (or at least appearing the same) from shot to shot.

Finally, keep light quality the same. Recall that "light quality" refers to the softness or hardness of your lights. This means you don't want your primary light to be a large, soft area light in one shot and in the next cut to the same source be represented by a hard spot.

Maintaining Continuity for the Digital Lighter

The most important thing you can do to maintain continuity between digital shots is to begin with the same lights. All of the lights in a scene together are known as a *lighting rig*. This rig can simply be exported from one scene and imported into another. On professional digital productions, the lighting for certain sequences is usually designed by a single artist, known as a lighting lead or sequence lead. This lighting rig provides a starting point for other artists. If there is no sequence lead, you still should begin from the lights taken out of a similar shot, if one exists. Following this workflow helps to ensure that the lighting design and technical approach do not differ dramatically between shots. Don't expect lights from another shot to drop into your shot without modification, however. On a rare occasion this may happen, but the vast majority of the time the lighting then needs additional adjustments to look its best. Beginning with the same setup, however, will help keep the shots consistent and hopefully reduce the amount of work that needs to be done. There is no need for each artist to begin from scratch when lighting similar scenes.

The next most important thing you can do to check for continuity is to view consecutive shots back to back, playing first one and then immediately following, the other. Don't just rely on your memory of last week's or even yesterday's work. An interesting thing about human perception is that differences between images may not be apparent if two images are viewed non-consecutively. This means that if you are working on a shot, and you think it matches another shot from what you remember, you may be in for a surprise. You need to view the shots or images sequentially in order to really see the changes. The CG supervisor views all of the work of the artists on his team, ensuring continuity, and you should also be doing the same on your own. Before starting a shot and while working on it, look at final rendered images from surrounding shots, especially those approved by supervisors, to see how your shot should be looking. Also, pay careful attention during daily critiques (known as *dailies*) to other shots in development that are in your sequence, to make sure all the shots are developing similarly. You often will hear a comment for a co-worker that helps out your shot or discover a technique you need to copy from their shot to yours.

Lighting ratio is usually determined by eye, by comparing back-to-back shots as noted. This method is usually sufficient because the digital artist rarely needs to know the *exact* lighting ratio in each shot. Experienced lighters can estimate the lighting ratio from the intensities of the lights. However, the lighting ratio isn't always exactly correlated to the light intensities. For why this is the case, refer to Chapter 9, "Light Intensity." When you need to know with complete accuracy the range of values in a scene, you should sample the luminance values of the final image. For specific technique, see Section 9.2.3 "Digital Measurements: Pixel Probes and Histograms."

SIX TIPS FOR MAINTAINING LIGHTING CONSISTENCY
1. The most effective way to match the lighting of one shot to another is to start with the same basic lighting setup.
2. View two shots back-to-back in order to check for consistency.
3. To maintain lighting continuity, the *lighting ratio* needs to remain the same rather than the exact intensities of the lights.
4. It is generally sufficient to estimate the lighting ratio from the intensities of lights in the scene "by eye."
5. When needed, exact *luminance values* may be determined by using a histogram or pixel probe.
6. The most accurate way to maintain *color consistency* is with precise RGB values (rather than matching color by eye).

In cases where you just need to match just the color (as when your streetlamps need to be the same shade of orange as your coworker's streetlamps), the best thing to do is to write down the exact red, green, and blue values that make up the color and copy these values into your light. I don't recommend estimating or "eyeballing" color. Color has a funny way of looking different in different situations, and matching color can be tricky even for those with an excellent eye for it. Best to keep it simple and play it safe—just write those numbers down.

7.2 GOAL 8: INTEGRATING DIGITAL ELEMENTS

"Integrating digital elements" means that all of the 3D characters, props, and/or backgrounds merge seamlessly with each other and with any live footage with which they are combined.

Integration of digital elements is the eighth goal of lighting, and it is the only goal that is unique to digital artists. Proper integration of elements maintains both cohesion and quality. When digital elements are not well integrated, the aesthetic quality of the piece suffers. Poorly done integration will also draw the viewers' attention to the illusion, in this case to the 3D itself, and distract them from the story. When integration is well done, it becomes invisible and the illusion is complete.

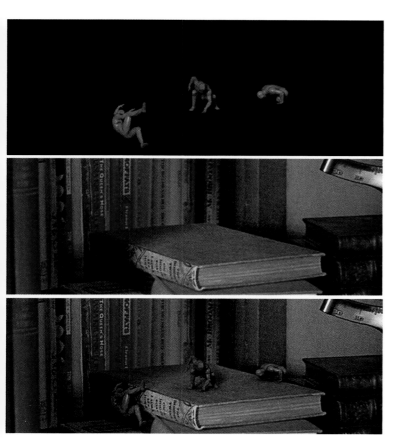

Figure 7.9 Digital elements (top frame) layered over a live-action background (middle frame). Final composite on the bottom. (Render and composite by Charles Trippe.)

Lighting plays an essential role in integrating digital elements into live-action footage. If the lighting on these different elements does not match, then the elements will not come together seamlessly. The elements won't look like they belong together and will look "cut out."

3D elements also need integration with each other. Many productions render different parts of the 3D scene into separate renders called *passes*. These passes may be of characters or props rendered separately from each other or their environment. At times different passes may use completely different lighting rigs from one another, yet when all the passes are recombined at the compositing stage, they should appear to be one render.

Seamlessly integrating digital elements involves many advanced techniques that are covered in later chapters throughout this book. The properties of real light are discussed in Chapters 8 through 11, techniques often used in visual effects productions are covered in Chapter 17, "Image-Based Lighting and More," and various compositing techniques are covered in Chapter 18, "Multi-Pass Rendering." As you can see, integration of digital elements isn't for the faint of heart—it requires a fair amount of technical skill and artistic sensibilities to be done well. Suffice it to say, in cases where digital objects need to be recombined with each other or with footage of real elements, integration is directly under the influence of the technical director and compositor.

7.3 GOAL 9: SETTING THE VISUAL STYLE

Style is a particular way of expressing something, characterized by a set of distinctive features. What kind of features depends entirely on the thing in question. For example, the writing in this book has a certain style of prose, while the style of a painting is defined by a set of visual characteristics such as painterly brush strokes and so on. Film style is defined by visual characteristics and by similar elements in narrative. Individual films have a consistent style in cinematography that creates visual cohesion for the entire piece. Each shot may look different, yet they all share traits that are consistent or reappear frequently.

***Visual style* is a particular look that is maintained throughout the entire piece**. For example, Francis Ford Coppola's *The Godfather* (1972) used warm sepia and gold tones throughout, and many scenes were shrouded in shadow. This visual style was carried throughout all three films in the *Godfather* trilogy and made such an impact that even today period pieces tend to use warm color schemes.

Goal 9 of lighting is to help establish the *visual style* of a piece. When dealing with the final appearance of 3D animation, the "look" is controlled in part by the rendering, shading, lighting, and compositing—all aspects that concern the technical director. This section concerns itself only with the visual aspects of style.

7.3.1 DEVELOPING A VISUAL STYLE

The development of a production's unique visual style is known as *production design* or art direction. Production design is headed up by a production designer or art director, who works closely with the director and director of photography or cinematographer. The art direction determines everything about how the production will *look*.

FILM NOIR AND NEO-NOIR

Sometimes classified as a cinematic style, other times a genre, film noir movies are crime dramas that were produced in the 1940s to 1950s. The film noir genre is largely (though by no means solely) defined by its lighting style. Film noir movies feature high-contrast lighting and strong shadows, often having single light sources coming from unexpected angles. Camera angles such as very high angle, low angle, or the Dutch tilt are used often. The plots feature murder and crime, and archetypes such as the femme fatale and hard-boiled detective are common (see Figure 7.10). The mood of the typical film noir is pessimistic with a sense of alienation and moral ambiguity. Famous film noirs include *The Maltese Falcon* (1941), *Notorious* (1946), *Sunset Boulevard* (1950), and *A Touch of Evil* (1958), to name but a few. Some examples of more modern films with a film noir flavor (called *neo-noirs*) are *Chinatown* (1974), *Basic Instinct* (1992), *L.A. Confidential* (1997), and *The Man Who Wasn't There* (2001). Neo-noirs can be futuristic, too, as in *Blade Runner* (1982) and *The Matrix* (1999). The film *Sin City* (2006) put a modern graphic twist on the film noir look by merging it with a comic-book style (Figure 7.11).

Figure 7.10 *Touch of Evil* (1958, Director Orson Welles) is a classic film noir film (courtesy of the Everett Collection).

Figure 7.11 *Sin City* is based on a comic of the same name by Frank Miller. Its distinct visual style draws heavily off the comic book and merges a film noir look with a graphic style. (©2005 Dimension Films. Courtesy of Everett Collection.)

Preliminary consideration of the overall style begins during the first phase of animation production, generally while the story is being developed. In some cases the style itself may be an inspiration for the story, as in a fine arts piece. Early development of a style consists of making decisions about the level of realism (see the following Section 7.3.2) as well as gathering together inspiration images, making concept drawings and sketches to flesh out ideas, and deciding on an overall palette for the production (Figures 7.12 and 7.13).

Figure 7.12 A mood board (assembled by Brenda Weede) used to develop a visual style.

Figure 7.13 A concept drawing and color palette for the animated short *Big Buck Bunny*. (Courtesy of Blender Foundation, www.blender.org.)

7.3.2 Level of Realism

When deciding on the style of a 3D animation piece, one of the first questions to answer is: How much realism is desired? The level of realism affects every aspect of production, from the way characters are modeled, to how they move and are textured, to lighting and compositing.

The level of realism may be divided into four broad categories:

◆ Realistic
◆ Stylized
◆ Cartoon
◆ Abstract

These categories aren't hard-and-fast rules. Some people may make somewhat different categorizations, and some works may straddle the line between categories and be hard to define. That being said, however, by making some generalizations, we can provide a framework with which to evaluate, compare, and discuss different levels of realism.

Realistic: The "Really Real" and the Hyperreal

***Realism* imitates, as closely as possible, the real.** Several styles may be classified as realistic. A *photoreal* painting, for example, is one that looks like a photograph. A photoreal digital render, likewise, will look like a photograph. It will leave you scratching your head and wondering whether it's actually CG (Figure 7.14). In film and video, the most realistic style of cinematography is the *documentary style*. The documentary style can appear rather no-frills, as if the film was shot with no special lighting or treatment of the scene. In other words, it looks as if someone pulled out a camera and began filming a real situation; nothing was set up, nothing was staged; nothing is artificial. Just because it appears no frills doesn't mean it is not exciting, however. A documentary look can draw the viewer in, making the action seem as if it is really happened. *Dog Day Afternoon* (1975), for example, had the look of live news coverage to give the audience the feeling they were viewing the hostage situation as it took place, thus heightening tension (Figure 7.15). Similarly, the low-budget horror film *The Blair Witch Project* (1999) was filmed and presented as a documentary, giving the feeling that the frightening events truly happened. The illusion of truly being real isn't limited to imagery. The original *War of the Worlds* was a 1938 radio drama directed and narrated by Orson Welles and was presented as a series of news broadcasts about an alien invasion. Some listeners believed the drama to be an actual news report, causing a panic.

Figure 7.14 A fully CG Song Hye Kyo by Max Edwin Wahyudi.

Figure 7.15 *Dog Day Afternoon* (1975) was lit in a natural, documentary style to enhance the impression that the drama was actually taking place (courtesy of the Everett Collection).

The documentary style represents realism at its purest. It looks as if the scene not only *could* be real, but that it *is* real, and furthermore that it *looks just as it would* if it were real. The last phrase may seem redundant, but it highlights an important distinction between *pure realism* (the "really real") and another form of realism—*hyperrealism*.

Hyperrealism **is an altered, enhanced, amplified version of reality**. Hyperrealism is different from strict realism in that it depicts reality and then some. Hyperrealism depicts things realistically enough to look as if they actually *could* and *do* exist, but upon closer inspection you will notice that these things *do not look as they would* if they really did exist. This style enhances certain characteristics and downright adds others in order to impart certain impressions on the viewer (Figure 7.16). Why not just be "really real" as in the documentary style? Because

Figure 7.16 Stylized light, color, and set design are all hyperreal in the futuristic classic *Blade Runner*. (©1982 Warner Brothers. Courtesy of Everett Collection.)

"really real" may not get you all you want. As Tony Apodaca stated in SIGGRAPH 92's *Writing Renderman Shaders*, "At times, something that is not correct, but is somehow similar to it, is even better than correct. Such things are often called *art*." The end result may impart certain emotions on the viewer; it may focus their attention on certain features; it likely furthers the story or simply adds beauty or interest.

Cinematically, the "classic Hollywood style" is hyperreal. The lighting has been heavily crafted, though done so in a way that the audience (hopefully) won't notice all the artifice. Special lights have been added purely for aesthetic reasons. Color may be added to lights or taken out with filters. All of these efforts help give stars their star power, enhance the story, and generally make the image more beautiful. It's also part of why if I take a picture of a Carl's Jr. burger it is likely not going to look anywhere near as appetizing as a burger on the commercial.

The difference between pure realism and hyperrealism is an important distinction for digital artists. The vast majority of the imagery we see in film, commercial, and television is hyperreal. Most films we might casually classify as realistic are, in fact, hyperreal. We see it so much, it has become invisible and we accept it as real, which is in fact part of the hyperreal illusion. It's also important to note for the digital lighter that in pursuit of a realistic image it's not always necessary to perfectly imitate life as seen in a documentary style. At times in the pursuit of the real, a digital lighter may say, "But this technique best imitates life and thus is better!" It's good to remember that film is not about reality; it's about the *illusion* of reality, and many times a crafted (hyperreal) image may suit the needs of the story better than a "really real" image. One is not better or worse than the other, it depends on what your story and overall style dictates. All is fair in love and war or, as another expression goes, "If it looks right, it is right."

Realistic styles are generally the most time-consuming to model, animate, shade, and light. If you want to opt for realism in your animation production, be sure you have the time, resources, and skill set to pull it off.

If the image deviates so much from reality that you no longer accept it as plausibly real, then it's not realistic, it's *stylized*.

Stylized: Plausible but Not Real

***Stylized* images have characteristics that are modified enough so that they no longer look like something that does or could exist** (Figure 7.19). "Stylized" is not so much a style as a broad collection of styles. When it comes to 3D art, stylized images still have plausible substance and volume and may look like they could be real in another fantasy or dream world. Most full CG features, such as *The Incredibles*, *Ice Age*, and *Horton Hears a Who* just to name a few, have a stylized 3D look that is common to most full 3D features. In stylized pieces the level of realism is less. Often things have been simplified, with unifying visual characteristics given to all the elements. A stylized look is often good for full 3D productions because it's generally faster to implement over a wide variety of elements. A certain "look" can be established and everything in the story gets that look, with only key characters and props having significant extra treatment. An important consideration when creating a stylized 3D element is that the style is convincing in terms of the whole image. In other words, that it fits in with all the other elements of the scene.

THE "UNCANNY VALLEY"

In 1970, Japanese roboticist Doctor Masahiro Mori published an article called "*Bukimi No Tani*" (不気味の谷) that roughly translates to "the uncanny valley." Dr. Mori's paper analyzed people's reaction to human-like subjects. He found that as something became more human-like, our reaction to it became more positive—until shortly before 100% likeness. When something is nearly human but just misses the mark, our reaction to it plunges sharply to be negative (Figure 7.17). This sharp plunge in our reaction is the "uncanny valley." The subject in question doesn't arouse empathy, but it has a sense of wrongness that makes us uncomfortable.

The uncanny valley is important to digital artists, for in our effort to faithfully represent a human likeness, if we miss the mark slightly our animations may fall into the uncanny valley. Notice in the graph that moving subjects provoke a larger response than nonmoving ones. A corpse is repulsive, but an animated corpse (zombie) is much worse. For animators, this makes the task of not falling into the uncanny valley even harder.

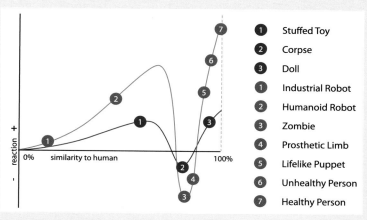

Figure 7.17 Diagram of the uncanny valley.

The first film thought to run afoul of this principle was *Final Fantasy: The Spirits Within* (2001). The characters fell just shy of realism; many viewers felt they appeared oddly stilted in motion and not quite lifelike enough in appearance (Figure 7.18). An ambitious step toward depicting CG humans for its day, while the film may have fallen short of the mark it pushed the envelope of what had been done and made several significant contributions to shading and lighting techniques. Another film that made great strides forward in a realistic depiction of humans but was still suspected of falling into the uncanny valley was the more recent *Beowulf* (2007).

Figure 7.18 *Final Fantasy: The Spirits Within* made great strides in the depiction of realistic humans but was accused of falling into the "uncanny valley." (©2001 Columbia Pictures. Courtesy of Everett Collection.)

Figure 7.19 *Big Buck Bunny* (courtesy of Blender Foundation, www.blender.org).

Cartoon: Flat and Graphic

Cartoon **images are 3D renders that have specifically been made to look like 2D cartoons or flat graphics.** These images may look cell-shaded or sketched, but the end result appears flat and two-dimensional (Figure 7.20). Achieving a 2D cell look involves special surface shaders and rendering techniques. Modern 2D animation (also called *traditional animation*) often incorporates 3D renders that have been made to look like 2D animations instead. 3D renders naturally show some volume, but one common problem is that when the elements move, they reveal themselves to be actually 3D.

Abstract: Form and Color

Abstract imagery doesn't try to look like anything recognizable. Abstract imagery focuses on form, shape, and color, often with the intent of purely conveying mood or visual interest. It may look realistic or graphic; it may be organic in form or scientific. An abstract style may be more suited to a fine arts piece or mathematical visualization, such as a procedural animation or render of a Mandelbrot (a mathematically derived fractal shape) (see Figure 7.21).

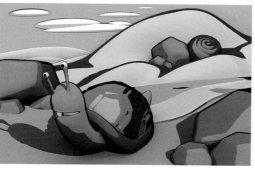

Figure 7.20 These images look like 2D drawings but are in fact 3D renders (Luke Heathcock).

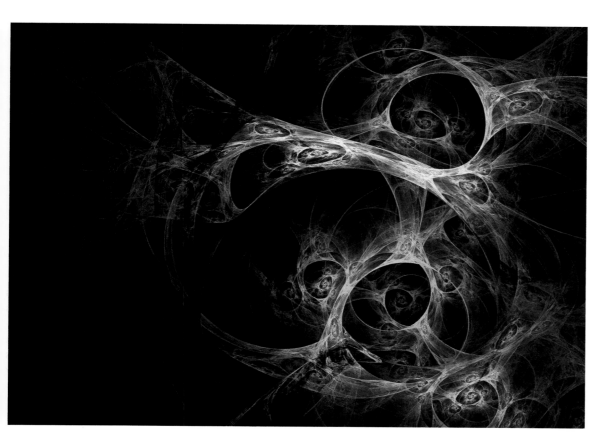

Figure 7.21 An abstract digital render.

7.4 GOAL 10: CREATING VISUAL INTEREST

We have now arrived at our final goal of lighting: creating visual interest. Although it's the shortest goal in the book, creating visual interest is an extremely important task of lighting. There just isn't too much to say about it.

An important role of lighting is simply to look good. Sounds like a shallow role, but no doubt about it, in the vast majority of cases an artist will make final lighting decisions based on visual interest. Sure, there are a few cases where this isn't a concern, but those are very few. The intent is usually to create compelling lighting that helps tell the story, doesn't distract, reveals or hides form as needed, maintains continuity as needed, etc.—and looks great doing it.

Beautiful lighting is often more important than accurate lighting, but it should never be more important than the story. To be clear, "beautiful" doesn't mean "pretty." It means visually interesting, and there is a difference. For example, one of the most famous paintings of the French Revolution, *The Death of Marat* (painted in 1793 by Jacques-Louis David), depicts the assassinated body of French radical journalist Jean-Paul Marat. It is powerful, aesthetically pleasing imagery. It has great visual interest, but I wouldn't call it "pretty."

Accomplishing the other goals successfully goes a long way toward creating visual interest. When the forms are well modeled, when a specific mood is evoked, when the eye is led through the composition, all this increases visual interest. However, this final goal has a great deal to do with the aesthetic abilities of the lighter. Learning all of the techniques in the world will not make you a great lighter unless you have some artistic ability, or the "eye" for it.

This final goal has no formula or technique, which is why discussion of it is so short. A technical director wishing to strengthen his or her skills in this area should study traditional visual art disciplines like painting, drawing, sculpture, 2D design, and color theory.

7.5 CHAPTER CONCLUSION

This chapter has covered several related goals and concludes Part II, "The Goals of Lighting." Most of this chapter has looked at the many ways lighting contributes to unifying a piece in order to maintain a believable story and to create an overall visual look. Also covered in this chapter is the role of lighting in creating visual interest.

7.5.1 IMPORTANT POINTS

◆ Maintaining continuity is one of the goals of lighting.
◆ Continuity may be broken for specific storytelling reasons.
◆ The lighting ratio is more important than the exact intensities of light when maintaining continuity.
◆ It is usually sufficient to match lighting ratios "by eye."
◆ Matching color often requires exact numeric values.

- The best way for the digital lighter to maintain continuity between shots is to begin with the same lighting setup.
- When checking continuity, view shots consecutively.
- Digitally created elements need to be integrated with live-action film and with each other.
- Integration of digital elements must be done well in order to maintain quality.
- Style needs to be considered early on in the development of a 3D project.
- The level of realism must be decided early on as it affects every aspect of animation production, from modeling to animation to lighting and rendering.
- Lighting plays a large role in developing visual style.
- Most visual storytelling presents an enhanced reality known as "hyperreal."
- Creating visual interest requires a good aesthetic sense.

7.5.2 TERMS

shot	style	hyperrealism
sequence	film noir	stylized
continuity style	realism	cartoonish
lighting ratio	photoreal	
live action	documentary style	

7.5.3 EXERCISES

1. Create a simple scene in which you use an ambient light and a spotlight. Create a lighting ratio of 2:1. Next, create a lighting ratio of 4:1. Render a frame from each scene and sample the shadow and lit areas. Write down your results.

2. Image gathering: Gather images that show digital elements integrated into a live-action film. Analyze each image: Is the integration seamless? What makes the image successful or not? Be prepared to discuss your images.

3. Image gathering/writing: Write a paragraph analyzing a film or video game. What are some of the repeated characteristics that make up the style? How does the style relate to the theme? Gather images that support your observations.

4. Research and develop a distinct style for an animated short. Gather inspiration and reference images that show traits representing your style or that are similar to your style. Design a storyboard that tells a story in four frames. Model, shade, and light and render these four frames. Your story should have a cohesive style, should be able to be told in four frames, and should use lighting as an integral part.

Another component necessary to achieving great lighting is to understand the *physics of light*. Traditional photographers and cinematographers spend time to learn about the properties of light in order to better control it. Understanding real-world lighting is even more important to the digital lighter, who must re-create it. The essential question to ask is *"What am I imitating with my lighting?"* Without a study of natural light, the digital lighter can easily create illumination that isn't plausible and that is unappealing. Even with nonrealistic styles, you will want to deviate from realism because you chose to do so, not because you don't know how to do otherwise.

When you understand real-world phenomena, you can better understand and control the many parameters and options in your 3D program. 3D applications have literally hundreds and even thousands of parameters. What does each one do? What is the ideal setting for each? Knowing the physics of real light helps the digital artist to better understand the choices available and what settings are best to achieve the desired result.

PART III

THE PROPERTIES OF LIGHT

(THE "WHAT")

"Look deep into nature, and then you will understand everything better."

—Albert Einstein, Physicist

Figure 8.1 Characteristic top-down light in *The Godfather* (1972) hides Don Corleone's eyes, making his thoughts inscrutable (courtesy of Everett Collection).

Chapter 8
Light Placement

"Everything should be as simple as it is, but not simpler."

—Albert Einstein

The *placement* of your lights is their position and orientation in space. Placement is usually the first thing set once the light is added to the scene, and in that sense it's rarely overlooked. However, achieving *correct* placement isn't without its difficulties. When lights are incorrectly placed, the resulting image will seem a bit "off" to the viewer. Avoiding incorrect placement is relatively easy if you know how to look for a few telltale signs.

This chapter goes over how placement affects your image and how to ensure the correct positioning of your lights.

By controlling position, the lighter controls how the light strikes the scene. Positioning of the lights affects many things: How many lights are needed, how accurate the image looks, how well your subject is shaped, how the shadows look and where they are placed, even the apparent softness and intensity of the light. Correct positioning is essential to a well-lit scene.

What is "correct positioning"? This means firstly that the scene looks right. Incorrect lighting may result in a scene that looks overly CG, lacks aesthetic appeal, and/or is disorienting. Correct positioning also means that the lights you use are minimal. Incorrect positioning often leads to more lights than would otherwise be necessary, making your scene harder to manage and likely increasing render time. Finally, correct positioning will satisfy the goals of lighting for that shot, such as shaping mood, or continuity.

The lighter has two primary considerations when positioning each light. They are (1) at what angle will the light rays be striking the surface, and (2) how far is the light from the surface?

8.1 DIRECTION

Direction **refers to the orientation of the rays coming from the light**. When you are positioning your light, the *number one* thing you are determining is the direction from which the light rays will strike the scene, known as the *incident angle*. Yes, it's that pesky incident angle again, just when you thought I was done with it—keeps cropping up, doesn't it?

The direction of the incoming light influences the brightness of the light upon the surface. Recall from Section 6.2, "Goal Five: Sculpting Volume," that when the light strikes the surface directly, at a 90-degree angle between the light ray and the surface, then the surface is brightest. If the light only grazes it, however, the surface will appear dim. In short, the more grazing the angle, the darker the light. When you move your light around to brighten one side versus the other, you may not have realized it but what you are doing really is changing the incident angle to affect scene illumination, which is one of the most important tasks of lighting.

This concept is important because it is how the lighter crafts his or her scene. We want more light in some areas than others, and the main way to accomplish this is by moving the lights around. You can apply this principle to your scene, for example, if you notice certain areas of your subject are still darker than you would like. *Rather than simply adding another light, first try repositioning the existing lights* to hit this area, keeping in mind that the more the illumination strikes the surface perpendicularly, the brighter the surface will be.

The direction of your light also affects the shaping of the subjects. Shaping is discussed in detail in Section 6.2.3, "Light Position and Sculpting Form," but here's a recap: A frontal light shapes the least, while a sidelight shapes the most.

Even a subtle change in position can substantially alter how a surface is lit. In Figure 8.2, the key has been moved to about a 45-degree front and side angle. This shapes the soccer ball nicely, but some of the faces of the diamond are blending together, and the square is disappearing into the background. To gain variance in tone on the diamond, we need to adjust our light so that it strikes either the front or the right side more directly. In Figure 8.3, the key was moved only a few degrees to the right. This small change provides a big visual difference—now both the diamond and cube have each face defined.

DIRECTIONALITY AFFECTS:
1. Light intensity
2. Shaping

Figure 8.2 (Left) Key at about 45 degrees front and side. Not a good angle, as many planes merge with each other and the background.

Figure 8.3 (Right) Key about 45 degrees top and 55 degrees right. A small change can make a big difference. This is a good angle for one light, as all planes have a different level of brightness and thus show shaping.

8.2 DISTANCE

One aspect of placement that often gives new lighters the most trouble is distance. A common problem is to place digital lights too close to their subjects, sometimes much too close. This problem arises in many ways because the digital lighter *can* place his lights anywhere he wants. Real-world lighters cannot place their lights just anywhere—real lights have mass. They have to be held up on poles or suspended from the ceiling. Even more exasperatingly, you can *see* them—the light source itself, that is. A light placed extremely close to the subject on a real set will probably be in view of the camera as well, unless the shot is very tight.

Digital lights, on the other hand, have no mass. Most of them are infinitely small, like spot- or point-lights, or are coming from everywhere and anywhere like ambient, directional, and environment lights. Even area and volume lights, which have dimension, aren't visible in a render. This frees the lighter to place lights just about anywhere and everywhere. And sometimes that's just what happens.

When digital lights are placed too close to their subjects, the scene often looks wrong or has other problems. Placing lights too close and having too many lights can go hand in hand, as the lighter may place many lights in every nook and cranny to illuminate each area just so, creating a scene that is very hard to manage and may begin to fall apart visually. To avoid this, make sure your lights are not placed on top of each object. Mentioned previously but a tip that bears repeating is to always work with your existing lights, adjusting their positions to get the most out of them, before you add another light. This will help to keep you from having too many lights in your scene.

Distance affects the range of illumination. When lights are very close, they generally don't illuminate as much of the scene. This means more lights, which, as noted, become harder to control. It also means that if your character is moving it may literally walk out of its light. Sounds funny, but I've seen this happen a lot. While working as a professional trainer at Sony Pictures Imageworks, the studio had a training shot with a mouse-sized character dancing around on a countertop. Incoming lighters would light this shot in order to learn the studio's tools. On many occasions, the first pass of the trainees' lighting had the character bound right out of his light sources. Oops! Two things were clear: One, the lighter had placed the lights much too close to the character, and two, the lighter had only tested the first frame of the animation when placing the light. The fix to such a problem is, similarly, two-fold. First, again make sure the light is the right distance away, and second, be sure to test more than one frame of an animation when lighting. (For more tips on lighting animations, see Section 8.3.2, "Positioning for Animation.")

The distance of the light will determine how parallel the rays are. We have seen several times now that very faraway lights contribute essentially parallel rays. Nearby lights, on the other hand, contribute radial rays. The presence of either radial or parallel rays will reveal to the viewer the distance of the light—even if the light isn't seen in the frame at all. Whether the rays are parallel or radial will be revealed by (1) the shape of the shadow and (2) the direct illumination on the subjects. If the light is near and the rays radial, the shadows will fan outward. Conversely, if the light is far and the rays parallel, then the shadows will be parallel. Notice how the shapes of the shadows reveal the position of the key light in Figures 8.4 and 8.5. Which image accurately portrays sun or moonlight?

Figure 8.4 The shadow shape from a distant light.

Figure 8.5 The shadow shape from a near light.

A visual cue that can be a bit harder to spot to the untrained eye is how the direct illumination strikes the subjects. If the rays are parallel, then all portions of the scene will be illuminated from the same direction. If the rays are radial, then the direct illumination will strike every portion of the scene from a slightly different direction (Figures 8.6 and 8.7). This is particularly important to lighters when illuminating an animated subject (and most of your subjects will animate). If the light is too close to the subject, then the direction may look great in one frame of the animation; but later when the subject moves, the angle may no longer be correct.

Figure 8.6 (Left) Distant light, showing even angle of direct illumination.

Figure 8.7 (Right) Nearby light, showing varying angle of direct illumination.

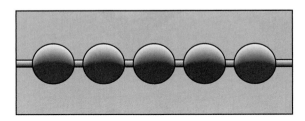

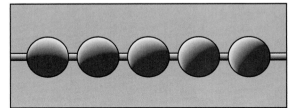

The distance of the light from its subject is also a factor in the softness of the shadow. All other things being equal, a near light will have a softer shadow than a far light. Knowing this can aid digital lighters in when and how much to blur their shadows (Figures 8.8 and 8.9).

Figure 8.8 Incorrect amount of shadow blur for distance.

Figure 8.9 Correct amount of shadow blur (any amount would be correct).

Finally, distance may affect light intensity if the light attenuates. If your light falls off in intensity with distance, known as attenuation, then distance will affect how much light is reaching the scene and how apparent the attenuation is, and be a clue as to if your light needs to have attenuation added to it or not. (Attenuation is discussed in detail in the next chapter, "Light Intensity.")

DISTANCE AFFECTS:

1. Range of illumination
2. The shape and quality of the shadow
3. Radial or parallel rays
4. Attenuation

8.3 MAKING IT RIGHT

When you're aware of the visual clues that reveal your light's position, then you can spot when your light is "off" (wrongly placed, that is). If your light doesn't look wrong, then it's not wrong. All is fair in love and war and digital lighting, as long as the illusion is maintained and the magician doesn't show his hand. Why is it crucial that the light be properly placed? If the light is incorrectly positioned, it will reveal itself. The light's position is primarily revealed in the following ways:

◆ The shape, direction, and quality of the shadow

◆ The angle of the incident rays (rays striking the surfaces)

◆ The position of the specular highlight

The audience will intuitively respond to these visual cues and will sense when the position of the light isn't right. A lighter needs to train herself to consciously think about these issues and to make sure these visual cues are in line with the light being imitated.

8.3.1 HOW REALISTIC SHOULD IT BE?

A question that sometimes comes up is—should digital lights be placed in the same position as their real-world counterpart, or does anything go? The answer is—that depends. It depends on the light's function, and even more, it depends on how it all looks.

The dominant light in a scene is known as the key. Correct positioning of the key is essential. It's usually best to motivate the key. A *motivated* light is one that has a logical source that exists in the scene, such as a lamp or window. This source may be in frame (in view), or it may be out of view, but it should make sense to the audience.

You will usually want to place a motivated key at or near where the real source would be. If the key doesn't match an obvious source, the image will appear wrong and will potentially distract the audience and take them out of the story. This isn't to say a lighter is locked into placing the key light exactly where a real source would be. The key light needs only to *appear* to come from the logical source. Its exact position is usually fudged to gain a desired aesthetic. Somewhat near the source is usually sufficient; a little cheating will go unnoticed by the viewer. Cheat too much and the illusion falls apart (see Figures 8.10 through 8.13, for example).

Figure 8.10 Before: This early work has multiple strong lights that do not make sense with where light might actually be in a real scene, resulting in lighting that is ambiguous. Several strong light sources compete for attention and create confusing shadows.

Figure 8.11 Scene file for Figure 8.10. Notice also how the lights are placed much too close to the subjects, a common mistake that leads to too many lights and will result in the scene lighting not working for animation.

Figure 8.12 After: In this reworked version, the position and number of lights have been adjusted so that all are plausible and relate to lights that could be in a real scene. The sunlight was chosen to be the dominant light.

Figure 8.13 Scene file for Figure 8.12. With the exception of one bounce light, all the close-up lights have been removed or repositioned.

A good workflow is:

1. Use a realistic placement as the starting point.
2. If needed, cheat the position to obtain a desired look.
3. If the illusion begins to fall apart—you've gone as far as you can—back up a bit.

…and of course, test-render often.

Other lights that aren't the dominant light often don't need to be motivated or are only loosely motivated. How realistic the placement of these lights needs to be depends on how well you notice their position. If the light is a lamp shining very obviously on a table in the foreground, by all means place your digital light right where its light will shine in the same way the real lamp's would. If the light is a window off-screen, then having your digital light just coming from that general direction should suffice.

Lights that aren't motivated can usually be placed about anywhere that gets the job done, provided you follow the general rules of not placing the light too close and placing the light for maximum effectiveness (as to avoid using too many lights).

It's important to evaluate your scene with a discerning eye. Look for the visual cues that reveal the position of the light and ask yourself, Does the light's position make sense? If the light is motivated, is it plausible? If it isn't motivated, does it need to be or is it fine if it's unmotivated? Don't skip asking yourself these questions.

8.3.2 POSITIONING FOR ANIMATION

When you're placing your lights in an animated sequence, be sure to test your lighting in a _variety_ of frames. If you don't, you may find that lighting that looked great in one frame falls apart when the subject or camera moves.

Figures 8.14 through 8.17 show how a light can reveal its position upon translation of the subject.

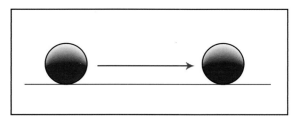
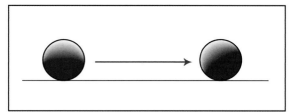

Figure 8.14 (Left) If the light is far, incident rays will not change as the subject moves. Where would the light be positioned in this figure?

Figure 8.15 (Right) If the light is near, the angle if incidence will change as the subject moves, altering the illumination. Where is the light position in this figure?

Figure 8.16 Frames 1 and 10—incorrect positioning. A fill light is placed too close, and when animated the frog passes through it, it produces an odd shadow that moves across the lily pad.

Figure 8.17 Frames 1 and 10—correct positioning. In this later version, the lights have been moved back from the character so they shadow correctly (*Drag'N'Fly* short, scene lighting by Huisoo Lee, SCAD-Atlanta Visual Effects student).

Ideally, you should have a few frames, anywhere from two to five, that you test regularly. Before beginning any lighting, view the animation in shaded mode with default lights. From this you can determine which the action of the shot is, which characters appear, and what frame you want to test first. This frame is not necessarily Frame 1. What frame or frames are best to test while you are placing your lights? I use a concept of *critical lighting moments*. These are frames in which the character and/or camera has reached a critical moment and has paused even if only briefly on some action. When the action of characters or camera slows down, the audience will have time to fully register the image on-screen, and so these moments should look the best. Usually I can identify two to five of these moments in any given shot. I begin lighting my scene on one of these frames, and the one I choose is the one that is most important to the story or that holds the longest.

Another important concept when deciding what to test is that of *lighting conditions*. Sometimes your subject moves from one kind of lighting condition into another during the course of the animation. For example, the subject moves from the shadows of a room into the light, or travels past different light sources, or walks from indoors to outdoors. Then, the animation should be tested at some point in each new lighting condition.

Don't do all your lighting on one frame—work for a bit testing one frame and then move to another of your "critical moments" to see how things hold up. Test-render another frame before spending any time finessing your lighting. I recommend interactively testing all or most of your identified critical frames before doing a long full-frame render so you can spot and correct potential problems. (For more on rendering workflow, see Chapter 14, "Rendering for the Artist.") Definitely don't drop the whole 200 frames into the render farm without checking the lighting in *at least* one other frame.

WORKFLOW TIPS FOR LIGHTING AN ANIMATION

1. First, view the unlit animation to see what you've got.
2. Select two to five frames to test based on critical lighting moments—pauses in the action or camera move when the scene is clearly seen. (Remember, Frame 1 is not necessarily a critical moment.)
3. If your subject moves through different areas of lighting ("lighting conditions"), select representative frames that test each area.
4. Write down these frame numbers so you don't forget them.
5. While placing lights, test these selected frames to see how the lighting holds up throughout the animation.
6. When things look good in your test renders for all these frames, render the entire sequence.

8.4 CHAPTER CONCLUSION

This chapter looked at a relatively simple property of light: position. Correct positioning of the lights in your scene is critical for a well-lit scene. Positioning involves two main characteristics: distance and directionality. The digital lighter needs to keep these factors in mind at all times when placing the lights.

By keeping an eye on the visual cues of how the light strikes your scene, you will be able to detect and correct for any errors in the positioning of the lights. Be especially mindful of the key and other strong light sources. Because they are easy to see and have a great influence on the image, correctly positioning them is essential.

Here is a checklist of things to look for and questions to ask yourself to help ensure correct light position:

✓ Look at the shadows: Do their shape, direction, and softness make sense for the light you are imitating?

✓ Check the direct illumination: Does the direction from where the light comes make sense?

✓ Is your light positioned to provide the amount of shaping you desire?

✓ Periodically check the distance of the lights from the subject: Are your lights too close?

✓ Consider the light source: Does your light need to be motivated? If so, does the position of the CG light match where the real light would be positioned?

✓ Do test-renders of multiple frames in your animation: Does the light position continue to look correct and satisfy your goals throughout the full frame range?

8.4.1 Important Points

◆ Light placement is rarely overlooked, but sometimes may not be evaluated thoroughly enough.

◆ An improperly placed light will not have the correct visual cues.

◆ Keep an eye on the visual cues to check your light placement.

◆ Light position can be checked by evaluating shadow shape and placement and how the direct illumination falls.

◆ Lights are often placed too close.

◆ When lights are too close, characters can move in and out of lights with unwanted results.

◆ Placing lights too close can lead to too many lights.

◆ Light placement will affect the shape, quality, and direction of the shadows.

◆ A nearby light will contribute softer shadows than a faraway light.

◆ In general, a faraway light has parallel rays; a nearby light has radial rays.

◆ Direction of the primary light source (key) is the most critical.

◆ Match the distance to a real light source where applicable.

◆ Not all lights need to be motivated, but it's generally a good idea to begin with a motivated position for the key.

◆ If you're cheating a light position, keep an eye on the scene to make sure you haven't gone too far.

◆ You will need to test the placement of the light in a variety of frames in an animation.

8.4.2 TERMS

position   parallel rays   motivated source
distance   direction
radial rays   incident angle

8.4.3 EXERCISES

1. Take a sample indoor or outdoor digital scene. Place the dominant light in the scene in a correct, motivated position. Now re-light the scene with the light moved until it becomes "incorrect." At what point did the light position no longer work? What were the visual cues you used to determine this? Save test renders along the way for discussion.

2. An exercise for two or more people. Using renders from the previous exercise, have another student show you two renders—one where the light position appears to be correct, and one where the light position appears incorrect. The other person should not tell you which they believe is correct. Evaluate for yourself which scene is "off" and even more importantly—why. Discuss your observations.

3. Image gathering: Looking online or in magazines, gather a variety of images that have single strong lights in them, but the light source itself isn't visible. Determine from the visual cues in the image where the light is coming from. Show images and discuss your observations in class. Did you find any digital renders that looked off to you? If so, save and discuss those as well.

Figure 9.1 Searing bright light in this scene from *The Chronicles of Narnia: The Voyage of the Dawn Treader* sets a surreal tone. (©2010 20th Century Fox. Courtesy of Everett Collection.)

<h1>Chapter 9
Light Intensity</h1>

"There are infinite shadings of light and shadows ... it's an extraordinarily subtle language. Figuring out how to speak that language is a lifetime job."

—Conrad Hall, cinematographer

Light intensity is the amount or quantity of the light. It is the brightness of light. Much of the work of the digital lighter is to control the brightness of the scene. We want light just where we want it and in the right amounts. We carefully place and adjust lights to achieve the results we desire. Adjusting the intensity is typically the second thing a digital lighter will do after roughly positioning the light.

Chapter 9 evaluates the various ways to control the brightness of our scene. It further looks at how we evaluate the results we are achieving and some additional considerations when finally capturing these values into a digital image. Both real and digital characteristics are examined.

9.1 CONTROLLING LUMINANCE

Digital lighters control the brightness of each light by adjusting an "intensity" parameter in their CG light. This parameter, or its equivalent, is found in every basic light. A higher number for the intensity makes a brighter light; a lower number makes a dimmer light. The ability to adjust brightness is a big advantage that digital lighters have over real-world lighters. We can make any light have any intensity we desire—even negative values! Real-world sources, in contrast, emit fixed or limited amounts of light. Photographers and cinematographers control light intensity by moving the source nearer or farther, by focusing the light (which makes it brighter), or by dimming it with screens or "dimmers."

When digital lighters think of light intensity, they naturally think of the "intensity" parameter in their CG light. In fact, the digital lighter may be tempted to think of light intensity only in terms of the intensity parameter, but in actuality, there's more to consider; otherwise, this would be a very short chapter indeed! Let's step back and take a broader view of the light in our scene.

9.1.1 RADIANT, INCIDENT, AND REFLECTED LIGHT

When working with light intensity, there are actually three kinds to consider:

1. The amount of illumination radiating from the light,
2. The amount of illumination falling upon the scene, and
3. The amount of illumination reaching the camera.

Radiance is the amount of energy released from the light at its source, known as *radiant light*. *Incident light*, the second kind of illumination, falls upon a subject. *Reflected light*, the third kind, bounces back off the subject (Figure 9.2).

Figure 9.2 Incident light travels to the surface, often coming directly from a light source, while reflected light travels away from the surface, some of it reaching the eye/camera.

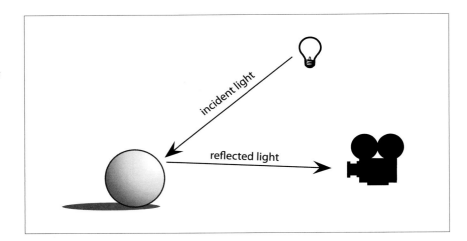

When we adjust light intensity, we are adjusting the amount of radiant light...but it's reflected light that makes the image. What really matters is the final image. Everything else is just getting there, and a lot can happen along the way, as this section will explain.

Reflected light isn't the same as incident light because reflected light is affected by atmospheric effects and surface material properties. Dark materials reflect less light; bright materials reflect more light. If, for example, the surfaces in your scene have a wide range of values, your final image will have high contrast, even under relatively even lighting conditions. Conversely, if a thick fog covers your scene, contrast will be low. This explains why digital lighters aren't just concerned with light. They are concerned with lights, material properties, compositing—pretty much anything that will affect the final image.

Similarly, incident light isn't the same as radiant light. How much light actually falls upon your subject certainly begins with the intensity of the light. After all, zero intensity means no light. But several other factors come into play as well.

9.1.2 FACTORS AFFECTING SCENE LUMINANCE

Editing the intensity parameter of the light is one way to control the amount of incident light in the scene. Other considerations include the interaction of lights in the scene, the incident angle, and attenuation.

The number of lights also affects the total luminance falling on the subject. Okay, when noted, this is rather obvious. Adding a light generally adds luminance, unless you reduce the intensities of the lights to compensate. The other factor to consider here is: How much do the lights overlap? When lighting your scene, you will want to evaluate in what places the illumination of lights is overlapping as well as the intensities of these lights to get an idea of how much total light is shining on any given area. Overlap also affects your key:fill or lighting ratio.

Here's an example: If my key is at an intensity of 1, and my fill is at an intensity of .5, what is my lighting ratio? Here's the answer: I don't know. It depends on how the lights are arranged. If the key and fill don't overlap at all, then the ratio is 2:1.

Key side = 1

Fill side = .5

Ratio = 1:.5 or 2:1

However, if the key overlaps completely with the fill, then the ratio is 3:1.

Key side = 1 + .5 = 1.5

Fill side = .5

Ratio = 1.5:.5 or 3:1

The following images show the effects of overlap on scene luminance (Figures 9.3 through 9.5). The only thing changing in these images is the position of the fill. In each image, the key comes from the right and the light intensities don't change (key intensity = 1.0 while the fill intensity = .5), yet the apparent intensity and lighting ratio vary significantly due to how the two lights overlap.

Additionally, by paying attention to how much the illumination from different lights overlaps, you may find that your lights are overlapping too much and that, in fact, one light could do the job, thus reducing the number of lights in your scene.

The angle of illumination is another factor influencing intensity. As we saw in previous chapters, if the angle of light to the surface is 90 degrees, then the illumination is at its brightest; as the angle of the light becomes more grazing, the effect of the light darkens. This simple fact is crucial to controlling the luminance of your scene. (For further discussion see Section 6.2.1, "Considering the Incident Angle," and Chapter 8, "Light Placement.") A light's intensity and its angle must both be considered when evaluating the light's effect on the scene.

Light *attenuation* also affects the amount of incident light reaching the surface. Attenuation is the decreasing intensity of illumination with increasing distance from the light source. In CG lights, attenuation may be called *dropoff, decay,* or *falloff.* In life, all light attenuates. Not all digital lights attenuate, however. If and how they do so is at the control of the digital lighter. If your light attenuates, then the distance of the light from the subject will greatly affect the amount of incident light. Closer to the subject and the light will be brighter; farther and the light will be dimmer. Attenuation is discussed in detail in the next section.

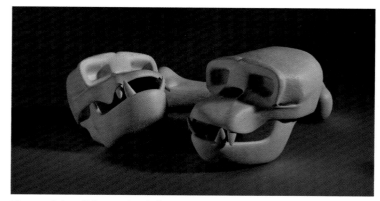

Figure 9.3 Fill from the left—the fill and key do not overlap. The fill adds to shadows only and reduces contrast.

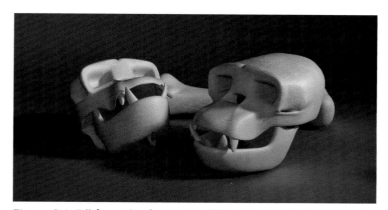

Figure 9.4 Fill from the front—the fill brightens the key as well as lifts the shadows, providing medium contrast.

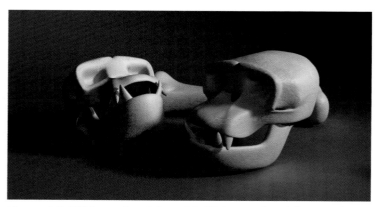

Figure 9.5 Fill from the right—this fill is mostly adding to the key without illuminating the shadow side, increasing contrast.

Finally, lighters have a number of specific techniques that will adjust the light intensity. They can work with the cone angle and penumbra of spotlights to control where the light is falling. (See Section 1.2.3, "Spotlight.") Also, by adjusting the softness of a light, they can control how much the light wraps around the surface. (See Section 1.2.4, "Area Light," and Chapter 10, "Light Diffusion.") Additional specific techniques discussed in Chapter 15, "Tricks of the Trade," include using special features such as "slides" or "barn doors," which can block out unwanted light or create patterns in the light's color and intensity.

Here are a few situations in which the information in this section could be put to practical use:

♦ If an area is too dark, adjust positions and intensities of the existing lights first to see whether an existing light can fill in the dark area. Don't add another light until you have gone through this step.

♦ If your scene is getting hard to manage, evaluate your lights to make sure that you don't have lights that overlap in illumination when fewer lights will do. Having too many lights is a common mistake amongst newer lighters.

♦ If your scene is becoming decidedly too hot in some area, yet each light doesn't have that high of an intensity setting, then you will certainly want to check to see whether you have a few bright lights overlapping. This will often solve the mystery.

♦ If you find your scene getting too bright in one area, try repositioning the lights to strike the offending surface more obliquely.

♦ If you add a light and seem to have no illumination from it whatsoever, check to make sure the light isn't attenuating by default without you knowing it. (Believe me, this will happen at some point.)

FACTORS THAT AFFECT INCIDENT LIGHT

1. Intensity (intensity parameter)
2. Overlap (the number of lights in the scene)
3. Angle (position)
4. Attenuation
5. Specific techniques, such as use of gobos and barn doors

You need to have a good grasp of each light's influence upon the scene—where it's striking and with what intensity, and how much overlap there is from different lights. Advanced lighters think about all of this intuitively when placing each light and thus have a rough approximation of the incident luminance throughout the scene. For both experienced and beginning lighters alike, the workflow is the same—tweak the light's position, adjust the intensity, add/remove lights—test rendering all the while to see the results.

9.1.3 ATTENUATION

attenuation (n.):
1. a lessening of the amount, force, or magnitude of something;
2. a dilution, thinning, or weakening of a substance.

Attenuation, as noted, is the decreasing intensity of illumination with increasing distance from the light source. As mentioned previously, attenuation is known by the following names: dropoff, decay, or falloff. Since different software packages use different names for this attribute, I'll stick with the scientific name "attenuation" to avoid confusion. In life, all lights attenuate. In the computer, however, most lights don't attenuate by default. If attenuation is desired it must be added by the digital lighter. Not all digital lights need to attenuate. This section covers real-world attenuation, informing the digital lighter as to when, if, and how much attenuation to add to each light, and then looks at the ways attenuation is imitated digitally.

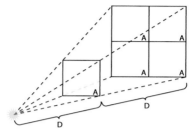

Figure 9.6 As distance doubles, light is spread out over four times the area, reducing intensity.

Real-World Attenuation

Attenuation in life follows what is known as the *inverse square law.* This formula tells us how quickly the light intensity will decrease with distance. This law states that, as a light source is moved away from a surface, it illuminates; the illumination decreases in an amount inversely proportional to the square of the distance. Specifically, when the distance from the light doubles, the amount of light reaching any given area of surface is reduced to ¼. Attenuation isn't due to the light "running out of steam" or energy; rather, it's due to the decreased number of photons per unit of volume. You can see in Figure 9.6 that as distance from the light source increases, there are fewer photons per unit of volume. When the distance doubles, the same number of photons are spread out over four times the area, thus reducing the density of photons and the intensity of light.

What does this bit of scientific information mean to you, the digital lighter, and how can we better understand it? Visual types will gain more from an image. Figure 9.7 shows a diagram of a light's intensity over a given distance. What you will notice is that closer to the light the intensity is at the highest; farther from the light, the intensity is very low. That makes sense—the farther from the light source, the dimmer the light. But even more notice the *rate of change,*

Figure 9.7 The inverse square law of light attenuation.

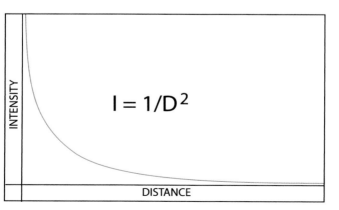

$$I = 1/D^2$$

INTENSITY

DISTANCE

as evidenced by the slope or the line. The steeper the slope, the faster the rate of change. Near the light, intensity drops off very quickly; far from the light, intensity drops off very slowly. At very great distances the rate of change is negligible and the light's intensity really doesn't change much at all.

The attenuation curve tells digital lighters when they should add attenuation to their lights and how much. When the light source is close in distance to the objects being illuminated (such as nearby lamps, overhead lights, wall sconces, and the like), the effect of attenuation will be noticeable. To maintain realism, it must be added by the CG artist. Conversely, if the light is very far away (such as sunlight or moonlight), then the effect of attenuation is negligible, and the digital light doesn't need it. As with so many things, knowing what happens in the real world will aid you in creating illumination that looks accurate.

The inverse square formula for attenuation represents an ideal situation, with the light source being a point. In reality, this ideal formula almost never holds exactly true. Different lights have slightly different attenuation rates. A focused beam will fall off more slowly. Light passing through fog or a transparent medium (like water) will fall off more rapidly. Uniformly scattered light (ambient light), on the other hand, has no decay. That being said, knowing how light falls off in an idealized situation is still very useful to digital lighters, but don't feel that you must stick exactly to this formula in all cases to stay realistic. Even in life actual attenuation rates vary depending on the light source and environmental conditions. Not only that, but a viewer will rarely notice whether a light falls off *exactly* how it would in real life.

Figure 9.8 The effects of light attenuation are clearly visible in this scene from *The Incredibles*. (©2004 Disney/Pixar.)

Digital lighters have several options for how to add attenuation to their lights. In computer graphics, many lights will have three options: no attenuation, linear attenuation, or quadratic attenuation.

No attenuation means that the intensity is constant and doesn't change with distance from the light. In Figure 9.9, no decay is represented by the green line. Many applications have this as the default for the lights. I prefer this setting initially, even with lights that I later plan to add attenuation to, so that I can roughly position the light without having to constantly adjust its intensity.

Linear attenuation decreases in intensity at an even rate. In Figure 9.9, linear decay is represented by the blue line. When using linear decay, the light will attenuate at the same rate whether it is near or far from the subjects being lit. Linear attenuation is less likely to produce hotspots near the light source since there is no dramatic change in intensity near the light. Linear is often a good choice for spot or point lights that are very near their subjects.

Quadratic, or exponential attenuation, has a falloff the most like real-world decay. It replicates the inverse square law. In Figure 9.9, quadratic decay is represented by the red line. While the most accurate to real-world point lights, this attenuation is often "too much" for the typical CG scene. The light falls off too dramatically, causing overly hot illumination near the light (called "hotspots") and not enough illumination farther from the light. In many cases, it doesn't look realistic; it looks overdone. When adding attenuation to a CG light, linear attenuation generally delivers a better look than quadratic.

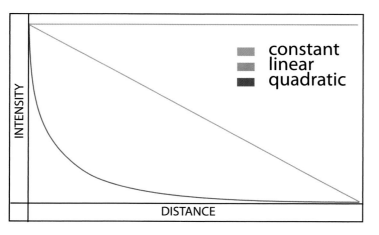

constant
linear
quadratic

Figure 9.9 Graph of common digital attenuation presets.

Figure 9.10 (Left) No attenuation.

Figure 9.11 (Center) Linear attenuation.

Figure 9.12 (Right) Quadratic attenuation.

Quadratic attenuation, like real light, falls off more rapidly when close to the source and less rapidly when far from the source. A light with quadratic decay that is near to its subject will fall off *extremely* rapidly (Figures 9.13 and 9.14). Yet when the same light is pulled farther from its subject, the rate of decay will lessen and begin to look like linear decay (Figure 9.15). If you were to pull the light far, far away, the rate of decay would become negligible and would appear like no decay. Savvy digital lighters can change the rate of decay by moving a light with quadratic decay farther or nearer and adjusting the light intensity accordingly.

Figure 9.13 (Left) Quadratic decay with a light very near.

Figure 9.14 (Center) Quadratic decay with a light far away.

Figure 9.15 (Right) Linear decay, any distance.

When adding attenuation, you will have to put a very high number in as the light's intensity setting, as the intensity finally reaching the surface will be much less. This can make it difficult to really know just how much illumination the light is casting relative to other lights or to estimate the lighting ratio. Such high numbers seem to have little relevance to the actual illumination in the scene. Experienced lighters can often estimate their lighting ratio just from the light's intensity setting, but this becomes much harder or even impossible when using a standard decay. One solution to this problem is what is known as *metered decay*.

Metered decay is a more advanced digital attenuation that allows for the lighter to set the intensity of the light at a specified distance. The light will become darker when farther than this distance and will likewise brighten in intensity when closer than this distance. The advantage of metered decay is that the lighter can specifically set the light intensity at the approximate distance the light reaches the subject rather than just "eyeballing" it. For example, if your light is 10 units from its subject and you want it to strike its subject with an intensity of 1, metered decay allows you to set the meter distance to 10 and the illumination to 1. If your light moves closer than 10 units, the light will brighten quickly. Metered decay often also has a maximum intensity setting for the light, so that the illumination never becomes higher than a certain intensity. Using metered decay and a max intensity will generally eliminate hotspots, another common problem with digital attenuation. Not all software has metered decay available.

Another option commonly available is *decay regions.* Decay regions allow you to specify certain distances from the light source for the illumination to begin and to stop. The light will decay inside these regions. The user can then set arbitrary ranges and craft the attenuation of his scene more artistically. One nice use for decay regions is to begin the illumination only once the rays have left the geometric model representing their source. This can be useful with spotlights when they are imitating a focused beam of light such as a flashlight or car headlights, especially if the entire beam of light is seen due to fog. In these cases you want the illumination to begin just when the light leaves the glass covering. To obtain the correct shape, you will want to pull your spotlight back a bit, then use decay regions to "turn on" the light right when it leaves the model of the light source. Look ahead to Figure 15.43 in Chapter 15 for an example.

As yet another option, some programs allow you to craft your light's intensity with distance according to a curve, similar to an animation curve but over distance instead of time. A feature such as this offers the maximum control. Not only can you specify the intensity of the light at every distance, you often can set the red, green, and blue channels independently, meaning the light can even change in hue with distance. When crafting your attenuation with tools such as decay regions or an intensity curve, be careful not to make your scene look unrealistic. The good news is that audiences will not notice if the attenuation is not 100% real and will easily accept a more creative version…as long as you don't deviate too far.

COMMON METHODS FOR CG ATTENUATION

- No decay
- Linear decay
- Quadratic decay
- Metered decay
- Decay regions
- Arbitrary decay

Tips on Adding Attenuation

- If the light is near, use attenuation.
- If the light is very distant, don't use attenuation.
- When using quadratic or linear attenuation, don't forget to greatly increase the intensity of the light.
- Quadratic attenuation, while the most realistic, is often too much for the average scene.
- Linear attenuation often gives better results than quadratic attenuation.
- The use of arbitrary decay provides the most creative control and, if not overdone, will not be perceived by the viewer as unrealistic.

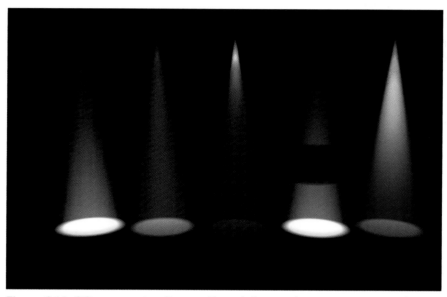

Figure 9.16 CG attenuation lineup. From left to right: no attenuation, linear, quadratic, decay regions, and using distance curves.

9.2 EVALUATING LUMINANCE

The digital lighter primarily just looks at his or her rendered image to evaluate lighting, unlike the photographer and cinematographer, who performs precise and careful measurements for the best results. This section looks at how both real and digital light sources are evaluated, with tips for digital lighters on how to be more precise when the need arises.

9.2.1 REAL-WORLD MEASUREMENTS

Real-world lighters cannot set the light intensity the way digital lighters can. Instead, they must measure the amount of light to find out how much of it they have. Luminance is measured in terms of candles-per-square-foot. Candles-per-square-foot (cd/ft2) is derived from foot-candles, which are a measurement of the amount of incident light energy emitted by a standard candle at one foot away. It was originated from the days when things like candles and feet were used as the basis for units of measurement and was used primarily in the United States. Europeans instead use candles-per-square-meters (cd/m2). One cd/m2 equals approximately 10 cd/ft2 (9.74 to be exact).

Photographers and cinematographers measure the light in the scene by metering it. A meter is a device that reads the intensity of the light. There are two types of meters: incident light meters and reflected light meters. A reflected light meter measures—you guessed it—reflected light. It is placed at the position of the camera and pointing into the scene. Most general-purpose handheld reflectance meters read about a 30% area and measure an average of all the luminance in the scene. When your camera automatically adjusts exposure, it's using a reflected light meter built inside it. In many cases, and certainly for the amateur photographer, an in-camera meter is sufficient. The more precise tool is the reflectance spot meter, which reads a small percentage of the scene, even only 1%. The spot meter is pointed at different areas of the scene to record the luminance of selected items, and it can be used to read high- and low-subject values. An incident meter, on the other hand, measures incident light. It's shaped as a hemisphere, placed at the position of the subject and pointed at the camera. Incident meters also read all of the incoming light, but they can be used to estimate the lighting ratio by flagging out part of the hemisphere pointing away from the key, then flagging out the key and comparing the two numbers. Incident meters eliminate the effects of background and surface properties that affect reflected light.

The next step for controlling the image when using a real camera is to set the exposure. This will effectively brighten or darken the resulting image overall. (Exposure and use of the camera are covered in detail in Chapter 13, "Camera Essentials.") Once it's all said and done, a look at the image produced will tell if it has been captured properly, but careful measurements are needed along the way. (For us amateurs, these "careful measurements" are being done automatically with that wonderful, if not always accurate, thing called "auto exposure.")

9.2.2 The Relative Nature of Luminance Perception

The process of digital lighting contains lots of adjusting of parameters, rendering, and looking. For the most part, we can trust what our eyes show us. However, it's good to be aware of a few facts about how we perceive luminance.

We are all familiar with the fact that our eyes adjust to large changes in overall brightness. I remember as a child coming in from the bright Florida sun and wondering why inside the house was so very dark. I even got a little worried that there was something wrong with my eyes! My parents explained there was nothing wrong with my eyes (to my relief) and that in a minute, my eyes would adjust and the room wouldn't seem so dark, as indeed happened. However, it wasn't until many years later, in film production, that I realized just how much "adjusting" my eyes were actually doing.

A little-realized fact is just *how much* our eyes will adapt to the luminance of whatever we are viewing. Human eyes will not only adapt to the amount of overall brightness in a scene, as is well known to all of us, but they also adapt to the brightness of even small areas of what you are viewing. What I mean by this is that if a certain area of your image is overall a bit darker, your eyes will compensate and you will actually *see* this area as a bit brighter than it really is.

Perhaps you enjoy optical illusions as much as I do, so here are a few to illustrate how your eyes may be fooled (Figures 9.17 and 9.18).

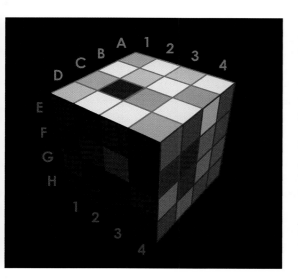
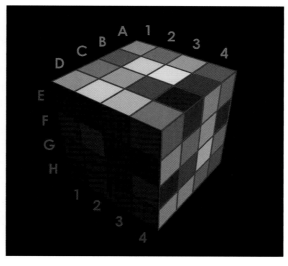

Figure 9.17 (Left) Which square on the front of the cube matches the value of the dark square on the top, square C2? The answer is at the end of this section.

Figure 9.18 (Right) Which square on the front of the cube matches the dark olive square on the top, square C4? The answer is at the end of this section.

Our eyes likely evolved this way in order to see continuous form, pattern, and color of objects under a variety of lighting conditions, even if in actuality the appearance of these things is changing greatly. Here's another illusion illustrating how we negate the effects of shadow when evaluating a pattern (Figures 9.19 and 9.20).

Figure 9.19 (Left) Would you believe that the lit portions of square A and the shadowed portions of square B are the exact same shade of gray?

Figure 9.20 (Right) Gray bars help reveal how the bars, A and B, are all the same value. (For similar optical illusions, see Professor Edward H. Adelson's website at http://persci.mit.edu/people/adelson.)

Our optical illusion illustrates two facts:

1. **Our eyes *are not* very good at evaluating the *absolute* brightness of things.** You cannot always trust your eyes: They don't make very good light meters. When you need to know with absolute precision the exact luminance of something, and not just an estimate of the ratio, then you will need to empirically measure it. You cannot just "eyeball" it.

2. **Our eyes *are* very good at evaluating the *relative* brightness of things.** We can with a fair amount of accuracy determine the *ratio* between two adjacent values, such as perceiving that one value is twice as bright as its nearest neighbor. This explains why evaluating the lighting ratio can often be done successfully by eye and also why the lighting ratio is more important than the absolute value of the intensities for maintaining continuity.

Additionally, our example provides a guideline for how you should view your images. Because the surrounding values will greatly influence how the values in your image are perceived, you should work on your image with a background and in a work environment similar to the one in which the final product will be viewed. Those working in film production know that digital film production artists often work in darkened rooms. Sounds gloomy, but it's the best way to view work that will ultimately be seen in a darkened theater. Never try to work with a glare on your monitor, please. It's okay to be a prima-donna in this area; you really cannot work like that. When in doubt, use a neutral gray background and medium-low lighting in your work environment.

Oh yes, and the matching squares for our optical illusions? Square F3 is identical to C2 in Figure 9.17, and square F2 is identical to C4 in Figure 9.18.

9.2.3 Digital Measurements: Pixel Probes and Histograms

Digital lighters don't have spot meters to precisely determine the amount of light in various parts of their scene. They do, however, have other means of measuring luminance precisely when they need to. When you need to be exact with how much reflected light you have in your image, you will want to precisely measure the luminance values found in your render. Two methods for doing so are to sample pixels ("pixel probe") or use a histogram.

Sampling the pixels in your image will tell you their exact values. This may be done with what is called a "pixel probe," where you can select individual pixels or marquee-drag around sections to get information on the min, max, and average values of the luminance and individual channels (Figure 9.21). To determine the lighting ratio, choose an object with an even material property, such as a uniformly gray surface (or drop one in your scene temporarily). Then probe the luminance value in both the shadow side and the lit side. A bit of simple math will determine the ratio for you. For example, if the luminance in the brights is .78, and the luminance in the shadow is .18, then your ratio is .78:.18. Okay, those numbers look rather uninformative; they need to be converted so that the second value is 1. Recalling some basic high school algebra reminds us that what we want to do is solve for "n" in this equation:

.78/.18 = n/1 or just n = .78/.18

So to convert the ratio to some number: one, the formula is

max value/min value : 1

Since .78 divided by .18 is about 4, the lighting ratio in our example scene is about 4:1. Using a pixel probe in this way is roughly analogous to using a spot meter.

Another option is to view a histogram of the image. A histogram is a graphical representation of the values of an image. The height of each bar in the histogram represents the number of pixels at a particular brightness. The values of the image are arranged from black to white, with black on the left-hand side and white on the right. To see the range of values in your image you will want to view a histogram of the luminance rather than individual red, green, or blue channels (see Figure 9.22). To see the lighting ratio, marquee-drag around just the lit and shadowed side for an area of relatively constant surface color (like just the face of the subject).

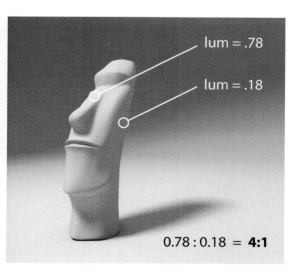

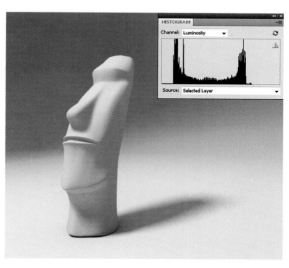

Figure 9.21 (Left) An image with selected areas sampled for value using a "pixel probe."

Figure 9.22 (Right) An image with a histogram of its luminance.

Histograms provide a graphical representation of the contrast and overall brightness of a scene. If an image is overall light, the histogram will bunch to the right. Conversely, if the image is overall dark, the histogram will bunch to the right. An image that has very little contrast will show a histogram that has bunched in the middle with few or no pixels in the high and low areas. And finally, an image with a high degree of contrast will show a histogram that dips in the center and is high on either side.

Both the histogram and the pixel probe are employed by digital artists when they wish to gain exact knowledge of the specific values or ranges of values in their images.

9.3 CAPTURING LUMINANCE

In the end, the luminance in your digital scene is captured (during render) into a digital file format. How this data will be stored is a final consideration when designing the lighting for your scene. It is analogous to considering the film when using a traditional camera. In your scene, you could craft a potentially limitless range of luminance values, yet digital files only contain a discrete and limited amount of information. Digital lighters need to be conscious of the limitations and work within them as needed.

9.3.1 CLIPPING

An important factor to consider is whether the luminance range in your scene is too large to be captured and reproduced. The basic fact is that our eyes can perceive a much wider range of luminance values than can be reproduced by your monitor, projector, printer, or on film. Anyone who has taken a photograph has likely experienced this. The world outside the camera looked great to your eyes, but when you photographed it, it became far too bright in some sections and became pure white, known as "blowing out," or conversely much of the photo was in grainy darkness. This happens because film cannot capture all of the values we can see. Above a certain brightness all of the values in a photograph will be represented as white, because the photo simply cannot get any brighter. Conversely, all of the luminance values below a certain point won't record at all, resulting in a uniformly dark area. Photographers and cinematographers deal with this limitation with every photo and film shoot. They carefully restrict the range of luminance and set the camera's exposure so that they can capture just the image they envision. (For more on exposure see Chapter 13, "Camera Essentials.")

When the value range in your digital scene is too large to be reproduced, then your image is said to have *clipped*. Clipping is when your image noticeably clamps all the values above a certain point to white, or all the values in a certain area to black. Clipping on the high end clamps all values to 1. The cause is too much light. Often lighters may overlap the illumination of several lights, resulting in the scene being much brighter than they realize. Clipping on the low end will clamp all of the values to 0, or black. Clipping at the low end occurs if certain sections of your scene have literally *no* light (nor incandescence).

Modern cinematographers sometimes deliberately choose to overexpose or underexpose their shoots for a particular mood, introducing areas of complete darkness or white. In the early days of Hollywood studio lighting, this was never done. One of the first modern films to deliberately underexpose some shots was *The Godfather* (1972). The film's cinematographer, Gordon Willis, was given the nickname "The Prince of Darkness" by one of his peers, Conrad Hall, because of his masterful use of low light conditions. Hall himself was not afraid to overexpose or underexpose, often blowing out some areas or reducing others to shadowy darkness for effect (Figure 9.23).

A bright surface will clip more easily than a dark surface due to the fact that a bright surface reflects more light. For example, a white surface will reflect 100% of the light that shines on it, while a perfectly black matte surface will reflect no light. Notice in Figures 9.24 and 9.25 how the white skull and white areas of the marble skulls clip under a brighter light, while the darker areas don't clip.

Figure 9.23 Cinematographer Conrad Hall uses a full range of luminance, from clipped white to inky black, in this dramatic pivotal scene in *American Beauty* (©1999 DreamWorks. Courtesy of Everett Collection).

Figure 9.24 (Left) A render of various surfaces, rendered with low light conditions. No clipping at the high end.

Figure 9.25 (Right) With the intensity of the lights increased, the lighter materials show clipping while the darker surfaces don't. Notice the flat expanses that have clipped on the white skull and white areas of the marble skull.

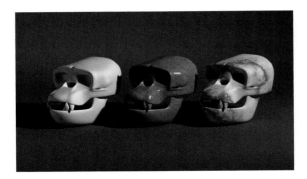 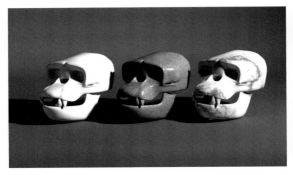

Similarly, highly saturated materials clip very easily. When a saturated surface clips, it may never go to white but will show it has clipped if its color flattens to a flat expanse when it should show some variation. The answer to why a material has clipped but not become white lies in the individual color channels. Digital images are represented by three black-to-white channels. If *any* of the channels clips to 1, then the image has clipped. (See Figure 9.26.)

Figure 9.26 In this example the luminance of the highly saturated cyan material never reaches white, but it has clipped because the green and blue channels have clipped.

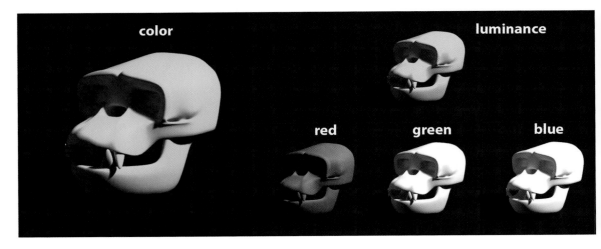

Another artifact of clipping is banding in the highlights. When different channels clip in different places, the image will often show rings of different colors around the highlights (Figure 9.27). For example, a pale peach color, such as that often used for flesh tones, creates a distinctive white-yellow-orange highlight if it clips. This type of banding is much more objectionable in digital files than real film. Film naturally rolls off the highlight to create a smoother transition and a better-looking highlight. Some advanced digital features will take this into account and attempt to imitate this more pleasing look by rolling off the highlights as opposed to abruptly clamping them.

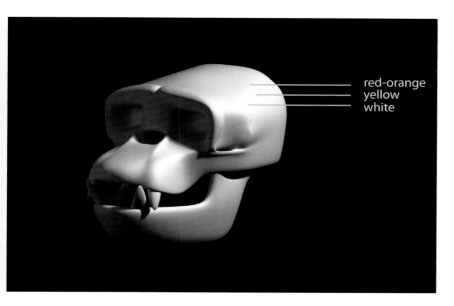

red-orange
yellow
white

Figure 9.27 Color banding in highlight regions from clipping.

Areas of your image that are to be black are often best rendered to be *near* **black—but not quite.** These areas will still look black and can easily be darkened in the composite if needed, but they still in fact have data in them. One way to accomplish this is an ambient or other light source with a very, very low intensity.

When it comes to digital renders, clipping is generally to be avoided like the plague. I have had many films in which my visual effects supervisor would change the gamma of a render up or down looking for clipping and probe the values of each suspicious area just to be sure. Why is clipping so objectionable in digital renders? It generally has to do with the fact that a render, especially for feature film, is almost always further manipulated in the compositing stage. If the desired look is to blow out an image to white or reduce it in areas to black, this can always be done in the composite. However, if the image has clipped when it was rendered, then the values aren't there to manipulate. You cannot bring any detail out in an area that has a uniform value of 0 or 1 (see Figures 9.28 through 9.31 for examples). If you try to adjust these areas you will only end up with a washed-out gray or flat color. That is, unless you have rendered to a high dynamic image range format, which is our next subject.

NOTE

Clipping on the low end is more objectionable for visual effects projects in which the blacks of the CG element need to be matched to the blacks of the live-action footage. In full CG projects, it may matter little if a render goes to black.

Figure 9.28 (Left) A render that has clipping in the darks.

Figure 9.29 (Right) The same render brightened in an image-manipulation program. Notice the lack of detail in the areas previously black: these areas will *not* be able to be lifted successfully without a re-light and re-render.

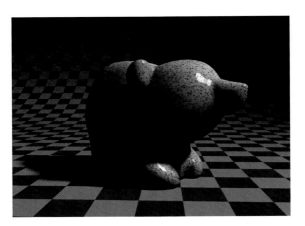

Figure 9.30 (Left) A render that has an imperceptible amount of light in the dark regions. No clipping.

Figure 9.31 (Right) The same image brightened in an image-manipulation program. The "black" areas still have some information in them that can be brought out later if needed, without re-rendering.

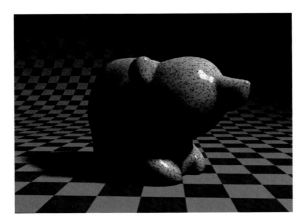

9.3.2 Introduction to High Dynamic Range Images (HDRI)

High dynamic range images (HDRI for short) are image file formats that can store a greater dynamic range than your standard image. What does dynamic range mean? It is the range of possible luminance, from the darkest possible value to the lightest possible value. As previous sections have discussed, the range of luminance in life far exceeds what can be captured on film or displayed by any display device in existence today. The human eye can also *see* a wider range of values than can be captured or displayed. Our vision perception is a remarkable thing. The human eye can expand or contract the pupil and adapt to a variety of light conditions. When adapted to dim light, at the lowest threshold we can see the equivalent of a candle at 30 miles on a clear night. We can more easily perceive dim stars, which have a luminance of about .001 cd/m2. On the other end of the scale, we can see details under extremely bright sunlight that has a luminance of 1,000,000 cd/m2. Luminance values too great will cause eye damage—don't look directly at the sun. You not only will fry your retinas, but you will not be able to see any detail either. The full luminance range of human vision is about a billion to one or even more (go eyes)! We cannot perceive all this range at once, however. Our eyes take a bit of time to adapt to dim light or a bright day. At any given time, the range we can see simultaneously is much smaller but it is still large enough to see all the details on a bright sunny day, in which the average contrast is about 10,000:1 but can reach up to 100,000:1.

Your average digital file, on the other hand, will only represent a puny range of about 256:1. You see the dilemma. For many years, however, high-end animation production has used file formats that will capture a higher range, about 65,000:1. This sounds sufficient, and in most cases it is. However, there are still cases where this falls short. In comes high dynamic range images. HDRI can capture the luminance range typically found in the real world or scene, all the way from dim stars to bright reflective highlights. Because of this, HDRI is known as scene-referred.

Two sources of HDRI are (1) the merging of multiple photographs each at a different exposure and (2) computer-generated renders. In this section we only cover the second source—rendering to an HDRI format. Common file formats that can store high dynamic range are radiance HDR (.hdr), 32-bit TIFF (.tif), and OpenEXR (.exr). OpenEXR, or just EXR for short, is widely used in the computer animation and visual effects industries. Developed by Industrial Light & Magic and released to the public as open source in 2003, EXR can store the equivalent of 30 stops of exposure. Among the first movies to use EXR were *Harry Potter and the Sorcerer's Stone* and *Men in Black II.*

When rendering into a high dynamic range format, the digital lighter needs to worry much less about clipping at the high end of the scale. The information will still be there. Values over 1 stored in a digital file are known as *super-whites*. Be aware, however, that just because the data is stored in the file, its viewability down the road still has limitations. Values over 1 will still appear to have clipped, because that is the brightest the display device, print, or film will allow. The range comes in handy, however, when you darken the image—magically all the detail appears out of the white (Figures 9.32 through 9.35).

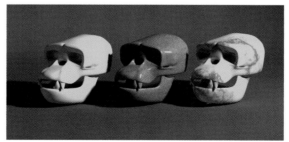

Figure 9.32 (Left) Original low dynamic range (LDR) render.

Figure 9.33 (Right) The LDR render darkened in an image-manipulation program. No information in the whites leaves flat gray when darkened.

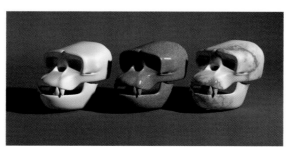

Figure 9.32 (Left) Original HDR render.

Figure 9.33 (Right) The HDR render darkened in an image-manipulation program. When darkened, data in the whites appears.

In addition to being a more robust render format, HDRI is commonly used for reflection maps to provide more realistic reflections, and used in image-based lighting (IBL). These topics are explored in detail in Chapter 17, "Image-Based Lighting and More."

9.4 CHAPTER CONCLUSION

While setting the intensity parameter in a digital light is simple, the total illumination of the scene involves several other factors. The lighter must take into consideration attenuation, overlap, and incident angle. For digital lighters, simply evaluating their image visually is usually sufficient, but be aware that sometimes your eyes can fool you and more precise testing is necessary. Finally, digital artists need to be mindful of how the scene will ultimately be captured—knowing the capabilities and limitations of the file format being used and keeping in mind the medium in which the image will be viewed.

9.4.1 IMPORTANT POINTS

- Our eyes adjust to local changes in value far more than we realize.
- When adjusting light intensity, also consider the effects of the incident angle and overlap with other lights.
- Attenuation refers to the decrease in light intensity with increasing distance.
- The rate of change of light intensity decreases with distance.
- If the light is very near, use attenuation; if the light is very distant, don't use attenuation.
- Quadratic attenuation is the most like real-world decay, but it's often too much for the average digital scene and linear is better.
- Attenuation can be artistically crafted, and the audience will not notice as long as the artist doesn't go too far.
- Our eyes don't make very good light meters, as they aren't able to determine absolute values very well.
- Our eyes are very good at estimating ratios.
- Pixel probes and histograms provide precise luminance measurements.
- The luminance range in life is limitless, while the luminance range of what we can capture or display is limited.
- Clipping occurs when the luminance range of the scene exceeds what can be captured or displayed.
- Clipping in the high end clamps values at 1; clipping in the low end clamps values at 0.

- Clipping at the high end will result in flat white or colored areas, and/or colored banding around highlights.
- Brighter and more saturated materials clip more easily.
- HDRI can contain information below 0 and above 1.
- HDRI capture more of the true luminance range.

9.4.2 TERMS

radiant light	metered decay	clipping
incident light	decay regions	super-whites
reflected light	reflectance meter	highlight roll-off
attenuation	spot meter	HDR
the inverse-square law	incident light meter	LDR
linear decay	pixel probe	scene-referred
quadratic decay	histogram	OpenEXR

9.4.3 EXERCISES

1. Working with just two lights, experiment with the different looks created when the lights are greatly overlapping or not overlapping at all. How does this affect the intensity of the lights and the lighting ratio? Render out a few images and discuss the lighting setup in each.

2. Experiment with both linear and quadratic attenuation in the software of your choice. Render out two images, using linear decay in one image and quadratic in the other. Which image do you like better? What was your experience in setting up the two scenes?

3. Continue to experiment with quadratic decay using the same scene from the previous exercise. Adjusting the position of the attenuating light, create two images: one where the light decays rapidly and another where the light decays much more slowly.

4. Set up a sample scene with a white surface, a dark gray surface, a highly saturated colored surface, and a low-saturation colored surface. Now render out a few images in which you make the dominant light progressively brighter (known as a wedge) while recording the light intensity for each render. At what intensity does each material clip? Write about your observations.

5. If you have rendering and imaging-editing software that creates and edits HDRI, experiment with rendering an image with super-whites to an HDR format. Then darken this render in an image-editing or compositing program that handles floating-point formats to see how values above 1 are stored in the image.

NOTE

Commonly found software such as Maya with Mental Ray and Photoshop or After Effects will handle HDR images. Refer to the software documentation for how to generate and edit HDR formats.

Figure 10.1 A soft frontal light keeps Arwen's face luminous and flawless in this scene from *The Lord of the Rings: Return of the King*. (©2003 New Line Cinema. Courtesy of Everett Collection.)

Chapter 10
Light Diffusion

"Only the photographer himself knows the effect he wants. He should know by instinct, grounded in experience, what subjects are enhanced by hard or soft, light or dark treatment."

—Bill Brandt, 20th-Century Photographer and Photojournalist

The *diffusion* of light refers to the hardness or softness of light. Light that is very diffused is soft, while light that isn't diffused is hard. A close study of what makes a light appear "soft" or alternatively, "hard," will aid the digital lighter in both when (or if) and how much to soften the lights in the scene. Lighters also need to know exactly how to soften their lights—more than one means exists to do this, each method having pros and cons. Diffusion is a property of light that is perhaps the least understood and most often neglected by digital artists. In contrast, photographers and cinematographers are usually well versed in how to control and use light quality. Digital lighters, too, need a solid understanding of this property.

This chapter looks at the differences between hard and soft light, and how much diffusion is appropriate for various lighting situations, and provides an overview of how digital lighters can control this property in their scenes.

10.1 OVERVIEW OF LIGHT DIFFUSION

Light diffusion, **sometimes referred to as** *light quality,* **describes how scattered the incoming light rays are.** Light that has little diffusion is not scattered much or at all, producing hard light (Figure 10.2). Conversely, diffuse light is very scattered and produces soft light (Figure 10.3). This scattering of rays has a dramatic effect on how the light looks. The best and fastest way to understand the difference between hard and soft light is to look at a few images.

The visual characteristics of soft versus hard lighting are very distinct from one another, as can be seen in Figures 10.4 and 10.5. When re-creating lighting in a digital scene, you need to be sure that the amount of diffusion of your digital light is appropriate for the type of light it's imitating. If a digital lighter uses a hard light source to imitate what in life would be a soft light, the audience will instinctively feel that something is off in the image, even if they cannot tell exactly what it is. Additionally, the moods created by soft or hard lighting are very different from each other. To create a convincing image and effectively set mood, you will want to keep in mind the light's diffusion.

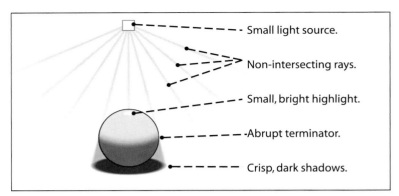

Figure 10.2 Hard light results from rays that aren't scattered.

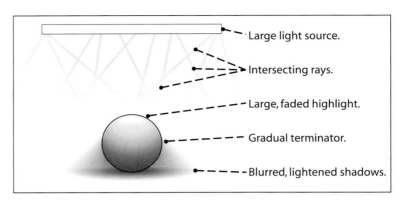

Figure 10.3 Soft light results from scattered rays.

Figure 10.4 Real-world hard light.

Figure 10.5 Real-world soft light.

10.2 HARD LIGHT

This section covers the visual characteristics of hard light, as well what kinds of light sources produce hard light.

10.2.1 DISTINCTIVE CHARACTERISTICS OF HARD LIGHT

Harsh transitions and crisp shadows are characteristic of hard light, due to the limited direction of incoming rays. Shadows typically are very dense, as there is little to no scattered light to fill them in and lighten them. On surfaces that are shiny, hard light will produce a highlight that is both small and bright. Hard light also has a distinctive terminator (the terminator is the area of the surface that transitions from lit to shadow side). Hard light produces a terminator that transitions abruptly and doesn't illuminate past half of the object (Figure 10.7).

Figure 10.6 A digital render of hard light.

Figure 10.7 This egg lit by a spotlight (yes, that's an egg standing up) is a good example of the sharp terminator and crisp, dark shadow produced by hard light.

Hard light has a decided directionality. We can clearly see where the shadow lies, where the highlight is positioned, and which side of the object is lit. From this we can deduce the light's position, even if we cannot see the light source itself.

Hard light reveals shape and texture. When coming from the side, all light will pull out form. We saw in Chapter 6, "Goals 4–6: Creating the Illusion of Dimension," that a hard light will still reveal form fairly well, even when coming from the front. Hard light that grazes the surface will bring out surface detail. On a minute scale, the clear impression of lit and unlit areas will bring out even the smallest bumps and irregularities of a surface, which is why hard light isn't a particularly flattering light for portraiture unless you want to pull out rugged features.

Hard light can contribute to mood as well. If the primary lights in a scene are hard, with few other lights, the result will be high contrast, harsh and dramatic, and will have much visual tension (Figure 10.8). Hard lights are often combined with soft lights. The softer lights fill in shadow areas and literally "lighten the mood," while the hard light sculpts shape and indicates the primary light direction.

Figure 10.8 Harsh top-down light makes these orcs seem even more menacing in *The Lord of the Rings: The Fellowship of the Ring*. (©2001 New Line Cinema. Photo by Mary Evans/Ronald Grant. Courtesy of Everett Collection.)

FEATURES AND CHARACTERISTICS OF HARD LIGHT

Three distinctive visual features of hard light:

1. Dark, crisp shadows
2. Small, bright specular highlights
3. Abrupt terminators that don't extend past one half of the surface

Characteristics and uses of hard light:

- Pulls out shape (volume) even when frontal
- Reveals texture (bumpiness) when grazing the surface
- Has a clear sense of directionality
- Creates a dramatic or harsh mood if it's the only light in the scene

10.2.2 SOURCES OF HARD LIGHT

In life, lights that are very small and/or far away produce hard light. Examples of real-world hard light are a bare bulb, a flash, or a spotlight. The sun, though massive in size, also casts hard light due to its great distance from the Earth.

Hard light in life comes from two kinds of sources:

- *Very small lights:* Very small lights emanate radial, non-intersecting rays (Figure 10.9).
- *Very faraway lights:* When lights are extremely far away, the rays that reach the surface are essentially parallel, with all other rays scattering off in other directions (Figures 10.10 through 10.12).

Some people define *size* as one of the properties of light, rather than diffusion, because the larger the light source, the softer the light. The issue isn't quite that simple though, because great distance mitigates the effects of size, making the light hard again (as we saw in the example of the sun). The absolute size isn't so important really. What is important is the *apparent size*. "Apparent size" is how large something appears from a certain vantage point—in this

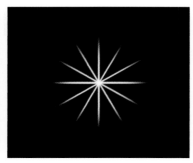

Figure 10.9 Radial rays produce hard light.

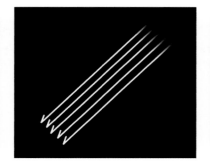

Figure 10.10 Parallel rays produce hard light.

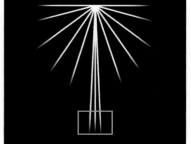

Figure 10.11 A small, faraway light contributes essentially parallel rays.

Figure 10.12 A large, faraway light also contributes essentially parallel rays.

case, how big the light looks from the position of the subject being lit. For example, if we were to put on our super-dark glasses and look at the sun, it would look rather tiny as it only occupies .5 degrees of the horizon. Its apparent size is very small—and so it contributes hard light (Figure 10.13). In the end, however, it isn't size that determines how the light affects the scene; it's the scattering of the rays. A large light is soft only if we are near to it. For this reason, the term "diffusion" is a better defining property of light than "size."

Figure 10.13 The apparent size of an object is how large it appears from a certain vantage point. Lights that are very far away appear small. The smaller the apparent size, the harder the light will be.

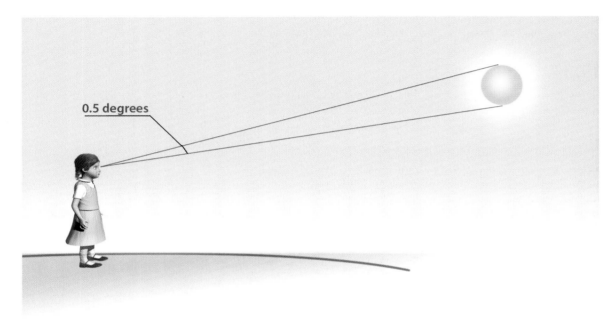

0.5 degrees

Hard light is easy to create digitally. So easy, in fact, that many times digital lighters will create hard light sources when, in fact, soft light would be more appropriate.

Commonly used CG lights that produce hard light are:

◆ *Point light*: Point lights cast rays radially in all directions from an infinitely small point. Because the origin of the light rays is infinitely small, this produces perfectly radial rays and perfectly hard light.

◆ *Spotlight:* Spotlights radiate light from an infinitely small point in a conical shape. Spotlights also contribute perfectly radial and perfectly hard light.

◆ *Directional light*: Also called *distant* lights, directional lights imitate sources that are very far away. These lights cast perfectly parallel rays in a specified direction throughout the entire scene. They contribute perfectly hard light.

◆ *Tiny area lights:* Area lights also will contribute hard light if they are very tiny and/or very far away.

Notice that all of these light types contribute *perfectly* hard light. In addition, digital shadows from these lights typically have default values of zero blur and 100% opacity, which means they too are perfectly hard. In life, nothing is perfect (don't we know it); even a bare bulb has a bit of volume to it and, therefore, a tiny amount of scattering of rays. Likewise, the sun passes through the atmosphere even on a clear day and diffuses slightly. For this reason, I recommend that no digital light ever be allowed to be perfectly hard in appearance, in order to avoid a telltale CG look. The easiest way to *slightly* soften a hard light (such as a point, spot, or directional light) is to provide a small amount of blur to the shadows, even for a very hard light. In the average situation, that is going to be good enough.

10.3 SOFT LIGHT

This section looks at the visual characteristics of soft light, and how soft light is created both in life and in the computer.

10.3.1 DISTINCTIVE CHARACTERISTICS OF SOFT LIGHT

Figure 10.14 A digital render of soft light.

Soft light has visual characteristics that are the opposite of hard light. It's important to note, however, that light can be very hard, very soft, or anything in between. Thus soft light sources can be anything from a little bit soft to completely soft and omni-directional. In general, the shadows produced by soft light will be very blurry and usually lifted in density because the light rays are occluded in an irregular manner and some bleed into the shadowed areas. The softer the light, the brighter and more blurry the shadows, until there may be no distinct shadow at all. Soft light also creates a highlight that is broader, often more blurred, and less opaque. The softer the light, the broader and less opaque the highlight, until there may be no highlight at all, even for a shiny surface. Similarly, the terminator created by soft light is more gradual and wider. Light will seem to "wrap around" the object, illuminating more than half of the surface. Again, the softer the light, the more broad and gradual the terminator, until there may be no terminator at all (the light truly comes from all directions).

Since soft light comes in from multiple angles, it has an indistinct directionality. The more scattered the rays, the less clear the location of the light source. Perfectly soft light literally comes from all directions and has no directionality. All these rays fill in the details of form and surface texture. For this reason, truly soft light will obscure surface bumpiness.

Soft light can be a calm, pleasing light. The gradual transitions between light and dark give a gentle mood (Figure 10.15). Soft light is often used for portraiture lighting of women, where seeing harsh detail is undesirable. Photographers and videographers use soft light extensively to provide gentle primary lighting or to illuminate areas without producing unwanted shadows or highlights. In other instances, soft lighting can be so uniform it becomes blah or boring. It can be deliberately used to set a mood of comfort, calmness, and in extreme examples, stagnation.

Figure 10.15 The gentle look of soft light is perfect for this photograph of a small baby.

FEATURES AND CHARACTERISTICS OF SOFT LIGHT

Three distinctive visual features of soft light:

- Blurry, lifted shadows to no visible shadows
- Large, dull highlights to no highlights
- Gradual terminators that wrap around the object to no visible terminator

Characteristics and uses of soft light:

- Frontal soft light obscures form and volume
- Hides surface texture (bumpiness)
- Indistinct to no sense of directionality
- Pleasing, gentle light, good for portraiture of women or calm, even stagnant scenes

10.3.2 Sources of Soft Light

In life, soft light can come from a variety of sources. Examples of soft light are sunlight on an overcast day, daylight passed through a curtain, a bulb covered by a lampshade, or light bouncing off a wall or ceiling. In general, real-world soft light comes from three kinds of sources:

◆ *Large and close light sources:* Large light sources that emit light from a volume produce soft light, such as from a tube light or a photographer's softbox (Figure 10.16).

◆ *Diffused light:* Hard light may be converted into soft light by passing the light through a diffuser, such as a cloud or cloth (Figure 10.17).

◆ *Reflected light:* Diffusely reflecting light will also soften it, such as bouncing light off of just about any surface except for a mirror (Figure 10.18).

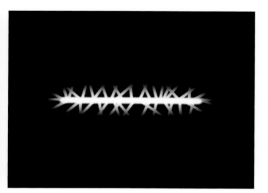 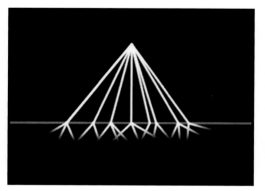 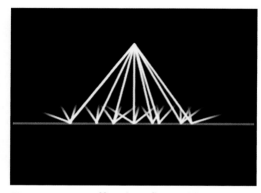

Figure 10.16 Area lights emit soft, scattered rays.

Figure 10.17 Diffused light is scattered and soft.

Figure 10.18 Diffusely reflected light is scattered and soft.

Most of the lighting we encounter in the real world is soft, having been either diffused or reflected. Consider the light in your room right now: Is it coming from a large source like a computer screen (soft), or has it been diffused through a lampshade (soft)? Perhaps your lamp points up, bouncing the light off the ceiling (also soft). Perhaps you're in an office with a fluorescent tube (soft, if not pretty). Is most of the light ambient, having bounced so many times it seems directionless (near perfectly soft)? If outdoors, you are either lit by direct sunlight (which is hard on a clear day, soft on an overcast day) or skylight (soft). You get the idea.

Various solutions to creating soft light are usually part of most animation software. Most of these are discussed in detail in later chapters but are mentioned briefly here.

Soft (or potentially soft) CG light sources and techniques include:

◆ *Area lights:* Area lights cast light outward from a user-defined geometric shape, typically a plane, which can be scaled, positioned, and rotated. This imitates soft light sources, creating many scattered and intersecting rays. The software calculates the illumination from the area light by actually calculating a multitude of point lights along the area light's surface. For this reason, the computation time required can be extremely long.

◆ *Ambient light:* A type of CG light that uniformly illuminates a surface evenly from all directions, regardless of surface orientation or the light's position. This is meant to imitate 100% uniformly scattered, perfectly soft light.

◆ *Environment light:* An environment light casts illumination into the scene from all directions, creating "real" uniformly scattered light. It is much more realistic than ambient light and likewise takes much longer to render. An environment light is often combined with high dynamic range imagery (image-based lighting) to create light that is less uniform and rendered with global illumination for the most realistic look (Figure 10.19).

◆ *Emissive geometry:* When rendering with some global illumination algorithms, any piece of geometry can emit light, based on its incandescence. This method is realistic, very controllable, and render-intensive.

◆ *"Real" diffuse reflection:* Realistically diffused bounced light can be created by global illumination algorithms such as radiosity and final gather.

Figure 10.19 A single environment light mapped with an image of three light sources.

Creating soft lighting and still maintaining reasonable render times can be a challenge for the digital lighter. Professional facilities have many tight deadlines. In the past, studios rarely used area lights, environment lights, or global illumination, as these weren't feasible due to time constraints. Instead, they relied on the knowledge and artistry of their employees to cheat the look of soft light by other means. In the past years, however, this approach has changed. Realistic soft light methods are more common, making the task of creating pleasing-looking soft light vastly easier, if more render intensive. While less common than before, techniques to cheat soft light are still quite useful to know, as they can dramatically reduce render time. (Methods to cheat soft light are covered in Chapter 15, "Tricks of the Trade.")

10.4 CHAPTER CONCLUSION

This chapter has provided a solid overview of light diffusion (also called light quality), how it appears in life, and the various options by which a digital lighter can control the amount of diffusion in their lights.

Digital lighters need to be aware of the softness of lights they are imitating—if they imitate this property incorrectly, the lighting won't be as effective. Light diffusion can be determined by several distinctive visual characteristics. When you understand that these looks come from scattered versus non-scattered rays, you can determine which lights should be soft.

In the computer, hard light is easy to create and hard light types are the ones most commonly used—yet in life, most light sources are soft. While creating soft light in life is easy, creating it digitally can be more difficult. Doing so requires skill and know-how on the part of the lighter and/or render time on the part of the computer.

The information in Table 10.1 serves as a summary of material presented in this chapter and may come in handy as a reference.

Table 10.1 Comparison of Hard and Soft Light

Attributes	Hard Light	Soft Light
Physical Properties	Direct lighting from a small light source, or far light source	A large light source, light that has passed through a diffusing medium, or light that has bounced off another surface
Real-World Examples	Cloudless sun, bare bulb, flash, spotlight	Neon tubing, fluorescent lighting, overcast day, shaded bulb
Ray Direction	Parallel or radial rays, nonintersecting	Scattered rays, intersecting
Shadows	Crisp, dark, directional shadows	Blurry, light shadows or no clear shadows at all
Specular Highlight	Smaller, brighter, more opaque	Larger, less bright, less opaque, to no specular at all
Diffuse Terminator	Abrupt transition, does not wrap past half of surface	Gradual transition, wraps around more than half of surface
Directionality	Defined directionality	Less defined directionality to no directionality
Effect on Shape and Texture	Brings out shape and texture	Obscures shape and texture
Mood/Uses	Harsh, dramatic, bold	Gentle, peaceful, pleasing
CG Light Types	Point, spot, parallel	Area, ambient, environment

10.4.1 IMPORTANT POINTS

◆ Hard light results from rays that aren't scattered, being either radial or parallel.

◆ Hard light comes from sources that are very small or very far away.

◆ Hard light has three distinct visual characteristics: (1) crisp, dark shadows, (2) abrupt terminators, and (3) small, bright specular highlights.

◆ Hard light can be harsh when it's the only light source.

◆ Digital lights creating hard light by default are point, spot, and distant.

◆ Hard light is easy to create in the computer and is often overused.

◆ In life, there is no *perfectly* hard light.

◆ Soft light results from rays that are scattered.

◆ Soft light comes from large and near light sources, diffused light, or diffusely reflected light.

◆ Soft light has three distinct visual characteristics: (1) blurry, lifted shadows to no shadows; (2) gradual terminators that wrap around the object to no terminators; and (3) large, dim highlights to no highlights.

◆ Most sources in life are soft.

◆ Soft frontal light will flatten form and minimize surface texture.

◆ Realistic soft light can be difficult and/or render-intensive to create digitally.

◆ Light in life can run the gamut from very hard to very soft.

10.4.2 TERMS

diffusion
light quality
hard light
apparent size

soft light
emissive geometry
environment light

10.4.3 Exercises

1. Using a camera, set up a real-world still-life scene in which you photograph simple objects (like eggs) under soft and then hard light. Remember, hard light can be created with a bare bulb, while soft light can be created with the same bulb shaded by fabric. Take two pictures. Identify the visual characteristics of light quality in each photo.

2. Image gathering: Gather a few photographs from magazines or online that are examples of hard or soft light. Identify the distinctive visual features of the lights in the image and discuss what kinds of light sources are in the scene. Now discuss what kinds of approaches you would use if re-creating this photograph in a 3D render.

3. Create a simple digital still life. Light the scene using a hard digital light source for the dominant light (such as spot, point, or distant) and a soft digital light source for the reflected light (such as an area light). Now try re-lighting the scene using global illumination and have the renderer calculate the reflected light for you.

4. Using the same still life from Exercise 3, re-light the scene using *only* soft light sources. Try using area lights, environment lights, and ambient lights.

Figure 11.1 A prism in multicolored light.

<h1>Chapter 11
Light Color</h1>

"It's terrible how the light runs out, taking color with it."

—Claude Monet, 19th-Century Impressionist Painter

Digital artists need to have a deep understanding of color. They not only need to understand the aesthetic uses of color and how pigments work, as does the painter, but they also need to understand how light works, as do the photographer and cinematographer. Even more, they need to understand how colors are represented digitally, a subject essential in all computer graphics.

This chapter covers many aspects of color. Chapter 4 covered how color affects mood. Here we delve deeper, looking into the science of light, vision, perception, and how color is represented digitally.

11.1 THE SCIENCE OF COLOR

color (n.)

1. a visual attribute of things that results from the light they emit or transmit or reflect.

The digital artist should have a general knowledge of the *science* of color. This section is a review of topics familiar but likely forgotten. Most of these topics we learned in high school physics or biology classes. This section will knock the dust off those old lessons. A few lesser-known facts will also be introduced.

11.1.1 THE VISIBLE SPECTRUM

Light is part of the *electromagnetic spectrum*, a continuum of wavelike energy. Waves of EM energy can be visualized much like waves in the ocean—they have troughs and peaks. The distance from peak to peak can be measured. This distance is the *wavelength* (Figure 11.2). How many waves travel past in a second is the *frequency*. Thus the smaller the wavelength, the higher the frequency is.

The electromagnetic spectrum is more familiar to you than you might think. Not only is light part of this spectrum, so are microwaves, radio waves, and the signals used by our cell phones. Even the thermal heat you feel when you put your cold feet on something to warm them is part of this spectrum.

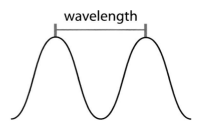

Figure 11.2 Measurement of a wavelength.

Figure 11.3 The visible spectrum.

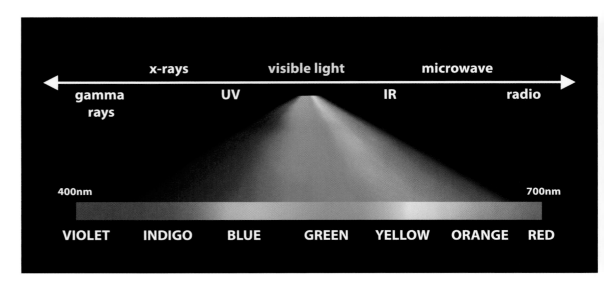

Light is the only portion of the electromagnetic spectrum that is visible to our eyes, and is thus known as *the visible spectrum* (Figure 11.3). Visible light ranges in wavelength from 380 to 750 nanometers (nm)—only a small portion of the electromagnetic spectrum. The visible spectrum consists of the colors that we see in a rainbow—from reds and oranges through blues and purples. Each of these colors corresponds to a different wavelength of light.

White light contains all the colors of the visible spectrum. When white light is passed through a prism (Figure 11.4), the light breaks into rays of differing wavelengths.

The color of certain objects results from the wavelengths of light reflecting off of them. When light strikes a surface, some of the wavelengths of light are absorbed, while others are reflected. The color an object appears to be is the color of light that is reflected by the object. For example, an object will appear red (like a cherry or apple) under white light if it reflects wavelengths of 700 nm (red) and absorbs all other wavelengths.

11.1.2 Color Perception

Color is a sensory phenomenon—it only exists because we perceive it. "Out there" in the universe are only electromagnetic waves. The interpretation of some of these wavelengths into color is unique to how our eyes and brain process visual information.

Rods and Cones

Our eyes contain special photosensitive cells that convert light into electrical impulses sent to the brain. We have two types of these cells: rods and cones. Cones are responsible for color vision and detailed vision. Humans have three different kinds of cone photoreceptors, each most sensitive to a different wavelength of light, corresponding to red, green, and blue (Figure 11.5). The fact that our eyes sample the spectrum at three locations is why we can use the RGB color system to represent color.

Figure 11.4 A prism splitting light into colors.

The other kind of light-sensitive cell in our eye is a rod. We have many more rods than we do cones. Rods are responsible for gross detection of movement, shapes, light, and dark. Rods are more than 1,000 times as sensitive to light, but they don't respond at all to red light. Rods cannot detect color; they allow us to only view objects in black and white.

As the light dims, we literally perceive less color, prompting the famous painter Monet to exclaim, "Terrible how the light runs out, taking color with it." In low light, our color-blind rods become more dominant in our vision. Additionally, of the three cone types, the one most sensitive in dim light is the cone that responds to blue. Thus in low light levels, we are less sensitive to reds and more sensitive to blues. This is partly why we perceive night as monochromatic and bluish, a phenomenon known as a *Purkinje shift*, or Purkinje effect (Figure 11.6).

Although this information might seem like a review of a high school science class, understanding how we perceive color explains the appearance of colored materials under colored light. Understanding the eye and how the images you see are translated to the brain also can help you to create images that capture your perception of what you saw, which will then help you better guide the audience's perception.

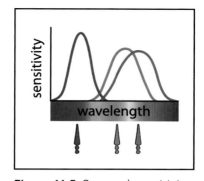

Figure 11.5 Spectral sensitivity of cones, cells responsible for color perception.

Figure 11.6 The Purkinje effect.

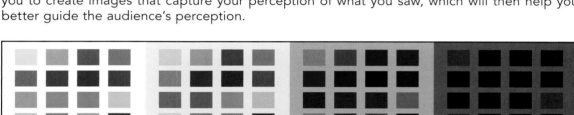

The Relative Nature of Color Perception

This section talks about how and why our perception of light color is not entirely, shall we say, accurate.

The human eye adjusts to overall hue in much the same way it adjusts to brightness. After seeing a color for a certain period of time, your eye becomes less stimulated by that color, effectively "seeing it less." If you doubt that your eyes are doing all that adjusting, try the optical illusion on the next page. First, glance at Figures 11.7 and 11.8. Notice that the image of the swan is decidedly two-toned. Next, stare at the dot in Figure 11.7, with the cyan and yellow swatches, and count to 10 slowly (one-one-thousand, two-one-thousand…). Then look back at the figure of the swan. Notice anything different?

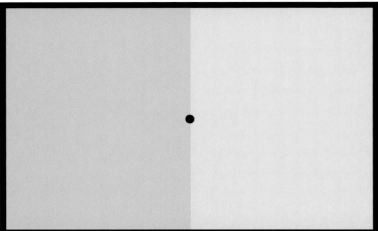

Figure 11.7 Colored blocks used in optical illusion.

Figure 11.8 Image used in optical illusion.

What has happened is that while staring at Figure 11.7, your eyes quickly adapted to the color you were looking at and removed a certain amount of this tint, a phenomenon is known as *chromatic adaptation*. This is what I mean when I say our perception of color is *relative*—it depends on the overall tint as well as the other surrounding colors. Chromatic adaptation explains why complementary colors, when adjacent, make each other seem more vibrant, a phenomena known as *simultaneous contrast* (explored extensively by Impressionist painters of the 1800s) and why you cannot reproduce colors with complete accuracy just by eye. It also explains why we perceive most of the light in ordinary situations as white or near white, when in fact common light sources are often rich in color, as we will see shortly.

11.2 COLOR TEMPERATURE

color temperature (n.)
the measure of the color of a light source by relating it to a theoretically perfect black body source of radiant energy, measured in Kelvin units (K)

In life, light sources are varied in color. It's very rare for all the light in an environment to be entirely white, as in nature this would require pure white light shining on only black, white, or gray objects. Chapter 3, "Goal 1: Establishing Setting," talked about common light colors in a general way. Here we take a closer look.

11.2.1 THE KELVIN SCALE

Common sources of light tend toward either orange or blue (Figures 11.9 and 11.10). Daylight is blue-tinted, while incandescent lamps, known as *tungsten lamps*, are yellow-orange tinted. Dusk is a deeper blue, while sunrise and sunset are in the red-orange part of the scale. This

Figure 11.9 (Left) Mixed lighting in this photo shows the different colors of light.

Figure 11.10 (Right) Warm lights in this interior contrast strongly with the blue daylight outside the window.

color can be mapped along a gradient from red-orange to deep blue, with yellow and white in the middle (Figure 11.11).

The color of light along this gradient is known as the light's color temperature, and it's measured in Kelvin units. The higher the number in Kelvin, the more blue the color.

The digital artist may be tempted to simply match the light source in his scene, such as a tungsten bulb, then look up the bulb's Kelvin number and match this with the corresponding color on a Kelvin chart. Danger, Will Robinson! Many charts you see are artistic approximations. Given an accurate chart an artist may indeed put in light colors in a paint-by-numbers way, and this approach may work at times. Other times, however, this approach will be too limited and not give satisfactory results, even with an accurate color chart.

10,000 K — **DEEP BLUE** — **Deep blue clear sky / Skylight** (10,000k - 20,000K)

BLUE — **Hazy sky / Average summer shade** (8000K)

— **Overcast sky** (6500K - 7500K)

— **Electronic flash** (5600K - 5500K)
5,500 K — **WHITE** — **Sunny day around noon** (5500K)

— **Early morning / Late afternoon sunlight** (4300K)

YELLOW — **1 Hour from dusk or dawn / Tungsten lamp** (3400K)
— **200W-40W Incandescent lamp** (3000K - 2680K)

— **Sunrise / Sunset** (2500K - 2000K)

— **Candlelight** (1500K)
1,000 K — **RED-ORANGE**

Figure 11.11 The Kelvin scale. Common light sources run the spectrum from red-orange to blue, with white in the middle, measured in Kelvin units.

To understand why, you only have to remember our friend, chromatic adaption. Recall that our perception of a color in fact varies depending on the surrounding colors and dominant tint of all the colors. A numerical representation, a measurement, does not vary. Thus at times a measured color (such as plug in 1, .2, .5 for 5000K) may be accurate to the color, but it will not be accurate to what we see. In this case, the color derived from a formula will be unsatisfactory. And of course, it doesn't leave room for artistic interpretation, which is often desired in visual storytelling.

COLOR TEMPERATURES OF COMMON LIGHT SOURCES

Common light sources run from red-orange to blue, with white in the middle, measured in degrees Kelvin.

The mid-range of these colors is relative, due to chromatic adaptation (the adapting of our eyes to color). Whichever temperature is perceived as white, the temperatures above appear blue-tinted, and those below appear orange-tinted.

Generally:

- 3500K and down appears warm.
- 3500K–6000K appears white. (In this range, relativity of temperatures is very important.)
- 6000K and up appears bluish.

Fluorescent lights are not on the Kelvin scale and appear greenish.

11.2.2 White Balance: Our Camera's Little White Lie

Cameras will capture the true range of colors and may produce images that have a decided cast to them—one that we don't remember seeing and that we don't want in our photographs. The camera is not mistaken; it faithfully records the light entering it, in all its colored glory. Be that as it may, we need the camera to be a little less faithful in its reproduction and to match our perception instead. To do this, photographers adjust what is known as the *white balance*.

Setting a *white balance* is selecting a particular tint to read as white in the photograph. The previous tint that now appears white is known as the *white point*, and all the other colors will be adjusted accordingly. If sunlight is set to look white, then indoor bulbs will look orange. Conversely, if indoor light is set to white, then exterior sunlight will look blue. This camera adjustment will match how our eyes adjust to overall color cast (Figure 11.12).

Digital cameras have much leeway with this. Just about any tint can be made to be white. Digital cameras are also set to automatically deduce an appropriate white point and set it, possibly without you realizing it or knowing exactly what white point it has set. Before the days of digital cameras, and if using a traditional film or photographic camera, the choices were more limited. Generally certain film stock is used, some film made for daylight that will capture sunlight as white, and other film made for interiors so that tungsten bulbs will appear white. These two temperatures on the Kelvin scale—5500K for sunlight and 3200K for tungsten—are the two common white-point settings in film. Photographic flashes are set to a color of about 5500K, the color of midday sun.

Figure 11.12 Various white balances show the different color temperatures in a mixed lighting situation (photographs by MacDuff Knox).

Additionally, photographers choose certain lights and/or place colored gels over light sources to change their color, often in order to minimize apparent color differences. Standard gels are designed to neutralize fluorescent light, exterior daylight, or tungsten by screening it with the opposite color on the color wheel. One look at these filters tells you just how tinted these light sources actually are (Figures 11.13 and 11.14).

Digital lighters, on the other hand, set their own light colors. They don't need to select special film, use gels, or set the white balance in a camera. The digital lighter still needs to decide "what is white" in his scene, however. When setting light color you will want to be aware of the gradient of colors in the natural world and decide how you will be representing these colors digitally. Will you set sunlight as white or the tungsten bulb? Or go in between? All other lights should be tinted accordingly. Because digital lighters can craft any color for their lights, I believe it's that much more important to be informed about the color of real lights. I don't believe lighters need to be bound to formulas or a paint-by-number approach using the Kelvin scale, but they do need to be familiar with the Kelvin scale and set the tints of their lights to be in accordance with it, or deviate by choice for creative intent.

Figure 11.13 Camera lens filters.

11.3 LIGHT AND PIGMENT

Color is learned early in life—purple and orange and yellow are pointed out along with circles and squares and the occasional hexagon. While working with pigments may be familiar, especially to those with a fine arts or painting background, light color and working with light color may not be. In fact, most people never really deal much with light color directly at all.

Digital lighters, however, need a solid understanding of both light and pigment color, as they will deal directly with the digital representation of both of them…and light color and pigment color act very differently from each other. Some things you may have learned about pigments may not apply to light, in fact, they are often exactly the opposite. In addition, some of the things we were taught as children about pigment aren't even correct.

This section discusses both pigment and light color, looking at how these colors interact and react when mixed with themselves and each other.

Figure 11.14 Common gel colors used to neutralize or give the appearance of daylight, tungsten, or fluorescent lighting.

11.3.1 Pigment Color

***Pigment* color refers to the colors of paints, inks, and dyes** (Figure 11.15). Our first introduction to color is through pigment. Not only do we look at the color of things (pigment), but we initially learn about color by mixing pigment. Every child, as soon as he or she can play with paint, sees that certain colors, when mixed together, produce other colors. Probably when you were a wee lass or laddie, someone showed you how to mix orange paint from red and yellow. This is basic color theory, and we learn it early on.

TIP

While 3D artists don't work with pigments, such as oil and acrylic paints, they should still have a solid understanding of the subject of color mixing. I'd recommend a good painting class to every digital artist.

Figure 11.15 Pigment.

Primary and Secondary Pigments, Then and Now

Long ago artists and scientists began their search for the minimum number of essential colors. Colors that, when combined, could produce all the other possible colors, but they themselves could not be mixed from any other pigments. Colors such as these are known as *primary colors*.

Most of us have learned that red, blue, and yellow are the *primary pigment colors.* Search on the Internet and you will find many, many examples of this basic supposition. It is also what is taught in grade school and in many art books. We are taught that from these all other pigment colors can be mixed.

Secondary colors are the colors mixed by even amounts of two primary colors. Most of us were taught that these secondary colors are orange (produced by mixing equal amounts of red and yellow), purple (produced by mixing equal amounts of blue and red), and green (produced by mixing equal amounts of blue and yellow). All of these colors can be evenly spaced on a circle with the primary colors equidistant and the secondary colors placed in between. This organization is the basis of color theory and is known as the *color wheel* (Figure 11.16).

One problem, however: *This information isn't entirely incorrect.* And so the confusion begins with light and pigment colors. Let's clear up the confusion and simplify the facts here. Several centuries ago, pigments weren't particularly pure, and the choice of colors was much more limited. Red, blue, and yellow were the best representations of primary pigments they had. It wasn't until modern chemistry that very pure dyes began to be produced. In the 20th century, modern chemists discovered a different set of colors that better represent pigment primaries.

All the modern person has to do to find out what these new, more accurate primary pigments are is to open up their home printer or take a trip to Office Depot. A look at the printing inks in a standard color printer reveals four inks in use: CMYK, standing for Cyan, Magenta, Yellow, and Black.

The three more accurate primary pigments are cyan, magenta, and yellow. These colors are more accurate because they produce a much wider range of hues than the old red-blue-yellow triad. RBY combinations cannot produce cyan or magenta. Furthermore, the greens or purples produced in RBY combinations are dull (Figure 11.17). CMY combinations, on the other hand, can produce all of the major colors found in the rainbow with clarity (Figure 11.18).

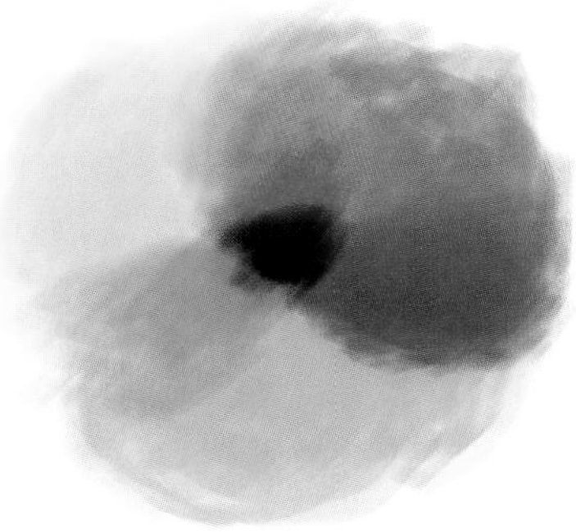

Figure 11.16 (Left) An artist's color wheel.

Figure 11.17 (Center) RYB. Painter's primaries—not accurate today, but the theory persists among artists. (The blue used is somewhere between blue and cyan, in order to mix both green and purple.)

Figure 11.18 (Right) CMY. Printing primaries—more accurate, discovered with modern dyes.

The secondary colors from the new pigment primaries are red (mixed from yellow and magenta), blue (mixed from magenta and cyan), and green (mixed from yellow and cyan). Orange and purple are in fact tertiary colors, which are formed from mixing a primary color with a secondary color.

NOTE

The CMY model doesn't produce *all* the colors we can see, however. In particular, it has a bit of trouble with vibrant orange. As a matter of fact, *truly primary pigments have never been found*, which is to say that no set of pigments can completely produce all the other colors we see.

The Color Wheel, Then and Now

The new pigment primaries affect how the color wheel is represented. With new primary and secondary colors in play, the positions of these colors on the color wheel change (compare Figures 11.19 and 11.20). A full consideration of what this means about the artistic merit of combining complementary colors, when many of our conclusions are drawn from colors which were *not* in fact complementary, is for the reader who is passionate about color to wonder on his own (Figure 11.21).

Figure 11.19 Color wheel arranged according to "old" painter's primaries. Magenta and cyan are left out, making dull greens or purples. Not truly primary—sorry, Sir Isaac Newton!

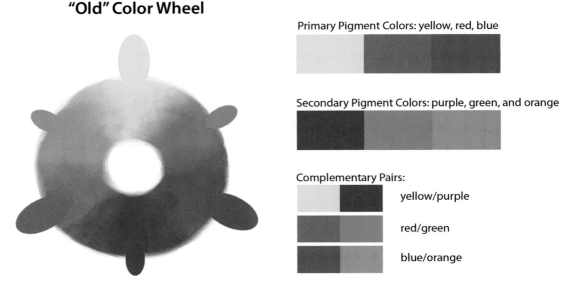

"Old" Color Wheel

Primary Pigment Colors: yellow, red, blue

Secondary Pigment Colors: purple, green, and orange

Complementary Pairs:

yellow/purple

red/green

blue/orange

Figure 11.20 Color wheel arranged according to "new" printing primaries. (Notice that orange and purple are tertiary colors.) Mixes most colors but not all.

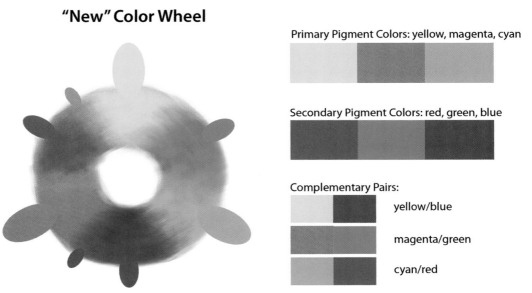

"New" Color Wheel

Primary Pigment Colors: yellow, magenta, cyan

Secondary Pigment Colors: red, green, blue

Complementary Pairs:

yellow/blue

magenta/green

cyan/red

Figure 11.21 Vincent van Gogh explored the effects of complementary color, using the "old" painter's color wheel.

Figure 11.22 Green and magenta, opposite on the color wheel, mix to black.

Figure 11.23 Yellow and blue surprisingly mix to black if they are pure in hue. On the other hand, yellow mixed with cyan produces bright green, while yellow mixed with cyan-blue makes a duller, darker green.

Subtractive Pigment

Pigments are *subtractive*, which means that mixing pigment colors together produces darker and darker colors. Mixing pigments produces darker colors because more wavelengths are absorbed when different colors of pigments are combined.

Mixing all colors of pigments together will produce black. Mixing just the three primary pigments together will also produce black. Specifically, layering magenta ink over cyan ink over yellow ink will yield black. Printers include black ink because to layer all colors is a lot of ink, and because the black produced by combining pigment isn't 100 percent dense. White comes from the color of the page—the absence of pigment.

Mixing any primary with the secondary directly across from it, such as magenta and green, will also produce black (or near black) (Figure 11.22). In fact, mixing *any* two pure pigment colors directly across from each other on the new color wheel will produce black. Even yellow and blue, if they are pure in hue, will mix to black (Figure 11.23). Amazing but true; try it out at home with some printing inks.

11.3.2 Light Color

Light is the source of all color, thus *colored light* is pure color (Figures 11.24 and 11.25). Pigments are a derivative of light. If you want to really understand color, then you will want to understand light. As a digital artist, you really *must* understand light color. Partly because when you light a scene you will work with light, but even more importantly because digital color is represented by light primary colors (discussed in Section 11.4, "Digital Color Representation"). Thus every digital artist dealing with images, from a matte painter to a compositor, needs to understand light color.

Figure 11.24 A string of colored lights.

Figure 11.25 A multicolored display of fireworks.

Light Primary and Secondary Colors

The primary colors of light are red, green, and blue (Figure 11.26). Unlike pigment, light *does* have true primaries. From these three light colors, all of the colors visible to the human eye can be mixed.

The secondaries for light are cyan, magenta, and yellow. You can see the secondary color formed by overlapping two light sources, one in each primary color. An interesting relationship you may have noticed is that the pigment secondary colors are the same as the light primary colors, and light secondary colors are the same as the pigment primary colors (Figure 11.27).

Light primaries = pigment secondaries (red, green, blue)

Pigment primaries = light secondaries (cyan, magenta, yellow)

Additive Light

Light is *additive*, meaning that as different colors of light are combined, the result gets lighter and lighter. When all colors of light are combined, the result is white or colorless light.

This relationship is again the inverse from pigment. Light is additive—all light colors together make white, while the absence of light makes black. Similar to pigment, a primary light color overlapping a secondary light color will result in white light. In fact, any two light colors exactly opposite on the new color wheel will produce white light when overlapped (Figure 11.28).

Figure 11.27 Another look at the new color wheel illustrates that light and pigment colors have an inverse relationship.

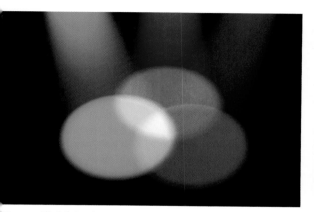

Figure 11.26 Light primaries.

Figure 11.28 Light colors opposite on the color wheel mixing to white.

LIGHT AND PIGMENT SUMMARY

Pigment Color:

- Primary hues: magenta, yellow, cyan
- Secondary hues: blue, green, red
- Subtractive—primary colors and opposites add to black

Light Color:

- Primary hues: blue, green, red
- Secondary hues: magenta, yellow, cyan
- Additive—primary colors and opposites add to white

11.4 DIGITAL COLOR REPRESENTATION

In life we can just look at a color and describe it, but when working on a computer, each color must be specifically qualified in order to be determined. In computer-land, as in science, things are often boiled down to numbers. Color can be represented numerically in a few different ways, known as *color models*.

11.4.1 RGB AND CMYK COLOR MODELS

The RGB and CMYK color models are ways of describing a color by numerically indicating the amount of primary color needed to mix it. The RGB model is a numeric representation of how much red, green, and blue light color is needed to mix the final color of the pixel you see. Similarly, the CMYK color model represents how much cyan, magenta, yellow, and black inks are needed to produce the given color. Because digital artists work almost exclusively with RGB, I will focus my examples on the RGB color model. The same principles hold true for CMYK as well, however.

The amount of each primary color needed can be represented on a scale of 0 to 1. Zero means none of the primary color is present, while 1 means full intensity of the color is present. In the case of RGB, these numbers are always stated in the order of red, green, and blue. Similarly, in the case of CMYK, these numbers are stated in the order of cyan, magenta, yellow, and black. Thus, a digital RGB representation of the primary light colors would be as follows:

Pure red = 1,0,0

Pure green = 0,1,0

Pure blue = 0,0,1

To see how other colors are formed from different RGB values, you only have to recall the additive properties of light. Recall the secondary light colors are equal mixtures of any two fully saturated primary light colors. Thus yellow is from equal mixture of red and green with no blue, while magenta is from equal mixture of blue and red with no green, etc. (Figure 11.29).

Benefits of really understanding RGB color include being able to predict what your color will do under certain situations, to understand why a color turned out the way it did, or to know in some cases how to correct the color of something. By understanding RGB, you will also know how to control your digital color to get the color you want.

Notice that the RGB and CMYK color models correspond to the three or four color channels in your digital image file. The channels are great ways to visualize the RGB (or CMYK) values of your color. For this reason working with these color models, and RGB in particular, really is inescapable. Luckily, like anything else, after a while RGB begins to be as familiar as the other way of describing color, that of using hue, saturation, and value.

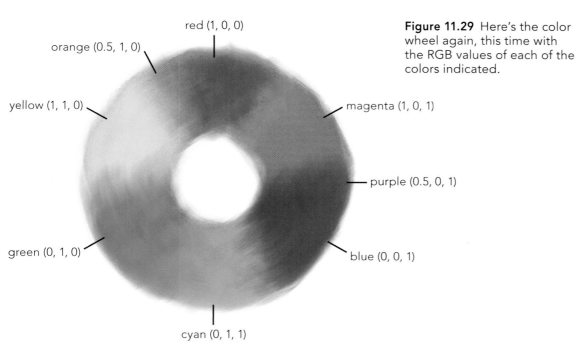

red (1, 0, 0)

orange (0.5, 1, 0)

yellow (1, 1, 0)

magenta (1, 0, 1)

green (0, 1, 0)

purple (0.5, 0, 1)

blue (0, 0, 1)

cyan (0, 1, 1)

Figure 11.29 Here's the color wheel again, this time with the RGB values of each of the colors indicated.

11.4.2 HSL AND HSV COLOR MODELS

Another way to describe color is by its basic placement in the spectrum, how dull or clear it is, and how light or dark it is. By describing these three qualities, known respectively as *hue*, *saturation*, and *lightness*, any color can be defined. Many artists find describing color in this way very intuitive. For example, we might start with a basic color like "blue" or more specifically "true blue," then describe it as a "light true blue." To further define the color, we will want to know if the blue is dull, like the color of a faded blue cotton shirt, or clear, like the color of the sky on a cloudless day.

Describing color in this way is the HSL (hue, saturation, and lightness) color model. HSV (hue, saturation and value) is a similar color model that is more commonly found than HSL. Thus *value* may be more familiar to some digital artists than *lightness*. The HSV color model is sometimes known as HSB (hue, saturation, and brightness), as the term "brightness" is interchangeable with "value." To understand how these color models work, we should be familiar with the terms used and how they can be indicated numerically.

Hue **defines a pure color according where it lies in the visible spectrum** (Figure 11.30). When speaking generally of a color, such as "blue" or "red," we are describing its hue. Numerically, hue is represented 0 to 1, or sometimes 0 to 360, where both 0 and 1 (or 360 degrees) indicates red, and values in between signify other colors on the wheel. Changing the hue changes the basic color.

Figure 11.30 Hue—the fundamental colors found in the visible spectrum.

Saturation **is the clarity or dullness of a color.** Some definitions of saturation mix a color with white, which is how many computer systems display color (Figure 11.31). In common terms, however, when a color or image is "desaturated," it is taken to gray, which is how we will refer to saturation here (Figures 11.32 through 11.35). A fully saturated color is its pure hue mixed with no gray, while a fully desaturated color is completely gray. The saturation scale typically ranges from 0 to 1, or 0% to 100%, where 0 or 0% is completely desaturated, and 1 or 100% is fully saturated.

Figure 11.31 Saturation may refer to mixing the original hue with white.

Figure 11.32 In common terms, desaturation occurs when mixing a hue with a shade of gray.

Figure 11.33 A fully saturated image.

Figure 11.34 Fifty percent saturation.

Figure 11.35 A fully desaturated image.

Lightness refers to how much black *or* white is mixed into the color (Figure 11.36). Lightness does not refer to mixing a color with gray, but rather with *either* black or white. Lightness is an intuitive way to think of color. It's measured on a scale of 0 to 1 or 0% to 100%. At 50% lightness, each color is a pure hue. As the lightness is reduced to 0, the color is increasingly mixed with black until it reaches pure black. Above 50% the color is increasingly mixed with white until pure white is reached at 100% lightness.

Figure 11.36 Lightness.

Value is a term related to lightness that describes how much a hue is mixed to black only (Figure 11.37). A color at maximum *value* contains no black. As black is added, the color's value is reduced until pure black is reached. Thus the lower the value, the darker the color. The value scale typically ranges from 0 to 1, or 0% to 100%. At 0 or 0%, the color is completely black. At 1 or 100%, the color contains no black. The term "brightness" is interchangeable with "value." A color may have a low value but still have a high saturation.

Figure 11.37 Value.

Luminance is the perceived brightness of a color. Sometimes confused with value, luminance differs from value in that all pure colors have a value of 1, but they do *not* all have the same luminance. Each color has an intrinsic *perceived* brightness, or luminance. The luminance values of an image can easily be seen by taking it to grayscale—the lighter the gray, the higher the luminance (as in Figure 11.35). Desaturated colors and grays, black, and white also have luminance; light gray has more luminance than dark gray; white has the greatest luminance of all, while black has none.

Figures 11.38 and 11.39 compare the HSL and HSV color models.

Many applications allow artists to switch how they are defining their color from RGB to HSV for a more intuitive adjustment when selecting color (Figure 11.40). H, S, and B are usually represented by sliders, and most find them easy to use. For others, RGB may be a bit easier. In the end, using HSV or RGB to select and adjust colors is a matter of preference.

Figure 11.38 (Left) HSL color representation.

Figure 11.39 (Right) HSV (also called HSB) color representation.

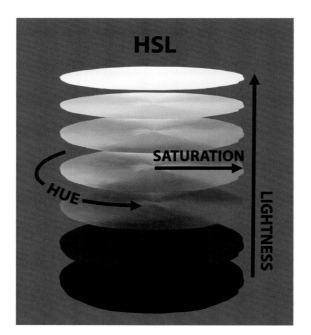

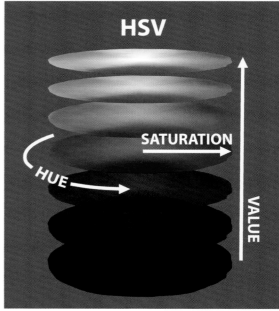

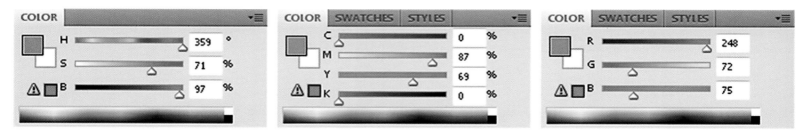

Figure 11.40 Most applications allow you to switch between color models when creating colors.

11.5 LIGHT AND SURFACE COLOR INTERACTION

The lighter deals with how light and surface color interact. Here we cover understanding the end result.

As noted, pigments produce color by absorbing some wavelengths and reflecting others. The reflected wavelengths are the colors we see. If a surface is under white light, what is happening is easy to understand and the resulting color is easy to predict (Figure 11.41).

When the lights are colored, on the other hand, only certain wavelengths are available to be reflected. This can produce some interesting results, and in some cases can lead to unexpected colors or an unexpected lack of color (Figure 11.42).

Figure 11.41 A yellow object under a white light will appear yellow (obvious, right?).

Figure 11.42 A yellow object under a magenta light will apear red.

To understand how the final color is achieved and to predict how things are going to look, the digital lighter only needs to keep in mind that the final appearance of the surface will be the surface color multiplied by the light color.

    light color * surface color = reflected color

This is the same formula for determining the color of bounce light, as both bounce light and the appearance of objects come from the same thing—reflected light.

Let's take a look at the simple math behind it. The math is simple because we're going to multiply sets of three numbers, and that will give us the resulting color.

    yellow * magenta = (1,1,0) * (1,0,1) = (1,0,0) = red

To illustrate how colored light can affect the color of surfaces, let's take a look at a scene with blue, red, green, yellow, orange, and white objects. Since the floor and backdrop are white, they will be our reference for what color light is shining on the scene. Notice how sometimes colors drop out, in other instances the scene becomes monochromatic, and still other times the colors change to something unexpected. I'll leave it as an exercise for you to determine how the light and surface colors multiply together, using the simple formula just given (Figures 11.43 through 11.49).

When both the surface and the light are highly saturated, some colors can drop out to black altogether. To avoid unwanted color dropout, slightly desaturate the light. Desaturating the light will put some values in all of the channels that will allow some reflectance for all colors (Figures 11.50 through 11.52).

Figure 11.43 Scene under white light.

Figure 11.44 (Left) Scene under blue light.

Figure 11.45 (Center) Scene under red light.

Figure 11.46 (Right) Scene under green light.

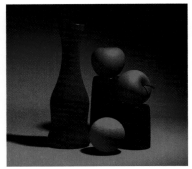

Figure 11.47 (Left) Scene under cyan light.

Figure 11.48 (Center) Scene under magenta light.

Figure 11.49 (Right) Scene under yellow light.

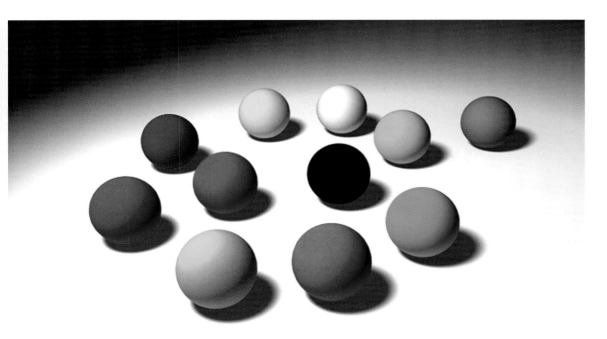

Figure 11.50 Colored balls under white light, for reference.

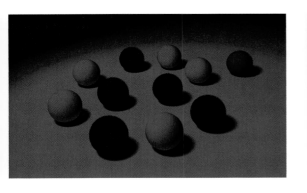 

Figure 11.51 (Left) Under a pure blue light (light color (0,0,1)), colors made with red and green drop out.

Figure 11.52 (Right) Desaturating the light puts value into the light's red and green channels (light color (.2, .2, 1)), avoiding complete color drop-out for colors made with red and green.

11.6 CHAPTER CONCLUSION

As you have seen in this chapter, there is a lot to know about color, and after extensive exploration, you may still have the feeling that you have just scratched the surface on this subject.

Color is our perception of light—it results from how we see different wavelengths in the visible spectrum. The basic digital representation of color is the RGB color model, which is based on light primaries. Digital artists will work almost exclusively with RGB channel images, and on top of this, digital lighters will deal extensively with light and surface color interaction with each scene they light. For this reason, a deep understanding of color, and in particular light color, is essential to the digital lighter. This chapter has covered a few well-known facts about color as well as a few lesser-known ones. A complete understanding of color aids digital lighters in creating and controlling the color in their images.

11.6.1 IMPORTANT POINTS

◆ Visible light is a small part of the electromagnetic spectrum.

◆ The wavelength of light determines its color.

◆ White light contains all the colors of the visible spectrum and can be split by a prism.

◆ Color exists because we perceive it.

◆ Photosensitive cells in our eyes called cones are responsible for our color vision.

◆ In dim light, we literally perceive less color. Light makes color.

◆ Common sources of light tend toward red/orange or blue.

◆ The color of light from red to blue is known as its temperature and is measured in Kelvin units.

◆ Our eyes adapt to color in the same way they adapt to light intensity.

◆ A light tint near white will look white without a true white nearby for comparison.

◆ Setting a camera's white balance adjusts the camera so it matches our perception better.

◆ Primary colors are those that can mix all visible colors.

◆ Secondary colors are mixtures of two primaries in equal amounts.

◆ Pigment primaries were once thought to be red, blue, and yellow.

◆ Modern pigment primaries are cyan, magenta, and yellow.

◆ There are no true pigment primaries—some colors are always left out.

◆ Pigment is subtractive—combining all colors makes black.

◆ Light primaries are red, green, and blue.

◆ Light is additive—combining all colors makes white (colorless) light.

◆ Light and pigment colors have an inverse relationship—light primaries are pigment secondaries, and vice versa.

◆ Digital color is represented by channels indicating the amount of primary color in each pixel.

◆ The RGB color model is based off light primaries and is a common way to describe color digitally.

◆ Digital artists need to become well versed in recognizing color described by the RGB color model.

◆ The final surface color reaching our eye is a combination of light and surface color and is expressed by the formula: final color = surface color * light color.

◆ Saturated lights and surfaces can combine to produce unexpected results until we understand RGB color representation.

11.6.2 Terms

electromagnetic spectrum
visible spectrum
wavelength
frequency
rods and cones
color temperature
Kelvin scale
chromatic adaptation

simultaneous contrast
white balance
white point
pigment
primary colors
secondary colors
CMYK
new color wheel

subtractive color
RGB
additive color
color channels
HSV/HSB color models
RGB color model

11.6.3 Exercises

1. Buy a few bottles of ink refills for your printer (you can find these sold online or in office stores). Working with these pure pigments, try mixing a variety of colors. Now get three tubes of paint from your local art store. Select three paint colors: true red (try cadmium red), a true blue (try ultramarine blue), and a pure yellow (try canary yellow). Now try mixing the same variety of colors. How many colors can you mix from magenta, cyan, and yellow? What about red, blue, and yellow?

2. If you have access to photography equipment, obtain a variety of colored gels from a photography or theater store and fit red, green, and blue gels over spotlights. If you do not have access to photography equipment, set up a 3D scene with a white ground plane, a white ball in the center, and red, green, and blue spotlights. Place these lights in a circle around the ball as a subject. Explain the resulting light and shadow color. Now try your own color combinations. Try overlapping any two colors opposite the color wheel. How about two primary colors? Photograph or render the results and explain them.

3. Using a standard digital camera, set the white balance for an interior and shoot photographs both indoors and outside. Now shoot another set with daylight settings and a final set with fluorescent settings. Evaluate and explain the colors of the resulting photographs.

4. Create a simple scene with a table lamp in a room with a window allowing in natural light. Add a light to the lamp and a directional light coming from outdoors. Set the colors of each of these two lights based on a chart of Kelvin colors. Render the result. Now discard these colors and creatively interpret the light color, keeping in mind the color *relationship* between the two lights. Which approach did you prefer? Be prepared to discuss your results.

5. Using real or digital objects and lights, place a variety of vividly colored surfaces under differently colored, saturated lights. Record and explain your results. Next, try predicting the results with a new set of surface and light colors. How accurate were your predictions?

The final ingredient of great lighting is *appropriate technique.* This is the *how* of lighting, as in, *"How am I going to get the job done?"* Learning technique is the technical aspect of knowing the software, tools, and various methods to produce certain kinds of looks. But what is meant by *appropriate* technique? That sounds rather stuffy. Appropriate technique simply means knowing not only technique, but also which techniques to use in a given situation. Choosing the right technique depends on being adept at a variety of techniques, knowing the advantages and limitations of each, and knowing the needs of the project.

Today's lighter has a wider variety of techniques to choose from than ever before. Advancements in the processing power of the computers have made more render-intensive approaches more feasible and much more common, such as the use of area lights, ray tracing, global illumination. Additionally, the computer lighting and shading community as a whole is moving toward more physically based and physically accurate lighting and shading models, such as the use of image-based lighting and high dynamic range imagery. While these advancements have revolutionized the lighting pipeline in the past 5 to 10 years, many older techniques still remain viable. Three-point lighting, which has been the foundation for lighting design since the early days of theater, has carried over into cinema and digital lighting and holds its own in combination with newer techniques. Many other long-held cheats and techniques remain, such as those designed to keep render time down and still produce high quality. Although used less frequently, they are well suited for certain effects and especially common on projects not demanding photorealism.

Part IV covers non-software-specific techniques spanning from traditional approaches to the latest cutting-edge 3D techniques. Pros and cons of various techniques are given to help artists decide which one is best suited for a given situation, as well as liberal tips on usage.

PART IV

TECHNIQUE
(MORE "HOW")

"True freedom in concept and visualization demands a refined craft."

—Ansel Adams, photographer, from The Negative

Figure 12.1 Margalo from *Stuart Little 2* lit with three-point lighting. (© 2002 Columbia Pictures Industries, Inc. All Rights Reserved. Courtesy of Columbia Pictures.)

Chapter 12
Three-Point Lighting and Beyond

An old adage says, "You should know the rules before you break them."

When first approaching a scene, lighters may initially have a hard time deciding where to place the lights in order to get the best look. There is no need to operate in a vacuum, however. The experience of countless digital artists and real-world cinematographers provides a valuable starting point.

The way your lights are organized in a scene—how many are used, where they are placed, and for what purpose—is known as a *lighting setup*. Throughout the decades, various schemes for organizing lights have been used—everything from one light to dozens and dozens. The most commonly known setup, however, is three-point lighting.

The concepts found in three-point lighting are the basis of many other lighting setups, both simple and more complex. Knowing the functions of each light, and why and how to use them, provides a wealth of knowledge to the lighter, whether he or she uses three-point lighting or not. For this reason, a solid understanding of this classic setup provides a foundation for expertise with lighting in general. This chapter looks in depth at the three-point lighting setup, then it goes on to extend this setup to many others, both more complex and more simple. This chapter covers both subject and environment lighting, explains the purposes of your lights, and suggests how they can be organized. Even more importantly for digital lighters, this chapter describes how traditional lighting concepts can be adapted for use in digital scenes.

12.1 THREE-POINT LIGHTING

setup (n.)
the way something is organized or arranged

The most common lighting setup and the basis for many others is the *three-point lighting* setup. Understanding this setup will give the digital lighter a deeper understanding of the purposes of his lights. For this reason, this chapter spends a great deal of time discussing each of the "points" in three-point lighting—because these appear in almost every other lighting setup in some form or another, whether it be three-point setup or otherwise. By mastering three-point lighting, the digital lighter is well on his way to mastering lighting in general. First,

Figure 12.2 Toy elephant lit with three-point lighting.

we'll look at the big picture of three-point lighting and provide an overview that is applicable to any lighting, CG or otherwise. Next, we'll look closely at each light in the setup with a focus on digital concerns.

12.1.1 OVERVIEW OF THREE-POINT LIGHTING

As the name suggests, in its purest form, three-point lighting uses three lights:

- ◆ Key
- ◆ Fill
- ◆ Rim

Each of these lights serves a specific function. (See Figures 12.2 and 12.3.)

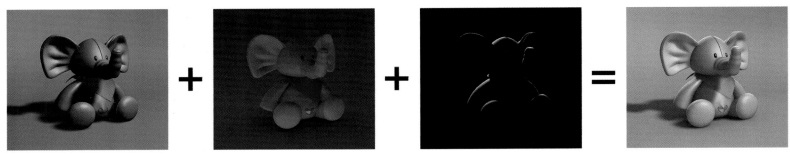

Figure 12.3 Key plus fill plus rim.

Overview of the Key Light

The *key light* is the dominant light in the scene (Figure 12.4). It sets the primary angle of illumination and has the greatest overall impact on the image. Its position and quality have a strong role in determining the mood of an image and shaping the form of subjects. It's responsible for most of the shadows. The key isn't necessarily the brightest light in the scene. The rim may be, and often is, the brightest. The key light is visually brighter than the fill, however. In an image, the key is usually easily identifiable.

Figure 12.4 Key light.

THE KEY LIGHT

Functions:

- Determines the primary angle of illumination
- Influences mood
- Shapes form
- Provides most of the shadows

Positions:

- About 30 to 60 degrees to the front and right of the subject

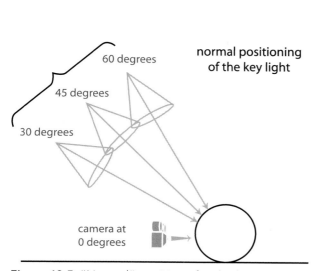

Figure 12.5 "Normal" positions for the key.

Figure 12.6 A still life lit with three-point lighting (Karen Chesney).

Generally, the key light is placed somewhere to the front and side of the subject, most often at a 30- to 60-degree angle of light to subject (Figures 12.5 and 12.6). This is by no means a rule, however.

Overview of the Fill Light

Fill light **is light that illuminates, or "fills in," the shadow areas**. Fill light (Figure 12.7) is always of lesser visual intensity than the key. In life, filling in of the shadows may be from secondary light sources, but it usually occurs from naturally occurring reflected and scattered light. Thus the quality of the fill is soft. The fill plays a supporting role to the key, yet the humble fill performs two important and related functions: controlling contrast and affecting mood. Images with little fill have higher contrast and more visual tension, while more fill has lower contrast and less visual tension.

A common position for the fill used in real cinematography/photography is in front of the subject relative to the camera and angled to the side opposite the key, thus illuminating primarily the shadow side of the subject (see Figure 12.8 for a diagram). Another common position is at or near the camera and pointed directly at the subject.

These positions, while providing a good starting point and valuable insight into the purpose of the fill, are often insufficient for digital lighters to get good results. Digital lighters have many special concerns when creating convincing fill. Section 12.1.3, "Fill Light," covers these concerns.

Figure 12.7 Fill light.

Figure 12.8 A common position for fill is roughly across from the key light and angled to the front.

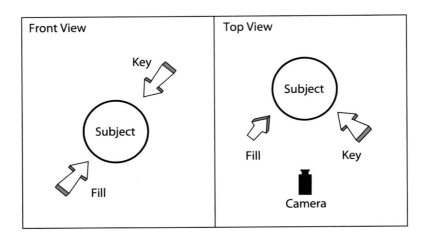

THE FILL

Functions:

- Controls contrast
- Influences mood

Positions:

- From the camera
- Across from the key

Overview of the Rim Light

Rim light **provides a thin line of illumination around the subject** (Figure 12.9). The primary function of rim light, or "backlight" as it's sometimes called, is to separate the foreground subject from the background. This separation both enhances the illusion of depth and emphasizes the subject by drawing the eye to it, similar to <u>underlining words</u> in a sentence.

Rim light is positioned almost directly behind the subject, relative to the camera (see Figure 12.10 for a diagram). Its position is angled up and/or over a small amount to achieve a thin line of illumination relative to the view.

Figure 12.9 Rim light.

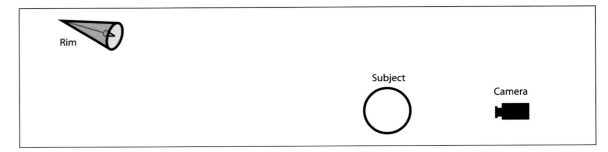

Figure 12.10 The position of the rim light.

THE RIM

Functions:

- Separates the subject from the background
- Emphasizes the subject
- Adds depth to the scene

Position:

- Behind the object relative to the view, angled up and over slightly

Why It Works

Three-point lighting has its roots in the early days of stage theater, long before the days of cinema. During this time, certain visual problems presented themselves. Actors needed to be seen and the audience oriented to the action (in came the key light). Obscuring the actors with too many dark shadows wasn't desirable (in came the fill light), and furthermore, the stage had limited depth, and the actors tended to disappear into their backgrounds (in came the rim light). Thus three-point lighting was born and remains a viable solution to these fundamental visual problems today. Countless theatrical productions, films, and photographs over the decades have used three-point lighting effectively to create outstanding imagery in a variety of styles. At the present time, every major digital film house uses three-point lighting in some aspect or other. But just how could this simple formula be so successful and adaptable? There must be more to it than initially meets the eye. Three-point lighting "works" for a few important reasons.

1. *Most scenes have a primary light source.* The concept of a *key light*, a single dominant light in a scene, is in line with our perception of the world. We live in a world with a single dominant light source—the sun. When creating imagery for film, often a dominant light will be set even if in life the light would be ambiguous. Why? To orient the audience. Is there always a primary light source? No, of course not. We will talk about these times and many other exceptions to the "rules" in following sections. Yet suffice it to say, the *majority* of the time there is a primary light source, which is why the concept of the key light came about and is used today.

2. *We need a way to control the amount of illumination reaching the shadow areas.* When telling visual stories we may need to better see the action taking place in the shadows or need to influence the mood by employing more or less contrast. Therefore, in cinema the amount of light reaching the shadows can't be left to chance, but rather it's carefully controlled. Introducing the *fill light*.

3. *We need ways to enhance the perception of depth.* When dealing with film, video, and photography, we are dealing with a two-dimensional representation of a three-dimensional subject. One of the tasks of lighting is to regain some of the sense of form and depth. One way to do this is with a *rim light*. Rim lighting is used extensively in modern film.

4. *Three-point lighting can be adapted to more or fewer lights.* This may be the most important point for lighters who are just learning three-point lighting. One reason the three-point lighting scheme is so adaptable is because it's not necessarily "three lights" at all! New lighters are often instructed to "put three lights here, there, and there" but often find it limiting, as it would be for most scenes. The reality is the lighting scheme can be modified in many, many ways. Practically speaking, there are often *more* than three lights, but other times *fewer* than the three are needed. In these cases, it's certainly arguable that these setups are then no longer three-point. When adding or removing lights, however, the three-point scheme is still the foundation, and thus is able to be modified for a variety of situations.

5. *The three-point lighting scheme gives us a vocabulary by which to analyze and discuss our lighting.* The importance of a common vocabulary of terms in a production setting cannot be underestimated. A large team of people working together must be able to communicate effectively. In digital production, supervisors need to be able to give feedback on an image in a way that everyone on the team understands. The terms of "key," "fill," and "rim" and the method of three-point lighting are commonly used and have become a means by which to analyze a shot. They also provide a useful basis for naming and organizing a digital scene.

6. *Three-point lighting ties digital lighting to the tradition of film.* By learning and mastering classic setup, the digital lighter builds an understanding of traditional cinematography and is also able to apply these techniques in the present day. Today's CG lighting has evolved out of early filmmaking and both have the same concerns—only the tools are different.

Students of lighting are usually introduced to three-point lighting early on. Because lighters typically only get a brief introduction to three-point lighting, they often aren't able to get it to work for them on a consistent basis. Lighters often then become frustrated and "throw the baby out with the bathwater," discarding the setup, and claiming that it's too formulaic to be useful. This is unfortunate, because they lose the advantages of a common vocabulary and a way to evaluate their lighting and images.

The fact is, three-point lighting in CG is not the same as three-point lighting in life. The problem for digital lighters is that they need more than a brief introduction to it in order to get the setup to work for them. By learning a few additional techniques, they will make their version successful. These techniques will be covered throughout this chapter. Now that we've gotten a basic understanding of three-point lighting, let's take a closer look at each light function.

12.1.2 KEY LIGHT

The key light ("key") is the most critical light in the scene. As the dominant light, all of its attributes—position, color, diffusion, and intensity—will highly influence the look. If the key isn't right, your lighting won't be right. In most cases, the first thing a digital lighter does when beginning to light the scene is to place the key.

Positioning the Key

When first lighting a scene, consider whether you have a dominant light, and if so, from where is this light coming? Knowing the direction and motivation for your light will let you know where it should be placed. When evaluating this, you will want to check any other shots in the sequence for continuity in lighting direction. Other important considerations when placing the key are the level of realism desired, the mood desired, the amount of shaping desired, and where the shadows are falling.

It's often best to give the key a realistic placement. When placing the key, begin by determining where the real light would be (consider both direction and distance), and then place your digital light roughly at this position. It's surprising how many CG lighters don't do this and arbitrarily place their key light, oftentimes too close to the subject. On occasion, however, the "rule" of motivating your key may be broken. For example, sometimes a light is added where it might not logically make sense but it is needed to illuminate the actors' faces. If your key is not motivated, however, carefully scrutinize its effect to make sure it is not so unrealistic as to be distracting. One might say the rule is not "motivate your key" but rather "motivate your key unless there is a reason to do otherwise."

When integrating a CG element into a live-action plate, the key lighting on the digital element *must* visually match the key in the plate or the element will not integrate. In these cases a properly placed key that matches the motivation in the plate is essential. (For details on how to evaluate and match a plate, see Section 17.5, "Evaluating a Live-Action Plate.")

The position of the key also strongly influences mood due to what is familiar. An overhead key feels normal to us, since the sun shines from above. This is why a common and pleasing direction for the key is at about a 45-degree angle to the subject, give or take about 15 degrees (Figure 12.11). On the other hand, if the light is coming from an unexpected direction or its shadows hide what we wish to see, we will find it unsettling (Figures 12.12 and 12.13).

Figure 12.11 (Left) "Normal" lighting is about a 45-degree angle to the subject.

Figure 12.12 (Center) Top-down lighting hides the eyes.

Figure 12.13 (Right) Up-lighting can give a sinister or disorienting feel.

Figure 12.14 This image is a good example of a carefully chosen key, both in terms of position and quality. The soft light keeps a gentle mood with the light carefully placed to sculpt the form. Lack of fill leaves much in shadow, lending to a sense of mystery.

As the dominant light, the key plays the largest role in shaping form. Section 6.2, "Goal 5: Sculpting Volume," discusses in detail how to position your lights to enhance or minimize the illusion of volume. Consider these principles when placing the key (Figure 12.14).

Finally, when placing the key, keep an eye on where its shadows are falling. The key's shadows are usually the dominant ones in the scene, and if not well placed they can be an unwanted distraction or hide the wrong elements. Properly placed, they will add to the mood and design of the image. In life, all lights have shadow. In CG, we can choose to shadow our lights or not. Your key light should be shadowed, and it's usually a good idea to turn key shadows on right away. Since shadows affect the look and sometimes even the intensity of the lights, this helps avoid unwanted surprises and having to redo some of your lighting.

TIPS FOR PLACING THE KEY
- Place the key first: The position of the key is vital.
- If integrating with live action, the key must visually match the plate.
- Position the key with a realistic distance unless you have a reason to do otherwise.

Checklist for the Key Light

In addition to the position of the key, you will want to pay careful attention to its other attributes, such as quality, color, and intensity. These attributes will play a large role in the mood and level of realism in an image. If the scene is realistic, then obviously it's a good idea to match these attributes realistically to the light source you are imitating, deviating only as needed to achieve a particular aesthetic.

Carefully consider whether the key light needs attenuation, how soft it should be, and what its color should be. It is helpful to ask yourself a few questions when setting up the attributes of the key. Here is a list of questions to get you started.

- ✓ Is the placement realistic? Do you want it to be? Is it motivated? Does it match the plate (if combining CG with real footage)?
- ✓ How does placement look throughout the animation?
- ✓ Is placement affecting shaping and mood the way you want?
- ✓ What is the intensity of the key relative to the combined effect of the fills? Is this setting the mood you want? Does it match the plate?
- ✓ Is the key intensity above one? If so, check for clipping.
- ✓ Does the key need attenuation?
- ✓ What color is the light source you are imitating and where is the white balance of the image?
- ✓ Consider the light quality. Is the light large and near, or small and/or far? How is quality affecting the mood and shaping in your image?
- ✓ Where are the shadows falling? What about during the course of the animation?
- ✓ Are the settings of the key's shadow(s) appropriate to its softness/hardness?

12.1.3 FILL LIGHT

The fill light ("fill") controls contrast, and thus greatly influences mood. Controlling contrast is done by adjusting the amount of fill relative to the amount of the key (Figure 12.15). In life, light that fills in the shadows occurs naturally. When crafting an image, however, the digital lighter does not leave the amount of fill light to chance, but instead carefully controls it. As Chapter 4 discusses, controlling contrast is one of the largest influences on an image's mood. In general, the intensity of fill is determined by the mood desired and doesn't need to appear to be realistic.

Figure 12.15 Key plus fill.

The Key:Fill Ratio

The visual intensity of fill light is always less than that of the key. You may have heard recommendations for the fill's intensity, such as "no more than half the brightness of the key." This isn't necessarily true. The fill can be any intensity—as long as it's visually less than the key. By "visually less," I mean how the fill *looks* compared to how the key *looks*, regardless of the numbers it took to get there. (For an example of how the same intensity setting in key and fill can result in different key:fill ratios, refer to Section 9.1.2, "Factors Affecting Scene Luminance.") This relationship is measured in the key:fill ratio.

The key:fill ratio is a measure of the total key illumination to the total fill illumination. It's analogous to the lighting ratio (described in Chapter 7, "Goals 7–10: Providing Cohesiveness and Visual Interest"). The key:fill ratio is stated in terms of the fill, meaning that the fill is set to 1 in the ratio. For example, a key at twice the brightness of the fill has a 2:1 ratio.

key:fill ratio = total luminance in areas lit by the key : total luminance in areas lit only by fill

Certain genres typically use common key:fill ratios because of the levels of visual tension associated with them. Examples of key:fill ratios:

TV news	1.5:1
Sitcom	2:1
Drama	4:1
Action sequence	8:1
Horror movie	10:1
Film noir	16:1

The lighting in a shot may be termed "high key" or low key" depending on its key:fill ratio. "High key" images have low contrast, which really means lots of fill. "Low key" images, on the other hand, have high contrast. Low key refers to little or no fill, and typically has many darks. The terminology can be a bit confusing. While critical to photographers and cinematographers, digital lighters usually need only a casual familiarity with these terms.

High key: Low contrast, lots of fill. Ratios less than 4:1.

Low key: High contrast, little to no fill. Ratios greater than 4:1.

It's important, however, to be aware of the key:fill ratio in a general sense, as it's a way to analyze and discuss your scene. When your supervisor says, "This shot is high key," or "Be sure to match the key:fill ratio," then you will know what he means.

Fill Quality

Most fill light has no particular sense of directionality. It imitates scattered environment light that has no motivating source. Occasionally a fill will come from a specific secondary source and have a sense of directionality, but most of the time it should seem to come from anywhere and everywhere, as to best lift contrast without drawing attention to itself. The best kind of light to accomplish this is soft light.

Softness is one of the most important properties of fill, yet it's the property most overlooked by digital lighters. Recall the features of soft light:

◆ Little to no specular contribution

◆ Blurry, lifted shadows to no shadows at all

◆ Gradual and imperceptible terminators

Figure 12.16 (Left) This apple render shows the fill specular and terminator without any modification. Notice that the fills' highlights are unrealistic and distracting, and that the terminator looks hard and leaves dark blotches in the center of the apple

Figure 12.17 (Right) Here the terminators of the fill lights have been wrapped and softened to provide smooth and even coverage, and the additional specular highlights have been eliminated.

These are the visual attributes of fill. Without these characteristics your fill light is almost guaranteed to give you trouble. (If you haven't yet read Chapter 10, "Light Diffusion," be sure to read it now for a full discussion of soft and hard light.)

Digital lighters have a variety of ways to create fill, each having its advantages and disadvantages. The tradeoff is usually realism for speed. Often a lighter needs a bit more know-how than a beginning level to get good results, and some methods for creating good-looking fill can be rather advanced. The next two subsections discuss various techniques for creating digital fill and provide pointers for their use.

Placing Traditional Sources for Fill

Digital lighters add lights into the scene to create fill, similar to how the cinematographer adds lights to a real scene. Out of the six basic light types discussed in Chapter 1, the area light most accurately imitates soft light. Hard lights may also be used, such as spotlights or directional lights, provided their look is softened by using special techniques. (For methods to imitate soft light with hard light sources, see Section 15.3, "Faking Soft Light.") This section goes over how to place these added lights.

In general, fill light is placed wherever it can best illuminate the shadow areas. In real photography, very soft fill is easily created with large light sources, diffused light, and/or reflected light. As noted, common positions are either opposite the key light or roughly at camera. Digital lighters who are taught the three-point lighting scheme strictly based on the positions used by real-world photographers may have a tough time getting satisfactory results from their fills. The reason for this has to do with the soft nature of fill light. Rarely do you want to see a strong sense of directionality from your fill, and you always want to avoid any odd dark spots, which hard light tends to have but soft light doesn't. Depending on how you are creating your fill light, accomplishing these tasks can be tricky. Creating good-looking fill light is arguably one of the more difficult tasks of lighting.

The most common position for digital fill placement is on the opposite side from the key and still on the camera side of the subject, a position we refer to as *cross-key*. A common practice for the real-world lighter is to place a bounce card on the side of the subject opposite the key. This will reflect the key's light back into the shadow side of the subject. Cross-key fill is angled toward the camera in order to cover more surface area relative to the viewer. Here it will illuminate mostly the shadow side of the object and provide a little shaping. This is the position often taught to students of three-point lighting. In this author's opinion, this is the best *starting position* for the fill. A cross-key fill is a good way to block in your lights' positions and your key:fill ratio. I say "starting position," however, because the problem with a single cross-key fill is that there is typically insufficient coverage. The fill doesn't wrap around the object enough, and some areas appear too dark (pointed to by dark arrows in Figure 12.18). Coverage isn't smooth and even. Using only a single fill light also has a decided directionality. For example, in Figure 12.18 it can be seen coming from the lower left-hand corner.

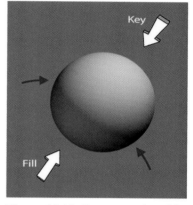

Figure 12.18 One cross-key fill. Notice the dark areas.

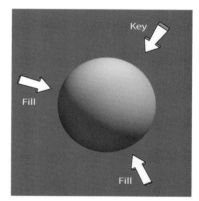

Figure 12.19 Two split cross-key fills. Notice that the coverage is even.

When using sources for fill, then you will almost always need more than one light to get full and even coverage of your subject. Just one fill in cross-key position generally won't cut it. To have even coverage, you will need to continue adding fills, adjusting intensities and positions as you go. Light can be made to wrap around an object more by replacing a single light with two lights, what I'll call a *split cross-key fill*. The illumination from these fills should overlap to look like one continuous light. In Figure 12.19, two cross-key fills are used, placed cross-key, and providing sufficient, even coverage. This setup has a number of advantages. For one, it can be achieved in any software package with a simple manual technique. Two, this setup, while simple, is highly modifiable for a variety of scenes. The positions can be modified to provide sculpting if desired, the intensities and/or colors of the fills can be varied from each other to reflect modulations in the environment lighting, more than two split fills can be used depending on need, and so on.

Figure 12.20 shows a more complex example of this arrangement. Three fills were used because this was the minimum number found to evenly light our character's more complex shape. A setup with three cross-key fills has an advantage for subjects on a ground plane: The two bottom fills are in perfect position to be used as bounce lights.

The other common fill position is to place a light at or near the camera, which I'll call an "at-camera" fill. Cinematographers and photographers may place very large light sources on either side of the camera, resulting in extremely soft light coming from the front. For the photographer, an important advantage of a frontal fill is that the shadows fall behind the subject and thus are hidden. After all, if you want your fill to seem sourceless, you don't want distracting shadows giving it away. While very useful for real-world lighters, placing a fill at-camera often doesn't work as well with CG lights. First, in CG we can turn shadows off, so unwanted shadows are not a concern and we lose this advantage. Even more importantly, in order for an at-camera fill to work, it must be a very, very soft light. A hard light placed at-camera produces dark edges around the subject that are not aesthetically pleasing and look unrealistic (Figure 12.21).

Figure 12.20 (Left) An example of three split cross-key fills.

Figure 12.21 (Center) Hard frontal fill plus key. Notice the unappealing dark edges around the subject.

Figure 12.22 (Right) This image has three lights—a key, an ambient with occlusion, and a greenish bounce. The occlusion density has also been lightened for the best look and ambient intensity adjusted.

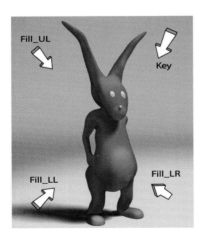

How many fills are enough? It depends on the complexity of your scene. I have found that when lighting a character with traditional lights, one fill light is rarely sufficient, and three to four is more typical. More than four and you will want to make sure that each light is essential; it is a common error to use too many lights. Of course, these numbers are far from rules, as each scene is unique. Just remember these two rules of lighting (and, yes, these are rules): (1) Only use as many lights as you need to get the job done, no more than that, and (2) always know what each light (and its shadow) are doing.

WORKFLOW TIP

When placing additional fills, you generally want to get rid of dark blotches. Look for these, and if (when) you find them, consider how you need to position your lights to get rid of them. Only if the existing fills cannot be angled to provide better coverage should you add an additional light.

Global Illumination and Fill

Rendering with global illumination gives the digital lighter a number of other options for creating fill. Global illumination algorithms calculate "real" bounce light, so your scene will naturally have more light filling in the shadows. When additional fill light is needed, you have a few additional techniques available, such as ambient light with occlusion, environment lights, or emissive geometry. Each of these approaches will be touched on here. Creating even-looking fill is generally easier when using global illumination, but requires more technical knowledge.

Using an ambient light with occlusion is a fairly straightforward way of generating an even, directionless fill. If you are incorporating ambient with occlusion into your scene, then ambient light can successfully be used to replace many fill sources. Ambient light produces no specular and is perfectly soft, but it needs to be shadowed by occlusion in order to keep from looking too look flat and unrealistic. Creating ambient occlusion is an intermediate-level skill—not too difficult but beyond the basics. When using ambient as fill, a suggested workflow is to add the ambient first, then add the key, then add any other fills and bounces you need. This is different from the usual workflow of adding the key light first. If you add the ambient last or near last, it will brighten all your other lights, and you'll end up having to do a lot of adjusting of all the intensities. You also may have added lights you don't need. Keep in mind, too, that ambient occlusion doesn't calculate any reflecting of light, it only darkens the scene. Reflected light will still need to be added if the scene calls for it (Figure 12.22). For an in-depth discussion of occlusion, refer to Section 16.4, "Ambient and Reflection Occlusion."

Environment lights are often used for fill. They are similar to ambient lights in that they simulate light coming from all around in the environment. Environment lights are more advanced in a few important ways, however. One problem with ambient light is that its color and intensity may be *too* uniform. Environment lights, on the other hand, can be mapped with an image so the lighting coming from them has variations in color and intensity. They also calculate "real" shadows, so if the map is brighter on one side, then the shadows will fall in the opposite direction, unlike occlusion shadows. Environment lights are then typically rendered with full global illumination, which adds reflected bounce light (Figure 12.23). For an in-depth discussion of environment lights, refer to Chapter 17, "Image-Based Lighting and More."

Figure 12.23 Our friend the bunny lit only in two lights: an environment light and a key. Global illumination is calculating the bounce. Notice the subtle variations in color (seen on the white cup).

A final technique for creating fill light is to use reflective or emissive cards. If rendering with a global illumination algorithm, a white card will bounce light the same as it would in life and can be used in the same manner—to reflect light back onto the shadow side of the subject. Emissive cards can also be used as soft sources of light. Many global illumination algorithms will calculate the emission of light from incandescent surfaces. Emissive cards can be uniformly colorized or mapped with images to provide specific control. For more detail on using cards as light sources, refer to Section 17.4, "Lighting with Cards."

Using cards, area lights, environment lights, and rendering with global illumination are all common techniques to achieve pleasing fill light. They require a large investment in rendering, however, so make sure you have time for them if you choose any of these options.

SOME TIPS WHEN WORKING WITH DIGITAL FILL:

- The intensity of fill can be chosen based on mood rather than realism.
- When working with lights that have directionality, more than one fill will be needed to create even coverage. This is especially true for hard lights.
- Large area lights make good choices for fill; hard lights have the advantage of rendering speed, but good results are more difficult to achieve.
- If using spotlights, keep your fills far from the subject.
- To quickly block in lights, a starting position for your fill is cross-key and cheated toward the camera.
- Set your key:fill ratio early, just after the key and fill are roughed in. This will be easier with fewer lights.
- Overlapping fills add intensities. As you add fills, reduce intensities to maintain contrast ratio.
- Remember that if the key is a high intensity, and fills/ambient overlap it, you may introduce clipping at the high end (values over 1) into your scene.
- Add/modify fills to keep from having dark blotches. Try splitting the fills to gain more coverage.
- Ambient with occlusion and environment lights are good sources of nondirectional fill and may be combined with IBL to increase their realism.
- When using ambient or environment lights as fill, place them *first* or just after the key, then adjust all intensities for the desired key:fill ratio.

12.1.4 BOUNCE LIGHT: A SPECIAL TYPE OF FILL LIGHT

Bounce light is a very specific type of fill: It's light that is reflected off one surface onto another surface. In life, bounce light happens naturally and doesn't need to be added. Most bounce light is due to the reflection of the key light off some surface. The most realistic bounce light will come from global illumination algorithms, such as radiosity or photon mapping, which will calculate bounce light for you. These algorithms take a long time to render, however, and while increasingly common, they are not always used. When not using GI, it is left to the CG artist to add bounce light with additional light sources. It's relatively easy to do if you follow a few simple guidelines. This section covers how to add your own convincing bounce light.

Both the intensity and color of bounce light are usually underestimated. Take a close look at many CG images you find in film and in books, and you will see that this is true: Not enough bounce light is one of the telltale signs of a CG image.

Like all fills, the quality of bounce light is soft, as it's diffusely reflected light. Bounce light is *always* softer than the original (non-bounced) light that created it. Unlike many other fills, bounce light *does* have a sense of directionality: It comes from the direction of the reflecting surface. Like other forms of very soft light, bounce light typically has no specular contribution, has indistinct shadows, and has very gradual terminators (Figure 12.24).

Figure 12.24 In this CG still life, notice the hard terminator from the key light, while the light reflected from the ground plane has a very wide, gradual terminator.

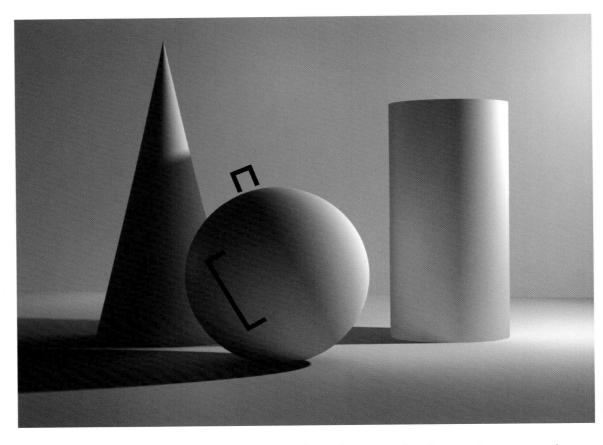

Reflected light takes on the color of the surface that it's reflecting, a phenomenon known as "diffuse color bleeding." For example, a white light shining on a green surface will reflect green light (Figures 12.25 through 12.27). It's not just the surface's color as found in its material setting, however. The bounce light color is the color the reflecting surface *appears* to be, when lit by the other lights in the scene. If you change the color of the other lights in the scene (especially the key), you will then need to adjust the color of the bounce light (Figures 12.28 and 12.29).

You can choose the bounce's color by eye, but matching colors exactly can be trickier than it seems, due to the unreliable optics of the human eye. It also isn't necessary. You can simply sample the color of the reflecting surface, which is much faster and more accurate. Then you can modify this color as needed. One modification you should make is to *set the value of the bounce color to 1*. This is to avoid having the color reduce the light intensity too much, making the actual intensity setting unclear. For example, a light with an intensity of .5 and a color with a value of .5 actually has an intensity of .25 (.5 * .5). See Figures 12.30 through 12.32 for examples.

Figure 12.25 (Left) Without bounce light, the duck is too dark on the bottom.

Figure 12.26 (Center) A white bounce isn't the right color and looks wrong.

Figure 12.27 (Right) A green that matches the floor is the correct color for the bounce.

Figure 12.28 (Left) A magenta key light. The bounce is the same green as the plane's material, but it's too green. Incorrect.

Figure 12.29 (Right) A magenta key light. Now the bounce's color is based on the color that the plane appears to be in the warm light. Correct.

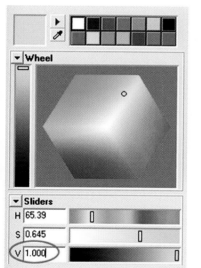

Figure 12.30 (Left) Set the value of the bounce color to 1.

Figure 12.31 (Center) The initial color sample of the reflecting surface (hue = 65; saturation = .645; value = .55).

Figure 12.32 (Right) The color of the bounce with a value of 1 (hue = 65; saturation = .645; value = 1.0).

Bounce light should be placed so that it seems to come from the reflecting source. It doesn't actually need to be placed at the reflecting source, however; it only needs to *appear* to come from the reflecting source. When using traditional lights (such as area lights, spotlights, or directional lights), an effective approach is two lights coming slightly from either side of the reflecting source and angled somewhat toward the camera in order to gain more coverage. An advantage of more than one light is that you can adjust the lights' intensity so that one side of your subject receives more bounce than the other. The shadow side of the subject would, in fact, receive less bounce, due to the cast shadow occluding some bounce light.

The closeness of the bounce light to the subject depends on the kind of light you are using. Area lights and emissive geometry give you the most realistic bounce light, due to their soft nature. Area lights used as bounce would be placed near the reflecting surface, or even closer to the subject if the subject isn't moving, to maximize their effectiveness (Figure 12.33). If keeping render times down to a minimum is a priority, then spotlights or directional lights may be used. Spotlights representing bounce light should *not* be placed at the position of the reflecting surface, but rather should be pulled very far from the subject (Figure 12.34). If spotlights are too close, they will reveal their hard, radial nature, which is not at all the light quality you are hoping to cheat. Directional lights can be placed anywhere, as long as they are angled correctly.

Figure 12.33 (Left) Area lights used for bounce should be placed near the reflecting source.

Figure 12.34 (Right) Spotlights used for bounce should be placed far from the subject.

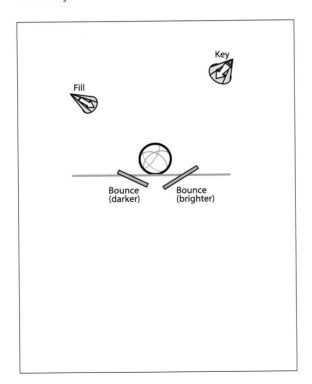

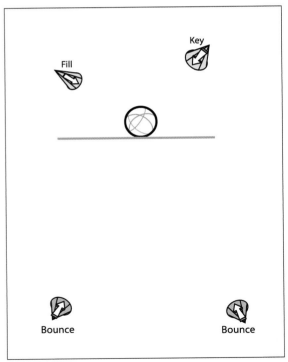

If your bounce lights are shadowed, be sure that they aren't shadowed by the reflecting surface. To correct for this, unlink the bounce lights from the reflecting surface or, if this surface is something like a ground plane or interior wall that doesn't need to cast any shadows anyway, just turn "shadow casting" off for this item.

Reflected light attenuates. Bounce light has attenuation beginning at the reflecting surface and falling off rapidly. Due to the very soft nature of diffusely reflected light, the rate of attenuation of real bounce is greater than an exponent of 2. CG bounce light without attenuation tends to "keep going" and looks odd on surfaces farther away. Area lights and emissive geometry placed near the subject will naturally fall off, and attenuation may not need to be added. If you are using spotlights or directional lights, on the other hand, you will need to cheat the attenuation so that it begins at the location of the reflecting surface and not at the origin of the light. If you don't do this, the attenuation will not fall off rapidly enough. To cheat where attenuation begins, you will want to carefully craft your light's attenuation. For methods to create digital attenuation, refer to Section 9.1.3, "Attenuation."

TIPS FOR CREATING YOUR OWN BOUNCE LIGHT

Creating your own digital bounce isn't that difficult if you keep the following in mind:

- Bounce light replaces some of the standard fills in your scene.
- Make sure the bounce light is very soft. It should be nonspecular, contribute little shadow, and have very soft terminators.
- Area lights and emissive geometry are the most realistic bounce lights, but spotlights and directional lights may be used to save render time.
- If using area lights or emissive geometry, place them near the reflecting surface. (They may even be cheated nearer the subject to gain more coverage.)
- If using spotlights, place them far from the subject.
- Try using two lights on either side and cheated toward the camera.
- Remember, less bounce comes from shadowed areas.
- Select the right color. Picking the color from a rendered image or background image is the most accurate.
- Add attenuation if needed, beginning at the reflecting surface.

12.1.5 RIM LIGHT

Rim light is one of the few lights that, by definition, is determined by placement. It's typically placed almost directly behind the subject relative to the camera, then cheated up and over a bit so only a thin line of illumination shows.

Rim light falls into the area of pseudo-realism. Its placement and intensity often do not really make sense. The position of the rim light may even move from shot to shot, so all subjects stay rim-lit. For example, two actors in a night scene may stay rim-lit even when the camera cuts from one over-the-shoulder shot to another (facing one actor then the other)—even though the light behind one actor should in actuality shine in the face of the other!

Rim light is often loosely motivated, meaning it has a motivating source when possible, but it can be unmotivated or cheated drastically. Unlike key light and bounce light, which have logical originating sources, rim light can and often is arbitrarily added to a scene. However, if there is even a faint suggestion of a motivating source, you should use it. For example, if there is a window in the background, the rim can seem to come from there, even if the window is in actuality too far away to contribute light on the subject (Figure 12.35). Other times, you can even add a rim that really makes no sense, if it's done for stylistic reasons. If you don't believe me, pay careful attention to the next film or television drama and notice how the rim crops up in all sorts of places it wouldn't normally be, even popping on and off between camera cuts.

Digital rim lights are often best placed pulled far back from their subjects. A good placement of the rim for many scenes is angled somewhat to the shadow side of the subject, though the placement will vary depending on the scene.

Rim Intensity

The intensity of the rim may be extremely bright. By "intensity" here I mean numeric value plugged into a digital rim's intensity parameter. Until you get used to it, it may be a higher number than you expect. In fact, it may be several times higher than the intensity setting of the key, even if visually it's not that much brighter. The reason for this is that the line of illumination

Figure 12.35 Even the suggestion of a light behind a character can serve as motivation for a rim (*Kung Fu Panda*, 2008, © DreamWorks Animation, courtesy the Everett Collection).

we see from the rim is very near the terminator, and therefore is only a fraction of the rim's full intensity. I often initially set the rim intensity about two to three times that of the key (for example, if the key is .8, try 2 for the rim). Of course, this serves only as a starting point and may be changed completely if needed.

Since the rim light is very bright, it needs full-density shadows. If you don't shadow your rim light or don't have full density on your shadow, you may end up with all sorts of light bleeding into unwanted areas. This is especially true for character lighting, where rim light can bleed into the mouth and light up teeth in a most unrealistic way.

Rim light is one that lends itself to light linking. It's not uncommon for different objects to have their own rim light with modified settings. By light-linking your rim light, you can have no rim contribution on some surfaces but keep it for others, or have a brighter rim on certain objects, such as the subject (Figure 12.36).

Figure 12.36 Rim light is shining *only* on the character in this animation by Leandro Ibraim.

Digital Concerns for the Rim

Creating digital rim has concerns specific to the digital lighter. The digital lighter really does need to know these concerns and some of their solutions in order ensure good-looking digital rim light. Digital rim is different from real-world rim in two significant ways:

1. Insufficient wrap
2. Can be too colorful

These differences can be problematic for the digital lighter, causing the rim to not look quite right unless he or she knows how to correct these issues.

Problem #1: Insufficient Wrap for the Rim

In life, rim light outlines most of the subject's silhouette. Digital rim, on the other hand, tends to wrap around a much smaller portion of the subject, which is what is meant by "insufficient wrap." This is primarily because real surfaces have fine surface details that scatter and transmit light, such as hair or fuzz on fabric. Digital surfaces don't have this microscopic detail, and thus the reaction of light on them is the same as a hard light on a perfectly smooth or flat surface, similar to lighting a bowling ball. This results in a small, tight area of illumination from the rim, regardless of the surface being imitated. This bright highlight, even when physically accurate, doesn't always make for the most pleasing rim light (Figure 12.37).

One solution to wrap light around an object is simple: Use more than one light. With the case of digital rim, it's often useful to use two rim lights that together look like a single rim with more wrap. If this method is used, it's often best to make the rim nonspecular, to avoid having two rim highlights that look odd and reveal the cheat (Figure 12.38).

Figure 12.37 (Left) With the digital render, the rim illuminates only a small area. The highlight from the rim exaggerates the problem, creating a small hotspot.

Figure 12.38 (Right) Render using two rim lights. Additionally, the rim lights have been made nonspecular. This technique is simple and can be accomplished in most software.

Another solution is custom light and/or surface shaders (Figure 12.39), which allow the user to manipulate both the thickness and wrap of the rim's illumination by adjusting material parameters rather than light position. While such custom shaders are standard fare in most production houses, few people have access to them in off-the-shelf software.

Figure 12.39 Custom shaders have long been used to improve the look of the rim light, as in this render from *Stuart Little*. (© 1999, Global Entertainment Productions GmbH & Co. Medien KG and SPE German Finance Co. Inc. All Rights Reserved. Courtesy of Columbia Pictures.)

Problem # 2: Incorrect Rim Color

The contribution from a digital rim is generally too colorful. What do I mean by "too colorful"? If you analyze rim lighting in life, you will find that rim contribution tends to be the color of the rim light itself, which is often white or near white, rather than the surface color (Figure 12.40). When lighting digitally, however, the addition of light merely brightens the existing surface color, so that a white light on a yellow surface makes a brighter yellow surface, not a whitish surface. When the digital light is brightened even more, the surface color in the rim area will simply clip. Possibly it clips to white, but this is an artifact and should be avoided. This problem is especially noticeable on highly saturated surfaces.

Figure 12.40 Notice how the color of the rim in this photograph matches the pale gold color of the light, not the green of the surface.

The simplest solution, if you have access to it, is again custom light and/or surface shaders that allow the lighter to adjust the color of the rim with material parameters. Figure 12.1 is an example from *Stuart Little 2* in which the character Margalo has highly saturated yellow feathers. In order to create a white rim effect, special shaders were used. Unfortunately, specialized shaders are not always available to the average user.

A solution that can be used by anyone is to render out a separate pass for the rim light. The rim pass can then be color-corrected as desired and re-integrated with the rest of the image in the composite (Figures 12.41 and 12.42). An advantage of this technique is that in addition to color, overall intensity and gamma can also be adjusted in the comp. The disadvantages include added complexity to your workflow and not being able to preview the result until the compositing stage. (For more on rendering passes, see Chapter 18, "Multi-Pass Rendering.")

Another solution sometimes proposed is to make the rim specular only, because the specular is the color of the light. I actually don't recommend this solution because it will only make problem #1 (insufficient wrap) worse. A specular highlight naturally covers a small area, making a tiny bright spot. Another disadvantage of this approach is that not all surfaces have specular.

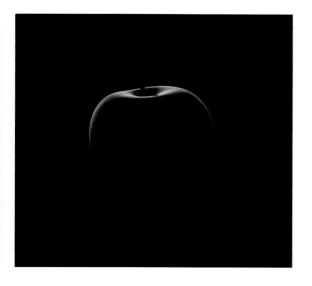

Figure 12.41 (Left) A desaturated render of the rim light only.

Figure 12.42 (Right) Composite image showing the apple with a rim pass that has been desaturated.

In general, specular contribution from a rim can at times be problematic. Due to the backward-angled position of the rim, rim specular will give bright specular highlights on horizontal planes, such as ground planes. Most lighters have experienced at one time or another the glare of a rim highlight on the ground plane. These highlights often end up too bright and distracting. As noted, rim specular will also exacerbate the problem of insufficient wrap and reveal the cheat if more than one rim is used. For these reasons, it's often best to reduce or eliminate the specular contribution from your rim light(s).

When using rim light, each scene is unique. A general observation is that in many CG scenes, the rim light needs special attention. By paying close attention to how your rim is illuminating the different objects in your scene and following some of the techniques here or others if needed, you should be able to make a successful rim each time.

TIPS FOR DIGITAL RIM:
- Rim lights may be loosely motivated.
- Most often pull the rim far back from the subject.
- Try placing the rim more on the shadow side of the key.
- Rim lights typically need full-density shadows.
- Two rims may be needed to wrap more.
- Color-correct the rim if it's too saturated.
- Reduce or eliminate rim specular if it's distracting.
- Make sure you know what the rim's shadows are doing.
- Link the rim to certain objects when necessary.

12.1.6 Section Summary: A Final Comparison

Here's one last look at two images. Figure 12.43 uses standard three-point lighting as one might initially be taught it, using just three lights in "recommended" positions and out-of-the-box settings, while Figure 12.44 uses the techniques we have discussed.

Figure 12.43 (Left) An apple lit with three-*light* lighting (just three lights) in "recommended" positions and no extra treatment. Ugh!

Figure 12.44 (Right) An apple lit with three-*point* lighting with some special techniques applied. Much better.

The techniques used in Figure 12.44:

Key

◆ No special techniques

Fill

◆ Three cross-key fills/bounces used.
◆ Specular contribution reduced in intensity and broadened in size.
◆ Terminator extended past 90 degrees and softened.
◆ Ambient with occlusion was used to lift key shadow and provide a contact shadow at the base of the apple. Occlusion is not at full density.

Rim

◆ Two rims used, one on either side.
◆ Rims made nonspecular.
◆ Rim contribution whitened.
◆ Rim light-linked to only shine on apple.

Table 12.1 Comparison of Key, Fill, Bounce, and Rim Lights

Function	Key	Fill	Bounce	Rim
Purpose	Dominant light in the scene. Provides shaping. Influences mood.	Controls contrast. Influences mood.	Special type of fill, adds realism. Not needed in real life or if using GI.	Separates foreground from background; emphasizes subject.
Position	Typically 45- to 30-degree angle. Placed near actual light source is best.	Wherever it can best illuminate shadowed areas; typically "cross-key."	Coming from the direction of the reflecting source.	Behind subject, far away.
Motivation	Typically motivated, unless there's a reason to do otherwise.	Not necessarily motivated.	Always motivated. Typically a reflection of key light off a surface.	Loosely motivated or unmotivated.
Intensity	Any brightness, brighter than the fill. Not necessarily the brightest light in the scene.	Less intense than the key.	Less intense than the key. Relative to key intensity and the brightness and proximity of reflecting source.	Brighter than fill, may be brighter than the key. Can be the brightest light in the scene.
Diffusion	Directional, soft or hard.	Soft, nondirectional.	Directional but soft.	Directional.
Shadows	Should be shadowed.	Very soft shadows to no shadows.	Very soft shadows to no shadows.	Should be shadowed at full density.
Digital Concerns	None.	Often need multiple fills unless using ambient or environment lights. Can be difficult to create directionless fill and keep render time down.	Often need two bounce lights to gain enough wrap. Often need cheated attenuation. Unnecessary if using GI.	Often need two rims to gain enough wrap. Often need to whiten contribution.

12.2 BEYOND THREE-POINT LIGHTING

So far we have been taking a close look at using three-point lighting in its traditional sense: using key, fill, and rim. We've seen that the three-point lighting scheme isn't necessarily only three lights, and that for digital lighters it often takes several lights to convincingly portray the look of one. The fact remains that while three-point lighting suits many scenes, it's not always the lighting setup that is best for a given scene, and it's certainly not the only lighting setup available. Using three-point lighting is far from a rule and more of a guideline.

For many CG artists, when three-point lighting doesn't apply to their scene, they opt for free-form lighting instead, simply placing lights here and there in the scene to brighten one area and then the next. However, this type of lighting often results in lots of lights, which may or may not work for a variety of view angles. The artist may then forget which functions his lights are performing. If the artist didn't assign a naming convention for his lights, he may have difficulty recalling on what "spotlight6" is shining without having to test it. Don't feel badly if this sounds all too familiar—most of us have been there.

Many scenes are variations and deviations of the classic three-point setup. In the next sections we will look at how three-point lighting can be modified to have more or fewer lights, forming the basis for many setups from simple to complex and thus fitting a wide variety of scenes. By building on the classic setup rather than discarding it, we maintain a sense of each light's function and retain the advantages of a common vocabulary and a means to organize our files.

12.2.1 WHEN LESS IS MORE: ONE- AND TWO-POINT LIGHTING

Many scenes use fewer than three "points" of light. While these setups are one- or two-point lighting, I tend to think of them as three-point lighting with fewer than three points. This is because these scenes have a subset of the three functions of lights as defined in the three-point lighting model. So instead of thinking, "This is a two-point lighting scene," where I'm not sure what those two points are, I instead think, "This is a scene with key and fill only, or a scene with rim and fill only." Describing the scene this way gives me more information about its lighting. The definition is relatively unimportant, however. Whether opting for a two-light setup or an eight-light setup, what is important isn't the exact number of lights, but their *uses*. By retaining the concept of "key" as primary light, "fill" as lifting the shadows, etc., we have a much better grasp of the *purpose* of each light.

The same guidelines apply to one- and two-point lighting as for three-point, in that it often takes multiple digital lights to create the look of a single light and so forth.

Key and fill only: A common setup is to have just key and fill. Rim light is cinematic and stylistic and largely optional. The popularity of rim light has waxed and waned depending on the times. Many scenes don't have a rim light. A rim shouldn't be forced into the scene if it doesn't add anything visually, isn't needed for realism or continuity, or doesn't fit the story.

Rim only/rim and fill only: A scene with rim only will have very little visual information and will feel particularly ominous or mysterious, since the subject is hidden but for an outline. Fill and rim combinations also lend a mysterious feel.

No fill/only fill: Scenes with no fill lend themselves to high drama due to the strong contrasts and many blacks. A scene with fill only, on the other hand, will be the opposite—very low-contrast and either peaceful or stagnant.

Key only: Using only a key will create strong contrasts, but it need not result in a harsh image. In life, and if using global illumination, a key will naturally produce bounce light. If not using global illumination, a true one-point setup with only key is rare, as bounced light will still need to be added.

12.2.2 When More Is More: Background Lights, Kickers, Eyelights, and Practicals

Many scenes call for additional lights whose purpose does not fall into one of the three primary categories of key, fill, and rim. Among these are background lights, kickers, eyelights, and practicals.

Background lights: As the name suggests, the *background light* does just that—illuminates the background. Sometimes the setup of key + fill + rim + background light is known as *four-point lighting.* As in the case of the other categories, you don't literally need one background light. It may be one, but it's often several. The important thing is that a background light's function is to illuminate the environment, or background.

Kickers: A *kicker,* or sidelight, comes in from the side/back. It differs from the rim in that the rim is placed mostly behind the subject, providing only a thin line of illumination, while a kicker comes in more from the side. Unlike a rim, a kicker provides extra definition and shaping to the subject (see Figure 12.45). Often kickers are lumped in with the rim by digital lighters, though their purpose and position are actually somewhat different.

Eyelight: An *eyelight* is used extensively in cinema and falls under the category of hyperrealism. It is a low-level light that is strategically placed to create highlights in the eyes of actors. No practical light that would actually cause such a highlight needs to be in the scene; an eyelight is purely for effect. Digital characters often look more lifelike with eyelights, and the digital lighter has the added advantage of being able to make the light contribute specular only (Figures 12.46 and 12.47).

Practicals: A *practical* imitates some real source of light that you can see in the scene. It may be serving the purpose of key, fill, rim, background light, etc. As such, it's not a light type per se, but it's still a term with which lighters should be familiar.

Figure 12.45 (Left) Use two kickers, one on either side, for an alternate lighting setup that sculpts form and provides drama.

Figure 12.46 (Center) Without an eyelight.

Figure 12.47 (Right) With an eyelight. The addition of an eyelight, while not realistic, can be used for effect.

12.2.3 Environment and Multi-Character Lighting

Three-point lighting lends itself well to subject lighting. However, when multiple characters and environments are involved, lighting setups tend to get more complex. Many environments need an approach that has been modified from basic three-point in order to be successful.

Full CG Environment Lighting

Lighting a full CG environment often does not follow a simple three-point setup, since an environment may or may not have one dominant light. Natural outdoor scenes often do have a key, such as a sun or moon. Indoor and artificially lit environments, on the other hand, often have several strong light sources with no single one dominating, such as a street with a row of streetlamps or a room lit by several lamps.

Additionally, environments often don't have rim light present throughout. The rim is typically reserved for emphasis on the subjects. (Remember that rim light separates foreground from background.) To indicate depth, environments instead often have *atmosphere* (fog) added, or in some cases, *defocus* provides a depth cue.

Most environments do still have some level of fill, as the task of controlling mood and contrast is relevant to the whole scene. Fill, in environments, illuminates the scene overall. If using global illumination, then bounces and much of your fill light will be calculated by the renderer. If not, additional fills and bounces are often added to correctly illuminate certain objects and may be light-linked to them.

Formulas for lighting an outdoor scene lit by natural sun or moonlight do not have to be particularly complex. Naturally lit environments usually have two kinds of light: a direct light in the form of the sun or moon and an indirect light in the form of scattered light. The scattered light in natural settings is known as *skylight*. The colors and intensities of both the direct and indirect light vary during the course of the day. (For specifics on natural light color, see Chapter 3, "Goal 1: Establishing Setting.") In terms of our friends from three-point lighting, the sun or moon provides either a key or rim, while the skylight provides fill: two-point lighting. For example, a common formula for night scenes is a low-level blue fill combined with a white rim and no key. A very cloudy, snowy, or foggy day will obscure the direct light, leaving just fill: one-point lighting. Other times the three-point lighting scheme is worked in, with the sun or moon as a rim and just a suggestion of a key to provide shaping, or the sun/moon acting as the key and the rim coming from some other source.

One easy, rather simple setup for natural outdoor exteriors is to use a directional light combined with an ambient with occlusion, plus a few bounces as needed. A directional light is a good choice for sunlight or moonlight because these lights imitate very distant lights that fill the environment. Ambient with occlusion is a good choice for skylight because, like skylight, it's completely diffused. Another option instead of ambient with occlusion is an environment map, which can be mapped with a gradient of color or image representing the sky.

TIP

Many outdoor scenes benefit from a subtle, soft top-down light as well. This light should have no specular and contribute only a very soft light shadow. This light can be used to enhance the feeling of top-down skylight or be used to extend the range of the key. Try adding one to your exterior scenes and see how it works for you.

Environments with many artificial lights are another matter entirely. These environments have several strong light sources placed throughout. In this case, consider the many practical sources in the scene, both in view and out of view. Lights should be placed throughout the scene to imitate these sources. Many of these sources will be motivated and will have placements that look to plausibly be coming from somewhere. Lights that are nearby to the surfaces upon which they shine should attenuate. Attenuation may be simply "turned on" to linear or quadratic or crafted more artistically, as described in Chapter 9, "Light Intensity." The overall level of fill should be designed based on mood—you will have a lot of leeway on what the audience will accept.

When you are dealing with an environment that has multiple lights, your scene can become complex very quickly. You will want to keep track of each of the lights you add and what light source it's representing. When your lighting setup is more complex (see Figure 12.48 for an example), keeping track of each light becomes critical in order to avoid confusion and maintain control. In these types of situations, naming everything descriptively and staying organized is essential.

Figure 12.48 A complex CG environment from *2012*. (© 2009, Columbia Pictures Industries, Inc. All Rights Reserved. Courtesy of Columbia Pictures.)

Digital Characters in Full CG Environments

Characters, in general, lend themselves to three-point lighting. You may wonder, if subjects lend themselves to three-point lighting and environments often do not, how do you light characters in CG environments? Do we use three-point or not? The answer is yes—and no.

Even if the lighting in the environment doesn't have a three-point lighting setup, the character may still be lit with this classic setup or some derivative thereof (Figure 12.49). While the environment may not have any single dominant source, any given character in this environment often *does* have a single light as dominant. This often has to do with proximity. Artificial light sources often show the effects of attenuation, so the closest appears the brightest. Thus, light that is closest to that character will be dominant and will become a key.

Additionally, just about any other light that is behind the character can serve as a rim, even if the light wouldn't really reach that far. Rim may be added to the characters even if it's not found throughout the environment or has only loose motivation. Mystery rims—rims that appear out

Figure 12.49 In this scene from *Arthur Christmas*, Arthur still manages to have key, fill, and rim, even when the environment does not. (© 2011 Sony Pictures Animation Inc. All Rights Reserved. Courtesy of Sony Pictures Animation.)

of nowhere—are surprisingly accepted by the audience. Remember, too, that rims are optional; not every scene needs one.

Finally, the fill throughout the environment will serve as the character's fill, completing a three-point setup for the subject. For example, a character on a street with several streetlamps will have as his key the lamp that he is standing under. A different lamp, store window, or moonlight behind him can all serve as rim if one is desired, while fill is from the dim blue skylight and perhaps bounce light. If the character is moving in and out of various strong sources, on the other hand, there is no single key, but there still may be rim and fill.

As a workflow, light the environment first. Next, place your character or characters in the environment and render to see how they look without any special lighting on them. Check your renders with your fingers crossed. Sometimes everything looks great with no further treatment, but chances are your characters will look only so-so in many cases. At this point you will want to specialize the lighting for them. You may need to split out separate linked lights for the characters, and three-point lighting comes into play for the subjects. On one character, the table lamp suddenly becomes the key light. Another character may have the same key, or may have as its key the light from the window, and so forth. If lights are split out for a character, it's best to name them according to the function they serve for that character.

A good rule of thumb when adding complexity is to add complexity only as needed. Remember, a lighter should never lose track of what each light is doing. If he does, chances are he has too many lights. Also, stay organized with your lights—group and name them logically in your scene to avoid confusion.

Multi-Character Lighting

When multiple characters appear in an environment, the lighting often becomes more complex. It's not uncommon for lighting that looks great on one character to not look quite right on another. When this happens, lighting for certain characters may be split out and made linked and exclusive. These lights are then tweaked slightly to gain the best look for each character.

Lights that are split out should still *appear* to come from the same source. For example, two characters may both be in sunlight, which is one light, but the lighting setup has each character with its own key. The attributes of each key are modified slightly for each character in order to achieve the best possible look. While this practice may seem a bit odd, it holds true for both CG lighting as well as real film. Remember, lighting for film or video isn't true realism, but it's hyperrealism, where reality is modified and adjusted for aesthetic and storytelling reasons. However, since splitting out linked and exclusive lights is not "really real," care must be taken on the part of the lighter to ensure that he has not gone too far, and the scene as a whole still has cohesion and is believable.

If the subjects lie on different planes (foreground, mid-ground, background), then varying their lighting can be an effective way to enhance depth. Sometimes, due to different luminance values of fabrics, a character's clothes need special lighting that is separate from his face. Sounds elaborate, but this is often done. At one time, cinematographers would regularly use a seven-light setup consisting of key, fill, rim, background, kicker, eyelight, and clothes light.

When lighting multiple characters it's best to follow this methodology: Start by lighting all the characters with the same lights. Render and evaluate the scene. If the light looks good on one character and not the other, try modifying the settings and positions of the light so that it looks good on all characters or as many as possible. Only after you have pushed a single setup as far as you can and are still not getting satisfactory results for some of your characters, should you then go the route of creating linked and exclusive lights on certain characters.

Characters may not share the same sources as their key or rim (Figure 12.50). For example, the same streetlamp that shines as a key on one character may serve as the rim on another depending on how the characters are positioned in the environment and the angle of view. This is all fine; the only dilemma is what to name the light. Anything is fine as long as it makes sense to both you and others and follows your naming convention.

Figure 12.50 In this shot from *Ice Age* (2002) the fire serves as a key on Manfred the mammoth, as a kicker on Diego the saber-toothed tiger, and as rim on Sid the sloth. (© 20th Century Fox, courtesy of the Everett Collection. All rights reserved.)

Digital Characters in Live Action

As noted, characters in general lend themselves to three-point lighting, and this holds true for characters of all kinds, be they real actors on a real set, full CG, or some combination thereof—like digital characters composited into a live-action set. What does change, however, are the techniques used and some of the concerns of the lighter.

The bottom line for lighting digital characters in a live-action set is that the character lighting must match the live-action set lighting. If the digital element doesn't match exactly, then the final product won't look right. Thus the focus of lighting a character for visual effects is not only making the character look good, but matching the plate with complete realism. How this integration is accomplished may be through a variety of techniques. In full CG, lights are built for the environment and then applied to the characters and modified as needed. In the case of the live-action set, and there is no CG environment or CG environment lights. Instead, lighting cues for the character or characters are taken entirely from the live-action plate (the real footage of the background).

Digital characters composited over live action are often lit with image-based lighting (IBL). By capturing an image from set (usually a high dynamic range image), the set lighting can be brought into the computer and used to light the digital scene. This method produces realistic and pleasing results as long as the image sufficiently matches the background plate. Using image-based lighting in this manner also helps ensure continuity between elements in a shot as well as shot-to-shot continuity.

Image-based lighting is not incompatible with three-point lighting, which is a common misconception. All image-based lighting does is provide a different means for delivering the light to the scene. This image may represent the fill, key, rim, practicals, or just about anything. You will want to evaluate the IBL in terms of three-point lighting. For example, you may ask yourself, "Am I getting a strong enough key from my IBL?" or, "Is this a good key:fill ratio for my shot?" and make adjustments as needed. IBL is discussed extensively in Chapter 17, "Image-Based Lighting and More."

12.3 CHAPTER CONCLUSION

This chapter covered much ground, looking in detail at the classic three-point setup with an emphasis on understanding how to apply this setup to your digital scenes. We've also looked at how this setup can be adapted to form the basis of other many other lighting setups. Once the functions of key, fill, and rim are clearly understood, these "points" of light can be used in any setup, from large to small, regardless of the technique used. Whether using all hard light sources and scanline rendering, or image-based lighting and global illumination rendering, the functions of key, fill, and rim have a place. Understanding how these lights function, what properties are suited to each, and how to implement them digitally will help you tremendously to master the art and technique of digital lighting.

12.3.1 Important Points

◆ Three-point lighting is a classic setup that is still often used and relevant today.

◆ Understanding three-point lighting will give the lighter a good foundation for understanding many other lighting setups.

◆ Digital three-point lighting isn't quite the same as lighting in life—a few special techniques are needed to be successful.

◆ Three-*point* lighting is not three-*light* lighting—more lights than three can be and often are used, as long as there appears to be only key, fill, and rim.

◆ The key light determines the primary angle of illumination, shapes form, influences mood, and provides most of the shadows.

◆ The fill controls contrast and influences mood.

◆ The rim separates planes and adds emphasis.

◆ The key light is the dominant light in the scene; however, it's not necessarily the brightest.

◆ Cross-key is a good starting position for the fill, but it usually needs further modification.

◆ When using traditional source lights for the fill, you will almost always need more than one fill to achieve sufficient coverage.

◆ Fill light is soft and usually directionless. Achieving soft fill with good render times can be a challenge for digital lighters.

◆ In general, position fill where it best fills in shadows.

◆ Environment lights and ambient lights can replace many fills.

◆ Bounce light is a special type of fill.

◆ Bounce light has a direction—from the reflecting source.

◆ Bounce occurs "for free" in life, but it must be added by the digital artist if global illumination isn't used.

◆ Bounce light is fairly easy to achieve if you follow a few simple guidelines.

◆ Rim light is only loosely motivated; rim light is largely stylistic and optional.

◆ Digital rim light doesn't wrap around the object as much as a real rim light would. More than one rim light will help to increase the wrap of digital rim.

◆ Digital rim light tends to be too saturated. Shader tricks can correct this, as can fixing it in the composite.

◆ Many other light functions round out most setups, such as background lights, eyelights, kickers, and practicals.

◆ Environments (other than natural day/night scenes) often don't lend themselves to three-point lighting.

◆ Characters *in* environments can still be lit by three-point if desired.

◆ As your lighting setup gets more complicated, staying organized becomes even more critical. Name your lights to avoid confusion and for when handing off projects to others.

◆ Remember to start simple: Light everything with only one rig and split out lights only as needed. Use as few lights as possible to get the job done.

◆ Never lose control of what each light is doing.

12.3.2 Terms

lighting setup	low key	four-point lighting
key	cross-key fill	background lights
fill	split cross-key fill	kicker
rim	at-camera fill	eyelight
key:fill ratio	bounce light	practical light
high key	one-point lighting	three-point lighting

12.3.3 Exercises

1. Image gathering: Find images from magazines and online that show a variety of lighting designs. Identify the lights in each image. Is the lighting three-point or another setup?

2. Light a simple plate of peaches or apples, or even just a plate of several spheres. (Use a rounded and not angular shape to better view your results.) Using traditional light sources and the techniques described in this chapter, light the scene with three-point lighting. Don't use environment lights, ambient lights, or global illumination.

3. Relight the scene from Exercise 2, but this time use an environment or ambient light with occlusion and global illumination.

4. Create your own still life, not spending too much time on modeling or texturing. Light the scene in two ways: (1) Use *fewer* than three "points," such as just rim and fill, key only, key and fill only, rim only, etc., and (2) light the scene with *more* than classic three-point lighting, incorporating background lights, practicals, eyelights, and/or kickers.

5. Create and light a simple outdoor scene with natural light. Using the techniques described in this chapter and the information about natural light found in Chapter 3, create a time-of-day animation, animating the light from dawn to dusk. Don't forget about bounce light—use global illumination or add it yourself.

6. Create an indoor environment scene with multiple lamps and one or two windows as light sources. First light and render the environment. Next place two characters in the scene, in different locations. Now light the characters, splitting out lights only when needed and using three-point lighting where applicable. Use additional light categories, such as background lights and practicals. Be sure to label the lights according to function and stay organized.

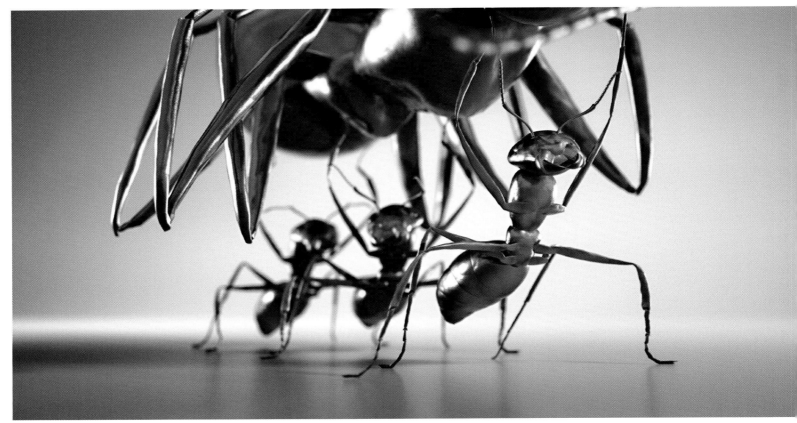

Figure 13.1 Shallow depth of field helps these ants appear tiny in this 3D render (Mark Evans).

Chapter 13
Camera Essentials

"The camera is the eye of the audience."

—John Alton, Cinematographer

On set, the person in charge of both the camera and the lighting is the cinematographer. The cinematographer (also called the *director of photography*) works closely with the director to bring the story to life visually. He or she selects the right camera angles and employs the right lighting to capture the story with memorable imagery. In the digital arena, however, tasks involving the camera are often divided. Many aspects of the camera, such as placement, movement, and framing, fall in the area of animation, while others, such as depth of field and motion blur, lie in the area of the lighting and rendering. For this reason, all 3D artists need knowledge of the camera. I highly recommend that every 3D artist have at least one photography and/or cinematography class under his or her belt to learn how things work on set and in the real world. Understanding how a real camera works is important because our virtual 3D camera often mimics its settings in order to produce the same look.

This chapter covers camera properties of greatest concern to the digital lighter, often with a comparison of how the real and virtual cameras differ. Aspects of the camera dealt with in other stages of the pipeline, such as camera continuity, camera motion, and so forth, are omitted. I encourage you to use other resources on these subjects. (Additional reading on these related topics may be found on the companion website, www.illuminated-pixels.com.)

13.1 LENS WORK: FIELD OF VIEW AND DEPTH OF FIELD

The 3D camera *imitates* many of the characteristics of a real lens but not all of them. With a real camera, many settings are interrelated in a rather complex way. In the virtual camera, on the other hand, many of the settings operate independently from each other. This gives the digital artist more freedom of expression but also means that when the real camera is to be imitated exactly, a fair amount of know-how is required.

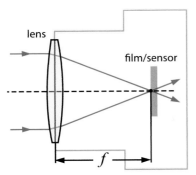

Figure 13.2 A simplified diagram illustrating light rays coming off a single point in space, focused by the lens into a single point on the film or sensor.

Figure 13.3 Photograph of a small subject using a long lens (photograph by MacDuff Knox).

13.1.1 THE LENS

The *camera lens* in a real-world camera is transparent optical device through which light passes when entering the camera body (Figure 13.2). Camera lenses are, in fact, made up of multiple lens elements, but to simplify things we'll refer to the camera lens as if it were only one element. In a simple point-and-shoot camera, like the one on your cell phone, this lens is very tiny and may be easy to forget about. In a camera with replaceable photographic lenses, the lens is much larger, usually a couple inches in diameter, and is shaped like a barrel in front of the camera. The job of the lens is to refract, or bend, the light as it enters the camera body, focusing and reducing the size of the image so that it fits onto the area captured by film (or the sensor in the case of a digital or video camera). (See Figure 13.2.) Without a camera lens, the light hitting the film won't result in an image, but instead it will be uniformly blurry.

13.1.2 FIELD OF VIEW

The *field of view* of a camera (FOV) is the angle at which the camera views the scene. This angle determines how much of the scene is in view. "Field of view" is sometimes simply called "angle of view," and it is measured in degrees. Deciding on the field of view is an important creative decision. It plays a large role in the framing of the subjects and the composition of the shot. The field of view should be decided early on along with camera placement. It does so because it affects the magnification of the scene as well as the amount of perceived distortion.

The field of view determines the magnification of the scene. If the angle is wide, much of the scene will be in view, which means that each object will be smaller (Figures 13.4 and 13.5). Conversely, when the angle is narrow, less of the scene is in view and objects will appear larger in frame (Figures 13.6 and 13.7). A wide-angle lens may be used when the scene is in a small room, for example, in an attempt to catch all the action and not have the view be too close to the subject. Very narrow angles of view are good for getting close up on tiny objects, such as coins or tiny flowers (Figure 13.3), or for enlarging sections of landscape far in the distance.

The angle of view also affects the perceived distortion of the scene (Figures 13.8 through 13.10). An angle of view on your camera that looks "normal" to us is about 40 to 60 degrees. For motion picture, the angle may be a bit less—anywhere from 25 to 55 degrees. Angles much larger or smaller than this will distort the scene. Very wide angles, such as 100 degrees or greater, will seem to enlarge space. A wide angle may be used to give a sense of a larger scale or presence to something. For example, a wider-than-normal view combined with an up angle will make a human figure seem more imposing and powerful. A wide angle may also be used to artificially distort the view for storytelling or aesthetic reasons. Conversely, very small angles such as 10 to 15 degrees will compress space. The distances between objects will seem shorter, and the perspective will flatten out. A narrower angle is generally preferable for close-ups of people, to avoid distorting the face.

Figure 13.4 A simple scene with a normal angle of view.

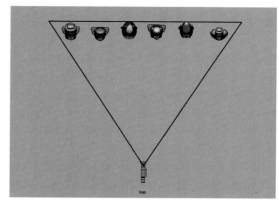

Figure 13.5 A diagram of the camera position and angle used in Figure 13.4. The camera FOV is 65 degrees.

Figure 13.6 The same scene as in Figure 13.4, but this time the camera field of view has been narrowed. The camera position hasn't been changed.

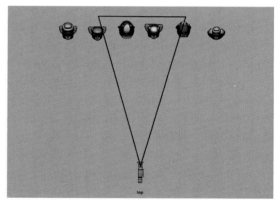

Figure 13.7 A diagram of the camera position and angle used in Figure 13.6. The position of the camera is the same, but the FOV is narrowed to about 30 degrees.

Figure 13.8 A scene with the camera placed far away and with a narrow field of view.

Figure 13.9 The same scene as in Figure 13.8, the only difference being the camera is now placed close to subject and with a wide field of view.

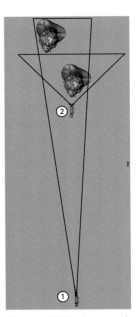

Figure 13.10 An overhead view of the cameras used in the previous two figures (Figure 13.8 used camera 1, Figure 13.9 used camera 2).

Figure 13.11 A variety of camera lenses.

Photographers and cameramen adjust the field of view by adjusting the *focal length* of the lens. "Focal length" is the distance from the lens to the plane in space at which incoming light rays are focused, which is typically the film or camera sensor. Different focal lengths can be seen in the differently sized barrels of photographic lenses (Figure 13.11). Focal length is measured in millimeters (mm). The relationship is: The longer the focal length, the narrower the field of view, and vice versa. This relationship can be seen in Figure 13.12.

A focal length may be long, normal, or short. A *long focal length* results in a narrow angle of view. Common long lenses for your average camera are from 80mm–200mm, such as 80, 85, 105, 135, 180, and 200mm. Telephoto lenses can range from 300mm to 1200mm! A *normal focal length* is one that approximates what a human eye sees. The angle of view seems natural, and objects don't appear flattened or distorted. A normal focal length is about 50mm. A *short focal length* gives a wider than normal view, resulting in greater distortion. Lenses that are known as "wide angle" are about half the length of normal. An extreme wide angle is known as a "fish-eye" lens and can be up to 180 degrees with extreme distortion. Common prime wide angle lenses for a 35mm camera are 35, 28, 24, 21, 18, and 14mm.

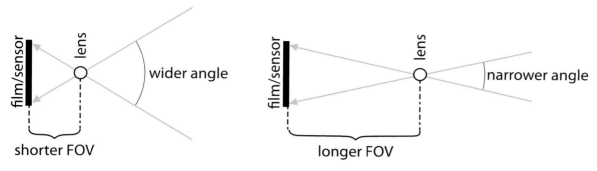

Figure 13.12 Diagram of the relationship between focal length and angle of view (treating the lens as if it were a pinhole).

When deciding the angle of view, the 3D artist typically may set *either* a "field of view" parameter *or* a "focal length" parameter. Since they are just two ways of doing the same thing, they are tied together—changing one automatically changes the other. The field of view parameter is fairly intuitive: It's the angle in degrees with which the camera views the scene. On the other hand, you set the focal length when you want to match a real camera more precisely.

THE FIELD OF VIEW/FOCAL LENGTH AFFECTS:

- Magnification
- Perceived perspective/distortion

13.1.3 Depth of Field

Depth of field (DOF) is the range around a focus point that is in acceptable focus. When a camera is focused, a certain distance away from the camera is seen most clearly. This distance is known as the focus point, or more accurately, the *plane of critical focus*. In front of and behind this plane, the sharpness will decrease. Objects gradually transition from sharp to blurry, and areas of the image will be slightly blurry but still acceptable.

Depth of field has a large impact on the appearance of an image. Having some areas in focus and not others will direct the viewer's gaze at the sharpest areas. Depth of field can be animated, forcing the viewer to look from one plane of depth to the next; an animated depth of field is known as a *rack focus* (Figure 13.13). Defocusing elements can keep them from being distracting, such as blurring the background of a portrait. Defocusing can also simply add visual interest. CG has its own considerations; defocus will add realism and may be necessary to match digital elements to a live-action plate.

Real-world cameras and virtual cameras handle focus very differently. In real cameras, the depth of field results from an interplay between the focal length and aperture. In the real camera, the *longer* the focal length, the *narrower* the depth of field is. This is why photography of tiny or far away subjects (which uses a long lens) has a very small depth of field (Figures 13.14 and 13.15). Also, the wider the aperture is (covered in Section 13.2.2), the shallower the depth of field is. This is why before the advent of faster film, very low light conditions that used very wide apertures often had very limited depth of field.

Figure 13.13 Changing the focus over the course of an animation is a way to control where the audience looks (images by Demorrius Sims).

Figure 13.14 This shallow depth of field is the result of a long lens and is typical of wildlife photography in which the animal being photographed is actually far away.

Figure 13.15 A shallow depth of field helps this CG render to imitate a small scale.

Digital artists can set their depth of field to anything they want, independent of any other camera attribute. This can be a blessing or a curse. It allows for more creative freedom, but it also makes matching a real camera a bit trickier. Depth of field generated by your virtual camera takes its settings from that of a real camera and imitates what a real camera is doing. Again, this is why understanding the real camera is very helpful, so that these settings make sense. Knowing how the real depth of field would look can be useful, as when trying to make objects appear small. When matching to a real camera, as in visual effects, accurate depth of field is essential. Unlike a real camera, which must be focused, the virtual 3D camera has all things in perfect focus all of the time. Depth of field has to be added if desired.

When adding depth of field as a 3D camera effect, the first step is to determine the distance at which you wish your camera to have crisp focus. This distance is the *focus distance*. Once you have set this distance, do a test render before proceeding to see how much defocus you have around this point and to make sure this distance is set where you want it. Next, adjust *how much* of the scene is in focus. In our virtual camera, the f-stop setting will determine the size of the depth of field. A smaller f-stop will give a smaller depth of field, meaning that just a narrow distance around the focal plane will be in clear focus. A large f-stop will give a larger depth of field, meaning that a larger area around the focal plane will be in focus. In short, the *smaller* the f-stop number, the *greater* the depth-of-field blur. I generally prefer to use one of the common real-world settings. Common numbers for f-stops are as follows:

f/1.4, f/2, f/2.8, f/4, f/5.6, f/8, f/11, f/16, and f/22

Many digital applications also give users an arbitrary multiplier on the amount of blur, so they can artistically increase or decrease the amount of defocus. This setting would be the last one to adjust, and only do so if you want to tweak the amount of defocus. If your depth of field isn't giving you what you want, check for these two common problems. (1) If everything in the scene is blurry, make sure that your point of focus is set to the correct distance. (2) Conversely, if everything still looks in crisp focus and you have depth of field turned on, make sure that your f-stop setting is low enough.

Adding depth of field to your render will significantly increase render time. Depth of field requires higher quality settings in order to not appear grainy. Because depth of field can add significant time to a render, it is rare that professional 3D animations calculate defocus in the 3D render. Instead, defocus is most often added after the render in the compositing stage. Defocusing in the composite is very fast and offers the most control over the final image. This technique is covered in Chapter 18, "Multi-Pass Rendering."

STEPS FOR ADDING DEPTH OF FIELD TO A VIRTUAL CAMERA
1. Turn it on (usually a check box found in the camera's attributes).
2. Select the distance of critical focus.
3. Determine the amount of blur around this distance by adjusting the f-stop. (Smaller f-stops create more blur; larger f-stops create less blur.)

13.2 CAMERA EXPOSURE

***Exposure* refers to the process of allowing light to strike the film or sensor** so that an image may be formed. The amount of light determines how bright or dark the final image will be. Photographers must carefully control the amount of incoming light so that the image is properly exposed. They work within the capabilities of the camera and film or sensor and properties of light.

Digital lighters don't have real cameras, real film, sensors, or existing light. They instead work entirely with added light in order to control the final luminance of the scene. This method of working marks a significant difference between digital lighters and real-world cameramen. In many ways, the digital lighter is freed from many of the concerns of the cameraman. But in other ways, a lighter faces some of the same limitations due to the fact that he or she is working with the same output medium (such as print or film) and is usually imitating the real-world properties. The digital artist should, therefore, understand how a real camera controls exposure.

Real-world cameramen control the film exposure with two controls:

- ◆ Shutter speed
- ◆ Aperture

13.2.1 SHUTTER SPEED

The shutter is the device in the camera that opens and closes to allow light to pass through the lens into the camera body, analogous to the door of a room. Most of the time, the shutter on a camera is closed. When a picture is taken or a video made, the shutter opens to allow light to reach and expose the film. For a video or movie camera, the shutter opens and closes once per frame. The amount of time the shutter is open is known as the *shutter speed*.

NOTE

Digital cameras may use a shutter or they may turn the sensor on or off. For the sake of brevity here, we will refer to only shutters and film, but the principles also apply to digital sensors.

Shutter speed is the amount of time the shutter remains open, and it's measured in fractions of a second, such as 1 second, 1/2 second, 1/4 second, and so forth. It's often notated by the denominator only (the number on the bottom of the fraction). For example, a shutter speed of 1/4 would be noted as simply "4." If the shutter is a disk, it may be described in terms of degrees; 180 degrees is a half disk, meaning the shutter is open half of the time. The longer the shutter is open, the more light reaches the film and the greater the exposure.

13.2.2 Aperture

How wide a shutter opens, known as *aperture*, **affects how much light reaches the film** (Figure 13.16). A good analogy for this is opening a faucet. If the faucet is open widely, it will fill a cup in a short period of time. If the faucet is only open slightly, allowing a dribble of water, then only part of the cup will be filled over the same period of time. Similarly, the total amount of light that is allowed in when the shutter opens is determined by both the size of the opening and how long it's open. The larger the aperture, the greater the exposure is. Aperture also effects depth of field. A wider aperture means a smaller depth of field and vice versa. Aperture is measured in f-stops.

13.2.3 This Business of "Stops"

An important term to cameramen and one with which digital artists should be familiar is "stop." The *stop* is the unit by which the light reaching the film is measured. To increase exposure by one stop means to *double* the amount of light reaching the film. Conversely, one stop less is *half* the exposure. The number of stops may be changed by adjusting by the shutter speed, the aperture, or both.

A more specific term is the f-stop. *F-stops* measure the size of the aperture. Just like with stops, each f-stop is double or half the size of the next, allowing in double or half the light (Figure 13.17). The number of the stop or f-stop isn't a simple "1, 2, 3, 4…," but rather f/2, f/2.8, f/4, f/5.6, f/8, f/11, f/16. Notice what is happening if you look a bit closer: Every other stop doubles the next: 2, 4, 8, 16. As the size of the f-stop number increases, the size of the aperture decreases. So, the *higher* the number of the f-stop, the *less* the exposure is.

Digital artists do not need to be concerned with the exact stop number; they do, however, sometimes work with relative stops. In other words, they may bring the intensity of their light "up a stop," which means they will double the intensity. When speaking of stops this way, the verbiage is more intuitive. "Up a stop" means more light; "down a stop" means less light. In professional circles artists will often hear the terms *stop* and/or *f-stop*. Supervisors will often ask to see the illumination "come up a quarter-stop" or "down a half-stop." They will often have viewing tools that allow them to view images "stopped up" or "stopped down."

When adjusting lights in terms of "stops," it's important that the digital lighter realize that the units of stops aren't in linear increments but are in logarithmically spaced increments. While a full stop is a nice tidy doubling of the light intensity, a half stop up is *not* going to increase the light by 50%, but rather only by 41%. When dealing with stops, Table 13.1 will be a useful reference.

Figure 13.16 Aperture—the size of the shutter opening.

 f/16   f/11   f/8   f/4   f/2.8

Figure 13.17 A diagram of various aperture settings, indicated by f-stop.

Table 13.1 F-Stop Multiplication Factors

Stop	Multiplication Factor	Stop	Multiplication Factor
Full Stop Up	2.0000	1 Stop Down	0.5000
3/4 Stop Up	1.6818	3/4 Stop Down	0.5946
2/3 Stop Up	1.5874	2/3 Stop Down	0.6300
1/2 Stop Up	1.4142	1/2 Stop Down	0.7071
1/3 Stop Up	1.2599	1/3 Stop Down	0.7937
1/4 Stop Up	1.1892	1/4 Stop Down	0.8409
1/6 Stop Up	1.1225	1/6 Stop Down	0.8909
NEUTRAL	1.0000		

To increase your digital light by a certain percentage of f-stop, refer to this chart. Look up the percentage of stop and then multiply the light's current intensity by the corresponding multiplication factor. For example, if your light intensity was .6 and you wanted to bring it up 1/3 stop, you would increase its intensity 1.26 times. In this example, the new intensity would be .6 * 1.26, or .756.

13.2.4 Film's Response to Light

Film has a characteristic response to light, which when graphed on a chart is noticeably nonlinear. What exactly do I mean by nonlinear? The best way to explain is to first look at a graph of how much the film responds when exposed to increasing amounts of light (Figure 13.18).

Figure 13.18 A graph of film's response to light.

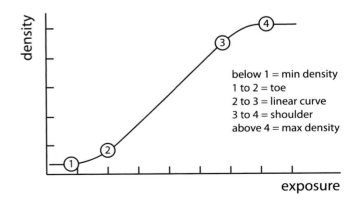

Characteristic Density Curve

below 1 = min density
1 to 2 = toe
2 to 3 = linear curve
3 to 4 = shoulder
above 4 = max density

When analyzing the graph, you'll notice that an even increase in light does *not* result in an even increase in the film's response. Initially, the film responds slowly, in that it takes a greater amount of light to produce a minimal change in density. This section of the graph is relatively flat and is known as its "toe." With the addition of even more light, the film begins to respond more quickly. In the middle section of the graph, a unit increase of light *does* result in a unit increase of film density, and the graph becomes linear at this section. As the film begins to reach maximum density (the point where it has completely reacted to light and where no more density is possible), the reaction slows down and the curve again flattens out. This range of the chart is known as its "shoulder." You may also notice that at all times a very small amount of the film has reacted, forming a slight density even with zero illumination.

The unique response of film to light has results in three distinct visual qualities. Firstly, an image represented on film will have *more contrast* than the original scene. Dark areas appear even darker than the original scene, since the film doesn't represent images as bright as they actually are at the very low end of the scale (in the "toe" area). Light areas appear even lighter in the shoulder area. This contrast in the appearance of film is sometimes referred to as a "film look." Each film stock has a different density curve, giving each film stock a unique and distinct film look.

Secondly, because of the gentle roll-off in the shoulder area, bright areas don't suddenly clamp to white, the way digital representations do. As noted in the Chapter 9, "Light Intensity," digital highlights don't roll off and are prone to abrupt clipping.

Thirdly, even in the absence of light the film will retain some value. Notice how the density curve never goes to zero. This means even in the darkest area, real film still retains a small amount of value and doesn't go to pure black (0,0,0). Digital renders, on the other hand, can and will go to pure black. When matching to a digital render to live-action film, the artist must make a conscious effort to integrate his or her renders so their darks have the same miniscule value, known as "matching the blacks." (Matching the blacks is covered in more detail in Section 17.5.2, "Seeing the Light.")

13.3 MOTION BLUR

The shutter speed affects *motion blur*. Motion blur is the blurring that occurs when objects move a noticeable amount during the time the shutter is open. The faster the motion or the longer the shutter is open, the greater the blur (Figure 13.19). Camera motion can also cause the image to move past the film or sensor during exposure, resulting in a blurring of the whole image (Figure 13.20). If the camera is tracking or panning with a moving subject, then only the stationary background will be blurred and the moving object being tracked will not (Figure 13.21). A camera moving forward quickly will result in radial blur (Figure 13.22).

Even though every real camera has motion blur, in digital cameras this feature defaults to off. This brings me to my first point on motion blur—don't forget to turn motion blur on for your animations. You really do need it. Without it, your animations won't look right. Yes, there may be the special occasion where you don't want motion blur for a theatrical effect, just like the real cinematographer, but unless you have a specific and compelling reason, you will want to turn on motion blur.

Figure 13.19 The foreground cars are motion-blurred due to their traveling during the exposure time.

Figure 13.20 Long exposure times can result in camera motion that causes the entire image to blur, as in this artistic example.

Figure 13.21 This camera was tracking with the car, resulting in the background blurring and adding to the sense of movement.

Figure 13.22 Radial blur from a camera moving forward very quickly.

Motion blur settings take their cues from how a real camera works. Motion blur is generally set in the render settings dialog box with a simple check box. Once it is on, a few additional settings become available that will control the look of the motion blur. Once motion blur is on, you should set *how much* motion blur (Figures 13.23 through 13.25). This is done by determining what percentage of the frame your virtual shutter is open. In life, for each frame of film, the camera shutter is open a certain percentage and closed a certain percentage of the time. How much it is open determines how much motion blur. Generally, a real camera is open 1/3 of the time and closed the rest. Virtual motion blur often defaults to having the shutter open for 100 percent of the frame, which is too much motion blur. It is generally best to reduce this amount. A good setting for motion blur is to have your virtual shutter open 35 to 50 percent of the frame. Greater amounts of motion blur will give a greater impression of motion; within reasonable limits, the amount of motion blur can be artistically crafted to give a sense of fast movement. Some applications indicate shutter opening by degrees. This is based on the fact that some real-life shutters are disks that rotate in front of the camera. A pie-sliced piece is taken out of this disk to allow light to enter once per rotation. In this case, 180 degrees would be open half of the time, while 120 degrees would be open 1/3 of the time.

Figure **13.23** No motion blur.

Figure **13.24** Motion blur of .33 (60 degrees).

Figure **13.25** Motion blur of .5 (180 degrees).

Figure **13.26** Linear motion does not accurately calculate trajectories that rotate or curve between frames.

The more motion blur you have, the higher your render quality needs to be to smooth out the result, increasing render time. On the other hand, the good news is that heavily motion-blurred objects need fewer shading samples, as you cannot make out much of the blurred surface anyway. (See Section 14.4, "Quality Control," for an explanation of shading samples.)

Another important setting for the digital artist to decide upon is how *accurate* the motion blur needs to be. As noted, motion blur adds to the render time, and most software has various options for calculating less realistic but faster motion blur. Digital motion blur often defaults to interpolating between the object's position at the start of the frame through to the object's position at the end of the frame, and is called *linear motion blur* because the motion blur of the object is calculated in a straight line between the start and end points. This is good enough in most cases but will be insufficient if an object is moving in an arc during the course of the frame (compare Figures 13.25 and 13.26). To accurately represent this, the position of the object in *between* the frame open and close must be taken into account. Motion blur that takes into account sub-frame positions is known as *multi-segment motion blur* (Figure 13.26). The artist generally can set how many sub-frame positions the renderer will account for. More sub-frame positions are more accurate but take longer, as you might assume, so be sure to use only as many as are necessary.

In spite of higher render times, for high-quality animations motion blur is rendered with the 3D scene as a camera effect. In-camera motion blur is the most accurate and is generally preferred. However, motion blur can be added as a post effect (in the composite) if speed rather than quality is the primary concern. Many compositing packages will add motion blur as a 2D effect, and some do a rather good—if not 100 percent exact—job of it. Some 3D packages will write out motion vector data that can be read into the composite to determine the motion blur.

TIP

A few miscellaneous tips when using motion blur—recall that depth-mapped shadows do not motion blur, while deep shadows and ray-traced shadows do. Turning motion blur off for test renders is one way to save render time.

13.4 CHAPTER CONCLUSION

For the cameraman, many camera properties interrelate. For the real-world cameraman, these relationships can become rather complex. If he wishes to change the angle of view and he changes the focal length, he will also affect the depth of field. He may then adjust the aperture to offset this, but that affects the exposure. So he adjusts the shutter speed to account for this, which results in a change in the motion blur. Phew. I'm getting fond of my point-and-shoot just thinking about it!

For the digital artist, things are simpler. The attributes are either set independently with purely creative interpretation or set deliberately to match a real camera. By knowing the real camera, you can better match it when you need to or create particular realistic looks if desired.

Table 13.2 Quick Comparison of Real and Virtual Cameras

Attribute	Real Camera	Virtual (3D) Camera
Angle of view	Determined by focal length and film gauge.	Set arbitrarily *or* realistically with focal length and film gauge.
Depth of field	Determined by focal length and aperture.	Can be set arbitrarily. Usually added in composite.
Exposure	Determined by shutter speed and aperture.	Set arbitrarily by adjusting light intensity.
Motion blur	Determined by shutter speed.	Determined by shutter speed and other user-defined parameters.

13.4.1 IMPORTANT POINTS

- Understanding real cameras is important in order to best control a virtual camera.
- The angle of view is an important consideration, as it determines the magnification of objects and the apparent distortion.
- Real cameras change the angle of view by adjusting the focal length of the lens.
- Depth of field is how much of the scene (in terms of distance from the camera) is in focus.
- Adding depth of field in the composite rather than the render saves significant render time.
- Film responds to light with a characteristic density curve that flattens at the low end (the "toe") and the high end (the "shoulder").
- Motion blur results from objects moving during the time the real camera is letting in light.
- Both depth of field and motion blur typically need to be turned "on" when used in digital renders.

13.4.2 TERMS

camera lens
focal length
field of view
telephoto lens
wide angle lens

normal lens
film gauge
depth of field
exposure
aperture

density curve
shutter speed
motion blur
f-stop

13.4.3 EXERCISES

1. Create a simple scene in 3D or set up a practical (real) still-life. Changing only camera placement, framing, and lens (changing the field of view and/or depth of field), create several compositions. The compositions should give different impressions of the subjects and create different moods. Be sure to experiment with the field of view.

2. Set up an animation with an object moving in an arc, or rotating as in the case of a fan or propeller. Try out both linear and full motion blur at different blur amounts. What settings worked best?

Figure 14.1 "Real" reflections and refractions require ray tracing.

Chapter 14
Rendering for the Artist

Creativity arises out of the tension between spontaneity and limitations,

the latter (like the river banks) forcing the spontaneity into the various

forms which are essential to the work of art or poem.

—*Rollo May, existential psychologist (1909–1994)*

Rendering is the part the computer does, so you may wonder how an entire chapter can be written on it for the artist. While rendering is when the computer makes the images, there is much that still involves the digital artist. Rendering is a process, and this process must be correctly set up and guided by a person. Sometimes things go smoothly, and sometimes not so smoothly. Technical directors are the ones to prepare renders, solve the problems when things go wrong, and oversee their jobs. How they approach their rendering can mean the difference between a successful and an unsuccessful job.

This chapter primarily looks at the artist's role in rendering. It describes a general workflow to maximize your chances of a successful render; it gives an overview of some common algorithms (scanline and ray-tracing) in order to better understand their processes; and it looks at some of the common problems that occur when rendering—and what to do about them. Additionally, this chapter looks specifically at how to set up and correctly render ray-traced reflections and refractions and includes some general guidelines for helping these materials look their best.

14.1 RENDER WORKFLOW

From your first render, you will want to have an approach to rendering (a "workflow") that maximizes your success. What constitutes a successful render? It's one that finishes *on time* and *with the quality level you desire*. A successful render workflow will allow you to "work smarter, not harder" as the saying goes.

14.1.1 THE NEED FOR SPEED

An extremely important task of the lighting technical director is to optimize his scenes for render speed. While this issue is of great concern to professionals, I find students often overlook this area almost completely. Bad habits often persist into early career years. I have even heard a less-experienced professional say the power of the computer was such that he didn't need to particularly optimize his scene. Quite the contrary! Render time is *always* an issue. The faster the computer, the more we'll ask it to do, resulting again in long renders, which need to be optimized. This is Blinn's Law, which first pointed out that as technology advances, we put more demands on it, resulting in a render time still equal to our tolerance level (some people are amazingly tolerant).

The longer the render, the more time your sequence will need in the *render farm* (many machines dedicated to rendering). If a show has not only your render but dozens and often hundreds of others to consider, and everyone has long renders, getting it all through the render farm on a nightly basis is going to be an issue. Having optimized renders becomes essential for the entire show to complete on time. Believe me, this is serious business. It's best not to wait until you have a problem to optimize your scene.

Fast Final Renders

Many, many factors control the speed of the final render. This section will take a look at some of the things you can do right away to speed up your renders. Efficiency tips that are specific to certain features will be discussed later in this chapter and throughout the book.

An important way to keep render times down is to judiciously select your rendering algorithm and techniques. Only use methods that take longer if you need their unique advantages and can afford the extra render time. To see the advantages of each render method, refer to the Table 1.2, "Comparison of Ray Tracing, Scanline, and Global Illumination Methods," in Chapter 1. There are no hard-and-fast rules on this one. Deciding when to cheat things in order to save time is something that is learned with experience and is influenced by the nature of the project and the resources available.

To save time, pre-calculate whatever you can, especially if it's something that takes a long time. Many studios incorporate more time-consuming render methods but pre-calculate the data. Shadows, reflections, occlusion, bounced light, and sub-surface scattering are all able to be pre-calculated or pre-rendered. Carefully adjust the render setting for passes to make sure they are also optimized. Make sure that you are not re-generating data unnecessarily, such as accidentally re-creating shadow maps. The decision on whether or not to pre-calculate data is influenced by what rendering method you are using. Ray tracing and ray-traced global illumination generally use much less in the way of pre-calculated data (if anything), while scanline and point-based global illumination make use of pre-calculated shadow and point maps.

Keep in mind render time while lighting, modeling, and texturing. Often decisions are made long before rendering that greatly affect how long things will take. Sometimes it is too late to go back and change them. Here are some things to keep in mind as you build your scene:

- ◆ Don't shade, texture, or model details you'll never see. Consider how large it appears on-screen, which is the detail level you need to model and shade. Don't use large texture files when small ones will do.
- ◆ Keep your geometry as lightweight as possible: Use polygons and subdivision surfaces with as few vertices as possible, and nurbs with as few isoparms as possible.
- ◆ Make your geometry single-sided.
- ◆ Use geometry your renderer likes: Some renderers work best with certain geometry types. RenderMan, for example, works more efficiently with nurbs and subdivision surfaces than polygons.

- Don't model geometric details when displacements will do; don't use displacements when bump mapping will do (Figures 14.2 and 14.3).
- Use as few lights as you can to get the look you want. More lights take more time to render, especially when they are shadowed. Don't light what you do not see.

Figure 14.2 The two oranges in this render look identical, but as Figure 14.3 reveals, they are in fact modeled very differently.

Figure 14.3 The orange on the left side has its surface detail created with a bump map (a displacement map wasn't necessary) and is made from a simple nurbs model, while the orange on the right side has small pores actually modeled into very high-resolution poly mesh. The poly-mesh orange is extremely inefficient; it renders much slower and has no visual advantage.

Keep your quality level *only as high as you need it*. General quality settings are discussed in detail in Section 14.4, many settings for ray tracing are covered in Section 14.3, and settings related to global illumination are covered in Chapter 16, "Global Illumination."

Fast Test Renders

Every lighter should have the "need for speed" while working; fast *test renders* are extremely important. Consider this: Achieving at the best possible look for your image requires many test renders. Each time you make even a small change, you need to re-render to see your change. If your render takes 15 minutes, then you can only get four test renders done in an hour. On the other hand, if your render is optimized and taking only a minute to render, then you can get about 40 images in an hour, subtracting time spent making changes. This will make a huge difference in how fast you can arrive at the image you want. In some situations, it pays to be impatient. I like to say, "Impatience is a virtue, if it means being efficient." In a professional environment, not optimizing your render times means one of two things—either you are going to have to regularly stay late to get your job done, or you'll miss deadlines. Yipes, I'm not liking either one of those options. This chapter discusses many ways to speed up your renders.

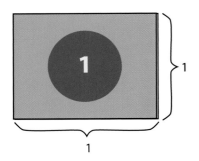

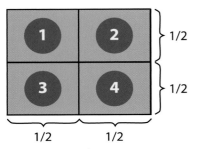

Figure 14.4 When an image is halved in size, it has only 1/4 the total number of pixels and takes about 1/4 the amount of time to render.

When rendering early interactive tests, you'll want to reduce the size of your test render to a fraction of the final render size. A render at half resolution will render not twice as fast, but *four times* as fast as full resolution (see Figure 14.4). Be aware that lo-res tests only can tell you so much. You should always do a test render at full resolution later to really see how things look. One workflow is to render lo-res, occasionally testing at hi-res, then switch to hi-res tests as you get near completion.

Another important time-saver when rendering interactively is to render cropped regions. Generally you just drag a box around the area you wish to see and test-render just this area. Why wait for the whole image to render when you just want to see one small part?

Only include geometry that you wish to see in your interactive render. Often the renderer has to calculate for geometry in the scene that you can't see, even when using a crop box. A "render selected" option is very helpful when available—you can pick the objects you wish to see and just render those. You can also set up render layers or geometry sets to easily hide the geometry you don't wish to render. Setting up layers is an extra step, but if you wish to hide certain objects frequently, it will be a worthwhile investment of your time. If using global illumination, you will want to make your selections carefully. Don't hide an object that you need for shadows, occlusion, or reflected light, or else you'll be in for a surprise when you turn everything back on. If you are unsure, do a test first to see what happens when you hide an object.

WORKFLOW TIPS FOR FASTER RENDERS

For faster final renders:

✓ Keep global samples as low as possible while still achieving the required quality.
✓ Limit more expensive algorithms to only where they are needed.
✓ Keep the number of traced rays for reflections and refractions down to the minimum number required for the scene (see Chapter 7, "Goals 7–10: Providing Cohesiveness and Visual Interest").
✓ Optimize all GI settings (see Chapter 9, "Light Intensity").
✓ Optimize all shadows and shadow settings (see Chapter 2, "Shadows").
✓ Pre-calculate whatever you can.
✓ Hide or delete geometry that isn't contributing to the scene in any way.
✓ Limit texture size and geometry detail to only what is needed.

For faster test renders:

✓ Use lower-quality settings for interactive test renders.
✓ Use a lower resolution for interactive test renders.
✓ Set motion blur to 0 temporarily.
✓ Crop areas for test renders.
✓ Render less geometry (turn geometry off by hiding or templating).
✓ Test-render the sequence first on 2s, 5s, or 10s, and at a lower resolution.

To get fast turnaround of early renders of the whole sequence, render them at lower resolution and/or don't render every frame. Early renders, if done at half resolution and only rendering every tenth or every fifth frame, will still tell you quite a bit about how everything is looking. Even when you are rendering at full resolution, you can tell much about the lighting and shading with every other frame, which renders, well, twice as fast. Consider this scenario: Say your full-resolution, full-frame render takes 15 minutes a frame for 40 frames. That is 600 minutes or 10 hours (on one computer). You should be able to get a test of that out over lunch on one machine, and here's how. First, at ½ resolution your render will take ¼ the time, so that's 10/4, which is 2.5 hours. Render every other frame, and you are at 1 hour 15 minutes. Okay, so that's lunch plus a cup of coffee, but still. Now imagine what you could do with a render farm.

Use low-quality settings while working, switching to higher-quality settings as your shot lighting progresses and you need to see more detail. You also can temporarily turn off motion blur or depth of field (if you have it) for your test renders, turning them back on later for more accurate test renders.

14.1.2 WORKFLOW FOR BATCH RENDERING

One of the first things to realize about rendering a series of frames ("batch rendering") is that just because the computer performs the rendering doesn't mean that the artist's job is finished. Far from it, in fact. The artist has many tasks to do during the process of a batch render, and this section goes over those tasks.

I have seen many students, freelance artists, and even small shops deliver substandard work (or worse, not be able to deliver!) because of the idea that when the artist has finished prepping the scene the work is done, and all that is left to do is for the computer to render the frames. Along with this idea is the mistaken belief that the process of rendering is a predictable process. I'd love to say it is, but in reality it isn't. Assuming your render will go off without a hitch is like assuming there will be no traffic…ever. You may get lucky some of the time with this approach, but it's guaranteed that at some point you will get into trouble. You will run into traffic. There is much an artist can do to ensure a successful render. See the sidebar "Five Ways to Ensure a Successful Batch Render" for the top ways.

While those are the top five tips, an artist can do even more to make sure the rendering process is a successful one by following these additional tips (and you thought I was done).

◆ *Communicate.* Communication and thoroughness are key. Many studios have people who monitor the render farm. If so, be sure to communicate with them. These people have your back and are your friends! Be nice to them and also communicate to them any details about your job. Also be sure to communicate any significant problems to your supervisor.

◆ *Check your work before delivery.* Never, ever deliver something to a boss or client "blind," meaning without checking it over first. If delivering a render to a client, you *must* look at each and every frame before delivery. Also be sure to check your work before passing it off to another person. It can irritate others to receive work that has avoidable problems (careless errors), which they then have to kick back, as this slows everyone's job down.

◆ *Include the details.* If sending a "help" ticket (which is a ticket sent to the technical support personnel), *include all of the details* about your problem—better more information than not enough. Not enough information can slow down the job of the support staff, who will then be slower to respond to you.

FIVE WAYS TO ENSURE A SUCCESSFUL BATCH RENDER

1 **Leave yourself enough time to render—*and re-render*.**

People less familiar with 3D (or those who know better but are in a huge hurry) will leave themselves only enough time for *one* full-frame-range, high-resolution render. This is dangerous. Unforeseen problems can occur, especially if all frames haven't been rendered before. It also leads to a lower-quality product artistically. Production houses render a shot many times in order to deliver a high-quality product. I recommend that artists leave themselves enough time for *at least two* full-frame, full-resolution renders. More is better, but I would consider two a minimum.

2 **Expect problems.** (You will be pleasantly surprised if you don't encounter any.)

Problems occur during rendering so often that you should not consider them an aberration but rather the norm, and *plan for them accordingly*. Problems can be anything—the server goes down; your render mysteriously hangs on several frames; weird things show up that were not in the interactive renders at all…the list goes on. Many times you won't encounter problems when rendering, but err on the side of caution. If delivering a project on time and with sufficient quality is at stake, you simply cannot risk it to assume otherwise. This is especially true if you are rendering an animation for the first time.

3 **Check your renders—repeatedly.**

Always check *at least one* completed frame from a batch or farm render before leaving a render to "cook." This will help eliminate any serious, avoidable surprises and wasted time. You don't want to come back the next day to find—oops, they were rendered at the wrong resolution (or camera or frame range). Also, during the render periodically check frames that have been completed so far, which is especially important for very long render jobs. You don't want your job to monopolize valuable resources, only to encounter problems that could have been caught hours ago (or days ago, in extreme cases).

4 **Estimate how long your render will take.**

Before rendering, do a bit of simple math based on the times of your test renders to figure out how long things will take, including how many processors you think will be allocated to you when rendering on a render farm. Once the job has started, let several frames finish and again estimate how long the entire job will take (some render farms do this for you). Make sure the job as a whole will not take too long. If you need it by morning, make sure it will be done by then. If it's clear from the beginning that the frames are taking too long, you will need to kill the job and optimize the render time before restarting it. When estimating the time for the whole job, be aware that not every frame takes the same amount of time.

5 **Render certain frames first, then fill in the gaps.**

Instead of rendering sequentially start to finish, render first on 5's or 2's and then fill in the gaps. For a render on 2's, for example, render the odd frames first (frames 1, 3, 5, 7, etc.); then when those are completed, your render will continue with the even numbers (frames 2, 4, 6, etc.). This way when the render is at the mid-way point you can see it play all the way through, every other frame, and have an excellent idea of how the whole thing will look.

- *Version up.* When showing your work to others, be sure to version up after every render. For example, your boss may ask you for the scene files of a render she just reviewed. If you overwrite your scene file, your boss will invariably ask, "Hey, can you go back to that version I saw from you last week?"

- *Stay busy.* It may be tempting to sit around while rendering, surfing the Internet or taking care of personal business. Bosses don't like this. While on their dime, it is best to be doing something productive, such as working on another task, checking your work, cleaning up files, or at the least going over work-related tutorials. Along these lines, plan to send off short renders at your lunch break and long renders overnight.

- *Keep logs.* Logs are records of your renders. Check logs automatically produced by the renderer and write down important details from them, such as render times. The situation may come up where what seemed like a small change in the scene results in render times that suddenly balloon out of control. You'll want to keep track of this so you can know what the changes are and when they happened. Logs are also useful for debugging problems.

- *Keep lists.* When trying to remember a variety of things, it's very helpful to have a checklist, such as settings to check, passes to render, and things to do. You may want a list of all the changes you intend to make. You definitely should write down all the changes your supervisor has requested so you don't forget one. (Supervisors don't like if you forget their instructions, and they give them verbally and usually only once.)

14.2 SCANLINE AND RAY TRACING "UNDER THE HOOD"

This section takes a closer look at how both scanline and ray tracing work. (Global illumination algorithms are discussed in Chapter 16.) As a digital artist you don't need to be a software programmer; however, you will want to have a general idea of what's happening behind the scenes while rendering. Knowing what each render algorithm does will give you a better understanding and control over the various settings and features associated with it.

14.2.1 SCANLINE RENDERING: SHORT AND SWEET

Scanline rendering gets its name from the way it processes the scene—successive lines on the screen are rendered one at a time. The main thing to know about scanline rendering is that it only calculates what is in view of the camera, known appropriately as *visible surface determination*. Scanline renderers convert all geometry to polygons at the time of rendering, a process known as *tessellation*. On a line-by-line basis, these polygons are then sorted for what's in front and what's behind. Only visible geometry currently being rendered is stored into memory; the rest is discarded. This makes scanline very fast but limits what it can do, and it is why scanline doesn't calculate real reflections or refractions. Scanline's memory requirements are very low even with complex scenes. During the render, the color of the polygons is calculated according to the materials assigned. Light calculations are done by the shaders, and only direct light is accounted for. The resulting color is projected onto the screen in a process called *rasterization*.

Scanline rendering is often used for animation and real-time graphics because of its speed. A popular implementation of scanline rendering is known as REYES, which stands for "Renders Everything You Ever Saw." REYES is the basis of RenderMan renderers, the most common of these being PRMan, developed by Pixar and used predominantly for feature film. REYES dices geometry into *micropolygons*, which are polygons about the size of a pixel or smaller. REYES primarily uses a rasterization technique similar to scanline. Pixar's PRMan also selectively incorporates both ray tracing and global illumination methods, making it a hybrid renderer. Various other RenderMan-compliant renders are Pixie, 3D Delight, and Aqsis. Aqsis and Pixie are completely free, while 3D Delight allows for one free license and integrates with Maya and Softimage.

14.2.2 RAY TRACING: A MATTER OF RAYS

Ray tracing accounts for hidden surfaces, meaning that even surfaces not directly in the view of the camera are included in the calculations. After all, they may appear in reflections or refractions, or be creating shadows (Figure 14.5). In classic ray tracing, all of the surfaces and textures must be loaded into the computer's memory all of the time. This can cause the renderer to have trouble or even not be able to render if the scene is very large and has much complex geometry, high-frequency displacement mapping, and many large texture maps.

Ray tracing gets its name from the fact that it traces the path of the light ray. Ray tracing is a more realistic approximation of how real light behaves. In life, light rays emanate from various sources, bounce off objects, and finally reach our eyes (Figure 14.6). Ray tracing follows this path, only instead of traveling from light to camera (the virtual eye), it traces from the camera back to each light (Figure 14.7). Why does ray tracing calculate backwards? Because doing so

Figure 14.5 An image rendered with ray tracing (by Steven Winters).

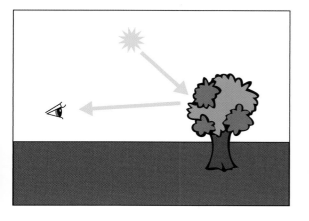

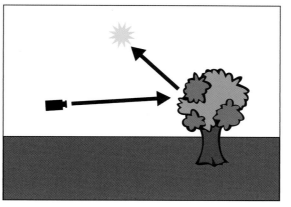

Figure 14.6 In life, rays travel from the light to our eye.

Figure 14.7 Ray tracing traces this path backwards, from the camera to the light.

is more efficient. In life, many, many rays of light radiate in directions other than toward our eyes. If light doesn't enter our retinas (or the camera), then it isn't seen. Since it isn't seen, ray tracing doesn't calculate for it.

A good way to imagine how ray tracing works is to think of the final image as a screen door with each square hole in the screen being a pixel (Figure 14.8). From each hole (or pixel) one or more rays are cast out to whatever objects can be seen from that hole. The color of the pixel is then set by what the ray "sees" in the scene.

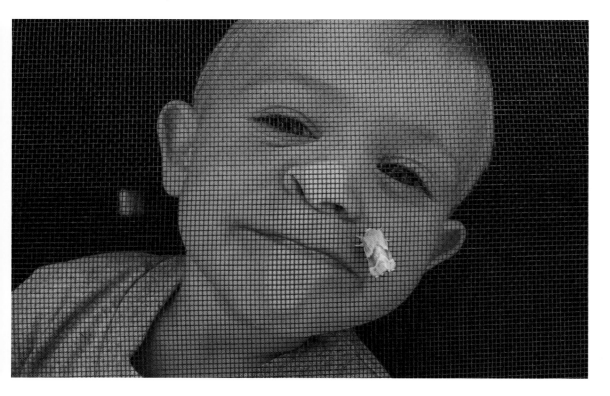

Figure 14.8 Each box in a screen mesh can be likened to a pixel, and our view through a mesh can be likened to how the virtual camera "sees" the 3D scene.

The ray doesn't stop when it intersects an object, however. From the object, more rays are spawned toward the lights in the scene in order to determine if the object is in shadow or not. For example, if the scene has three shadow-casting lights, then at least three new rays are spawned. If the scene has reflective surfaces, then another ray is bounced off looking for what appears in the reflection. Similarly, if the scene has transparent refractive surfaces, then more rays are generated to travel through the surface.

The first ray is the one coming from camera, sometimes called the *camera ray*. The number of camera rays has the largest impact on render time, as all of the other kinds of rays are spawned off each camera ray as needed. Thus a higher number of camera rays will multiply all other rays in the scene. As rays traverse the scene, each time they bend or bounce a new ray is created. For example, when the camera ray bounces in search of a reflection, a reflection ray is created. Figure 14.9 illustrates how many rays split off from a single camera ray in a simplified scene. You can see how the number of rays can quickly increase. More rays means more calculations, and longer renders.

NOTE

Some ray-tracing algorithms continue rays to search for indirect light in the scene, and thus fall under the category of global illumination. They are called *path-traced global illumination* or *ray-traced global illumination* and are discussed in Chapter 16.

Figure 14.9 A diagram tracing the splitting of one camera ray coming from one pixel.

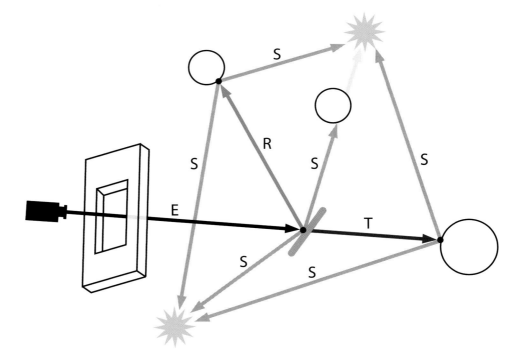

14.3 RAY-TRACED REFLECTIONS AND REFRACTIONS

"Real" reflections and refractions are accomplished through ray tracing, and they are some of the major features of ray tracing (Figure 14.1). Recall that "real" reflections are those in which a reflective surface truly mirrors the other objects around it. "Refraction" is the bending of light as it passes through a transparent medium, distorting the view of what is behind. Without refraction, transparent surfaces look dull and unconvincing. Both reflections and refractions take a bit of additional know-how in order to render correctly.

Getting started with traced reflections is relatively easy—just make sure that ray tracing is on in your render settings, and also that your material has a reflective parameter greater than zero. Expert use of reflective materials requires more know-how, however. In addition to ray tracing, reflections may be mapped or rendered as a separate pass. This section will cover ray-traced reflections and refractions only. Mapped reflections and refractions are covered in Chapter 17, "Image-Based Lighting and More" while reflection passes are covered in Chapter 18, "Multi-Pass Rendering."

Setting up refractions takes a few additional steps. Simply making your material transparent doesn't give you refractions. Since digital refractions take extra processing time and need to be adjusted to be correct, they default to off. To get refraction in your materials, you will want to make sure that you are ray tracing, and that refractivity is "on" in the transparent material. Additionally, you will need to set the refractive index.

The *refractive index* is a measure of *how much* light bends when it passes through a transparent surface, and thus distorts the background. In life, each kind of material has a unique refractive index. Water is 1.33, while glass is about 1.5. Diamonds have a very high refractive index at 2.4. You can look up a material's true refractive index—the Internet is a great resource. A refractive index of 1 means the ray doesn't bend at all. A number slightly over 1 is usually about right, like 1.1 to 1.5 (Figure 14.10).

TIP

If you turn on refractions and nothing happens, make sure the refractive index is not 1.0.

14.3.1 RAY LIMITS

One of the most important tasks when ray tracing is to limit the number of rays. Too many rays result in overly long render times. Too few rays, on the other hand, will result in render artifacts, or you may not get the effect you are looking for. *Ray limits* refers to the number of times the ray bounces or bends in its journey from the camera outward into the scene.

Rays can be limited in three main features:

1. Ray-traced shadows
2. Ray-traced reflections
3. Ray-traced refractions

In a scene without traced reflections or refractions, ray-traced shadows need only one ray bounce. When reflections or refractions are present, however, they will need more. Ray-traced shadows were discussed in Chapter 2, "Shadows," and are further discussed in this section.

Figure 14.10 The higher the refractive number, the more distortion through the transparent surface. From left to right, refractive index of 1.25, 1.1, and 1.0. Notice that 1.0 effectively turns off refraction.

The *reflection ray limit* is the number of times the renderer will generate a new ray in search of reflections. A new ray is generated each time the ray bounces off a surface. Setting up the correct rays limits is essential because without them your reflections may not appear (too few rays), or your renders may take unnecessarily long (too many rays). To determine the correct number of reflection rays, just count up the number of bounces the ray must do before reaching the object that appears in the reflection. With one reflective surface, one bounce is likely sufficient (unless you have a lot of inter-reflections of the same surface with itself). In fact, in the majority of cases, one reflection ray is going to be enough (Figure 14.11 and 14.13). If you have two objects reflecting into each other, then you want your reflections to bounce as many times as you can see reflections within reflections (Figure 14.12 and 14.14).

Figure 14.11 (Left) Ray-traced reflection with one additional reflection ray needed.

Figure 14.12 (Right) To see reflections within reflections, you will need more than one additional ray. In this example, two additional reflection rays are needed.

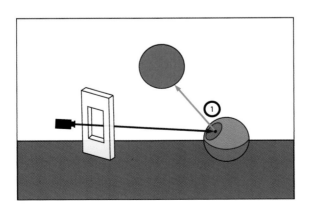

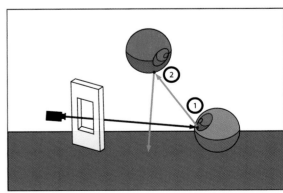

Similarly, the user needs to limit the number of rays the renderer will spawn in search of refractions. During the course of traced refraction, new rays are spawned each time the ray intersects a surface, and the ray bends. To determine the maximum number of necessary refraction rays, just count up the number of times your view goes through a surface before finally ending up on a non-refracting, non-reflective surface. Keep in mind that a solid object is represented in CG by *two* surfaces—the front side and the back side. For example, if you were looking through a glass plate, then the number of refraction rays would be 2, one for each surface representing each side of the plate (Figure 14.15). If two plates are stacked in front of each other, then the number of bends would be four (Figure 14.16). If you have multiple transparent objects all stacked one in front of another, the number of refraction rays can get to be quite a lot. As usual, more rays means a longer render.

If you don't have enough refractive rays, then your ray may stop short before it reaches the background, resulting in objectionable black patches within the transparent surface (Figures 14.17 and 14.18). Renders such as Mental Ray handle refractions in this manner. Other renderers, such as RenderMan, simply continue the ray on but without refractions, which is preferable as often the lack of additional refraction isn't noticeable.

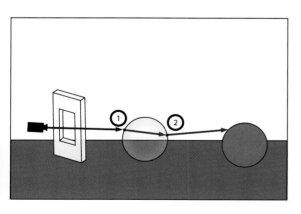 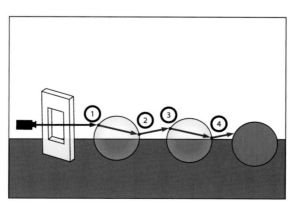

Figure 14.15 (Left) Two refraction rays will pass through two sides of a surface.

Figure 14.16 (Right) Four refraction rays are needed to pass through two surfaces, each with two sides.

Figure 14.17 (Left) Not enough refraction rays results in the ray stopping short, leaving black spots (two refraction rays, rendered with Mental Ray).

Figure 14.18 (Right) With enough refraction rays, the surface is correctly transparent (four refraction rays).

If your scene has both reflective and refractive materials, then you will need to total up all of the bends and bounces for both the reflection and refractions rays. For example, if a mirror is behind a refractive glass ball, then it will need three reflection rays and refraction rays—one for the initial bounce, and another two to get through the glass ball (see Figures 14.19 through 14.21 for examples). Some testing may be required to determine the optimum number if you have many reflective and transparent objects in the scene.

TIP

When working with a refractive and reflective surface, I highly recommend turning off one component while you work on the other——so you can better see what you have.

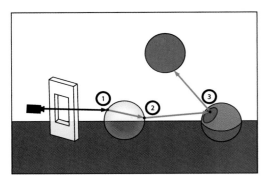

Figure 14.19 Three reflection rays and three refraction rays are needed here in order to see the reflections and refractions properly.

Figure 14.20 One reflection ray isn't enough to pass the reflections through refractions. Rather than seeing reflections, the pawn behind the glass is black.

Figure 14.21 With three reflection rays, the reflections on the pawn are now passing through the glass.

If you have a ray-traced shadow that is appearing in reflections or through refractions, you'll need to increase your number of *shadow rays* as well. Ray-traced shadows appearing in reflections need the number of reflection bounces *plus one* (see Figures 14.22 through 14.24 for examples). If appearing behind refractions, then the number of shadow rays is likewise the refraction limit plus one (Figures 14.25 and 14.26). If your ray-traced shadow is unfortunate enough to be showing up in a reflection and through a refractive transparency, then it needs the total number of bounces *plus* bends *plus* one. Mapped shadows, on the other hand, will show up in all reflections without any additional calculations, which is another way their render time can be faster.

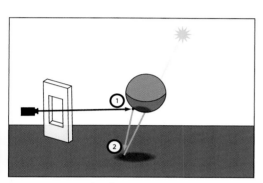

Figure 14.22 Shadows appearing in reflections will need more rays as well—one plus the number of reflection bounces; in this diagram two will do.

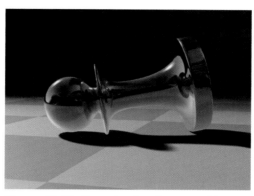

Figure 14.23 One shadow bounce. No traced shadows in reflections.

Figure 14.24 Two shadow bounces. Traced shadows appear in reflections.

Figure 14.25 (Left) This image doesn't have enough traced shadow rays to make it through the refraction.

Figure 14.26 (Right) Two additional shadow rays pass the shadow through the refractive transparency.

Reflection and refraction ray limits are set in both the material and the render settings. The number of shadow rays is also set both in the global render settings and in each light. The renderer will use the *lesser* of these two numbers. For example, if your reflective material is set to allow six ray bounces, but your render setting is 1 (because you are on a low-quality preset, for example), then you will never have more than one bounce with any material. When setting the number of rays, place the maximum you will ever need in the render settings, then make each individual material as low as possible.

14.3.2 BLURRED REFLECTIONS AND REFRACTIONS

Blurred reflections and refractions are known as *glossy* (Figure 14.27 and 14.28). A blurry refraction looks like frosted glass. Ray-traced glossy reflections and refractions blur realistically—the farther away the object is that appears in the refraction or through the refraction, then the greater the blur. True glossy reflections and refractions are costly in terms of render time. They will need many samples in order to smooth out and not have grainy artifacts (Figures 14.29 and 14.30).

The blurrier the reflection or refraction, the more samples you'll need. If your reflection or refraction isn't blurry, then you only need one sample. Samples are different than limits. Ray limits refer to the number of times the ray bounces or bends, while samples are the splitting of the ray into many other rays upon a single bounce or bend (Figures 14.31 and 14.32). Each of these samples represents a new ray and continues to trace.

Figure 14.27 Glossy (blurred) reflection.

Figure 14.28 Clear versus glossy transparency.

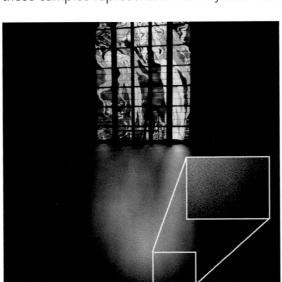

Figure 14.29 Insufficient samples. This reflection has noise that will sizzle objectionably upon animation.

Figure 14.30 This blurred reflection has been smoothed out with many more samples.

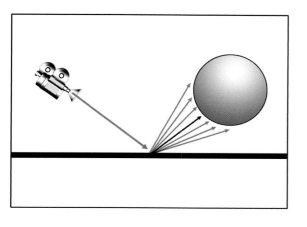

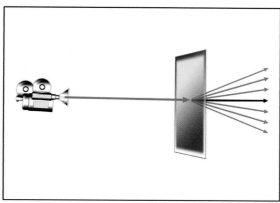

Figure 14.31 (Left) Reflection samples (bouncing off a glossy ground plane).

Figure 14.32 (Right) Refraction samples (passing through a glossy vertical plane).

14.3.3 THE FRESNEL EFFECT

Many reflective and transparent surfaces demonstrate the *Fresnel effect* (named after the scientist who first documented it). The Fresnel effect describes how the reflectivity and/ or transparency of a surface varies depending on our angle of view to the surface. When light strikes a surface dead-on, it tends to scatter back diffusely or pass through. On the other hand, when light strikes a surface at a grazing angle, it tends to bounce off in the direction of the reflection (Figure 14.33).

To the observer, this means that reflectivity and specular intensity increase with increasing angle of view (Figure 14.34). In some surfaces, the Fresnel effect is negligible and can be ignored. For example, mirror-like objects are so reflective, they are considered fully reflective at any angle. The Fresnel effect is most noticeable with surfaces that exhibit partial reflectivity, such as water, car paint, or glazed ceramics. Adding Fresnel to these types of surfaces will greatly enhance their realism.

Fresnel Effect

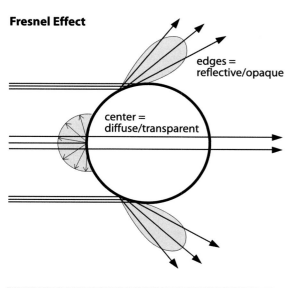

edges = reflective/opaque

center = diffuse/transparent

Figure 14.33 (Left) Diagram of the Fresnel effect.

Figure 14.34 (Right) These digitally rendered colored metallic balloons show the Fresnel effect, becoming more reflective at their edges.

Figure 14.35 This photograph demonstrates the Fresnel effect. Notice how at the horizon the water reflects the sky, while nearer the viewer, the surface is less reflective and more transparent, allowing us to see the sand.

In terms of transparency, a semi-transparent object will appear most transparent when our view of it is dead on, and is least transparent when our view of it is oblique (Figures 14.35 and 14.36). An example of this is a bubble, in which the edges look more opaque than the center. A lake or ocean provides another good example. When you look straight down into the water, you can see below the surface; when you look at the water at a grazing angle, such as looking to the horizon, however, you see the sky reflected.

14.3.4 ARTISTIC CONSIDERATIONS

Reflective objects are much more interesting when they have something to reflect (Figures 14.37 through 14.40). "Real" ray-traced reflections will accurately depict what is around them in the 3D scene. 3D scenes are typically built only for what is visible. A highly reflective traced object will reveal the set nature of your, well, set. For example, if your room is missing its roof or a few out-of-view walls (like the one behind the camera), then a reflective object in the room will reveal this. To solve for this, reflective surfaces may have objects placed in the scene for the sole purpose of providing more accurate or more interesting reflections. Cards mapped with pictures of more complex geometry may be used, in order to mimic geometry out of view without having to add geometric complexity. In this case, make the cards "visible in reflections" only, non-shadow-casting, and map their incandescent parameter.

Figure 14.36 As these squares turn sideways, they become less transparent and more reflective.

Figure 14.37 (Left) Without anything to reflect, the tall vase is disappearing into the background.

Figure 14.38 (Right) The apple on the right and a white card placed off-camera on the left help to define this mirrored vase.

To add interest and shape your objects, pay careful attention to the placement and size of your highlights and reflections. You also may need to add specular-only lights to craft additional highlights just where you want them. Another option is to provide mapped reflections. Mapped reflections are covered in Section 17.2, "Mapped Reflections and Refractions."

Figure 14.39 (Left) This render illustrates the importance of reflection for visual interest and shaping.

Figure 14.40 (Right) Car photographs and digital renders typically use large area lights (or reflective cards) that provide interesting highlights over much of the car.

Refractions don't have to be truly accurate to be convincing. For this reason, the index of refraction of a digital material can be artistically crafted. For example, in Pixar's classic short *Geri's Game*, the refraction of Geri's glasses was designed to make Geri's eyes look large and angelic when he was being the good version of himself, rather than being exactly physically accurate (Figure 14.41). I often start with the material's true refraction index number, then adjust it creatively until it looks about right.

Figure 14.41 In *Geri's Game* (© 1997 Pixar Animation Studios), the refraction in Geri's glasses was artistically crafted to give him an innocent appeal.

TIPS FOR WORKING WITH REFLECTIVE AND REFRACTIVE SURFACES

- Set the minimum necessary number of reflection and refraction rays. (For one reflective object, one reflection ray is usually enough.)
- Set the minimum necessary number of refraction rays. (At least two refraction rays are needed for one solid refractive object.)
- Check to make sure you have enough traced shadow rays, if applicable. (Count up the number of bounces plus bends plus one.)
- Be sure to set number of ray limits in each material and the render settings.
- Set the minimum necessary number of reflection/refraction samples for glossy reflections/refractions. (For non-glossy, one is sample is enough.)
- Determine the desired index of refraction. (Setting it to 1 does nothing; set this number between 1 and 2.)
- Remember that refraction can be dialed in creatively.
- When ray tracing reflections, make sure your surfaces have enough to reflect.
- Add the Fresnel effect to your semi-reflective and transparent surfaces for the best look.

14.4 QUALITY CONTROL

Quality, **when it comes to digital renders, doesn't mean the excellence of something, but rather how artifact-free the render is**. Artifacts, those tiny imperfections introduced by the renderer, are the bane of every digital 3D artist. Early in the book, Chapter 1 included a general discussion of quality settings found in the render settings dialog box (refer to Section 1.4.2 "Introduction to Render Settings" for review). Recall that most software packages have various presets for low quality ("draft") or high quality ("production"). Low quality is good for test renders, while high quality is needed for final renders. Presets are a great way to get started, but they aren't always sufficient for your scene. Sometimes a preset doesn't correct your artifact. Other times the preset is *more* than you need, resulting in excessive render times. Quality presets found in the render settings also only control global settings; these settings affect the entire render. A number of other quality settings are material-specific or object-specific and are found in an editor associated with that material or object.

To achieve *optimum settings* you will want to adjust various parameters individually. "Optimum settings" are *always* those that give you the quality you require—and no more, to keep render time as low as is possible. Determining what is good enough requires a bit of testing. This section takes a closer look at render quality, gaining a better understanding of what actually is happening when artifacts are created and specific parameters and means to correct for them.

Be warned, quality control isn't about the art, it's about the (computer) science; and by necessity, it gets a bit technical. Sometimes tracking down a solution to a pesky render artifact can be frustrating and make you want to pull your hair out. Be prepared to problem-solve. Don't despair, someone out there has already seen it and been there, I promise. Your best resource is actually a knowledgeable friend or co-worker. Barring that, try software documentation, books, and online forums.

14.4.1 ALIASING: THE PROBLEM OF SAMPLES

No matter how the final image is calculated, all renders sample the scene. A sample is a test to ask, "What do you look like here?" Depending on the answer, the renderer colors the point or pixel.

Imagine if you were viewing an alien planet from a pinhole camera, and you could only see one tiny area of information at a time. Now imagine that from this pinhole camera you took several photographs in random directions to get an idea of what this alien world looked like. If you had just a few pictures, you may not have enough information to really know. For example, if you took only two photographs and both happened to point up to the sky, you might erroneously decide the world is all sky. On the other hand, if your camera shot thousands of pictures, you would have a very good idea of what the world looked like (Figure 14.42).

Figure 14.42 The more pictures we have, the more accurately we can re-create the scene.

And so it is with your renderer. The more times it samples, the more accurate the result. In our analogy, each snapshot represents a sample. A difference is that the snapshot can encompass a large area, while a computer sample just grabs one tiny dot of information. Now you see why the renderer needs to take lots and lots of samples to create an accurate 2D image from the 3D scene you have built. The quality of the final render is directly related to the number of times the renderer has sampled the scene. More samples are more accurate but take more time. This is the time versus quality trade-off we see over and over again.

14.4.2 Aliasing Artifacts

When there aren't enough samples to accurately rebuild the scene, artifacts known as *aliasing* **occur**. Aliasing can be introduced at various places in the render process. Likewise, it can be corrected in a variety of places.

Aliasing may manifest in any of the following forms:

◆ *Stair-stepping* ("jaggies") along edges
◆ *Graininess* in areas that should be smooth
◆ *Sizzling/flickering* of small details and objects upon animation
◆ *Strobing* of fine, repeating patterns

When aliasing is visible in a single frame, it's known as *spatial aliasing*. "Spatial" means "of or relating to space." Other artifacts show up when animated, known as *temporal aliasing*. "Temporal" means "of or relating to time."

TIP

Be wary of temporal artifacts that don't show up in a single test render: Be sure to test a series of frames before launching a long render to make sure your images are artifact-free.

The most common form of aliasing is stair-stepping around the edges of objects or areas of high contrast, known as "jaggies" (Figure 14.43). Jaggies can be seen in a single frame. Like other forms of aliasing, they occur from too few samples. Imagine a black object on a white

328   Chapter 14 | Rendering for the Artist

background, for example. If there is only one sample per pixel, jaggies are sure to occur as the sample either hits or misses, and the pixel is colored black or white with nothing in between. If more than one sample is sent out per pixel, however, some pixels will have some samples returning black and other samples returning white, averaging to gray pixels along the border. These pixels of intermediate value will smooth out the transition (Figure 14.44).

Grainy-looking areas are another form of aliasing. Grainy areas have speckles in regions that should be smooth. This results from too low of samples that are jittered (Figure 14.45). Grainy areas will sizzle upon animation. Grain can also appear in areas like the edges of shadow blur and in ray-traced blurred reflections and refractions as well. While these artifacts aren't typically considered aliasing, they are in fact the result of the same problem—too few samples. Shadows, reflection, and refractions are covered in the previous Section 14.3, while overall issues with grain or grainy textures are addressed in this section.

Too low of sampling also may result in "sizzling" of tiny objects or details. Sizzling refers to flickers in the render that are the size of a pixel. This sizzling won't show up in an individual frame but will be apparent in a series of frames. Grainy noise will sizzle upon animation. Tiny objects tend to sizzle, like hair or thin branches or objects that appear small because of distance. In this case, the samples are sometimes hitting the tiny target, registering its color in that pixel or missing it. Sizzling may also occur from tiny specular hits when shiny surfaces have small details, such as a fine bump or displacement.

A final artifact caused by too low of samples is strobing and incorrect frequency for regular patterns (Figure 14.46). Regular repeating patterns tend to show aliasing the smaller they appear on-screen. How many times a pattern repeats over a given distance is known as its *frequency*, which is just a fancy way of saying how small it is as far as the visual artist is concerned. A high-frequency pattern (one that is small, having many repeats over a given area) needs more samples than a low-frequency pattern (one that appears large, having few repeats over a given area) (Figures 14.47 and 14.48).

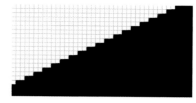

Figure 14.43 An edge that demonstrates stair–stepping, magnified many times so the individual pixels can be seen.

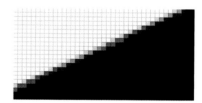

Figure 14.44 An edge that has been anti-aliased, magnified many times so the individual pixels can be seen.

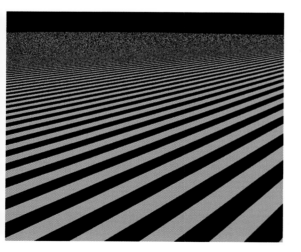 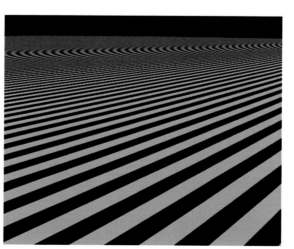

Figure 14.45 (Left) This pattern has been reduced to noise in the distance—a typical artifact from too low of samples. This graininess will sizzle upon animation.

Figure 14.46 (Right) Another artifact of too few samples is an incorrect reconstruction of the pattern.

Figure 14.47 (Left) Too few samples, and the result will not be accurate. Note that the samples in this diagram are identical to Figure 14.48 in number and placement, but the frequency of the pattern is greater. High-frequency patterns need more samples in order to accurately be reconstructed.

Figure 14.48 (Right) Stripes in the far distance have resolved to an incorrect frequency and rotation. This banding will strobe or swim (move around) upon animation.

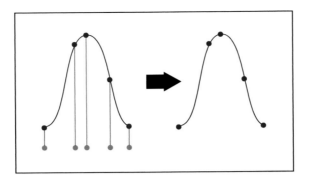 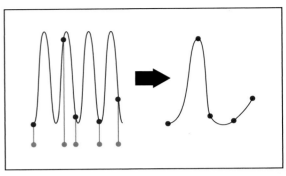

NOTE

For the geeky, the number of samples needed to correctly reconstruct a regular pattern is at least two times that of the frequency and is known as the *Nyquist limit*.

14.4.3 Anti-Aliasing: Solving the Problem

Eliminating aliasing problems is known as *anti-aliasing*. Since the problem is too few of samples, the solution is usually—you guessed it—more samples. But where and which ones? And if more samples increase render time too much, are there other options? This section answers these questions. When your scene has aliasing problems, a bit of debugging and careful testing are often needed to determine what solution is best.

The renderer samples the image at many stages in the process, but a few settings have the most impact and are useful for solving aliasing problems.

Samples per Pixel

The most fundamental sample the renderer takes is the one that comes from the camera, from each pixel. Depending on the renderer, this parameter can be called "pixel samples," "anti-aliasing samples," "camera samples," "camera rays," or something similar. I'll refer to this setting as "pixel samples," which is the name used by RenderMan renderers.

Adjusting pixel samples will affect the entire image as a whole, and it has a large impact on render time. Pixel samples is a global setting and is found in the render dialog box. One sample per pixel turns off anti-aliasing and is good for very early or very fast tests. One sample per pixel means the renderer queries only once per pixel, "What does the world look like out there?" The answer determines the color of the final pixel. Only one sample per pixel is sure to produce the stair-stepping seen in Figure 14.43. More than one sample per pixel is known as *super sampling* and is required for higher-quality renders. When multiple samples are sent out per pixel, these samples are averaged to determine the color of the pixel. About 16 samples per pixel is high quality, but even higher numbers may be needed on occasion to solve problems.

CAUTION

Be careful here! When setting the number of samples per pixel manually, don't overdo it. The actual number of samples may be greater than the number input into the parameter. For example, if using RenderMan's pixel samples, a setting of 4 and 4 means a 4 *times* 4 grid of samples, which is 16 samples per pixel (high quality), while a setting of 10 and 10 means 100 samples per pixel. In Mental Ray, a sample level of 2 is 16 samples per pixel, while 3 jumps up to 64! Refer to your software's documentation for details and suggested values.

If your problem is due to tiny geometry, increasing the pixel samples is often the solution. Also, when grain results from calculating motion blur and depth of field in-camera, more pixel samples are usually needed. More pixel samples will increase render time, sometimes dramatically. If your values are very high, make sure you really need them that high, that there aren't other solutions to your artifacts, and that your scene will still render on time.

Pixel samples are filtered across a small number of pixels to further reduce artifacts. The user can often control the width and type of the filter. Different filters have different looks. Gaussain produces good results and results in a softer, blurrier image. At times it may be too soft. Catmull-Rom has a sharper look, while a narrow Box filter is fast will have a hard-edged look. (See Figure 14.49.)

If you are having trouble with aliasing and increasing the pixel samples isn't enough, try additionally experimenting with the different filters and the width of the filter (Figures 14.50 through 14.52). A filter width of 2 is common.

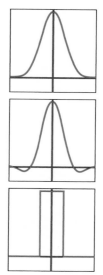

Figure 14.49 Three common filters from top to bottom: Gaussain, Catmull-Rom, and Box. The red line represents how much the surrounding pixels affect the final color of the pixel being shaded, which is positioned in the center.

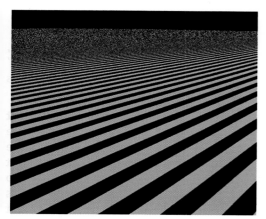

Figure 14.50 Here is our example with grain again. Pixel samples of 2×2.

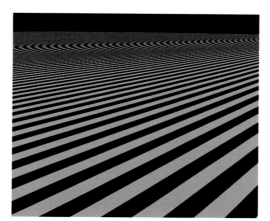

Figure 14.51 Pixel samples were increased to 10x10 to eliminate the noise, but banding has occurred. More and more pixels samples are only increasing the render time, and a new kind of artifact results. Filter used is Catmull-Rom with a filter width of 2.

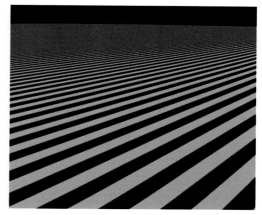

Figure 14.52 Pixel samples of 10x10 eliminate noise, and filter type of Gaussian with a filter spread of 3 smoothes out the result. The pattern is so small that it has blended to a uniform color, which is the correct result. Problem solved.

Samples per Shading Area

Many renderers (but not all) also sample each *surface* a number of times to determine how the surface is shaded, called "shading samples," "shading," "shading rate," or the like. I'll refer to this setting as "shading samples," the term used in Mental Ray.

While shading samples may at first seem similar to pixel samples, they are in fact different. The number of pixel samples is a global setting, while the number of shading samples is surface-specific. This is good news when the rest of your scene renders great but for one surface. Rather than cranking up the pixel samples for whole scene, you can adjust just the shading samples on just the one surface.

Shading samples evaluate the materials and textures applied to the surface specifically. This means that if your surface has aliasing due to a fine bump map, or a high-frequency color pattern such as a fine wood grain, then increasing shading samples for this surface may solve the problem. If the aliasing is the result of tiny but smoothly colored geometry (such as hair for example), then more shading samples will *not* help—you will need to increase the pixel samples instead.

Shading samples are generally set globally in the render settings for all objects in the scene, then overridden individually for certain objects or materials as needed. When used as a global setting, shading samples have a great effect on the quality of the image as a whole and also a large impact on render time. You can adjust the global settings to affect render time and to get quick tests. When individual objects have difficulty rendering due to the material, try increasing their shading samples. Conversely, if they have smooth and even material properties, reduce the number of shading samples for faster renders.

A shading sample of 1 means the surface material is evaluated once per pixel, which is usually good enough. To solve a problem with a particular surface, you may need more (Figure 14.53). Conversely, surfaces with very uniform color and bump may need fewer shading samples (Figure 14.54). Individual surfaces can have their shading samples set explicitly, typically done through a dialog box associated with them. If an explicit value is set, it will override what is in the global settings for that surface only, regardless of whether this number is higher or lower than the global setting.

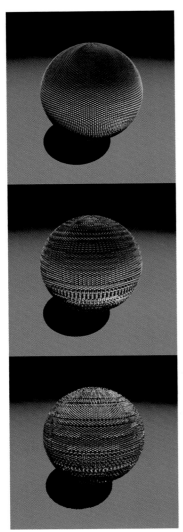

Figure 14.53 Fine displacements, in particular, need a high number of shading samples. These examples are rendered in RenderMan with the following settings: shading rate from top to bottom: .1, 1, 5 (recall that a higher shading rate means fewer samples).

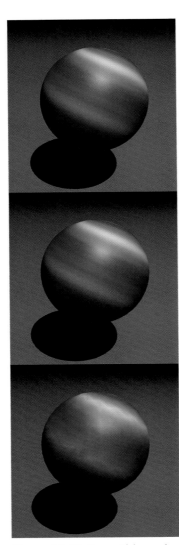

Figure 14.54 Smoothly and evenly colored surfaces need fewer shading samples. These examples are rendered in RenderMan with the following settings: shading rate from top to bottom: 1, 100, 1000 (recall that a higher shading rate means fewer samples). Notice that even a shading rate of 100 delivers a good result due to the smoothness of the material color.

RenderMan's "shading rate" parameter controls the number of shading samples. A *smaller* shading rate means *more* samples. Note that shading rate settings are opposite than those for pixel samples. When using RenderMan, to increase render quality you would *decrease* the shading rate and *increase* the pixel samples.

Figure 14.55 A mipmapped texture.

In contrast to pixel samples, objects blurred by motion blur and depth of field need fewer shading samples, because you cannot see them that well.

Anti-Aliasing Textures

Texture maps have filtering methods that are very effective and fast. For this reason, mapped texture files have fewer anti-aliasing problems than small geometry or some types of procedural textures.

If you're finding your renders have persistent problems such as flickering or sizzling, and your samples and render times are already very high, consider replacing the geometry with maps. For example, if the problem is strobing of a fence seen far in the distance, consider replacing the fence geometry with a card mapped with a render of the fence. Or if the problem is a procedurally generated starfield in which the stars flicker on and off (more than a twinkle), try converting the procedural texture to a file.

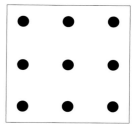

Figure 14.56 Non-jittered samples.

Some applications make use of *mipmapped* textures (Figure 14.55). Mipmapped textures are pre-filtered by storing a variety of texture resolutions all in one file. Thus, when the file appears smaller and smaller on-screen, the renderer doesn't have to do all the work to filter the results; rather, the renderer looks up the smaller version of the texture file stored in the mipmap and does a bit of clean-up on the result. Even without the use of mipmapped textures, texture files can be filtered in the software to help with their aliasing.

How the Renderer Helps

Renderers often jitter their samples so they are not shot out in a regular grid (Figure 14.56) but rather in a random pattern (Figure 14.57), known as *stochastic sampling*. Irregular sampling patterns are better at tricking the eye into believing there is no artifact present. They break up artifacts like banding or stair-stepping and replace them with noise. While noise itself is also an artifact, for some reason the human visual system notices it less. When noise is very pronounced, it becomes noticeable and looks grainy.

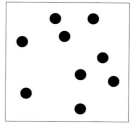

Figure 14.57 Jittered samples.

An optimization technique that is often combined with stochiastic sampling is called *importance sampling*. This sounds fancy, but all it really means is that the samples are weighted in the direction that is "most important," such as bright, detailed highlights (Figure 14.58). Importance sampling is used with image-based lighting to make the sampling of the IBL map more accurate and better reproduce the look of hard light, such as that cast by a small but very bright sun for example. Image-based lighting is covered in Chapter 17, "Image-Based Lighting and More." Samples also can be *adaptive*, meaning that when the renderer finds higher contrast, it shoots out more samples. Adaptive sampling has a minimum and maximum number of samples that the user can set.

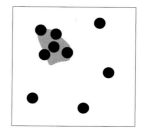

Figure 14.58 Adaptive sampling.

14.5 CHAPTER CONCLUSION

Rendering is an essential part of creating 3D, one attributed to the computer. While the computer does the labor, the artist still has much work to do; a person needs to guide the process. A successful render takes good workflow, problem-solving, and time-management skills. The process of rendering isn't always as predictable as we'd like it to be. Often artifacts or other errors show up. By understanding how the renderer calculates the final image we can better eliminate artifacts and speed up our workflow when needed.

Ray reflections, refractions, and shadows take a general knowledge of how ray tracing works in order to be set up correctly. When working with ray-traced reflections and refractions, the most important aspect technically is getting the number of traced rays correct. This usually requires some testing. These rays interact with each other and also with any traced shadow rays in the scene, so the user needs to consider all the rays for reflections, refractions, and shadows in order to get the correct results.

14.5.1 IMPORTANT POINTS

- Rendering requires active monitoring on the part of the artist to be successful.
- A successful render is one that completes *on time* and *with the quality desired.*
- Be sure to optimize the modeling and texturing of your scene early on for efficient renders: Keep textures *only as large as they need to be* and geometry *only as detailed as it needs to be.*
- Fast test renders will help you get your job done with minimum time spent waiting.
- Problems when rendering are common: Expect them and leave yourself enough time to deal with them.
- Leave enough time to render at least two full-frame, full-resolution, full-quality passes before the due date.
- Check your work while it's rendering. Look at whatever frames finish first and keep an eye on render times.
- Scanline is fast because it only renders visible surfaces, but this limits what it can do.
- Ray tracing "traces" rays through the scene, which gives it its added functionality (and takes longer).
- The artist must control the number of traced rays in order to optimize render time.
- Traced rays are controlled in three main areas: reflections, refractions, shadows.
- "Real" reflections and "real" refractions require ray tracing.
- To determine the correct number of rays, count up the number of surfaces the rays must bounce off of and pass through.
- To determine the correct number of traced shadow rays, count up the number of surfaces the shadow must bounce off of or pass through, plus one.
- Reflections and refractions can be glossy (blurred). Glossy reflections and refractions need more samples, which increases render time.
- Adding Fresnel to your semi-reflective and transparent materials will greatly increase realism.

- Optimum quality settings are always those that give you the quality you require—and no more.
- Aliasing is the problem of too few samples, and anti-aliasing is any method used to fix it.
- Aliasing can manifest in a variety of ways.
- Aliasing is generally corrected by increasing samples in the problem area, which increases render time.

14.5.2 TERMS

render farm	reflection samples	pixel samples
visible surface determination	refraction	shading rate
tessellation	refraction ray limit	stochastic
rasterization	glossy refractions	importance sampling
REYES	refraction samples	adaptive sampling
micropolygon	refractive index	mipmapped
camera rays	Fresnel effect	"jaggies"
reflection ray limit	aliasing	frequency
glossy reflections	anti-aliasing	Nyquist limit

14.5.3 EXERCISES

1. Write a paragraph about the most difficult render you have experienced so far. What problems did you encounter? What solutions did you implement to make it successful? What did you learn from the experience?

2. If you had a render that had 1/2 test resolutions taking about 5 minutes each, how long would a 100-frame animation take? How many processors would you need to get the job done overnight? When would you need to begin in order to get *two* full-frame, full-resolution renders completed (and on how many processors)?

3. Let's say you have an animation that has been rendering for 30 minutes on three machines, and you have 6 frames done. If your job has 250 frames, then how much longer would it take if you don't have access to any additional machines? What if it's 8 p.m. and your job needs to be completed by 8 a.m.? Will it finish on time? If not, how many more machines would you need (assuming all machines have the same number of processors)?

4. Create a still life with both reflective and refractive materials. Create a range of materials: highly reflective (like chrome, mirror, or brass), glossy reflections (dull metal), semi-reflective (like ceramic or car paint), clear transparent (clear glass), partly transparent (colored glass), and glossy transparent (frosted glass). Try your hand at creating all these materials. Be sure to add Fresnel to your semi-reflective and refractive materials and, for good measure, ray trace your shadows.

5. Assign a grid shader to a ground plane and increase the repetitions until the grid begins to alias in the distance. Work with the render settings to eliminate the aliasing. Now try animating it. Does it still hold up? If not, adjust the settings until your animation is artifact-free. What settings did you use? What was your process of problem solving?

Figure 15.1 This romantic scene from *Tangled* (2010) features glowing lanterns and depth cueing to achieve its magical feel. (© Disney. All rights reserved.)

Chapter 15
Tricks of the Trade

"If people knew how hard I worked to get my mastery,

it wouldn't seem so wonderful at all."

—Michelangelo Buonarroti, Italian Renaissance Sculptor, Painter, and Architect

This chapter presents a collection of techniques that are used to gain control and craft a better look or as special effects. These techniques range from intermediate to advanced. Many are commonly used (some daily) in high-end production, yet some are almost unknown among average users.

This chapter seeks to share the wealth, so to speak, and give each lighter some information about techniques they may not otherwise have known about, as well as serving as a reference—a buffet of techniques—for the more experienced lighter.

These techniques can be used in combination with a variety of rendering algorithms as needed. Additional techniques specifically associated with global illumination are covered in Chapter 16, "Global Illumination."

15.1 SHAPING LIGHT

"Glory be to God for dappled things…"

—Gerard Manley Hopkins, 19th-Century Poet

In life, the intensity of light varies across the scene. In CG-land, on the other hand, things tend to be rather uniform—too uniform. CG renders have a tendency to look too smooth, too even, too perfect. It's often a good idea to "muck it up" a bit, and to vary light intensity throughout your scene. Not only can this look more realistic, it can provide visual interest as well.

Real-world light varies in intensity for a variety of reasons. In many cases, it's due to how light is reflected and bounced around. Reflected light takes on the color of the surroundings. It's less intense if reflecting off darker surfaces, more intense when reflecting off lighter surfaces, and has subtle shadowing due to occlusion. When using global illumination, you'll get these interactions "for free" (well, for the cost of additional render time). If not using global illumination, you will need to add them for yourself. Other times, light variation is caused by shadows. One example of this is the dappled light on a forest floor (Figure 15.2). Another example is sunlight on a partly cloudy day. At times the light source itself may be the cause.

Figure 15.2 Dappled light in a forest.

Additionally, artificial light sources have "throw patterns," which are variations in light intensity intrinsic to certain kinds of bulbs.

15.1.1 GOBOS, SLIDES, AND BARN DOORS

A fairly straightforward way to vary the intensity of your lights is with a projection map, such as a gobo or slide.

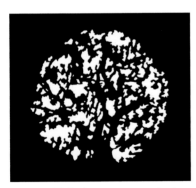

Figure 15.3 A pattern typical of a real gobo.

In life, a *gobo* is a card with some shapes cut out of it used to shadow a light. Gobos are also called *cookies* (short for "cukaloris"). Gobos imitate the shadow of something off-screen. They are often used to add visual interest. Many gobos have random patterns and simply break up the light much like leaves on a tree (Figure 15.3). Gobos such as these are used to provide interest to otherwise flat areas, such as a plain expanse of wall (Figure 15.4). A gobo with a regular pattern could be used to create the shadow from window panes or Venetian blinds (Figure 15.5). Gobos and slides can also be used to break up rays of light that are visible due to fog (Figure 15.6).

The digital gobo and slide are the same in principle. In the case of the digital gobo, a black and white *texture file is supplied as the light's color*. The light is then darkened according to this file without having to actually shadow anything. You don't need to place a card or other object in front of the light. Using a gobo to create the look of a shadow will render many times faster than generating a real shadow. Whenever a shadowing object is off-screen, consider replacing it with a gobo to speed up your render (Figure 15.7).

Figure 15.4 These shadows are from a real tree, but a similar effect could be accomplished with a gobo.

Figure 15.5 In this photo, the look of Venetian blinds was created with a gobo.

Figure 15.6 A simple dot pattern placed in a single digital light. The fog shows how the color is projected out from the light. (Fog is a separate effect.)

Figure 15.7 The dappled light in this scene is created using a digital gobo (*Drag'N'Fly* short by SCAD-Atlanta students, lighting by Ross Cantrell).

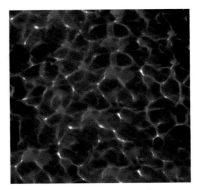

Figure 15.8 An image of a caustic pattern, used as a gobo in Figure 15.9.

Figure 15.9 The caustic pattern in this CG underwater scene is created with a gobo. The texture can be animated to move the pattern realistically.

A *slide* **is essentially the same thing as a gobo; the only difference is that a slide has color.** Using a slide in your light is a lot like adding a slide to a projector. It will colorize the light along the length of the ray and project an image of the texture onto whatever surface it hits.

Unlike a real gobo or slide, a digital one can be easily tiled, repeated, rotated, and mirrored by the artist. Digital lights can use 2D texture files as slides and gobos, and they can also use *procedural textures*. Procedural textures are ones that the 3D software makes for you, such as fractal noise or a grid.

Digital gobos and slides can also be animated (Figures 15.8 and 15.9). To animate a 2D texture, use a file sequence rather than a single frame. Procedural textures are animated by key framing their parameters.

A variation of a slide available to digital spotlights is to vary their color based on the ray direction. Sounds fancy, but it just means that the center of the spotlight is a different color than its edges, which can be accomplished by using a circular ramp as the light's color (Figure 15.10). This technique can also be used to precisely control the penumbra and drop-off (brightness at the center) of the light as well.

***Barn doors* are another technique used to block light.** Barn doors work with spotlights and are specifically shaped to flag the light off along the outside edges into a quadrilateral shape. Often this is done to imitate light coming through a window (Figure 15.11). Other times they are used just to flag off any light from unwanted areas. Barn doors usually have controls for softening the edges, how far into the center each side goes, and the angle of each side.

Figure 15.10 The color of this spotlight is based on a circular ramp.

Figure 15.11 Barn doors are used here to create the look of light coming through a window.

15.1.2 VOLUME LIGHTS, 3D TEXTURES, AND BLOCKERS

Digital lighters can also vary the intensity and color of light throughout a volume. Using volumetric controls will vary the light based on something that exists in three dimensions in the scene. Volumetric variations are not realistically calculated; they are purely artistically crafted and should be used with care.

A few means to sculpt light within a volume are:

◆ Volume lights
◆ 3D textures
◆ Blockers
◆ Projected textures

Volume lights are a way to sculpt light and can be used to either add or remove illumination within their volume. Volume lights were covered in Chapter 1, "First Things First," which also included a few tricks on how to use them. Volume lights have lots of fun uses, such as adding ambient light confined to just one portion of the scene, creating fake soft shadow (when set to a negative intensity), and confining the illumination to specific shapes. Refer to Chapter 1 for examples.

3D textures are another good way to break up illumination. Unlike a 2D texture (a gobo or slide) that is projected from the light, 3D textures occupy three dimensions. 3D textures can be placed in the light's intensity or color parameter in order to break up the illumination. 3D textures are procedural, and the most common one is fractal noise. The use of 3D fractal textures is especially helpful if the entire beam of light is visible, as in when passing through fog (Figure 15.12).

Figure 15.12 The spotlight has a 3D texture placed in its color. A fog light is used to better show the volume of the texture. (Fog is a separate effect.)

Blockers are an advanced method that can be used to sculpt the intensity of light throughout a scene. Similar to volume lights, blockers come in standard 3D shapes of cone, box, cylinder, sphere, and also cards. Unlike volume lights, which are their own light source, blockers work in conjunction with an existing light to modify various attributes of that light. Blockers can change a particular light's intensity only inside their volume, or conversely only outside their volume. Blockers are an advanced feature not commonly found in standard software.

A projected texture, available in most software, can imitate the simplest form of a blocker—a card. Those who are familiar with texture mapping know that textures can be projected along their own coordinate system. This method is similar to a slide or gobo, but the texture projects along an arbitrary axis positioned in the 3D scene, rather than along the rays of the light (Figure 15.13).

Figure 15.13 In these renders of bones, the bounce light's color has been mapped with a gradient projected down the z-axis. The top render has a colorful gradient (shown top right) to see the effect, while the bottom render uses a gradient that fades to black (shown bottom right) to darken the bounce light as it gets farther from the ground plane.

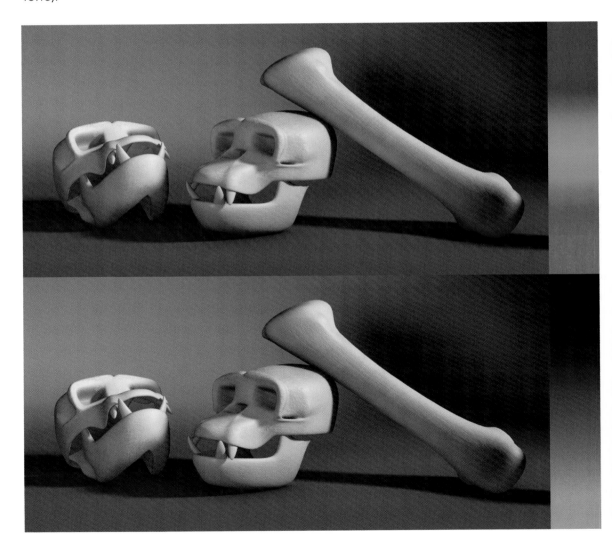

A method discussed in the Chapter 9, "Light Intensity," and worth reminding here, is that a light's color and intensity can be crafted based on the distance from the light. This technique can be used to gain precise control over the attenuation of the light, for artistic reasons, or when you only want your light to begin after a certain distance (see Figure 15.43 in Section 15.6.1 for an example).

TECHNIQUES TO SHAPE LIGHT INTENSITY

- Gobo: A black-to-white texture file placed in the light's color or intensity.
- Slide: A colored texture file placed in the light's color.
- Barn door: A standard feature in most spotlights.
- 3D textures: Procedurally created volume textures placed in the light's color or intensity.
- Blockers: An advanced form of 3D and projected texture not commonly found in most lights. Typically affects intensity and shadow parameters.
- Projected textures: Two-dimensional textures projected down an arbitrary axis, placed in the light's color or intensity.
- Distance curves: Varying color and intensity based on the distance from the light.

15.2 ADVANCED SHADOW TECHNIQUES

This section discusses advanced shadow techniques that can be used to give your shadows a better look and/or save render time. Topics include deep shadows, advanced mapped shadow techniques, and a few tricks that can be used with any shadow type.

Shadows were previously introduced in Chapter 2, "Shadows," which covered in-depth the basic use of the two most common shadow types: ray-traced shadows and depth-mapped shadows. Refer to Chapter 2 for details on these topics. Deep shadows were also briefly introduced, as was ambient occlusion.

Here's a quick recap of shadows and where they are discussed in this book:

- Ray-traced shadows are more realistic and are easier to use, but at the price of slower execution speed (covered in Chapter 2).
- Depth-mapped shadows are fast but have a number of limitations. They are sufficient to produce good results in many situations (covered in Chapter 2; advanced techniques covered here in this chapter).
- Deep shadows combine the benefits of depth shadow maps with some of the features of ray-traced shadows (introduced in Chapter 2; covered in detail here).
- Ambient occlusion imitates the shadowing of fully scattered indirect light (introduced in Chapter 2; covered in detail in Chapter 16).

15.2.1 Using Deep Shadows

A type of shadow that is becoming more commonly available is the deep shadow. While there is nothing intrinsically difficult about deep shadows, they are included in this section because at the present time their use is still relatively uncommon among average users due to the fact that they aren't available in many off-the-shelf packages. Deep shadows have a number of advantages, however, and are frequently used by many animation and visual effects production houses.

Deep shadows have features in common with both ray-traced and depth-mapped shadows. Like depth-mapped shadows, deep shadows are a kind of shadow map; they can be pre-calculated, and the data is stored for later use. Deep shadows have resolution in pixels width and height. Like depth-mapped shadows, these files are always square. Their general method of generation and techniques for optimizing are the same as for regular depth-mapped shadows.

Deep shadows also have some advantages normally associated with ray-traced shadows. Deep shadows motion blur. Deep shadows will also take into account surface properties, which means that unlike depth-mapped shadows, deep shadows will correctly shadow stained glass. Deep shadows allow for partial transparency, which makes them ideal for shadowing volume effects like billowing fog and clouds (compare Figures 15.14 and 15.15).

Figure 15.14 (Left) Pre-calculated depth-mapped shadows are fast but don't work at all for this smoke plume (render time: 1 minute, 43 seconds).

Figure 15.15 (Right) Pre-calculated deep shadows look much better and also render quickly (render time: 1 minute, 57 seconds).

Furthermore, deep shadows anti-alias. Recall that each pixel of a mapped shadow stores information about if the ray shot from that pixel hit a surface or not, and if it did, how far away that surface was. In a depth-mapped shadow, each pixel either has a hit or not, which will produce jagged stair-stepped edges if the map resolution is too low. In the deep shadow map, on the other hand, pixels around object edges may store partial hits, smoothing out the boundary between shadowed and non-shadowed regions (Figures 15.16 through 15.18).

Figure 15.16 Notice the lack of transparency in the shadows and the chunky look of the hair shadow in this render using a pre-calculated depth-mapped shadow (render time: 1 minute, 6 seconds).

Figure 15.17 Ray-traced shadows, used here, deliver an accurate look, but at the cost of a much longer render time (render time: 1 hour, 15 minutes, 52 seconds).

Figure 15.18 Deep shadows, used here, render quickly like depth-mapped shadows but accurately shadow transparency and fine detail like the ray-traced shadow (render time: 1 minute, 7 seconds).

Since deep shadows anti-alias, they can generate good-looking shadows for fine geometry such as hair. To achieve a similar result with a regular depth-mapped shadow, you would need to dramatically increase its resolution to capture all of the detail.

Deep shadows store more information per pixel and can be rendered at a much lower resolution than depth-mapped shadows. For example, in cases where a depth-mapped shadow might need to be 2k (2048x2048) or 4k (4096x4096), a deep shadow of the same subject may only need to be 512x512. Because deep shadows store more information, they take longer to render and are larger files in terms of the disk space they need than depth-mapped shadows.

As a limitation, by default deep shadows don't blur with distance the way traced shadows do, but rather blur uniformly like a depth-mapped shadow.

Because of their added functionality and their ability to be pre-calculated, deep shadows are frequently used in animation and visual effects productions. Since they take longer to generate, they should only be used if you need their distinct benefits.

SUMMARIZING DEEP SHADOWS

Benefits:

✓ Can be pre-calculated (faster to render)
✓ Motion blur
✓ Correctly capture transparency
✓ Correctly shadow volumes
✓ Ideal for very fine geometry

Limitations:

• Require some setup
• Don't blur realistically with distance

Workflow Tips:

• Only use deep shadows if you need their advantages, because they take longer to render.
• Remember that deep shadows generally can be much smaller in size: often 512x512 is sufficient.

15.2.2 MAPPED SHADOW TECHNIQUES

Here's the truth: Getting a good look out of mapped shadows can be difficult. Depth-mapped shadows have many limitations and are more prone to artifacts than the other shadow types. These artifacts are avoidable, but doing so takes a bit of know-how and experience. Refer to Chapter 2 for how to solve common artifacts and basic techniques for using and optimizing depth maps.

Some advanced techniques can transform the look of depth-mapped shadows from merely adequate (or even at times insufficient) to good enough to achieve photorealism in many cases. These techniques are equally applicable to deep shadow maps as well. Advanced lighters in film-production houses are well versed in these tricks, but their use is almost completely unknown by lighters restricted to off-the-shelf software. One of my first motivators for writing this book was to share some techniques seemingly restricted to an elite group with students of lighting in general. Mapped shadow techniques are in this category.

Every digital lighting artist needs a solid command of mapped shadows in their arsenal of techniques. While ray-traced shadows are much more common now than in the past, the mapped shadow still has a place and is often used. Due to their fast speed, mapped shadows can be combined with other more render-intensive techniques like global illumination and sub-surface scattering. Wouldn't a production spending time on these techniques just go ahead and ray trace everything? Not necessarily. Some productions do, and some productions don't. The preferred technique depends to a large degree on which rendering algorithm you are using. If you are ray tracing your entire render, then you are likely to use mostly or only ray-traced shadows. If you're using primarily scanline and incorporating ray-traced and global illumination features selectively, on the other hand, then you'll likely use mapped shadows mostly and resort to ray-traced shadows only when absolutely necessary or not at all. Another consideration is the level of realism desired as opposed to the amount of artistic control. When combined with advanced techniques, mapped shadows provide a greater degree of artistic control and are thus the common choice for stylized full CG animation.

Multiple Mapped Shadows

One of the most fundamental ways to improve the look of depth-mapped shadows is to have more than one of them per light. This may come as a surprise to those who haven't had this option, but there is nothing to say that a light can only read in one mapped shadow. We have seen that each point light generates and pulls back in six depth-mapped shadows, one along each of the positive and negative directions of each axis. The fact is, any light can pull in multiple shadow files—as long as the light shader is designed to do so. Advanced usage of mapped shadows allows for several different depth maps to be put into any given light.

When using multiple shadow maps, the user must actively manage the generation and reuse of each shadow. Rather than letting the renderer do it all for you, the lighter must set up specific shadow map renders and explicitly pull each of these renders back into the light once they are complete. Getting the hang of generating your own shadow maps takes a bit of practice. Once you get used to this technique it becomes fairly easy, but accomplishing it still remains another step in the process. More intermediate steps are the drawback of this feature.

The visual advantage of this is that each of these shadows can have its own blur, bias, color, and density settings (Figure 15.19). When creating convincing mapped shadows, and depth-mapped shadows in particular, this additional control is a tremendous help. You can even mix shadow types. For example, hair on characters is often split out into a deep shadow map, while the body of the character is shadowed with a depth-mapped shadow. Each of these shadows typically has very different settings from the others.

One practical advantage of multiple shadows is that the shadow of static objects can be decoupled from the shadows of moving objects. As an example, suppose you have an animation with a character moving throughout a full CG environment. If using multiple mapped shadows, the artist can render one shadow map for the environment without the character, and another shadow map with just the character. For the non-moving environment, only one frame needs to be generated and reused for the entire animation. On the other hand, the character's shadow would be rendered every frame. If the animation on the character changes, only the character's shadow needs to be re-rendered.

Another practical advantage is that each of these shadows can be optimized by centering it on its subject, which brings us to the next advanced usage of depth-mapped shadows— shadow cameras.

Figure 15.19 Each fish in this image has its own depth-mapped shadow, each with its own blur and color settings.

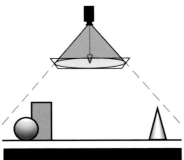

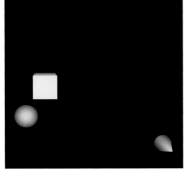

Figure 15.20 Using one shadow map in a scene with objects spread out produces a depth map with much wasted space.

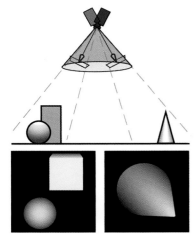

Figure 15.21 By using multiple shadow maps each generated from a different camera, each subject can be optimized in its own depth map.

Shadow Cameras

In order to make effective use of multiple shadows, each of these shadows should be optimized for its own subject. Imagine an overhead light in the center of a large room with two different characters, each standing in a different side of the room, as in Figure 15.20. Let's say that each of the two characters has its own shadow map. Initially, neither one of these depth maps is going to be very optimized—each shadow map will have a lot of empty space on one side or the other. To be efficient, you will want the subject to fill up the map with as few black, wasted pixels as possible. To accomplish this, you will need to render each map from its own camera and have each of these cameras pointing *directly at its subject*. In this way each map can be tightened in around its subject and optimized, as in Figure 15.21.

But wait, you say, I thought the light itself generated the depth map? Well, no, actually, it doesn't. Your renderer has been making it simple for you. At render time, unbeknownst to you, your renderer has been making a camera on the fly, placing it at the position of the light, orienting it down the axis of the light, and using the light's cone angle to determine this camera's field of view (or a user-supplied angle if you have this option). This camera has been used to generate a depth-mapped shadow, then discarded when the map is rendered—all behind the scenes. A bit of rendering sleight of hand.

Advanced users often make their own cameras from which to render mapped shadows. These cameras are known as *shadow cameras*. I'll sometimes refer to them as "shadcams" for short.

Setting Up a Shadow Camera

Spotlights are the easiest light types from which to generate and control mapped shadows. For this reason, let's start by explaining how to set up shadow cameras in combination with a spotlight.

First, match the position of the shadow camera to the position of the light in order for the shadow to correctly line up. Usually, the easiest way to accomplish this is to point-constrain the shadcam to the light. If the shadow camera is point constrained, you can move the light around, and the shadow camera will automatically follow along. The orientation (rotation) of the shadow camera does *not* need to match that of the light, however. The shadow camera can aim in an entirely different direction, and its shadow will still exactly and correctly line up with the light, a fact which may be a bit surprising at first.

The aim of the shadow camera should be centered on its *subject*. Once the shadcam is aimed at its subject, the angle of view of the shadow camera should be narrowed until the subject fills the frame, optimizing the shadow far more efficiently than one depth map covering everything ever could. Another advantage of this setup is that the aim of the shadow camera can be animated, even while the aim of the light remains constant. You can track the aim of the shadow camera along with a moving subject. It's often best to constrain the aim of the shadcam to the subject. If the aim is constrained to the subject, it will track automatically. This allows you to keep the angle of view tight in around the subject so that the shadow remains well optimized even when the subject is moving (Figures 15.22 through 15.24).

Figure 15.22 A character moving across a scene like this one is a good candidate for a dedicated shadow camera (set and character model by Brenda Weede).

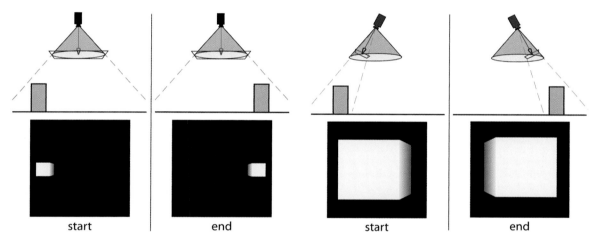

| start | end | start | end |

Figure 15.23 (Left) With one static shadow camera, a moving subject only occupies a small area of the depth map.

Figure 15.24 (Right) If the shadow camera is animated to point at the moving subject at all times, the shadow map can be better optimized.

A final constraint you may choose to set up is the field of view of the shadow camera to the bounding box of the subject. This constraint means that the field of view will dynamically adjust so that the subject never pops out of the shadow. If you don't have this constraint set up, then you will want to carefully check different frames to make sure that the subject at no time moves out of the shadow. The savvy lighter may ask, won't the changing field of view mean that the subject gets bigger and smaller in the shadow file, and won't this affect my blur settings? The answer is YES, good thinking—it could. But this only becomes a problem if the subject changes dramatically in size in the shadow map. For example, in my own experience the only time this came up was on the *Matrix Reloaded*, when the Sentinels (those who saw the film may recall they were machines with *very* long tentacles) animated from being wound-up balls to fully extended. In this case they changed size within the depth map so dramatically that the blur animated noticeably. Other than a situation like this, you'll likely not notice any problem.

When setting up a shadow camera for a directional light, match the orientation of the shadow camera to the orientation of the light and then position the camera to best frame the shadowing objects. The correct camera type for a directional light is an orthographic camera, which renders with parallel rays. If you are using a perspective camera as the shadcam for a directional light, however, be sure to pull the camera far back from its subject and use a very narrow field of view to imitate parallel rays.

Workflow Tips When Using Shadow Cameras

When creating your own shadow cameras, it's very important to *check your shadow renders before using them,* at least the first time you render your shadow passes. Doing so will allow you to catch any errors before integrating the shadow into the primary render, and it will save you headaches down the line. Shadow maps cannot be viewed by ordinary image viewers; you will need a special utility that can view shadow maps. RenderMan's "sho" will view mapped files, for example, but it will only view single frames, not play animations.

When working with shadow cameras and multiple mapped shadows, you should split out shadows only as needed. Multiple mapped shadow passes add complexity to your scene, and remember the rule for adding complexity: Only do it if you gain a needed advantage. If one shadow is working fine for all of the objects in your scene, then one mapped shadow is all you need! Never add complexity "just because," which is a common pitfall for both experienced and new lighters alike.

Also, as when adding any kind of complexity, you'll need to stay organized and follow a good naming convention. You will want to name the shadow map so that the light it's associated with is clear, as well as its subject. For example, for a light named "lgt_key" the shadow camera may be called "shd_key." If there is more than one shadow camera, which is often the case, additional modifiers would be added to the name to indicate the unique subject of each shadow. For example, the shadow camera rendering the hair of the character Chris would be "shd_key_chris_hair." The maps rendered should follow the name of the shadow camera. Inside the scene, it's helpful to group the shadow cameras with the lights and name the top node something descriptive.

As a final workflow tip, be sure to optimize the render settings for the shadow passes. When you're in charge of generating your own shadow passes, you'll have control over all these settings. In addition to the resolution, you should set the number of samples (1 is fine for depth-mapped shadows since they don't anti-alias). You even can (and should) render out your scene with more streamlined materials. Complex shaders that load many color maps are unnecessary for depth-mapped renders and for deep shadows that aren't calculating transparency. Bump is also unnecessary. You should keep displacements, as these need to be calculated in with the shadows. Assigning more simple materials for your shadow renders will speed up the rendering of these passes.

Production studios have scripts that facilitate the process of creating and implementing custom shadow maps; otherwise, the process is very step-intensive. Additional scripts often organize the shadow maps so that each frame of a particular shadow resides in its own folder. You can do this without scripts, of course; the process is just a bit more work. The payoff, however, is *much* faster renders than with traced shadows and *much* better-looking mapped shadows than when you use only one default shadow map per light.

Realistically Blurring and Fading Mapped Shadows

Another feature not commonly available to the average user is the ability to blur and fade mapped shadows realistically with distance. Realistic blurring of mapped shadows can be accomplished by rendering several mapped shadows around the position of the light. The light shader then interpolates between all of these shadows to create a soft-shadow look. That is, if you have a light with this capability. Advanced software allows the user to indicate the width and number of shadows, and the software does the rest. Pixar's RenderMan for Maya Studio Pro makes this technique available and easy to set up through the use of Slim. Studios, such as Disney and Pixar, often use blurred mapped shadows. They use special light shaders that allow the artists to set how much blur and even density they want at specified distances from the shadow-casting object. This allows the lighters greater creative freedom and allows the look of the shadows to be fully art directed (Figure 15.25).

A deep shadow that is blurred realistically with distance looks just like a ray-traced shadow, having all of the same visual advantages—realistic transparency, motion blur…and realistic blurring and fading with distance. All able to be pre-calculated and reused at a fraction of the render cost of a ray-traced shadow. The disadvantages are that the lighter has to set up his or her own shadow map passes and manage more data.

A similar, if more limited, effect can be set up by using 3D blockers that affect shadow parameters. Blockers, mentioned in the section on sculpting light intensity, can also affect the blur and density of a shadow. When correctly set up, the blocker can improve the realism of a mapped shadow by increasing its blur and decreasing its density as the shadow gets farther from the shadow-casting object. Since blockers are positioned in the 3D scene, this effect is best used when neither the light nor its subject is moving, such as with elements in an environment or figures that are relatively static.

Figure 15.25 Disney's *Bolt* used advanced soft-mapped shadow techniques to be able to realistically blur shadows with distance but still pre-calculate them (©Disney).

Figure 15.26 These depth-mapped shadows have been made to blur and fade with distance, using distance curves.

Another option is to use distance curves. A little known fact is that, in some applications, the various parameters of the light can change based on the distance from the light. You are familiar with a change in intensity with distance, known as *attenuation*. In the digital world, however, any parameter can be made to change with distance, including shadow parameters like blur and density. Because of this, distance curves can be used to craft a shadow that seems to blur and lighten with distance from its subject. This technique has a number of limitations and is only recommended on static objects, such as non-moving environment props, but it's a fun option with which to experiment and may have use in some situations (Figure 15.26).

15.2.3 SHADOW-ONLY LIGHTS

Most of the shadow techniques we have been discussing so far require special shaders or special features that aren't, alas, commonly available in a wide variety of packages. You can, in most cases, accomplish similar results with off-the-shelf packages if you are willing to use other cheats, however. Here is another technique, *shadow-only lights*, which can be used in most any package.

Shadow-only lights are lights that do not provide any illumination; they only shadow. To set them up you will want to first create a spotlight and shadow it. Next set the light's intensity to a negative number. Negative light intensities will suck light out of the scene. In order to remove light only from the shadow area, set the color of the light to black and the color of the shadow to white. With this bit of magic, the light can be made to cast no illumination, only removing light from its shadow (Figures 15.27 through 15.29).

Figure 15.27 The original scene with one shadowing light and no added shadows.

Figure 15.28 The same scene with an additional spotlight placed over one statue in preparation for adding a shadow-only light.

Figure 15.29 The scene again with the additional spotlight converted to a shadow-only light.

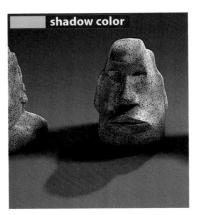

Figure 15.30 A tinted shadow from a shadow-only light.

Sample settings in a shadow-only light might be:

◆ Light intensity: –.5 (must be a negative number, best between –1 and 0)
◆ Light color: black (light color must be black)
◆ Shadow color: white (shadow color cannot be black)

The color of a shadow-only light can be tinted, but the color the shadow actually appears is opposite on the color wheel to the shadow color you have input into the light. So if you want a red shadow, you'll need to put cyan into the shadow color parameter (Figure 15.30).

This technique is equally effective with mapped as well as ray-traced shadows. An advantage of this technique is that each shadow light can be optimized around its subject. To optimize a shadow-only light, constrain its cone angle tightly around its subject. Each shadow can have its own blur and density settings as well. To lighten the shadow, change the intensity of the light so it's closer to 0.

Shadow-only lights can be paired with directional lights with good results. Recall that spotlights offer the most control over mapped shadows, and directional lights the least. You can turn off shadowing in the directional light and pair it with one or more shadow-only spotlights pointing in the same direction as the directional light. (Be sure to pull each shadow light far back and narrow its cone in order to make its rays close to parallel.) This gives you highly controllable shadows coming from shadow lights instead of only one potentially problematic shadow generated by the directional light.

As a word of caution, shadow lights are complete fake and should be used with care as to not produce odd-looking and unrealistic results. As a drawback, shadow lights aren't associated with any one light—they suck illumination out from *all* lights, which may not be desirable. Overlapping shadows from multiple shadow lights will darken each other further. This will look like shadows from two separate lights, as opposed to looking like one continuous shadow from one light.

15.3 FAKING SOFT LIGHT

Soft light, easy to come by in life, is render-intensive to create in the computer. Both area lights and environment lights deliver soft light but cost in render time. For this reason the look of soft light is sometimes cheated rather than more realistically created. Sometimes there simply isn't time to use area lights, or environment lights, or global illumination. Additionally, if a production or artist is using depth-mapped shadows, then spotlights are preferred over area lights both because they render quickly and because they offer the most shadow control.

Cheating soft light takes some skill and know-how on the part of the artist. Firstly, the artist needs a solid understanding of this light property. As a brief recap, here are the three visual characteristics of soft light:

1. Broad, low specular to no specular at all
2. Soft, lifted shadow to no shadow at all
3. Gradual, wrapped terminator

Each of the characteristics will need to be imitated to fully capture the look of soft light. Next, the artist needs to be familiar with a few methods to cheat it. There are two main ways to cheat the look of soft light:

1. Multiple light sources
2. Custom light and surface shaders

15.3.1 Using Multiple Light Sources to Soften Light

Multiple hard lights (such as spotlights) can imitate the look of a single soft light source. In this cheat, two to several hard lights are placed in an arc roughly covering the area of the imagined single soft light source (Figure 15.31).

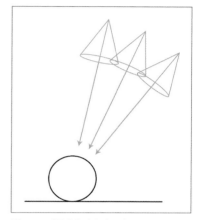

Figure 15.31 Multiple spotlights can be used to imitate the look of a single soft (area) light.

When using this technique, you would start with a single hard light and position it as desired. Then to soften it, duplicate the light and roll it around a bit so that the new light's illumination extends that of the original light. For example, if you had a key at an 80-degree angle to the subject, then the new light could be placed top-down. The illumination from this light will blend in with the key, and both lights will appear to come from one source. The advantage is the illumination will wrap around the object more and soften its appearance. The intensities of the additional lights should be low, as their illuminations overlap.

Adding multiple lights in this fashion will wrap the terminator past half of the object. This method gives the artist much control over the look of the terminator. This technique can also be used to provide a slight color shift to the light as it wraps around the object. For example, the key could be white while the additional light is slightly tinted.

Since the illusion is that these two lights make up one source, you only want one apparent specular. If you can see multiple specular highlights, you will need to turn some of them off, as multiple highlights will give your cheat away. If you wish to cheat the look of a larger highlight from your arc of lights, then you could use an area light as a specular-only light and make the other lights non-specular. This would render fairly quickly, as the only contribution from the area light would be specular.

Likewise, there should only be the appearance of one shadow. Blur each light's shadow in order to have all the shadows visually blend together into one soft shadow. In some cases, you may lighten or turn off some of the light's shadows, if you are okay with the shadow being lifted.

EXAMPLES OF SOFTENING ILLUMINATION BY USING MULTIPLE LIGHTS

Even a single additional light can soften the look of your illumination (Figures 15.32 and 15.33). A more complex approach uses more than one additional light (Figures 15.34 and 15.35).

Example 1: Adding a Top-Down Light

Figure 15.32 This key light still looks harsh even with a very blurred shadow (key light only, angled at about 60 degrees from the side and with an intensity of 1.2). Notice the hot specular, dark shadow, and crisp terminator.

Figure 15.33 Adding the top-down light still looks like one source from the right, but it seems like softer light now. Notice that the wrap is increased, the specular is less hot, and the shadow has a subtle gradation from light to dark (key reduced to .7 intensity; top light at .6 intensity). Both lights contribute specular, and the top light has a very blurred, lightened mapped shadow that provides a contact shadow.

Example 2: An Arc of Lights

Figure 15.34 A single key light with one depth-mapped shadow (key intensity at .8).

Figure 15.35 Three depth-mapped shadowed lights act as the key, intensities ranging from .5 to .2. Notice the blurrier shadows and softer terminators.

15.3.2 USING SHADERS TO SOFTEN LIGHT

The best and most efficient solution to cheating soft light is to use custom shaders that have parameters to imitate its look. This method is commonly found in professional studios, especially those that use RenderMan. The problem is that few artists have access to such shaders.

Creating a soft shadow is easy and common to find in most any light shader—just blur the shadow and possibly lift the density. The problem becomes the other two visual qualities—the highlight and the terminator. When only the shadow is blurred and these other two qualities remain hard, something looks "off" to the viewer; something looks "CG," but it's difficult for the audience to figure out for sure what it is. Custom soft light shaders allow the artist to manipulate these other two attributes as well, so that shadow softness, terminator softness, and highlight size are all in line with the desired level of light diffusion.

To achieve a soft light look, the highlight needs to be modified on a per-light basis. Any 3D package will allow you to modify the size and intensity of the specular highlight for the entire surface. This is the surface property of *roughness*, and these controls are found in the surface shader. Unfortunately, this doesn't help to give you a sense of each light's quality. Recall that hard lights contribute relatively small and bright highlights. Soft lights, on the other hand, contribute relatively broad, dim highlights. In most software packages, lighters can only turn off the specular highlight from a given light, which is rather limited. A custom soft light shader, however, will fully control the look of the highlight coming from each light. When adjusting the highlight, keep in mind that just broadening or just dimming it alone isn't accurate; you need to adjust these two parameters together—both broader *and* dimmer.

To cheat soft light, you also need to adjust the look of the terminator on a per-light basis. Recall that hard lights have abrupt terminators. Soft lights, on the other hand, have gradual terminators that wrap around the surface. Custom soft light shaders will allow the artist to control the look of the terminator coming from each light. When adjusting the terminator, you must adjust two features—firstly, wrap it so light shines on more than half of the subject. Next, soften the edge of the terminator, usually with something similar to a gamma function.

In order for the wrapped light to work, you *must* adjust the shadow as well. If your faked soft light has no shadow, as in the case of a low-level fill or the like, then you are in luck; you can wrap away with no problems. However, if your light has a shadow, then you must use a depth-mapped shadow with this cheat, and you must both blur and bias this depth-mapped shadow a great deal. This will soften the edges of the shadow and allow your wrapped light to bleed around. Luckily, this works fine because soft light should have a blurry, indistinct shadow anyway. If you don't blur and bias your shadow, it will cut off your wrapped light, producing an even harder and more odd-looking terminator than the one you were trying to avoid. You cannot use a ray-traced shadow with an artificially wrapped terminator. Ray-traced shadows are too realistic, and they will always cut off any light wrapped in the shader.

TIP

When artificially softening a light, carefully check to make sure you haven't carried your cheat too far and shown your magician's hand.

Figures 15.36 through 15.38 illustrate how special shaders can transform the look of spotlights from hard light to soft light without any increase in render time.

Figure 15.36 A single spotlight in this scene uses default shading values, creating hard light.

Figure 15.37 The same spotlight now looks soft due to adjusted shader parameters that soften and wrap the terminator, enlarge and dim the highlight, and blur the shadow.

Figure 15.38 The finished image uses only spotlights with a variety of soft light settings. Notice how some spotlights contribute hard specular highlights, others soft highlights, and still others no specular at all. All spotlights have softened terminators.

SHADER PARAMETERS TO CHEAT SOFT LIGHT

On a per-light basis, adjust these settings:

- Increase terminator wrap *and*
- Decrease terminator gamma.
- Increase specular size *and*
- Decrease specular intensity.

If the light has a shadow:

- Increase shadow blur *and*
- Increase shadow bias.
- Possibly decrease shadow density.

Note: You cannot use a ray-traced shadow with a light using this technique.

Important Tips:

- All these parameters must be adjusted together!
- Be aware of how your shadows are interacting with your cheat, so as not to introduce artifacts.

15.4 SIMPLE EFFECTS: FOG LIGHTS, ATMOSPHERE, AND GLOWS

A few effects are simple, and it's highly likely that you'll use them at some point. Among these effects are fog lights, atmosphere, and glows. All of these effects make light and air visible. These effects are relatively easy to implement and are handy to know about. They imitate real effects found in nature (see the photographs in Figures 15.39 through 15.41).

Figure 15.39 Real-world visible light rays (fog light).

Figure 15.40 Photograph of morning mist (atmosphere).

Figure 15.41 Photograph demonstrating light bloom (glow).

15.4.1 Fog Lights

A *fog light* **imitates the effect of a particular light becoming visible due to passing through suspended particulate matter,** such as dust or mist or…fog. We are all familiar with this when driving on a misty evening and seeing car headlights. In CG we often want to imitate the look of light as it shines through smoke, mist, or other fine particular matter, and there are a few ways to do this.

Most applications allow for a somewhat realistic creation of fog within certain lights. Exactly how this is accomplished depends on the software and light shader used. Mental Ray allows you to set up what is known as a *participating volume*, and inside this volume indicated lights will be visible as if shining through fog. Other applications allow you to select fog as an option in a particular light and adjust various density and color settings. Refer to your software's documentation for how to create fog for certain lights only.

When creating fog lights, be wary of making your fog too uniform. Since all of the light's illumination becomes visible, your light may need attenuation in order to stay realistic or visually interesting. A bit of noise within a fog light often adds visual interest. Three-dimensional fractal noise breaks up the look of fog nicely (Figure 15.12). This fractal noise should not move with the light, but rather be in a fixed position in the world. Remember the light is to be shining through a fog that exists as part of the environment, not taking fog with it everywhere it goes. If you are adding noise to your fog, make sure the noise is calculated in world space, so that it does not move with the light. The noise in the fog will look best if it animates over time to imitate the subtle movement of air.

Gobos and shadowing objects also add interest, as they break up the fog into beams of light (see Figures 15.6 and 15.42 for examples).

If your light is coming out of a visible light source, such as a flashlight or lamppost, you may have the problem of part of the cone of light showing up where you don't want it. To solve for this, you'll want to work with custom decay regions. This is the time to have the intensity of your light off until it reaches a certain distance. If your light has no illumination until a certain distance away from the CG light source, then the real position of the light will not be revealed (Figure 15.43).

Figure 15.42 Underwater shot from *Drag'N'Fly.* (SCAD-Atlanta student short. Lighting and compositing by Visual Effects student Steve Dinozzi.)

Figure 15.43 The lamppost on the left has illumination and fog showing above the lamp geometry, while the middle lamppost attempts to solve the problem by lowering the light source below the lamp geometry; neither solution produces good results. The far-right lamppost uses decay regions to turn off illumination until inside the bulb geometry, so that light correctly seems to begin inside the bulb.

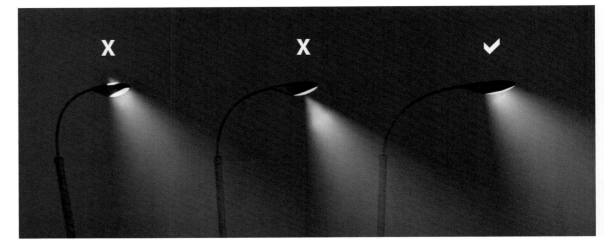

Fog can even be modeled as geometry in the scene. In the case of a spotlight, just model a cone and constrain it so that its tip matches the position of the light and the axis of the cone is oriented along the axis of the light. Ideally, the width of the cone is further constrained so that it matches the cone angle of the light's illumination. To get this cheat to work, you'll need a special material assigned to the fog cone. The geometric fog cone should be incandescent and semi-transparent. Fade out the transparency as the cone moves toward both the base and the sides for the best result. This approach isn't very realistic but has the advantage of rendering quickly.

15.4.2 ATMOSPHERE

Atmosphere **is an effect similar to fog only instead of being confined to particular lights, atmosphere is everywhere.** Creating a bit of atmosphere is extremely common in production, especially film, as it enhances the illusion of depth (Figure 15.44). Real cinematographers often add a bit of atmosphere by using fog machines on set, as adding even just a tiny bit helps separate foreground and background.

Figure 15.44 Disney's *Tangled* made frequent use of atmosphere as a stylistic choice. In this still, atmosphere enhances setting, creates depth, and separates the character from the background. (©Disney. All rights reserved.)

The most common way to create atmosphere is to incorporate it in the composite. This method is fast and even more importantly is easy to control and adjust without having to re-render the scene. To add atmosphere in the composite, you'll want to render out a z-depth pass. The z-depth pass is then used to control the density of a uniform color (your fog), which gets laid over the rest of the render. For how to integrate atmosphere in the composite, see Chapter 18, "Multi-Pass Rendering."

Atmosphere can also be rendered in with the 3D scene. How this is implemented varies greatly from software to software. It can be accomplished with a particle effect or it can be a 2D effect that is added by the renderer. Generally, atmosphere isn't rendered in the 3D scene unless it has a sense of substance, as with mist that curls around the bases of trees and rocks. In this case, it may be generated as a particle effect.

15.4.3 GLOWS

In the digital arena, a *glow* is anything that has a halo of luminance around it, and/or is visibly seen to emit light or *seem to* emit light. Glows give presence to the light. Repeated use of glows as part of the visual style can impart a certain magical or luminous feel (refer to Figure 15.1).

Lights, surfaces, and highlights can all be made to glow. When it comes to light, a glow is a halo around a source of light, making the source visible beyond the boundaries of the light (a halo around something is also known as "bloom"). Similar to bloom are flares and stars, which appear at the position of the light and imitate optical lens effects. In terms of surfaces, a glowing surface is one that appears to emit light, such as the body of a firefly. Sometimes just the highlight of a surface can be given a bit of bloom, which imitates an optical effect inside the lens. For example, the film *The Polar Express* used bloom around all visible lights and around the highlights in very shot to help give the film a storybook look and feel.

Glows can be accomplished in a variety of ways. Incorporating glow involves three visual characteristics:

◆ Making the surface appear self-illuminated
◆ Making the surface actually shine light on objects around it
◆ Giving the light or surface a bloom or halo

Depending on the look you're trying to create, you may want one, two, or all of these visual characteristics (see Figures 15.45 and 15.46 for examples). The following paragraphs describe the various ways to achieve these looks.

One way to add glow is to create it in the 3D scene. When working with glowing surfaces, you'll need to make them appear as if they are self-illuminated. To do this, add incandescence to the surface. Incandescence, found in every basic material, brightens the surface regardless of any light striking the surface (Figure 15.48). However, it's important to realize that when rendering with either scanline or ray tracing, making a surface incandescent will *not* make it actually cast light into the scene.

Figure 15.45 Added light sources, incandescent materials, and bloom are all used in this render to create a glowing effect.

Figure 15.46 This 3D render combines an incandescent material with a light source.

When scanline rendering or ray tracing, if you want your surface to cast light, you'll need to pair it with a CG light source as well (Figures 15.50 and 15.51). On the other hand, when rendering with most global illumination methods, an incandescent surface *will* actually illuminate the objects around it (Figure 15.52), which provides more realism and some interesting lighting possibilities (more on lighting with global illumination is in Chapter 18).

Additionally, most digital surfaces and lights have a simple "glow" option that adds halo around the light or surface (Figures 15.49 and 15.50). This halo does not actually shine any light on anything around it, however. Even though your 3D renderer is making it, this kind of glow is a 2D effect added on top of the image after it's rendered. Glow added in this manner is easy to implement, but offers little control to the artist and sometimes has objectionable artifacts (such as unwanted flickering upon animation). If you want bloom but need precise control, try adding it in the composite instead.

The advantage of adding bloom-type glow in the composite is that you have more control. You can also change the glow without re-rendering the entire scene. The disadvantage is that it's an extra step. This method is the one most often chosen when the visual look of the glow must be high quality. Adding glow in the composite is described in Chapter 18, "Multi-Pass Rendering."

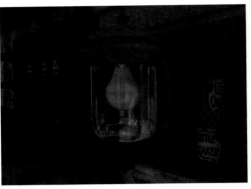

Figure 15.47 With no special treatment, this light is clearly not glowing.

Figure 15.48 Adding an incandescent material is a start but still no glow.

Figure 15.49 Adding 3D "glow" adds a bloom around the bulb and brightens it, but no light is actually emitted— something is missing.

Figure 15.50 A light source is added to cast illumination into the scene. Now we have all three together—illumination, incandescence, and bloom.

Figure 15.51 This version removes the bloom around the bulb. In this case, it may not be needed.

A final down-and-dirty way to add bloom is to fake it with special geometry in the 3D scene. The technique is the same as when using a cone of geometry to imitate a fog light. To fake a small round halo, place a sphere in the scene and map it with both incandescence and transparency. Give the sphere more transparency around the edges. This method has the advantage of being highly controllable by the user, who can modify the color and scale of the glow easily. This kind of glow will scale with distance, because the spheres are smaller when farther away.

Figure 15.52 This render of neon tubing uses only incandescence and is rendered with global illumination.

GLOWS CAN BE ADDED TO:

- Lights
- Surfaces
- Highlights

Visual characteristics:

- Self-illumination of the surface (accomplished with incandescence in the material)
- Bloom/halo around the glowing object (a simple "glow" accomplished in the 3D material or composite)
- Light emission onto nearby objects (may need to add an additional light source)

Methods to create glow:

- Added by the renderer (an option in the material or light)
- Added in the composite
- Faked with special geometry

Tips when working with glow:

- Remember that with most renderers, an incandescent material must be paired with a light source to truly emit light.
- The most controllable glow (bloom) is done in the composite.

15.5 CHAPTER CONCLUSION

In today's climate, a wider variety of techniques are in use than ever before. Often the decision on which technique to use is based on the level of realism desired, the skill set of the people involved, and last but not least, the amount of time able to be spent on rendering. A common trade-off is artist time versus computer time. This chapter has covered several techniques of lighting that have been in use for years and still find widespread application today. Most of these tricks involve "artist time," requiring skilled artists to implement. Later chapters will cover additional techniques involving global illumination and image-based lighting, which are increasingly being used and rely more heavily on the renderer.

While one approach may be more in favor than another depending on the production house or the lighter, every lighter should be versed in a variety of techniques. By knowing a variety of ways to create an effect, the lighter can choose which one best fits his or her situation and, in turn, better serve the needs of potential employers and clients.

15.5.1 IMPORTANT POINTS

- Natural light varies in intensity throughout the environment, primarily due to reflection and shadowing.
- Digital light tends to be too uniform and needs more variety in intensity.
- A number of methods can be used by artists to vary their light intensity throughout their scene, some more realistic and others less so.
- Gobos, slides, and barn doors block light much like real-world shadows and projections.
- Digital lighters should take advantage of gobos to cheat shadows from objects off-screen, in order to save render time.
- Less realistically based methods for sculpting light intensity include 3D textures and blockers, which must be used with care to avoid looking unrealistic.
- Deep shadows combine many of the benefits of both depth-mapped shadows and ray-traced shadows.
- Deep shadows work well for semi-transparent objects, such as clouds, and fine geometry, such as hair.
- Mapped shadows can deliver a high-quality look if the lighter has the right tools and know-how.
- Generating more than one mapped shadow per light is an important means to improve the look and optimization of mapped shadows.
- Shadow cameras are used to render and optimize multiple mapped shadows.
- Constraints on the shadow camera will help you optimize each shadow.
- Advanced lighting tools allow for mapped shadows to blur and fade with distance.
- Shadow-only lights allow the lighter to place shadows precisely where they are needed, but they must be used with care to avoid unrealistic results.
- Using multiple hard lights can cheat the look of a single soft light, a technique available to anyone.
- Custom soft light shaders are the most efficient means of cheating soft light but are not commonly available.

◆ Fog, atmosphere, and glows are common effects with which every lighter should be familiar.

◆ Fog lights often benefit from being made less uniform by adding textures into the lights' color or intensity.

◆ Atmosphere can be generated in 3D but usually is created in the composite instead.

◆ Glows involve three features: incandescence, illumination, and bloom. Any or all of these things may be incorporated into a "glow" effect.

◆ Surfaces, lights, and highlights can all be made to glow.

◆ Bloom-type glow is generally best done in the composite for the most control.

15.5.2 TERMS

gobo	3D texture	deep shadow	atmosphere
cukaloris ("cookie")	light	shadow camera	glow
slide	blocker	shadow-only light	bloom
barn door	projected texture	fog light	incandescence

15.5.3 EXERCISES

1. Create a digital gobo (a black-to-white texture) that imitates a dappled forest. Render a sample scene that uses your gobo. To build a grayscale texture as a gobo, I recommend starting with some pictures of leaves and branches and manipulating them in a paint program.

2. Create a simple scene that imitates light coming in from a window just out of view. Create the square shadow of the window with barn doors. Give the window Venetian blinds with a procedurally generated gobo.

3. Use a projected texture to change the color and intensity of your light as it goes upward in the y-axis, regardless of light angle.

4. If your renderer has deep-shadow capability, perform some timing tests between depth-mapped shadows, deep shadows, and ray-traced shadows on a variety of subjects. What were the advantages and disadvantages you experienced? How did each look?

5. Set up a simple scene with three or more subjects at different distances from the ground plane. Using either multiple shadow renders or shadow-only lights, create a different-looking shadow for each object.

6. If your software has the capability for multiple shadow passes, practice setting up and rendering a custom shadow camera. Practice this several times until you feel comfortable with it.

7. Set up a simple still life, and using the soft light techniques described in this chapter, cheat the look of soft light with either a top-down light or a few additional spotlights.

8. Using your software's documentation, look up how your software implements fog light. Create several fog lights with different textures in them.

9. Create a scene with one or more glowing objects. As a suggestion, try either a light bulb or fireflies. Practice adding glow to these objects. What features did you implement and why?

Figure 16.1 *Shrek 2* was the first feature film to use full global illumination (2004, ©DreamWorks, Courtesy of Everett Collection).

Chapter 16

Global Illumination

"The challenge is always balancing realism with cinematic drama...

we still have to get there in a creative and interesting way."

—Jay Redd, Senior Visual Effects Supervisor at Sony Pictures Imageworks[1]

In the past several years, one of the largest changes in lighting has been the whole-sale adoption of global illumination as a practical rendering solution. Global illumination methods have been around for a long time, but up until recently were considered too computationally expensive to be of much use in CG production. The choice of whether or not to implement global illumination, and if so by what means, has been a defining aspect for studios in the past few years when selecting and developing their rendering pipelines. The general trend in lighting has been toward greater realism (or at least more physical accuracy in the case of stylized pieces), and global illumination has been a part of that move.

In common usage, *global illumination* (GI) refers to any rendering algorithm that calculates indirect light. Global illumination was briefly introduced in Chapter 1, "First Things First," and Chapter 14, "Rendering for the Artist." In this chapter, we'll take a much more in-depth look. Occlusion is considered a subset of full global illumination and is also discussed. Global illumination can be tricky to implement unless you have a general understanding of how it works "under the hood." This chapter will take a look at the different ways global illumination can be created as well as some pointers for its usage.

16.1 DEFINING GLOBAL ILLUMINATION

Global illumination includes a group of algorithms that calculates for *indirect light*. This light may be coming directly from another surface, known as *bounce light* or *diffuse reflection*, or it may come generally from the surroundings, known as *skylight* or *environment light* (Figures 16.2 through 16.4). Calculating indirect light is the primary feature of global illumination. This is a big advantage to the artist, removing the need to add much if any bounce light and most fill light.

Global illumination methods can also be used to calculate *caustics*. Recall from Chapter 1 that caustics are the bright spots of light formed when light is focused upon reflection or refraction (Figure 16.5). Refracted caustics occur when light bends and is focused upon passing through a transparent material. Reflected caustics occur when light bends and is focused upon reflecting off a shiny material. Students of lighting are often eager to learn caustics because

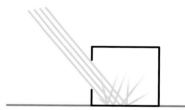

Figure 16.2 Diagram of direct light and bounce light.

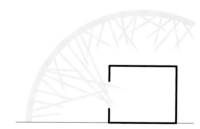

Figure 16.3 Diagram of skylight.

---

[1]Animation World Network (AWN). "Shine On, Global Illumination and 3D Environments." December 30, 2005.

Figure 16.4 (Left) Real-world direct light, reflected light, and skylight.

Figure 16.5 (Right) Real-world caustics.

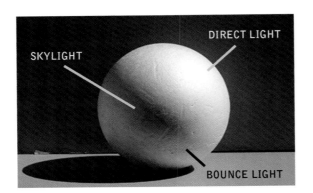

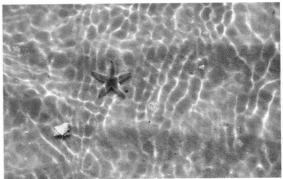

they look cool. Caustics happen only occasionally, however, and should be considered a bell and whistle, not an essential technique.

16.1.1 Definition Madness

Before going further into this chapter, I'd like to take a moment to clarify some confusion on the usage of terms. Many people may be a bit confused by what "global illumination" means, as they may hear the term used in a variety of contexts.

As noted, in common parlance, global illumination is taken to mean any rendering method that calculates indirect light, as we've been discussing here so far. The problem is that the real definition of the term actually means *any algorithm that accounts for hidden surfaces in its calculations* (hidden surfaces are those not seen directly by the camera), which can cover quite a lot. This broader definition includes ambient occlusion, reflection occlusion, even ray tracing. Many things are fair game to be called "global illumination," which isn't incorrect but can be confusing when the term is used in different ways by different people. Ambient occlusion and reflection occlusion are often referred to as "global illumination" in today's literature, and this is correct—they are, however, only *partial* calculations. Standard ray tracing, the kind that calculates reflections and refractions but not indirect light, is no longer referred to as a global-illumination technique (though in some much older literature you may see it referred to this way). However, there *is* a ray-tracing algorithm that calculates indirect light as well, which is discussed later in this chapter.

Adding to the confusion, Mental Ray, a renderer commonly used in software such as 3DS Max and Maya, uses the term "global illumination" to refer to one very specific algorithm: photon mapping. Photon mapping is indeed a global-illumination technique, but so are final gather and several others. Through the use of Mental Ray, many people say "global illumination" when they mean just "photon mapping," and think final gather is something else entirely, they just aren't sure what. Similarly, the term "radiosity" is sometimes used to mean diffuse reflection of bounce light in general, but this is incorrect. Radiosity is yet another global-illumination method. (I know, there are a bunch of them, aren't there?)

To avoid confusion, in this chapter the term "global illumination" or "full global illumination" refers to *any* rendering algorithm that calculates bounce light. Photon mapping, radiosity, and final gather are all different means of doing this and are covered in Section 16.2. Occlusion techniques are covered separately in Section 16.4, and are referred to as "partial global illumination." And if this section made absolutely *no* sense to you, try coming back to it after reading the chapter.

16.1.2 (VERY) BRIEF HISTORY OF GLOBAL ILLUMINATION IN ANIMATION AND VFX PRODUCTION

In the early days of global illumination, it was commonly used only by architectural firms for pre-visualization. These firms often needed only single frames, and showing the realistic propagation of light in their architectural designs was a priority over speed. In animations, which can have more than a hundred thousand high-resolution frames to render, however, speed was (and is) a priority. At the beginning, global illumination was simply too slow to be used in animation production.

The first movie to use full global illumination was DreamWorks' *Shrek 2*, in 2004 (Figure 16.1). Next, ILM used global illumination to render its CG characters, such as Davy Jones, in *Pirates of the Caribbean: Dead Man's Chest* (2006), and later that same year, Sony Pictures Imageworks used full global illumination for the first time with *Monster House* (Figure 16.6). At that time, most other films didn't use full GI; it was only as recently as 2010 that Sony made the switch to global-illumination as standard workflow for all of its feature films. Pixar began employing a limited global-illumination calculation known as *radiance*, which calculates one bounce of diffuse reflection and color bleeding, beginning with the film *Up* (2009). Several other large studios have followed a similar route, first employing global illumination in a limited capacity and then more recently using full GI in more and more films. This transition has revolutionized the lighting pipeline in animation and visual effects film production. Many cheats that were the norm are no longer used; new techniques that are more physically accurate and physically based are now standard.

Increased use of global illumination has been made possible primarily by two factors. The first is the *faster processing speed* of computers. Second are *more efficient algorithm*s. These algorithms not only help speed up render time and reduce artifacts, but they allow the renderer to handle more complex scenes.

Figure 16.6 *Monster House* was the first film created at Sony Pictures Imageworks using full global illumination. (©2006 Columbia Pictures Industries, Inc. and GH One LLC. All rights reserved. Courtesy of Columbia Pictures.)

16.1.3 Pros and Cons of Global Illumination

Global illumination appeals to artists because it can make the task of achieving good-looking lighting easier. By calculating both the color and intensity of reflected light, global illumination eliminates many of the lights artists previously had to add. Realistic light is calculated by the renderer, as opposed to being cheated by the artist. This means that a satisfactory result can usually be achieved in fewer iterations and in less time.

Physically accurate lighting and shading helps shot continuity. Physically accurate light holds up from a wider variety of angles as opposed to just looking good from the angle of the camera, which means that one lighting setup can be shared among multiple shots more effectively. Because it needs fewer cheats, there is less tweaking by individual artists on the different shots, which also leads to better continuity.

Large studios prefer global illumination for reasons having to do with the profitability of their business. Without global illumination, studios rely on their artists' knowledge and ability to accomplish the same or similar looks. Switching to global illumination pushes much of the labor of realistic rendering from the artist to the computer. Carl Ludwig, Blue Sky's R&D Vice President, is quoted as saying, "An hour of a person's time is worth hours of a computer's time. These machines run 24 hours a day, especially now that they're cheaper and faster. It's a person's time that you have to value. That's how we keep our costs under control."[2] Here's how the numbers break out. In the past, one shot in a feature film would typically take two weeks to light and composite, and now the average time is one week. Stan Szymanski (former long-time Senior Vice President of Creative Resources/Digital Production at Sony Pictures Imageworks) once told me that half as many lighters were needed on shows using global illumination versus shows that didn't use this technique. Half is a compelling number.

Computers are even cheaper now too. In the 1990s, the kind of computer needed to handle complex 3D graphics was the extremely expensive SGI (short for the company that made them, Silicon Graphics International). When home computers like Windows and Mac became powerful enough to run 3D applications, the writing was on the wall for SGIs. SGIs ran on the UNIX operating system. A switch from the UNIX operating system to the open-source (free and open for development) Linux operating system only sealed the deal. Now studios can stock up on extremely fast, more powerful, and less expensive computers than ever before.

Another advantage for the studios is that they don't need to hire as many experienced technical directors but instead can manage with a greater percentage of less experienced (read "less expensive") ones. With less specialized techniques being used on global-illumination projects, fewer experts who are able to get "under the hood" and tinker are needed. That's good news for those new to the industry or who are looking to get in, but not so good for the old pros who find more competition for fewer jobs.

Before you sign on the dotted line, remember that the main drawback to global illumination is the length of time it takes to render. It takes a lo-o-ong time. Currently, for feature-film high-res images and complex scenes using global illumination, about 4 to 11 hours a frame

---

[2]digitalcontentproducer.com. "Photoreality." Ellen Wolff. August 1, 2005.

is common, and that's on an 8-core machine. When I was working on the film *2012*, an eight-hour frame was doing great. The average render time per frame on *Cars 2* was 11.5 hours, and the same with Sony's *Alice in Wonderland*. With very complex scenes, render times can climb much higher, however. On *Green Lantern*, the render times on some shots reached about 100 hours *per frame*, according to a technical director who worked on the show. In the past these render times would have been unacceptable. Two hours per frame was more common, and 30 minutes was considered pretty speedy. The idea is that the increase in time is at least partly offset by the fact that global illumination needs fewer passes and iterations—but still, that's a long time. With 32- and 34-core machines predicted on the horizon, this number will certainly come down. To accommodate these long render times, the large studios have huge render farms. (A render farm is a network of computers dedicated to rendering.) And when I say huge, I mean really huge. Pixar ramped up to 12,500 cores for *Cars 2*.[3] During the making of *Avatar*, Weta's render farm was said to be "the fastest supercomputer in the southern hemisphere."[4]

Not all the advantages weigh in for every project, however. Sometimes the visual advantage is minimal, while the render cost is still high. For example, if your scene is overall dark and there's little reflected light, then there won't be as much advantage to using full GI. However, the render time will be just as long as if you were working on a project with a lot of complex inter-reflections. Sometimes, the style of your project just doesn't call for global illumination. Frankly, not every studio is a large studio, nor is every job a movie.

Most importantly, many small to midsize studios and freelancers don't have access to the huge render farms the large studios have. Sure, one can always rent time on a render farm, but then you're paying for the time, and that can get expensive. For many projects, complex global illumination is still too time-consuming to render. A friend who is a freelancer likes to keep his renders down to a handful of *minutes* to get his jobs done with the quick turnover the client wants, and another friend who works at a small studio says sometimes they don't even have time for ray tracing, much less global illumination. It is likely that one day global illumination will be able to be used by everyone, but right now that's still in the future. For this reason, a lighter should know how to light both *with* and *without* global illumination as to not be handicapped.

ADVANTAGES AND DISADVANTAGES OF GLOBAL-ILLUMINATION METHODS

Advantages

✓ Calculates realistic indirect light and diffuse color bleeding
✓ Calculates caustics (some methods)
✓ Requires fewer cheats on the part of the lighter

Disadvantages

• Extremely slow
• Can be prone to artifacts
• Uses more memory

---

[3]"New Technology Revs Up Pixar's *Cars 2*." Daniel Terdiman. CNET News (new.cnet.com). June 20, 2011.

[4]"Tech Tussle: Cloud Wars." *Variety*. February 2011.

16.2 COMMON MEANS OF GENERATING GLOBAL ILLUMINATION

Global illumination can be calculated and implemented in a number of different ways. Some of these methods are:

- Radiosity
- Final gather
- Photon mapping
- Path-traced global illumination
- Point-based global illumination

Each has its advantages and disadvantages. This section discusses how each algorithm works generally speaking, noting advantages and disadvantages and giving some tips on usage. You'll want to refer to your software's documentation for specific parameters and steps.

16.2.1 RADIOSITY

The first widespread algorithm for global illumination was *radiosity*. Radiosity calculates only for diffuse reflection and color bleeding (Figure 16.7). Radiosity works by dividing the geometry into small polygon meshes (Figure 16.8). Light is then bounced off these meshes. The user can specify the number of times to bounce and the complexity of the mesh. The finer the mesh, the more accurate the lighting calculations.

Some limitations of radiosity are that it calculates all surfaces as if they are fully matte, and the light bouncing off them is fully diffused. It doesn't calculate either caustics or reflections. Also, due to the nature of the algorithm, the computational time is proportionate to the geometric complexity of the scene. Thus it is best suited for large expanses of simple geometry with relatively even expanses of diffuse lighting.

Radiosity isn't common for animation productions because it's too slow when working with complex geometry. However, radiosity is much more common in architectural pre-visualizations. Because radiosity stores the lighting calculations with the geometry, the data doesn't need to be recalculated if only the camera moves. This means architectural fly-throughs only need one single calculation. Currently AutoCAD (architectural and industrial design software), LightWave, and 3DS Max, among others, include radiosity as advanced render options.

16.2.2 FINAL GATHER

Another algorithm that calculates diffuse reflection and color bleeding is *final gather* (Figure 16.9). Similar to radiosity, final gather doesn't calculate caustics. Final gather will evaluate light coming from areas illuminated by direct light, from a skydome representing fully scattered environment light and from incandescent surfaces.

Final gather works from the shaded point backwards. First, the direct illumination is calculated as in a normal render. Then the indirect illumination is calculated by shooting a number of rays out from a variety of points on each surface. The rays are sent in a quasi-random pattern into the hemisphere above each point. What these rays hit will determine how much indirect

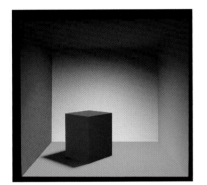

Figure 16.7 Radiosity render.

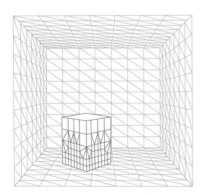

Figure 16.8 Diagram of a radiosity mesh.

Figure 16.9 Image rendered with final gather (Charles Trippe).

light is calculated for that point: If the rays hit many bright surfaces, then there is more indirect illumination; if the rays don't hit many other bright surfaces, then there is less indirect illumination (Figure 16.10). Specular highlights aren't included in the calculation. Not every surface point is evaluated either, as this would be far too time-consuming. Rather, results of each ray hit are averaged for the point, then those results are interpolated over the other non-calculated points on the surface. For each bounce, the process is repeated and summed with the previous calculations and with the direct light. Final gather can stand alone as a global-illumination solution, or it can be combined with other methods as a final step.

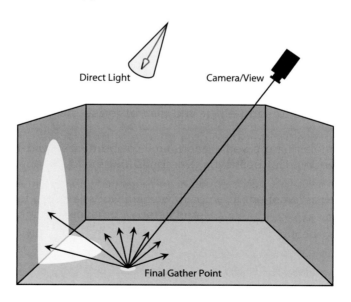

Figure 16.10 Diagram of final gather sample. The brightness and color of the surfaces hit by the sampling rays determines the brightness and color of the point being shaded.

An advantage of final gather is that it's fairly fast. The calculations aren't based on dicing the geometry, as in radiosity, but rather on random sample points. This means that it's geometry-independent: Increasing the complexity of the geometry won't increase the render time.

As is often the tradeoff, one drawback is that final gather is less accurate than some other methods. Because it's less accurate and often smoothes the results over larger areas, it works well when the indirect illumination varies slowly. Final gather may also not create as much occlusion-type shadow as it should.

Final gather can be easier to control than some other algorithms. When working with final gather, there are three main settings the user can control:

1. The closeness of each point, and thus the number of points (sometimes called *density*)
2. The number of rays from each point (sometimes called *accuracy*)
3. The amount of smoothing between points (sometimes called *interpolation*)

Some workflow tips when using final gather:

◆ To increase the speed of the render, lower the number of rays and/or the number of sample points.

◆ To smooth out the results, either increase the number of rays (which will be more accurate but will take longer to render) or increase the interpolation (which is faster but less accurate).

◆ If the results need more detail, increase the number of sample points or decrease the smoothing.

◆ Final gather can be combined with a short-distance ambient occlusion to improve its speed and still maintain a good look (compare Figures 16.11 and 16.12). Incorporating occlusion allows you to use fewer points and smooth the results, which is fast but less detailed. Occlusion helps to visually bring the detail back.

◆ Final gather is a good choice for evaluating an environment light, and it also calculates real glow from incandescent cards.

Final gather is a frequent choice for animation production, as its results are deemed "good enough," and it's relatively fast.

Figure 16.11 (Left) Final gather alone can be too bright in some areas.

Figure 16.12 (Right) Final gather plus ambient occlusion helps provide detail in corners and darken inaccuracies while still keeping samples down.

16.2.3 Photon Mapping

Photon mapping calculates indirect illumination by shooting virtual photons from each light source into the scene. This imitates life—for those who recall the particle theory of light from high school science class, light is composed of packets of energy called *photons*. The brightness of any surface is determined by the number of photons falling on it. Photon mapping roughly imitates this process.

Photon mapping calculates both diffusely reflected light (color bleeding) and specularly reflected light (caustics) (Figure 16.13). It is a two-step process. First, photons are shot into the scene from each light, bounced around the scene, and their positions stored in a map (thus the name photon *mapping*) (Figure 16.14). This map is written to disk and saved for later use. In the second step, the image is rendered and the map is read back in to determine the indirect illumination. The final step of evaluating the points is generally done with final gather. Final gather can be omitted and the photon map used without this estimation, but the result has more artifacts unless a much higher number of photons is used (see Figure 16.15). Final gather used in this capacity is calculating the last bounce of the indirect light. Direct illumination is typically calculated with ray tracing, which provides ray-traced reflections, refractions, and shadows.

One disadvantage of photon mapping is that the maps can be extremely large, especially for large scenes. If the map is too big, it cannot be read back in. Reading the map back in requires that it be loaded into the computer's memory. If the size of the map exceeds the size of the free memory on the computer, then you'll have a problem. The size of the photon map is based on the number of photons shot into the scene. In this way, it's independent of geometry complexity, though more complex or larger scenes may require more photons and affect map size in that way.

Photon mapping is more accurate than final gather, but it also takes longer to render. It is not favored in animation productions, and it's generally only done when needed. Those creating architectural simulations, on the other hand, often prefer photon mapping because of the increased accuracy.

Figure 16.13 Photon mapping calculates both bounce light and caustics.

Figure 16.14 Visualization of the photon map.

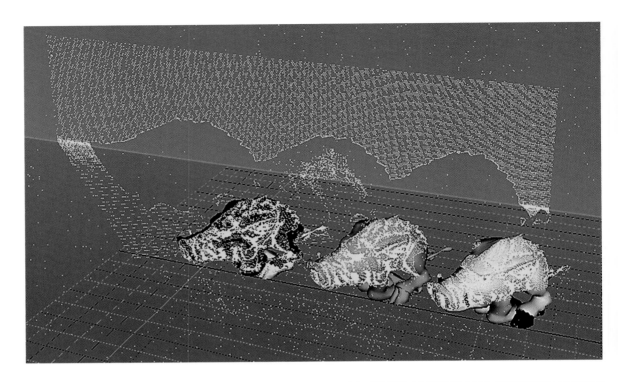

Figure 16.15 A render with no final gather shows the photon calculation.

Standard renderers such as Mental Ray have both photon mapping and final gather as rendering options. Note that final gather can be used alone or in combination with photon mapping to smooth the results.

The user can control a variety of settings, which require iterative test renders to get right. Four main factors control the quality and look of photon mapping:

1. The intensity of the photons (makes the indirect light brighter, doesn't increase render time)
2. The number of photons emitted from each light (increases render time, more accurate)
3. The radius size of the sampled area (can be imagined as larger photons, doesn't increase render time—see Figure 16.16)
4. The number of photons sampled at each point during the final summation (increases render time and quality)

An important control for the user is determining which lights are emitting photons and carefully scaling and positioning these lights for maximum effectiveness.

Figure 16.16 Three renders with differently sized photon radii and photon density.

Some tips when using photon mapping:

◆ When using photon mapping, remember to turn it on in two places: in the render settings and in each light.

◆ Not all lights need to cast photons. Limit the number of photon-emitting lights to speed up render time. For example, lights that are small or far away may not add much indirect light to the scene and thus may not need to emit photons.

◆ Position the lights so the photons are used most effectively. You don't want to have light coming in a window that has the majority of its photons lost due to bouncing off the outside wall, for example.

◆ Carefully control the total number of photons. The greater the number of photons, the longer the render and the larger the photon map. The total number of photons is the sum of all the photons from the photon-emitting lights in the scene. Test to see what is the correct number for your scene. A good number to start with is 10,000; 200,000 to 1,500,000 is not uncommon for a medium-sized scene; a complex scene may need tens of millions of photons.

◆ While working, reduce the number of photons you're using to half or less to increase the speed of your test renders.

◆ Combine photon mapping with final gather in order to smooth out the results and decrease the total number of photons needed. If you're using final gather in this capacity, only one final gather bounce is needed.

◆ Specify which objects cast and receive photons to reduce render time.

◆ Model more realistically, with the light in mind. For example, don't let your interior models have missing walls, or the photons will escape from these openings and not illuminate the interior enough. Interior corners should be beveled to avoid having the photons get trapped along the edges, causing inaccurate results (see Figure 16.17 and 16.18).

Figure 16.17 (Left) Photons often get caught in sharp corners.

Figure 16.18 (Right) A slight bevel fixes the problem in seen Figure 16.17.

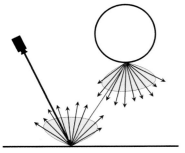

Figure 16.19 Diagram of how path-traced global illumination splits into many rays to calculate indirect illumination at each point.

16.2.4 PATH-TRACED GLOBAL ILLUMINATION

Path-traced global illumination takes a different approach. It's based on Monte Carlo ray tracing, in which the renderer shoots jittered rays from the final pixel (from the camera) backward through the scene. This path bounces around the scene accumulating interactions between the surfaces. Because this algorithm is based on standard ray tracing, it may also be called *ray-traced global illumination*. The main difference from standard ray tracing is that upon striking a surface, many quasi-random rays are then shot outward, which accumulate indirect light upon striking another surface. If more than one bounce of indirect light is calculated, then this process continues for each and every bounced ray (Figure 16.19).

Path-tracing has the advantage of being simple. There aren't a lot of knobs to tune—just the number of samples. Path-traced global illumination is a one-step process. It doesn't precalculate and store data. Rather, the entire scene is calculated and rendered at each frame. Path-traced global illumination also naturally calculates realistic reflections, refractions, and caustics.

On the other hand, it's very sample-intensive, which can lead to very long renders. Like standard ray tracing, each time a ray hits something it splits into new rays, and now this includes illumination from other surfaces. This method tends to have trouble with small bright lights and specular highlights; both of these tend to cause sizzling in the final image. A high number of samples may be needed to eliminate artifacts, and a high number of samples slows down the render, sometimes dramatically. Recent advances in *importance sampling*, in which more rays are directed at problematic areas of small bright lights and highlights, have helped to solve this issue.

Path-traced global illumination can also sample luminance from skydomes and incandescent cards, which will contribute a real glow. Since skydomes and cards are already part of the indirect light calculation, adding them doesn't take much additional render time.

An example of path-tracing is the Arnold renderer, developed by Solid Angle. Sony Pictures Imageworks uses its own version of Arnold, which can be seen in films such as *Cloudy with a*

Chance of Meatballs, Green Lantern (Figure 16.20) and *Men in Black 3*. Another renderer that will ray trace is Pixar's PRMan. Beginning with version 16, it integrated an option for a ray-traced global illumination solution that can completely bypass its native REYES algorithm. (This is in addition to its point-based approach, discussed in the next section.)

Some tips for working with path-traced global illumination:

◆ Efficient use of sampling and keeping the total number of samples down is critical when using this method.

◆ Increasing the number of samples from the camera causes the greatest increase in sampling time, as each of these rays is divided further by all other samples in the scene. Keep the number of samples from camera as low as possible for the fastest render.

◆ Use incandescent cards to add controllable soft light, as cards will add much less render time than area lights.

◆ Select and omit certain geometry from secondary light calculations to save render time.

◆ Omit tiny incandescent surfaces from the indirect light calculation to help avoid "sizzling."

◆ Sizzling in the indirect bounce can be lessened by increasing the specular roughness, an approach that doesn't increase samples or render time.

Figure 16.20 *Green Lantern* used path-traced global illumination (2011, ©Warner Brothers Pictures, courtesy of Everett Collection).

16.2.5 Point-Based Global Illumination

A relative newcomer on the scene is point-based global illumination (Figure 16.21). First developments of the algorithm were developed by Arnauld Lamorlette (who won an Academy of Motion Picture Arts and Sciences Technical Achievement Award for his contributions) and were used in DreamWorks' *Shrek 2*. Later developments of this algorithm were by Pixar, who integrated it into their renderer, Pixar's RenderMan (PRMan).

Figure 16.21 Example render of global illumination using a point cloud.

Point-based global illumination writes out lighting information into a 3D data file known as a *point cloud,* called this because the information looks like a cloud of points in space. Point-based global illumination is a three-step process. First, the direct illumination is pre-calculated and recorded into a point cloud (Figure 16.23), a part of the process known informally as "baking out the direct lighting." Actually in the case of GI, the point cloud doesn't contain points at all but little disks. Each disk, known as a *surfel*, represents a small area of surface on the geometry in the scene. Each surfel records the illumination as well as surface color of that area. In the next step, the data in the point cloud is optimized into what is known as a *brickmap*. The purpose of the brickmap is to offer more efficient access to the data and to perform better filtering to reduce noise and other artifacts (Figure 16.22). The final step is to render the scene (Figure 16.24), in which the brickmap is called in and used to calculate the indirect illumination. The point cloud can be read in directly, but this is less efficient.

Figure 16.22 Three levels of detail in a brickmap, generated from Figure 16.23.

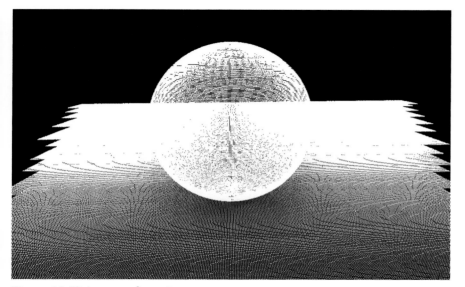

Figure 16.23 Image of a point map.

Figure 16.24 Simple scene that generated Figures 16.22 and 16.23.

Point-based global illumination has the advantage of being relatively fast. Since much of the data is pre-calculated, global illumination doesn't take any longer than an ambient occlusion calculation. The point-based approach is immune to complex geometry and textures. This means that point-based global illumination also can handle ultra-large data sets that would simply be too large for the ray-traced approach. Additionally, the intermediate step of the brickmap helps with data access. Due to how the brickmap functions, only parts of the calculation are loaded into memory as needed, which also means larger scenes can be handled. Finally, this method is less prone to artifacts than some others. The surfels are distributed evenly (unlike photon maps), which makes for smoother calculation of the indirect light, and the data has been pre-filtered in the brickmap.

As an added advantage, point clouds and brickmaps can also store and reuse data other than just direct and indirect illumination. They can be used to solve other complex rendering issues in a manageable amount of time, such as ambient occlusion, reflection occlusion, sub-surface scattering, area light illumination and shadows, environment map illumination, and more. Due to the advantages and application to other areas, point-based calculations are a common choice for animation studios.

Point-based global illumination has a few disadvantages, however. One disadvantage is that it's not as accurate as ray tracing. Ray tracing is needed for fine detail, such as mirror reflection, sharp refraction, and sharp shadows. Also, point-based global illumination is resolution-dependent, meaning the point cloud has a certain number of data points (the surfels). This is a disadvantage because if you were to move too close to an object with too few surfels in the point cloud, then the calculations won't hold up. Conversely, you don't want too many data points. If you calculate many more than you need, this takes up unnecessary disk space and memory.

Some tips for working with point-based global illumination:

◆ Don't make your point clouds and brickmaps too large. These files take time to generate, and large ones take even longer. If your files are larger than needed, you are wasting precious processing time.

◆ Be sure to manage your data. Baking out point clouds and generating brickmaps requires organization and artist management, as does any kind of intermediate pass.

◆ Reuse your baked-out lighting as long as possible. If your lights have only changed a little, as when you are fine-tuning, you can reuse your previous point cloud/brickmap. If your lights are changing a lot, as when you are making larger adjustments to position and intensity of the key light, then you will need to regenerate your point clouds and brickmaps in order to keep things looking accurate.

16.3 WORKING WITH GLOBAL ILLUMINATION

Rendering using global illumination has a few special concerns. Some of these are algorithm-specific and have been mentioned previously. This section gives some helpful tips for working with global illumination in general.

16.3.1 GETTING STARTED WITH GLOBAL ILLUMINATION

Getting global illumination to work correctly can be confusing to the new lighter. You may think, "But I thought lighting was easier with global illumination." Global illumination requires fewer cheats, but setting it up can be complex. There are a variety of algorithms, each with its own way of doing things and its own set of parameters the user can control. It's important to have at least a general knowledge of what the computer is doing behind the scenes so that the different parameters make sense. Without this understanding, getting your global illumination to look right, or in some cases work at all, can be difficult.

When first learning global illumination techniques, start simple. Try a pared-down scene (like a ball on a ground plane), then add a single light and get indirect illumination working (Figures 16.25 and 16.26). Refer to your software's documentation for specifics. The good news is that once the methodology is up and running, then the actual lighting part is usually easier.

Figure 16.25 Without global illumination.

Figure 16.26 With global illumination. Notice the diffuse color bleeding.

16.3.2 GENERAL TIPS WHEN USING GLOBAL ILLUMINATION

◆ When using global illumination, remember that even items out of view may be contributing light. You won't be able to turn items' visibility off during the course of an animation.

◆ Many elements have to all be rendered together. Because all the geometry is interacting with inter-reflections and real occlusion, you often cannot remove elements without losing a needed shadow or bounce.

◆ Items out of view that are still contributing light can be replaced with simplified versions to reduce render time.

◆ Keeping control of your render times is a priority. It's critical with global illumination that your scene be optimized, or it may not even render at all.

◆ Global illumination makes real bounce and occlusion possible: Don't forget to add bounce cards and flags to your arsenal of tricks, the way real-world photographers and cinematographers do (Section 17.4, "Lighting with Cards").

◆ Don't just accept the defaults. Unlike real-world lighters, digital lighters can edit how the reflected light looks. Surfaces can be made to reflect more or less light, or even reflect light that is a different color. (I wouldn't deviate too far, however.)

◆ Optimize the reflected-light calculation. In some applications, the reflected light can be calculated with a more simplified version of the color texture. For example, if the reflecting surface has a complex wood grain, then the reflecting color can simply be brown. This speeds up calculations and helps reduce artifacts.

◆ Model more realistically. For example, if your interior environment is missing some walls because these walls are behind the camera, the room will likely not have enough reflected light.

◆ One bounce of light is often good enough.

◆ When using global illumination, you'll need far fewer lights. As a general rule, you won't need to add much if anything in the way of bounce light and will need far fewer fills.

◆ Global illumination has a number of parameters that affect the quality and eliminate artifacts. Unless you're absolutely sure of what each parameter does, adjust only one parameter at a time, test rendering often, until you find the right settings.

◆ Choose your render algorithm carefully. Do timing tests before committing.

◆ If the environment isn't moving (such as a camera flythrough), render just one frame of global illumination data and reuse this for the rest of the animation.

◆ In general, pre-calculate whatever you can to save render time.

16.4 AMBIENT OCCLUSION AND REFLECTION OCCLUSION

Ambient occlusion and its lesser-known cousin, *reflection occlusion,* are two techniques that are used to increase the realism of ambient light and reflections, respectively. Ambient occlusion and reflection occlusion are cheats. They are not physically accurate, but rather they approximate what ambient shadow and reflections should look like.

Figure 16.27 Ambient occlusion.

Figure 16.28 Ambient occlusion is an important feature in this render of eggs (lighting by Howard Ross). The left side has no occlusion, while the right side has occlusion, greatly improving the realism of the render.

16.4.1 CREATING AMBIENT OCCLUSION

Ambient occlusion is the shadow created by ambient light (Figures 16.27 and 16.28). More specifically, it's the kind of shadow generated by light that comes from all directions. Light that comes from every direction appears to be non-directional, and its shadow is likewise non-directional. Ambient shadow occurs when one surface is close to another, and by proximity excludes (or *occludes*) the scattered light—thus the name *ambient occlusion*.

Generating ambient occlusion is a type of global illumination. It's not a full global-illumination calculation, however, as it doesn't calculate for all light scattered in a scene; it only calculates an approximate *shadowing* of scattered light. Thus as global illumination techniques go, it's relatively efficient and fast. Furthermore, the calculation can be pre-generated and stored for use later in a variety of ways, further increasing efficiency and its appeal to animation productions. Using ambient occlusion was the first foray into global illumination by many production houses in the early 2000s.

How It Works

The renderer calculates ambient occlusion by shooting rays out from each point on the occluded surface. These rays are shot out randomly within a full hemisphere. Depending on how many of these rays hit another surface, the original point gets darkened by a certain amount (Figure 16.29). If all of the rays hit another surface, then the point is shaded black. If none of the rays hits anything, then the point is shaded white. If some of the rays hit and not others, the point is shaded some value of gray. The calculations of an ambient occlusion render go from black to white. To darken surfaces that are in close proximity to one another, this "shadow" needs to be multiplied into the light contribution, which is calculated separately.

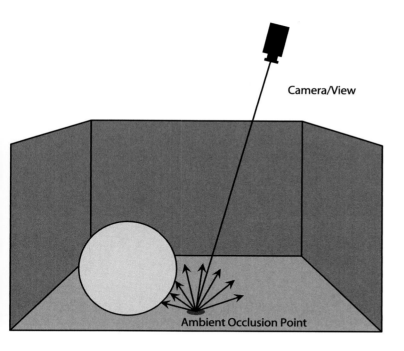

Camera/View

Ambient Occlusion Point

Figure 16.29 Diagram of how ambient occlusion calculates shadow. Each point being shaded sends out a hemisphere of rays to see whether there are any occluding surfaces nearby. The darkness of the point being shaded is determined by how many rays have struck an occluding surface.

Creating Occlusion without Occlusion

The look of ambient occlusion can be accomplished by other means worth mentioning here. Since ambient light with occlusion cheats the look of multi-directional light plus shadow, you may realize that you can *actually* put light in the scene coming from all directions, *actually* shadow it, and achieve the same results.

The look of ambient light with occlusion can be created using just traditional lights. This can be manually set up by placing many lights in a hemisphere pattern around the scene, and then shadowing these lights with very blurred shadows. If depth-mapped shadows are used, the shadow calculation can be pre-generated and stored, saving some render time. We'll call this the "bunch-of-lights" method (BOL) (see Figures 16.30 and 16.31). Computationally expensive, this is the closest to calculating what is truly happening with real-world ambient—real light is coming from all directions, and this light has shadows. While this method has been used in the past, it isn't particularly common as more efficient means are now available. However, its advantage is that anyone can do it, in any software, with no special rendering capabilities. I'm sure someone reading this will find the perfect use for it. Conceptually, the "bunch of lights" method helps one to understand what ambient occlusion is imitating.

Ambient light with occlusion isn't necessary if the scene uses an environment light. An environment light also essentially casts light from all directions into the scene and is typically represented by a large sphere around the scene. Environment lights can be shadowed, producing ambient-with-occlusion type effects if the color and value of the environment light are uniform

(Figure 16.32). This is similar to the "bunch of lights" method in that light provides both illumination and shadow at once, but it's more streamlined as there is but one light to edit. It also renders faster as it is calculated more efficiently than a "bunch of lights."

Figures 16.31 through 16.33 show a comparison of these three methods: a "bunch of lights" (BOL), a uniform white environment light, and ambient occlusion. Figures 16.31 through 16.33 all use a simple white lambert material.

Figure 16.30 A scene using the "bunch of lights" method.

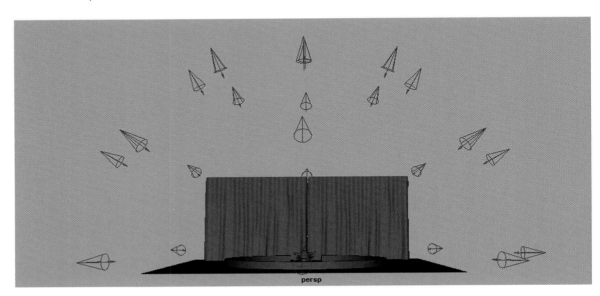

Figure 16.31 A BOL render.

Figure 16.32 A uniform white environment light render.

Figure 16.33 Ambient with occlusion.

16.4.2 Storing Occlusion Data

An advantage of ambient occlusion is that the data can be pre-calculated and reused later, saving time during the primary render. The data can be stored in a variety of ways. How a production decides to store and reuse the data depends on the software/tools available to them and their needs. Occlusion can also be used without pre-generating and reusing the data as well, though this is less efficient, as it must be recalculated with each render.

Here are a few ways ambient occlusion may be stored and reused:

◆ **Render an occlusion pass:** A common option for ambient occlusion is to render just a black-and-white image sequence with just occlusion values, known as an *occlusion pass*. This pass can then be used in the final composite. It also can be brought back into the 3D scene by projecting the pass from the camera's perspective and multiplying it with the ambient light intensity, a method that requires special light and surface shaders. These methods are *camera-dependent*, meaning the camera must be in the exact same position for both the ambient occlusion pass and the beauty pass. If the render camera is moved, the ambient occlusion won't line up properly during the render of the beauty pass. This method allows for great flexibility and control of how the occlusion is used and how it looks, but requires many render passes, compositing, and a pre-determined decision on camera placement. Many large productions meet these requirements and thus use this technique.

◆ **Store point-cloud data:** The occlusion information can be written out as point-cloud data. The point-cloud file is referenced when rendering the beauty pass to create the ambient occlusion. This method is camera-independent.

◆ **Generate a surface texture:** The information can be written out as static surface texture, which can then be reapplied with 2D mapping to various parameters of the material. The drawback of this is that the texture will then not animate when objects move closer together or farther apart. (An animated texture file could be used to solve this problem.) A non-animated texture file can be useful, however, for stationary objects or in applications that need maximum efficiency, as with video game textures. This method is camera-independent, meaning the render camera may be moved and the pre-calculated ambient occlusion contribution will still line up correctly.

16.4.3 Bringing Ambient Occlusion Back In

The occlusion needs to be combined with the lighting calculations to be a part of the final image. An artist has several options on how to bring occlusion back in, which can be a good thing if you know what you're doing, but may be a source of confusion if you are unsure. This subsection seeks to clear up some mystery on the "right" way to use occlusion data and what your options are.

In general, occlusion can either be re-incorporated back into the 3D scene, or it can be rendered out as a pass and integrated into the composite. If brought back into the scene, the occlusion calculation can be incorporated into either the light or surfaces. This leaves us with three ways to use an ambient occlusion calculation:

1. Integrate it into the composite (use a 2D pass, pre-calculated because it's pre-rendered).
2. Shadow the lights in the scene with it (pre-calculated or not).
3. Darken the materials in the 3D scene with it (pre-calculated or not).

No matter which approach you choose, the "right" way to use occlusion is to multiply it with the ambient contribution. I put "right" in quotes because I'm of the opinion that *if it looks right, then it is right.* But chances are a lot better that it will look right if it's implemented as realistically as possible, then you deviate from that if you have an artistic need to do so. Since ambient occlusion is the shadow of fully scattered (ambient) light, then this is the component it should darken.

The best way to illustrate this is to look at how things are done in a composite. Figure 16.34 illustrates how the occlusion would be multiplied with the ambient contribution in a scene lit with only an ambient light. Ambient times occlusion equals shadowed ambient. It's pretty straightforward when all you have is an ambient light.

Figure 16.34 Ambient occlusion should be multiplied by the ambient contribution to shadow it. From left to right: the ambient pass only, the occlusion pass only, and the resulting ambient times occlusion.

When the ambient light is combined with other light sources, which it usually is, you need to pay close attention to what the occlusion is affecting. The occlusion should *only affect the ambient contribution*, not all of the lighting. Figures 16.35 and 16.36 show the difference.

Multiplying the occlusion into everything is a common mistake, and it happens in a couple of ways. Often lighters implement occlusion in the composite. They render out two passes, one pass with all the lights and another pass containing the occlusion, then they multiply the two together as in Figure 16.37. This is incorrect, however, because then the occlusion affects everything and ends up looking overdone.

Figure 16.35 The occlusion is affecting the ambient contribution only—correct.

Figure 16.36 The occlusion is affecting everything—incorrect.

Figure 16.37 A common mistake is to multiply the occlusion by the entire lighting, which leads to too much occlusion (incorrect).

In the case of the composite, to correctly use occlusion you need another pass. You need to render the ambient light, the direct light, and the occlusion all separately so you can multiply the occlusion by the ambient contribution only. Figure 16.38 shows how the three components (ambient light, direct light, and occlusion shadow) are combined.

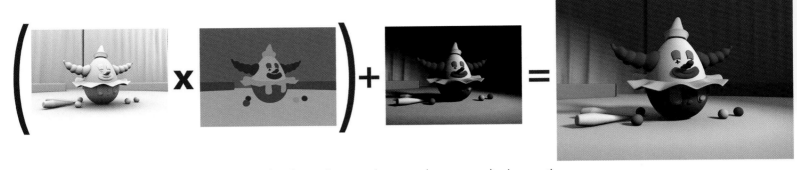

Figure 16.38 Multiply the ambient occlusion by the ambient only to get better results (correct).

When incorporating ambient occlusion back into the 3D scene, the principle is the same. You want it to affect the ambient contribution. If the ambient occlusion calculation is read in by the ambient light, then it will darken the light appropriately as a shadow. In some applications, you can turn ambient occlusion on directly in an ambient light. In my opinion, this is the most understandable implementation. No ambient light, then no shadow from that light, right?

If you are incorporating the occlusion as a texture, the most accurate implementation is to have the occlusion darken the material's response to ambient light. If you have no ambient light in the scene and no ambient component to the material, occlusion can be multiplied with the *color* of the surface, or the *diffuse* parameter. This is the down-and-dirty method, because it works and is often fast to implement, but it isn't exactly correct. Many times doing this will result in occlusion that doesn't seem dark enough in the cast shadow areas but looks too dark under direct light. Consider for a moment and you may realize why... well? Yes, it's because this also effectively "shadows" everywhere the same amount, in both directly and indirectly lit areas, and will appear like Figure 16.36.

In whatever way you use your occlusion, it will likely need to be adjusted to look its best, which is what is covered in the next section.

16.4.4 Tips on Using Ambient Occlusion

You'll rarely want to leave occlusion at its default settings. The user can typically adjust these settings: the number of rays shot from any given point, the length of these rays, the density and color of the occlusion, a gamma on the final result, and the cone angle at which the rays are shot into the scene. All of these settings will determine the final look and quality of the occlusion.

◆ **If your occlusion is speckly or blotchy, increase the number of rays** (Figure 16.39). The default setting usually is low quality and needs to be increased quite a bit. It's a good idea to do a short test render before launching your entire job, as sometimes artifacts only show up when a series of frames is rendered. More rays mean a longer render, so don't let your occlusion rays be too high either—only high enough to eliminate artifacts.

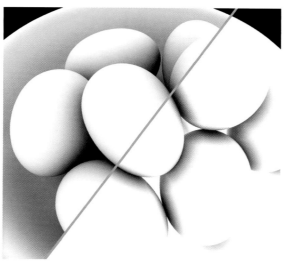

Figure 16.39 (Left) A low number of rays results in artifacts (left side of the image) while a high number of rays takes longer to render but smoothes the result (right side of the image). Test carefully to determine the lowest number of samples you need.

Figure 16.40 (Right) A longer ray distance results in more occlusion, suitable for a small subject (left side of the image), while a shorter ray distance means the occlusion is limited to very nearby objects (right side of the image). Measure your scene and use this to determine the best ray length for your occlusion.

◆ **If your occlusion affects too much, try shortening the rays** (Figure 16.40). Often the default is to look for hits into infinity. This is much too far; it wastes calculation time and ends up giving your scene more occlusion than it needs. Figures 16.41 and 16.42 illustrate how shortening the rays will result in fewer hits. This brings me to the next tip….

◆ **Occlusion should be calculated with scale in mind.** For example, an ABC block may have occlusion from a tabletop all along its side, but a skyscraper isn't going to have occlusion from the sidewalk all the way up to the 10th floor. You can control this by limiting the length of the occlusion rays. The lengths of occlusion rays are based on world units. Measure your scene to get an idea of how big things are, then estimate how far away you think things will be and still shadow each other, and enter that distance as the ray distance. Then render, evaluate, and adjust as needed. Remember that a small scene will show more occlusion than a large one.

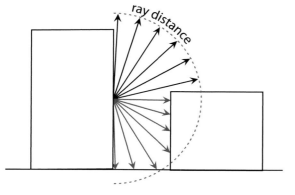

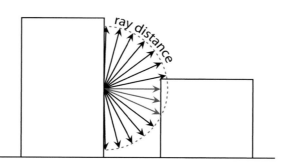

Figure 16.41 (Left) Longer rays result in more hits, resulting in darker occlusion at the point being shaded.

Figure 16.42 (Right) Shorter rays result in fewer hits, resulting in lighter (or no) occlusion at the point being shaded

Figure 16.43 Occlusion at its default distance and black color is too much for these eggs.

Figure 16.44 The final render has a light orange occlusion color with a limited ray distance. Much better!

Figure 16.45 To help debug your occlusion if it's incorporated into the render, turn it a vibrant color. My favorite debugging color is magenta.

◆ **Don't let your occlusion go to full density.** This is a common error when using occlusion. Most of the time, density that goes all the way to black is too dark (compare Figure 16.43 and 16.44). Of course, the density you need depends on your scene and on the materials used.

◆ **Consider the material.** Materials that have translucency, such as a cotton shirt or crumpled paper, won't occlude much light. Transparent materials won't occlude any light at all. This means not all the materials in your scene will have the same look to the occlusion. Notice how the eggs in Figure 16.43 look like fossilized dinosaur eggs (i.e., rocks) due to the very dark occlusion, while the eggs in Figure 16.44 have a lighter, translucent look.

◆ **Consider tinting the occlusion.** Occlusion often looks better if it's tinted, not just black or gray. One trick is to tint the occlusion with the color of the surface, so that a green object has saturated dark green occlusion, not black occlusion. Or tint it with a variation of the surface color, such as a pale yellow surface having an orange-ish brown occlusion (as in Figure 16.44).

◆ **To help debug your occlusion** if it is incorporated into the render, turn it a vibrant color. This helps to clearly see what is occlusion and what is not (as in Figure 16.45).

16.4.5 REFLECTION OCCLUSION

***Reflection occlusion* imitates the occluding of light from one object to another in a reflection.** Reflection occlusion can help the realism of a digital reflection by making it darker in places where it's too bright. Due to how digital reflections are calculated (they are just added to the rest of the lighting), CG reflections can look too bright. Reflection occlusion helps to correct for this (Figures 16.46 and 16.47).

Figure 16.46 Typical calculations *add* the reflection, which can be at times overly bright (left side). Reflection occlusion darkens the frog's reflection only, producing a more realistic image (right).

Figure 16.47 Reflection occlusion used in Figure 16.46.

Reflection occlusion is calculated like ambient occlusion but instead of looking for object hits in a full hemisphere above the point being shaded, it uses a narrow cone of directions oriented around the direction of the reflection. Reflection occlusion can be blurred (Figures 16.48 through 16.50). The amount of blur in the reflection occlusion should match the amount of blur in the reflection itself. If the cone is very narrow, the reflection occlusion will look very crisp. The wider the cone, the more blurry the reflection occlusion. Reflection occlusion can be pre-calculated just like ambient occlusion.

Figure 16.48 A series of reflection occlusion renders, showing increasing amounts of blur.

Figure 16.49 Reflection occlusion used in Figure 16.50.

Figure 16.50 Digital renders of a frog both without (left side) and with (right side) blurred reflection occlusion. The amount of blur in the reflection occlusion needs to match the amount of blur in the reflection itself.

Reflection occlusion gets multiplied by the reflective component to darken it. As with ambient occlusion, this may be done in the composite by splitting out passes, or incorporated into the materials at the time of the render. Most often it's accomplished with passes (Figure 16.51).

Figure 16.51 Reflection occlusion is multiplied by the reflection.

Reflection occlusion can be used to darken ray-traced reflections, mapped reflections, and/or reflections that are captured onto a live-action background image. Reflection occlusion was originally designed to work with mapped reflections. (Mapped reflections are covered in Chapter 17, "Image-Based Lighting and More.") Mapped reflections have the problem of reflecting the map in areas they shouldn't, namely in areas where the object would be reflecting into itself instead of the environment map. In these cases, just darkening the reflection in these areas solves the visual problem and looks pretty good without necessitating any ray tracing. Glossy ray-traced reflections in particular are very render-intensive; a blurred reflection occlusion can sometimes substitute as a cheap glossy reflection. Reflection occlusion also works well when combining a digital reflection to a live-action plate. Simply adding a digital reflection can brighten the plate too much, and better results are obtained if the plate is first darkened by a reflection occlusion pass (Figure 16.52). Sometimes, just darkening the plate or render with reflection occlusion is enough, and an actual reflection isn't needed.

Figure 16.52 An example of using reflection occlusion to darken a live-action background image. If the digital reflection is simply added, it may be too bright (left). Darkening the plate first with reflection occlusion produces better results (right).

16.5 CHAPTER CONCLUSION

Global illumination makes the task of creating soft fill and bounce light vastly easier, but the render times can be formidable. Global-illumination techniques were once avoided in animation production due to their long render times, but now enjoy much greater use thanks to the faster processing power of today's computers. While a variety of GI algorithms are available, ones commonly found in animation and visual effects productions are ray-traced GI, point-based GI, and ambient occlusion. Which method to use depends on if you need strict realism and ease of use (as with path-traced methods) or faster renders and more creative control (as with point-based and occlusion methods). Having knowledge of how the algorithm you are using works "under the hood" will help you to understand how to use its settings.

16.5.1 IMPORTANT POINTS

- Global illumination calculates indirect light.
- Global illumination has been around for a long time but only recently has become feasible for animation production.
- Several different methods can calculate global illumination.
- Global illumination has several advantages, the biggest one being that it makes the job of lighting easier (in most cases).
- Global illumination's one significant disadvantage is that it's very render-intensive, which makes it unsuitable for certain projects.
- When first learning global illumination, start simply.
- Different methods have different settings. Change only one setting at a time to best control and understand the results.
- Radiosity was one of the first global-illumination algorithms in common use, but it doesn't handle complex geometry well so it's not common in animation production.
- Final gather gives relatively fast results and is easy to dial in, but is less accurate.
- Photon mapping is very accurate and controllable but very render-intensive, so it's used little to sparingly in animation production.
- Ray-traced global illumination is gaining in popularity. It has few settings, so it's easy to use and highly accurate but very render-intensive.
- Point-based global illumination is very common in animation production. It can be pre-calculated and renders relatively quickly, but it's less accurate than ray tracing.
- Ambient occlusion and reflection occlusion are partial global-illumination calculations that can be pre-calculated.
- Ambient occlusion and reflection occlusion are cheats used to increase the realism of a digital scene.

16.5.2 Terms

global illumination

indirect light

direct light

skylight

caustics

physically accurate

SGI

render farm

radiosity

final gather

photon mapping

path-traced global
  illumination

point-based global
  illumination

point cloud

brickmap

ambient occlusion

reflection occlusion

16.5.3 Exercises

1. Using your software of choice, light a simple scene with one white ball and one light. Make the ground colored so you can see the diffuse bleeding. Add global illumination. If your software calculates caustics, then add another ball, make it transparent, and render with caustics.

2. Light an indoor scene with the strongest light coming through the window. Use global illumination to calculate realistic scattered light throughout the room.

3. If your software calculates it, practice using ambient occlusion with an ambient light. Try implementing it into the render without pre-calculating it. Next try implementing it in the composite, rendering out passes. Which way do you prefer? What were the advantages and disadvantages of each for you?

Figure 17.1 Beginning with *Iron Man 2*, Industrial Light & Magic made extensive use of image-based lighting techniques. (©2010 Paramount. Courtesy of Everett Collection.)

Chapter 17
Image-Based Lighting and More

"Human subtlety will never devise an invention more beautiful, more simple or more direct than does nature because in her inventions nothing is lacking, and nothing is superfluous."

—Leonardo da Vinci, 15th-Century Scientist and Artist

This chapter focuses on techniques and skills often used to integrate 3D elements with real-world footage. Foremost among these techniques is *image-based lighting*, a technique that uses an image to control the lighting in the scene. Image-based lighting, combined with global illumination, produces highly realistic rendering as it closely replicates the properties and behavior of real-world light. In the past several years, image-based lighting has gained widespread use in visual effects films. Skills such as the ability to evaluate a live-action image for lighting cues remain necessary, however. These skills demonstrate a fundamental understanding of how light works. For that reason, this chapter also covers how to evaluate a live-action plate "by eye."

The techniques in this chapter can be used in full CG animation as well. For example, the use of mapped reflections is common to both full CG animation and visual effects. Certainly Section 17.4, "Lighting with Cards," is just as useful. This chapter contains something for everyone interested in digital lighting, regardless of whether your primary interest is stylized full CG or photoreal visual effects.

17.1 IMAGE-BASED LIGHTING

Image-based lighting (IBL) is a technique that uses an *image* to drive the color and intensity of light. Most typically, an image is mapped to a special environment light that is shaped like a dome, sphere, or cube. Illumination is calculated as radiating inward from the environment light into the scene. This image is known as an *environment map* because it is coming from all directions and distant from the subject (Figure 17.2). IBL used in this manner will not be able to imitate a bright lamp between two CG subjects, for example.

Image-based lighting can also be used to drive the entire lighting for the scene, or just part of it in combination with other traditional CG lights (Figures 17.3 through 17.5). "Traditional lights" are one of the basic light types, such as point, spot, directional, or area light. In addition to the direct light, the maps used for image-based lighting can also be used to contribute to reflections, refractions, glossy highlights, and/or ambient illumination.

Figure 17.2 In IBL, lighting takes its color and intensity from an image file.

The maps used in IBL are usually photographs taken from some real-world location. Often they are high dynamic range (HDR) in order to produce a wide enough range of luminance values. While HDR maps are typical, IBL can be used in combination with normal low dynamic range (LDR) images, but a LDR map will not be able to reproduce strong light sources in the scene. (For an introduction to HDR, see Section 9.3.2 in Chapter 9, "Light Intensity.").

Figure 17.3 A render using two lights—an environment light mapped with an HDR image and a single distant light. Rendered with global illumination. All items on the table are digital.

Figure 17.4 A close-up render of *just* the CG elements from Figure 17.3, including captured shadows and reflections (blurred background is the IBL map).

Figure 17.5 The map used to light Figures 17.3 and 17.4.

IBL is also typically associated with global illumination methods. It is important to note, however, that IBL does not have to be used in combination with global illumination, nor does it have to be mapped onto an environment light. Whether or not you combine your IBL with HDRI and/or GI depends on what you need your IBL to do (whew, that is a lot of acronyms!).

17.1.1 Advantages and Disadvantages of IBL

Image-based lighting offers a few unique advantages over traditional lighting methods. On the other hand, IBL has a few disadvantages. IBL isn't necessarily the one-stop lighting solution for easy, great lighting some initially may hope for. At times the technique can fall short of what you want it to look like in terms of style, or what you need it to look like in terms of integration or quality. Here are a few of the common benefits and problems.

Advantages of IBL:

✓ **Better integration with live-action sets.** The maps used for IBL can be taken from photographs of the set to ensure a match between live elements and later digital renders.

✓ **More realistic soft light.** IBL lends itself to soft light. As noted, soft light can be difficult to imitate unless large area lights and/or elaborate cheats are used. Environment light, on the other hand, can create soft light easily.

✓ **Natural-looking color shifts.** By using a map with varying intensities and colors, the lighting can have subtle shifts of intensity and color that are difficult and time-consuming (in terms of the artist's time) to reproduce with traditional lights.

✓ **Getting started is easier.** IBL gets you much of the way there. Your goal is to get the rest of the way there, which may entail filling in the gaps of what IBL doesn't do well or dealing with quality issues.

✓ **Helps provide consistency between scenes.** If two shots use the same IBL, then they will have come a long way toward looking alike. Artists need to tweak less on an individual-shot basis, providing better shot-to-shot continuity in less time.

✓ **Provides a guideline for the placement of any traditional lights put into the scene.** If other lights are added to the scene (as they often are), then a look at the IBL dome, which can be visible in the scene, will show you where these lights actually were in the real-world setting, helping with placement.

✓ **Easy to swap out.** Having a map that changes all of the lighting in one fell swoop is a great way to quickly test out different lighting scenarios (assuming you have a variety of accurate maps). During the making of *Avatar* (2009), for example, the artists used IBL maps to test how a scene looked at different times of day. This allowed the director to quickly pick the lighting that was best suited for that story point, a process that would be very time-consuming if each new lighting scenario had to be built by hand.

IBL has particular benefit for visual effects productions. When creating digital elements that are to be combined with live action, all of the lighting from the set must be re-created inside the computer. Lighting for visual effects must be very realistic and it *must match* the lighting in the live-action footage, or the two will not integrate. IBL allows a way for us to literally take the set lighting and bring it into the computer to light our digital elements with it.

WHAT ARE VISUAL EFFECTS?

The term *visual effects* is sometimes misused, causing some confusion about its exact meaning. Many people believe the term *visual effects* refers to *effects* added to film, such as explosions, snow, tidal waves, buildings crumbling, and the like. These things, however, are known simply as "effects" (FX), and the artists who make them are known as FX artists. In particular, they are dynamic or particle effects, but that is another book. Visual effects (VFX) often includes dynamic or particle effects but also includes a whole lot more.

Visual effects is, in fact, an extremely broad category meaning any artificial manipulation done to live-action footage to create a new result. The purpose of it is to create imagery that would have been impractical or impossible to shoot all live, or all "in camera." By definition, visual effects are integrated in some way with, or applied to, existing real footage. And they include lots of things, from footage that is colorized (to make day look like night, for example), to full CG characters added to live-action backgrounds (such as *Transformers*), to full digital backgrounds around real actors (such as *Alice in Wonderland*). Visual effects can be computer-generated (nowadays most of them usually are), or they can be generated without a computer (known as "practical" effects). Visual effects are today's "movie magic."

If it doesn't have a live-action component, then it's not visual effects. In general, feature films can be categorized in two main divisions: full CG feature (such as *Toy Story*, *Shrek*, *Tangled*) and visual effects films (such as *Avatar*, *Pirates of the Caribbean*, *Transformers*, *The Chronicles of Narnia*).

Most color and lighting technical directors will work on all kinds of productions, since just about everything 3D and CG needs shading and lighting. In my career, I have worked on commercials, music videos, full CG features, VFX features, video games, and even an interactive kiosk. My advice is to look past the labels of animation and visual effects and look instead to the skill sets, knowing that you will quite likely be working on all of the above.

Disadvantages of IBL:

◆ **Doesn't imitate hard light well.** Lights that should be hard in IBL look softer than they should, cause sizzling in the render, or both. IBL has trouble with hard light because of the way it's calculated. Very tiny and very bright sources are difficult to accurately sample. Importance sampling helps with this, but in many cases sizzling remains an issue.

◆ **High-frequency IBL maps cause sizzling.** This has already been noted in terms of a small bright light for hard light, but this holds true for any fine detail on the map. Fine detail needs a lot of samples to accurately reproduce, or else the results show artifacts.

◆ **Less creative.** While some feel that IBL frees them to focus on more creative issues, other lighters may find that at times they spend more time wrangling maps than lighting. In general, the more that is done for you, the less control you have over the look.

◆ **Less flexible.** When working with traditional lights, the artist has many clearly defined parameters in each light and its shadow in order to adjust the look of each light. In traditional lights, separate parameters control intensity, color, and so forth. When working with IBL, however, changing the IBL itself requires repainting the map. Painting a map is a far less intuitive way to light, and it can be difficult to visualize what the results will be.

- **You need an accurate map.** For the lighting to look correct, the map must be correct. In visual effects, accurate photos of the set need to be taken at the time of the shoot (not at a different time when the lighting is different). For the average person who is trying to find a suitable image from, say, scouring the Internet, these images may or may not work for your needs. The best map is one custom-made to represent your environment.

Luckily, each of these problems has a solution. In general, finding a solution often means backing off a bit from pure IBL, modifying the map, or working with the quality settings. To find out specifics, keep reading to the next section.

17.1.2 Working with IBL

IBL is most often combined with traditional lighting to get the best of both worlds. IBL is used for what it does well—creating realistic soft light and getting the artist much of the way there. Traditional lights are then used to fill in the gaps. Traditional lights can be used to imitate the hard light sources in the scene and provide more creative control. When using this approach, the bright hard lights in the IBL map are painted out, often leaving the bloom around the light behind (Figures 17.6 through 17.10). You can use the location of the bloom or the light before it was painted out to help you accurately place your added light. Some studios use plug-ins that can quickly extract a light source from a map, automatically generating a light with the correct brightness and color, and remove the corresponding values from the map. The trick is striking the right balance between IBL and traditional lights, depending on the needs of the scene.

TIP

In some cases when adding traditional lights, it's best to paint out the light source from the diffuse map only, leaving the light in the reflection map.

Figure 17.6 (Left) The scene that generated Figure 17.7, showing the unmodified IBL map.

Figure 17.7 (Right) This render uses the unmodified HDR environment map and no additional lights. The quality of the sun is too soft, and the scene looks like a cloudy day rather than a bright, clear day.

Figure 17.8 (Left) The scene that generated Figure 17.9, showing the added light and the modified IBL map.

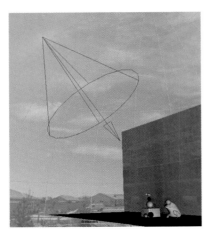

Figure 17.9 (Right) Here the sun in the map was painted out and replaced with a traditional spotlight to better imitate a clear day. Notice the crisp shadows and strong contrasts.

Figure 17.10 On the left is the original environment map; on the right, the sun has been painted out.

Another common practice is to blur the environment maps used for diffuse lighting to help reduce artifacts. As noted, highly detailed maps are prone to sizzling. One way to correct for this is to simply *blur* the map, which helps to eliminate sizzling of the diffuse light contribution without increasing the number of samples or increasing the render time. You may wonder— but if my environment map is blurred, then won't that make my mirror reflections look incorrect? The answer is that yes it will, so two maps are generally used—a blurry, low-resolution map for diffuse lighting and a crisp high-resolution map for sharp reflections (Figure 17.11).

Maps can be color-corrected. Sometimes to get an accurate result, the map just needs a bit of overall color tweaking, like a slight tint or brightening. In some cases a map that doesn't have a high enough dynamic range can be made to look like more by dramatically increasing its value (15 times or more). Color-correction is generally available in the 3D software and doesn't require bringing the map into a paint program. If the map still isn't giving you what you want, however, you can always paint it. This may not be the most intuitive of methods, but it certainly works. You may want to paint in certain colors or values for artistic reasons.

Figure 17.11 On the left is an unrevised map, used for crisp reflections and refractions. On the right is the blurred map, used for diffuse lighting (maps by Alex Kozeki).

TIP

If using final gather, to get a faster render decrease the number of rays ("accuracy") and increase the smoothing ("interpolation") of the environment IBL. This result may be too smooth, so it can be combined with a short-range occlusion to get some details back. This is not completely accurate lighting, but it will look correct in many cases.

17.2 MAPPED REFLECTIONS AND REFRACTIONS

Environment maps contribute to more than just image-based lighting, however. Environment maps have long been used to cheat reflections and in some cases refractions as well. A mapped reflection or refraction comes entirely from—you guessed it—a map, rather than what's around the reflective or refractive object. This map is a texture supplied by the user. Mapped reflections and refractions may be less familiar to some new lighters, who may be unsure how to get the best results from them. Because mapped reflections are far more common than mapped refractions, they will be discussed first.

Mapped reflections and refractions can be very effective. Knowing how and when to use them instead of ray tracing will allow you to save render time, match a live-action plate, and fill in the gaps where your digital set leaves off.

17.2.1 MAPPED REFLECTIONS

Mapped reflections are and have been common as a way to get reflections from the real world onto our digital characters and/or save render time. The maps used for reflection are known as *reflection maps* or *environment maps*. The environment maps used for mapped reflections can be the same as those used for IBL, and their method of obtaining them is the same. (See Section 17.3 for how an environment map is made.)

Mapped reflections render very quickly because they don't need to be ray traced. Scanline renderers can *only* make use of mapped reflections, while ray-traced renderers can use both traced and mapped reflections. Blurred mapped reflections also render very quickly, as they need no additional reflection samples and do not add to the render time, unlike ray-traced blurred reflections. Blurring a mapped reflection is easy—just blur the map. A mapped reflection blurs uniformly, however, meaning it blurs the same amount regardless of distance from the reflecting object. It is not a "true" blurred reflection.

The key to effectively using mapped reflections is having the right map (compare Figures 17.12 and 17.13). If the reflective material is very shiny and the reflection distinct, then you'll need a highly accurate map likely supplemented by ray-traced reflections of nearby elements. On the other hand, if the reflection is indistinct, as when you need to provide some glints on a mildly reflective surface, then something just representative will likely be fine. In the latter case, you may just need to color-correct a found map so it fits into the scene.

Figure 17.12 (Left) An accurate reflection map will integrate well—this CG ball has its reflection entirely from a map created from photographs of the actual location.

Figure 17.13 (Right) The wrong reflection map will stand out like a sore thumb. This reflection map was clearly taken in another location.

Maps can provide reflection when the CG scene doesn't actually have the objects to reflect. This is particularly the case in visual-effects films. It would be highly impractical to model, texture, and light a replica of the entire real-world set just to have a reflection of it in our digital element. So instead, photographs are taken of the actual set, and these photographs are used to generate an accurate environment map.

Mapped reflections can be combined with ray-traced reflections. For highly reflective objects, this generates the best results. The ray-traced reflection will provide realistic self-reflections (reflections of the object within itself) as well as realistic reflections of other objects in the scene. Then the mapped reflection will fill in the gaps (Figures 17.14 through 17.16).

Figure 17.14 This CG ball gets its reflection entirely from the map and is missing nearby elements—the notebook and phone—that weren't present when the reflection map was created.

Figure 17.15 This ball has ray-traced reflections of nearby objects. The table, notebook, and phone are modeled in the 3D scene (as simple cubes) and visible only in the reflection.

Figure 17.16 By combining both ray-traced and mapped reflections, we can capture the reflection from nearby objects (which have been modeled in 3D) and then fill in the gaps with the mapped reflection.

The most realistic reflection maps are high dynamic range (HDR). HDR reflection maps deliver much more accurate results since they preserve the information in the brightest area of the maps. You will notice this difference when your reflection isn't at full intensity (Figures 17.17 and 17.18). When using a regular low dynamic range map, the highlight area grays out and loses detail when the reflectivity isn't at full intensity. In life and when using an HDR map, these areas will stay bright and full of detail. Also notice that when an HDR environment map is blurred, the brightest areas correspond to the specular highlights that come from traditional lights. This clearly shows the relationship of the specular highlight to reflectivity; the highlight is a reflection of the light itself. This is another way HDR environment maps are more realistic.

NOTE

When using IBL as well as mapped HDR reflections, the specular highlight comes directly from the environment map and is tied to the reflectivity of the surface.

In most 3D software programs, mapped reflections are added to surfaces through an attribute on the surface itself. High-end studios, however, often use something called a *reflection light*. This is a "light" in the scene that doesn't actually cast any illumination; rather, it passes the information on what map to use to *all* of the reflective surfaces in the scene. This works well for large projects that may have many reflective surfaces appearing in different shots, each with different environments (and thus different reflection maps). Rather than having to swap out the reflection map in many different materials each time—a time-consuming process—only the reflection light needs to be updated. When using IBL, the reflection may come directly from the IBL map. However, as noted, the map used for diffuse lighting is usually blurred. In this situation, a better approach is use the blurred IBL map for diffuse illumination only, and use a non-blurred map with standard reflection mapping for the reflection.

Figure 17.17 The vase in the center has a reflectivity of 1, with an HDRI environment map. The two vases on either side each have a reflectivity of .2, but the vase on the left uses a normal low dynamic range (LDR) map, while the vase on the right uses an HDR map. Notice the LDR map on the left doesn't maintain its brightness in the highlight areas, while the HDR map on the right does.

Figure 17.18 When blurred, the HDR environment map blooms in the highlight areas, while the normal LDR map loses even more information.

17.2.2 MAPPED REFRACTIONS

Like reflections, refractions can get their look from an environment map as opposed to a "real" background. This approach is particularly useful in visual effects work in which there is no actual background to refract. Refraction maps need to show what is behind the object and are best if they are a full 360-degree view of the scene.

Although almost every standard surface shader has a way to input a mapped reflection, not all of them have a way to input a mapped refraction. If your shader does not have this capability, another option is to map the environment texture into the incandescent parameter of a large sphere placed around the scene. Make sure that incandescence is the only property of the sphere (no diffuse, specularity, reflectivity, and so on). Set this object to be visible in refractions only and then ray trace (Figure 17.19).

Figure 17.19 Example of an environment map appearing only in refraction. This technique is needed when the object is rendered out as a separate pass and then composited over a background.

17.3 CREATING ENVIRONMENT MAPS

Environment maps are added into the 3D scene with special environment projections. What kind of environment projection depends on the kind of reflection map you are using. Environment maps come in two basic flavors: spherical (also known as *lat-long*) and cubic (or *cross*).

Lat-long or *spherical* maps are designed to be used with a spherical projection. They wrap around the sphere and pinch at the poles. Lat-long maps are often created by unwrapping a photograph of a steel ball (Figure 17.20). Special software is used to unwrap a steel ball photograph (try Paul Debevic's HDR Shop, which is free and available online). When unwrapping a photo of a steel ball, the reflection map generated will be missing a view from the back (Figures 17.21 and 17.22). However, if the CG scene is mostly from the view that the photograph was taken, this is fine. A skilled artist can paint in a back view if needed. Full 360-degree lat-long maps can also be stitched together from multiple views of the set. Building a complete 360-degree panorama takes many images, each with a bit of overlap so the images can be stitched together seamlessly, again using special software (Figure 17.23).

Figure 17.20 Photograph of a real stainless-steel ball used on set to capture light and reflection information.

Figure 17.21 The lat-long map created from unwrapping the chrome ball in Figure 17.20. Notice the sides pinch (pointed at by arrows) due to the back not actually being seen in the photograph of the steel ball (map by Alex Koziki).

Figure 17.22 Pinching of the map in the back, which is fine as long as you don't see it. This kind of map would not work as a refraction map.

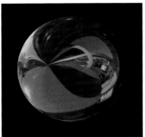

TIP
Be careful when using spherical maps that you don't have pinching in the back or at the poles.

Figure 17.23 Full-panorama lat-long (map by Alex Koziki). This map would work equally well for IBL, reflection, or refraction.

Cubic or **cross** **maps** are generated from a series of six images, one in each of the six directions matching the six sides of a cube: up, down, right, left, front, and back (Figure 17.24). These directions are often described in terms of the 3D coordinate system.

- up = positive y (py)
- down = negative y (ny)
- right = positive x (px)
- left = negative x (nx)
- front = positive z (pz)
- back = negative z (nz)

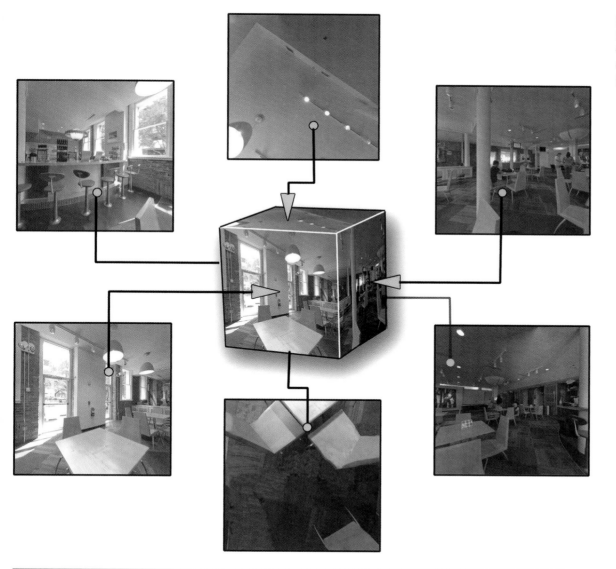

Figure 17.24 Six images used in a cubic environment map, each projected into the scene along the face of a cubic projection.

To generate the images for a cubic or cross map, take a photograph in each of the six directions with a camera having a 90-degree angle of view. For a cubic environment map, each image is mapped to the six sides of a cubic projection. For a cross map, the images are stitched together in a cross formation (Figures 17.25 and 17.26). Which one you use will depend on what your software requires. Software that uses cross maps often comes with a utility to stitch the six images together. In both cases, the software will project these images into the scene along the six faces of a cube.

Figure 17.25 (Left) Diagram of layout of six sides for a cross-environment map.

Figure 17.26 (Right) A cross-environment map (by Alex Koziki).

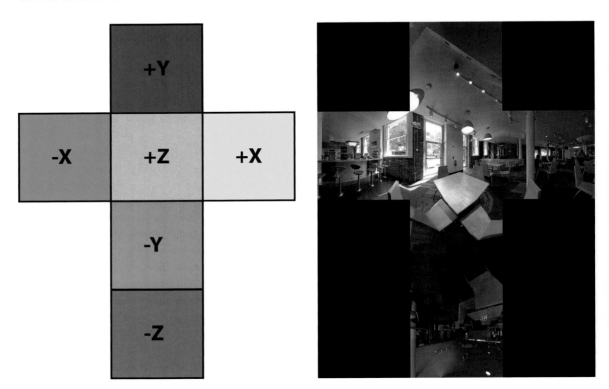

To create an HDR map from a set, a series of photographs are taken at multiple exposures (known as *bracketed exposures*). Usually a minimum of six and up to about nine exposures are taken, each one stop apart (Figure 17.27). This series of photographs can be combined digitally into a single HDR image in an application such as Photoshop. The resulting HDR image is then further processed to create the environment map.

Environment maps can be created by taking renders of a 3D scene as well. In this case, multiple exposures aren't needed; rather, just render the scene into a high dynamic range format, such as an EXR file. This technique is often employed by studios such as Industrial Light & Magic in shots where much of the environment is actually a 3D set. These environment maps can be used for IBL or to supplement and speed up reflections and even refractions. In some cases environment maps can even be painted entirely by hand (Figure 17.28).

Figure 17.27 A series of exposures that can be combined to create an HDR environment map—in this case a lat-long map (photos by Alex Koziki).

Figure 17.28 Simple painted maps can be effective, too (render on top, map used on the bottom).

17.4 LIGHTING WITH CARDS

An new technique that is part of more realistic lighting is to use cards (simple flat surfaces) to help light the scene. This technique is analogous to how a real-world lighter works.

Dark cards can be inserted into the scene to flag out unwanted indirect light. This light may be reflected from a surface or light coming from the environment. Inserting a card with the desired value and color is a useful way to modify light coming from the environment instead of painting the map (compare Figures 17.29 and 17.30).

Figure 17.29 (Left) An IBL image lit with an environment light only, for comparison with Figures 17.30 through 17.33.

Figure 17.30 (Right) A card on the right side of the image blocks illumination from the environment light.

Figure 17.31 (Left) Bounce cards can be placed in the scene to add fill, just as in life.

Figure 17.32 (Right) This scene has been relit entirely with cards—a blocking card, a bounce card, and an incandescent card. The background was color-corrected in the composite.

Conversely, bright cards can add soft light to the scene. White cards can be used to bounce reflected light into a certain area, just like a real-world photographer uses a bounce card (Figure 17.31). Cards that are incandescent or mapped with HDRI will emit light when rendered with most global illumination methods (Figure 17.32). These cards will act much like area lights, only they render faster as they are calculated along with the reflected light in the scene.

Using cards mapped with imagery is a highly controllable form of IBL. Each card can be scaled, rotated, carefully positioned, and brightened or darkened individually to achieve just the result you want in the area you want. Additionally, because the illumination is provided by a card rather than an environment light, the objects in your scene can react to it like a local light source. They can walk past it and be affected by it based on proximity, unlike an environment light that is always distant. The cards can be made invisible so that only their interactions are seen, not the cards themselves (Figure 17.33).

Figure 17.33 Unlike life, the cards' primary visibility can be turned off. This render still has the cards affecting the light in the scene, but the cards themselves are no longer visible.

17.5 EVALUATING A LIVE-ACTION PLATE

Being able to match a digital element to real footage ("live action") is an essential technique. This section covers how to analyze and interpret lighting found in a live-action plate. When using IBL, the digital lighter has less need to be able to determine the lighting just by looking at the background plate—he can see it in the environment map. However, being able to evaluate an image for lighting cues is still extremely important for a number of reasons. Even with IBL, completing the integration of digital and live action relies on the skill of the lighter. Sometimes the IBL isn't a perfect match or requires modification based on the creative needs of the shot. Although most visual effects shots use IBL today, not all do, and some use it only in a limited sense. Without IBL, you will have *only* your own skill.

Additionally, being able to look at an image and see what is happening with the lights has application beyond just visual effects. This skill will allow you to better determine what is going on in your scene or someone else's, just by looking at the render. The results of your renders won't be a mystery, as you will understand what each light is doing and know what to change in order to make improvements. For those who aspire to leadership or supervisory roles, this will allow you to give informed feedback to lighters on your team, for projects ranging from stylized and full CG to photoreal visual effects. Students are often surprised that I usually know where their lights are placed just by looking at their renders. I can tell when a light is incorrectly positioned, and furthermore where it *should* be positioned, usually without opening the scene file. This comes from practice and training, from years of studying lighting cues.

This section focuses on skills needed by the artist that will allow him to confidently build upon IBL or to match a digital scene without it if need be.

17.5.1 REFERENCE IMAGERY

Before you begin, it's helpful to have reference imagery. Reference imagery is any imagery gathered that helps to explain how the lighting on set actually looked.

A variety of references may be available, such as:

◆ **Photographs of reference balls**. Reference balls are chrome, white, and 18% gray balls that are shot on set. The white balls show the colors and qualities of the lights clearly. By looking at the chrome ball, you can literally see the lights reflected in its mirror finish. In all cases, the shadow can be evaluated for light quality, the number of direct lights affecting the scene, light direction, and overlap of illumination. The chrome ball can be used to create environment maps as well (Figure 17.34).

◆ **A model or "stuffy" pass**. Imagery of models and maquettes placed on location help you determine how the light should look on your digital model. These models are made to look like the CG object that is to be created. They may even be actual models that appear in other shots in the production.

◆ **Lighting diagrams**. These are diagrams of where the real set lights were placed. Notes on type, size, and color of the light source are indicated.

Even without these references, in most cases you can determine the lighting just from the live-action plate itself. It may be more difficult and require some study on your part, but you can do it. You just have to learn how to read the signs, like a tracker finds a trail once he knows what to look for.

Figure 17.34 Various reference imagery, shot on location.

17.5.2 Seeing the Light

Light reveals itself, even when you cannot see the source of it. We intuitively respond to these visual cues, which is why any person can tell you if your CG lighting looks "right" or not—he just may not be able to tell you why. As digital lighters, we just need to bring to our conscious mind what these visual cues are; then we will be able to "see the light" so to speak, even when the source itself is out of view. Here is how to determine all of the properties of light by looking at the plate, or any rendered image for that matter.

To integrate a digital element into a live-action background, the lighting must visually match in the following properties:

◆ Direction
◆ Diffusion
◆ Color
◆ Lighting ratio
◆ Black levels

We need to evaluate each property and match the properties of the lights in our CG scene to those we identify in the plate. Notice that the first four of these areas correspond to the four properties of light—light placement, diffusion, color, and intensity—discussed in Part III of the book ("lighting ratio" corresponds to light intensity). The fifth one, "black levels," refers to a property of real film and is explained in Section 13.2.4 in Chapter 13, "Camera Essentials."

Determining Light Direction

Light direction can be determined by three visual cues:

- The direction of shadows
- The placement of highlights
- The placement of diffuse illumination

Shadows in the scene are the easiest to evaluate. If shadows are apparent, be sure to study them, as they will easily reveal the direction of the light, and to a certain extent its distance from the subject as well. Sometimes I draw a line from the shadow to the shadowing object and then just keep extending this line to where I think the light would be. This will give you the approximate height of the light (Figure 17.35).

The position of the direct diffuse illumination will also reveal the position of the light, both in terms of height (Figure 17.35) and front-to-back placement. If the illumination on the surface is *less* than half of the surface, then the light is coming more from the back. If the illumination on the surface is *more* than half of the surface, then the light is coming more from the front (Figure 17.36).

The specular highlight also reveals the position of the light. While determining light position from a highlight may be a little less intuitive, the specular highlight is very helpful, especially if your material is very dark and has little diffuse information (Figure 17.37).

Don't forget to evaluate how far away you think the light is when placing your digital light. Remember that a near light will produce radial rays and demonstrate attenuation while a far-away light produces parallel rays and little to no apparent attenuation. Also, use your common sense based on what light you are imitating. If the light you are imitating is the sun, it's extremely far away; either place your light far away or use a directional light. On the other hand, if the light you are imitating is an overhead light, determine how high a ceiling would be in your scene and place your light there. Remember from Chapter 12, "Three-Point Lighting and Beyond," that fill lights can be placed anywhere that gets the job done, while rim lights (if you have them) are typically far away and near a motivating source you can see or imagine. For more on direction and distance, see Chapter 8, "Light Placement."

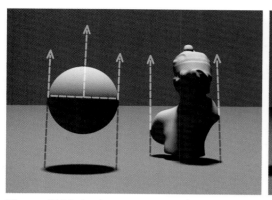 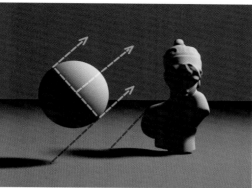 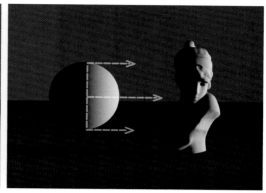

Figure 17.35 In this sequence of images, both the angle of the diffuse illumination and the direction of the shadows reveal the angle of the light, high or low.

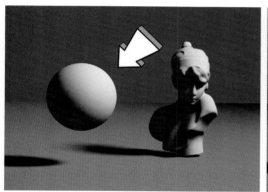 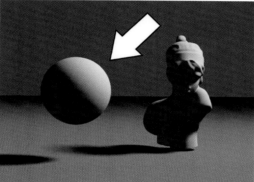 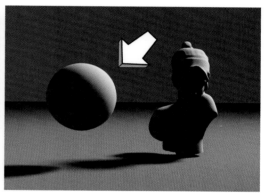

Figure 17.36 Looking at how the diffuse illumination curves across the surface will reveal whether the light is positioned in *front* of the object or *behind* it. If the illumination curves like a crescent moon, the light is somewhere behind the subject. If the illumination covers exactly half the subject, then the light is exactly to the side. If the illumination curves to cover more than half of the subject, then the light is angled toward the front. Of course, the direction of the shadows reveals this, too.

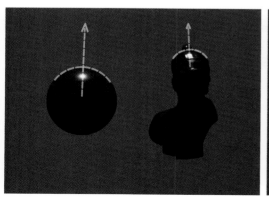 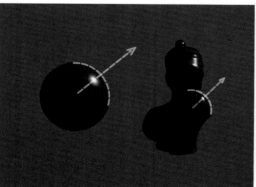 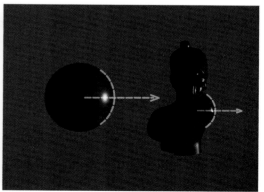

Figure 17.37 Even devoid of other visual cues, the position of the specular will reveal the angle of the light.

Determining Light Color

You can see light color in:

◆ The colors of white objects;

◆ The specular color on shiny or reflective objects; and

◆ The color of the reflecting object (if bounce light).

If your plate has white objects or you have white reference balls, then you are in luck; you can see the color of the light in them. Remember that the colors add up, however, so if a blue light overlaps a red light, then you'll have magenta light. If there are many colors of lights, you'll want to understand how light colors mix. (See Chapter 11, "Light Color," for more on light and surface color.)

Light color can best be determined from specular highlights and reflective objects. Remember the specular highlight is a reflection of the light, and it takes on the color of the light. If you have a mirrored reference ball, an environment map, or just reflective objects in the scene, you can literally see the lights and their colors in reflection.

To set light colors from the plate or reference imagery, sample white objects and highlight areas with a color picker tool. If you are determining the color of a bounce light, remember that you can sample the reflecting object and this will be the hue and saturation exactly. You should sample a variety of areas, as each will likely be a bit different. Choose the color you get the most often and then turn the color's value to 1 in the light.

Determining Light Diffusion

You can see light diffusion (also called *light quality*) in:

◆ The blur and density of shadows;

◆ The relative size and intensity of highlights; and

◆ The hardness and wrap of the terminator.

If the shadow is blurry and lifted, the terminator gradual, and the specular (if there is one) large and possibly dim, then the light is soft—it's large and likely near. Conversely, if the shadow is dark and crisp, the terminator abrupt, and the specular (if there is one) small and bright, then the light is hard—it's small and/or far away.

Determining the softness of the light is perhaps the easiest of those mentioned so far and also perhaps the most overlooked by digital lighters. For many examples of how soft and hard light appear, refer to Chapter 10, "Light Diffusion."

Determining Lighting Ratio

Contrast ratio will determine the relative intensities of your digital lights (how bright you make your key relative to all the fills, for example). We don't need to know or match the exact brightness of the set lights, only their ratio. Contrast ratio is usually judged by eye—just by looking. Of course, you would also determine if the scene is overall bright or overall dark, so that your CG element fits in. Contrast ratio is usually visually matched by adjusting the intensity of the fill relative to the key. For further reading on the lighting ratio, refer to Section 7.1.3, "Light and Continuity," and Section 12.1.3, "Fill Light."

Determining Black Levels

Determining black levels refers to making sure the black in your digital element is exactly the same value as the black in the plate, and is otherwise known as *matching the blacks*. This step is typically done in the composite and is applicable only to visual effects integration.

Real film never goes to black. It may look like it's black, but upon closer inspection there will always be a tiny bit of value even in the darkest areas. Your digital render, however, can and does go to pure black (0,0,0 in all channels). To complete the integration of values, you need to make sure that your CG render has the same infinitesimal bit of black as the plate. You cannot do this by eye! You must measure the black in the plate with a color picker and then color-correct your digital element to match. Raising your digital blacks from pure 0 is known as *lifting the blacks*. To match the blacks, in the composite lift just the darkest values of your 3D render so they match with those in the plate—and I mean match *exactly* (Figure 17.38).

If your blacks aren't matched, you may not notice it right away. When working with film, however, differences barely detectable while your image is in its high-quality glory may become very apparent when the image is processed and the quality reduced, as when you're converting to video. In video, blacks that aren't matched become readily apparent, though if the difference is very large it can be seen in film as well. Supervisors (and you, too) will often gamma your image up or down dramatically to check for details they may have a hard time seeing otherwise. They will be looking, among other things, to make sure your digital render, once composited with the plate, doesn't ever go to true black.

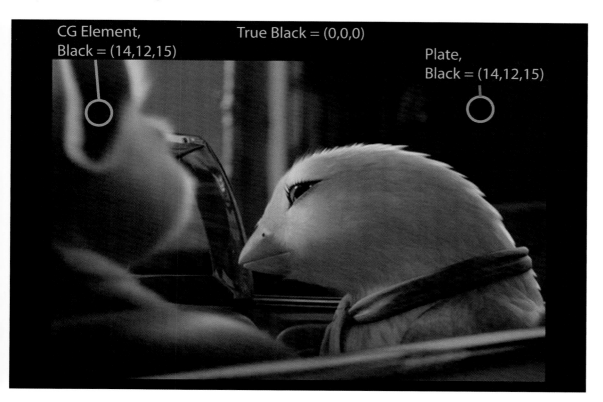

CG Element,
Black = (14,12,15)

True Black = (0,0,0)

Plate,
Black = (14,12,15)

Figure 17.38 The blacks in the digital element have been carefully matched to those of the plate. (*Stuart Little 2*, ©2002 Columbia Pictures Industries, Inc. All Rights Reserved. Courtesy of Columbia Pictures.)

CASE STUDY: EVALUATING AN EXAMPLE PLATE

The lights in this image can be determined entirely from the visual cues on the plate. (Figure 17.39 is the original background plate.)

The direction of the key can be determined from the shadows formed on the lid of the first-aid box; it's coming from the top left, a bit low. We know this is the key because the left side of the box is brighter than the right side. The specular from the key can be seen on the left side of the metal clip on the handle of the box.

A *top light* is evidenced by three cues: one, the countertop is rather bright, indicating more light than just the key; two, the shadow along the top rim of the lid is darker than that along the side, indicating another shadowing light; and three, the metal clip has an additional specular coming from, you guessed it, the top. The top light is rather bright.

Fill light comes from the left. We know we have a fair amount of fill as the key:fill ratio is low.

Bounce light will need to be added coming back up from the countertop unless rendering with global illumination.

Rim light comes from the window. In actuality, no real light would reach from the window to the counter, but we can use the window to loosely motivate a rim if desired.

Figure 17.40 shows the positions of the lights as determined by an analysis of the plate.

The colors of the lights can be determined by sampling the plate with a color picker. With this plate, we are in luck. We have both white and reflective objects, both that will reveal the colors of the lights. Generally, it's a good idea to sample a variety of areas to get an idea of the light's color. Notice which areas are sampled to get the color from each light. You want to either sample highlights directly or sample areas in which the light in question is providing most of the illumination. Bounce light is the color of the reflecting object itself. Be sure to turn the sampled color's value to 1. For more on setting bounce-light color, see Section 12.1.4, "Bounce Light: A Special Type of Fill Light." Figures 17.41 and 17.42 show the colors of the lights as samples from various areas on the plate. In each swatch, on the left is the original sample; on the right is the color once the value is set to 1.

A look at the final composite reveals that the digital characters are well integrated using the light properties determined from an analysis of the plate (Figure 17.43).

Figure 17.39 The plate.

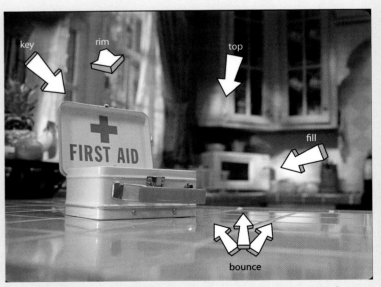

Figure 17.40 These lights have been determined entirely from a study of the plate itself.

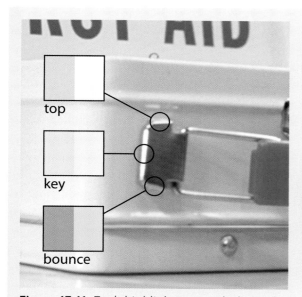

Figure 17.41 Each highlight is sampled. On the left in the rectangle is the original sampled color; on the right is the color with its value adjusted to 1.

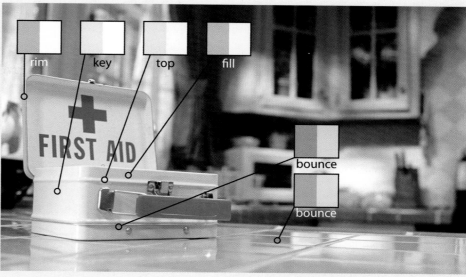

Figure 17.42 The light colors can be determined by sampling colors on the plate.

Figure 17.43 The finished composited image from *Stuart Little 2*. (© 2002 Columbia Pictures Industries, Inc. All Rights Reserved. Courtesy of Columbia Pictures.)

17.6 CHAPTER CONCLUSION

The trend in today's digital lighting and rendering is toward accurate and realistic replication of the behavior of light and materials, known as *physically based lighting and shading*. Visual effects productions in particular have moved toward more realistic and more render-intensive techniques, such as ray tracing, ray-traced global illumination, and image-based lighting. While lighting for visual effects utilizes many of the same techniques as full CG, it has the special concern of realism and matching the live-action component, and therefore uses image-based lighting techniques far more often.

Several long-held cheats still apply, however, adapted to meet today's demands. For example, reflections and refractions can be successfully mapped, provided you have the right environment map. These maps are often the same as or similar to those used for IBL. Mapped reflections and refractions don't need ray tracing and can be used to provide better integration and reduce render time.

Realistic rendering is not a substitute for artistry and skill. The foundational skills of good lighting, such as being able to determine lighting from an image, are applicable in situations from photoreal to stylized and should be mastered by serious students of lighting.

17.6.1 IMPORTANT POINTS

- Capturing high dynamic range imagery (HDRI) on set for later use with image-based lighting (IBL) has become a common practice in visual effects lighting.
- IBL usually is rendered with global illumination for the most realistic result.
- Environment lights can use environment maps to drive the lighting of an entire scene.
- The environment maps used for IBL are the same as or similar to those used for mapped reflections.
- IBL does an excellent job of simulating soft light, and not so good of a job at simulating hard light.
- Recent advances in importance sampling have helped improve the simulation of hard light from IBL.
- IBL is often combined with traditional lights to get the best results.
- Both reflections and refractions may be mapped. Mapped reflections and refractions can be rendered using scanline methods.
- Mapped reflections and refractions are especially important to visual effects shots.
- Mapped reflections are helpful in full CG as well, to fill in where your digital set leaves off and reduce render time.
- The specular highlight is a *reflection* of the light source.
- Using cards to light a scene imitates how a real-world lighter would work.
- Being able to evaluate a plate to determine the lighting is a valuable skill.
- Lighting needs to match in all of its basic properties: position, color, diffusion, and lighting ratio.
- Integrating CG with live action is completed in the composite.

17.6.2 Terms

physically based lighting
image-based lighting (IBL)
visual effects (VFX)
special effects (FX)
practical effects

mapped reflection
environment map
lat-long or spherical map
cubic map
cross map

bracketed exposure
black levels
matching the blacks

17.6.3 Exercises

1. Create a simple outdoor scene with at least one matte object and one reflective object and light it using IBL. Find or make an HDR environment map that represents a sunny day. Make blurry diffuse maps for your scene. Use the blurry map for direct light and the clear map for reflections. Paint out the sun and add in a directional light to replace it. What were the differences?

2. Light a scene using only an environment light and cards. Starting with a mapped environment light, use cards to relight the scene. Use cards with high incandescent values or mapped with HDR images as additional light sources, and dark cards (no incandescence or HDRI) to flag out unwanted light. Use white cards to bounce light into shadows like a real photographer would. For this exercise, don't use any traditional lights.

3. Select a photograph, one that doesn't have an environment map or lighting diagram. Evaluating the lighting cues described in Section 17.5, what lights can you see? Determine each light's direction, color, and diffusion.

4. You and a friend evaluate each other's CG renders. Without looking into each other's scene files, see if you can determine what lights your friend is using. Try to determine the lights' approximate placement, color, and level of diffusion. Next, discuss your observations with your friend. How accurate were you?

Figure 18.1 Many passes surround the central composite in this photo montage (model and set by Brenda Weede).

Chapter 18
Multi-Pass Rendering

"Maybe because it's entirely an artist's eye, patience, and skill that make an image and not his tools."

—Ken Rockwell, Modern Photographer, from "Your Camera Doesn't Matter"

While any 3D scene can be rendered in its entirety, a common practice is to split a scene into various parts and render each part separately. These separate renders are then reassembled into a single image sequence either by being reintegrated into the 3D scene or by being combined in the composite (Figure 18.1). In the composite, each 2D image pass can be further adjusted in hue, saturation, and so on, before being recombined, allowing for more control of the final image. The technique of separating a single render into different passes is known as *multi-pass rendering* or more simply *rendering in passes*.

This chapter presents rendering in passes from the lighter's point of view, focusing primarily on what passes are common to split out, when and how to split out passes, and how to recombine them. This chapter doesn't go into detail about compositing, but rather it assumes that the reader either has or will obtain information about specific compositing technique. For further reading on compositing, I recommend Ron Brinkman's *The Art and Science of Digital Compositing, Second Edition*, itself a 600+ page tome of good information. This chapter concludes with a discussion of linear workflow. While not exclusive by any means to rendering in passes, linear workflow is an advanced topic of concern to both lighters and compositors, so it is included here.

18.1 OVERVIEW OF PASSES

"Pass" is an general term that can sometimes be a bit misunderstood. In its broadest sense, a "pass" is just about anything that is generated by the renderer and is later used to make the final image. This can be a 2D render or it can even be data stored in other formats, like depth maps and point clouds, which get re-integrated into the 3D scene. For example, a pre-rendered depth-map shadow is known as a *shadow pass*. Passes involving data are usually pre-calculations done to save time later. This chapter focuses on image passes, not pre-calculated data passes.

Professional digital lighting artists often split all but the most simple scenes into passes. Why are they so common? The best way to answer this is to look at their advantages and disadvantages.

18.1.1 ADVANTAGES OF RENDER PASSES

Rendering in passes is common professional practice because it offers several distinct advantages *in certain situations*. There are any number of reasons why something may be split out as a pass, but generally doing so saves render time or provides some sort of needed control that improves the final image.

Here are the main advantages of passes:

- ◆ **Easier:** Some things are just easier to do in the composite. Fine-tuning the lighting, which would normally take a lot of time, can be easily adjusted in the composite. Or an effect that is difficult to create in 3D may be simpler to create in 2D.

- ◆ **More control:** Sometimes you have more options in the composite than you do in 3D. Changing the color of atmosphere at certain distances or dialing in a very specific glow effect are two examples.

- ◆ **Better results:** There are times when the 2D approach can provide better results. Renders can be prone to artifacts like aliasing or flickering, such as a sizzling highlight or flickering glow effect. In some cases, generating a pass can help solve problems or be a less error-prone approach.

- ◆ **Faster:** Many things are simply faster if split into passes and done in the composite. Changes can be made in the composite relatively quickly—a composite may take only a few minutes compared to the hours per frame of a 3D render. Depth of field, in particular, is faster when done in the composite. Also, if objects are separated into passes and a change is requested to one of them, then only the pass with that object needs to be re-rendered. Other times, an element that isn't moving (like a static background) can be split out and only one frame rendered, then this frame held in the composite. Additionally, passes that pre-calculate data speed up render time by reusing those calculations multiple times.

- ◆ **Necessary:** Some things simply cannot be done any other way. For example, when integrating digital with live action you'll need certain passes in order to composite different aspects with the live-action plate. In another example, if a scene is too large or complex, it may not render all together and must be split up.

The advantages of passes can be summed up in two words: faster and better. However, remember that passes should only be used "in certain situations." Not all passes are needed all of the time. The benefit of a pass depends on the situation. Productions often have certain passes they render for almost every shot, while other passes are only implemented on a case-by-case basis.

18.1.2 DISADVANTAGES OF PASSES

The main disadvantage of passes is that they add complexity. Added complexity always comes at a price. When you add complexity, you have more data to set up and manage. The key is to have the benefits outweigh the drawbacks of complexity. Only use passes if they give a specific advantage. If they don't have an advantage or if you're not clear about that advantage, then don't use them, which brings me to another point…

A potential problem of passes is improper use. Rendering in passes isn't a basic skill but rather an intermediate to advanced skill. To properly set up and use passes, you need to have an in-depth knowledge of your 3D scene, know some compositing, and be organized. Without these things you may easily render out unnecessary passes that will add to total render time without any benefit, or worse, recombine the passes incorrectly, resulting in an image that looks "wrong." This will make your work slower/worse—which is the exact opposite of what you want!

Remember the Rules of Good Lighting Technique: *Only add complexity as needed* and *the bigger the cheat, the more knowledge needed.* For this reason, I encourage new lighters to not delve into rendering in passes until they feel fully confident and comfortable with lighting without them. Added complexity is the only real disadvantage of passes, but this creates several difficulties.

Here are the main difficulties of passes:

◆ **Passes require additional setup**. Each pass must be set up by you or someone else. A way around this is to use presets, but then you are limited to the functionality of the preset. Some of your own setup is usually unavoidable. Properly setting up a pass can take time and requires that you know what you are doing.

◆ **(Some) passes can result in increased render time**. When passes are generated as separate renders, each of these renders takes time. The time needed to render the pass needs to be offset by its visual advantage, or the time you will save later. If improperly used, separate passes can add to render time without benefitting the scene.

◆ **Passes require more organization**. When working with passes, you have more files to keep track of. A bit like juggling, you'll have many balls in the air. Without organization, you are likely to lose track of where things are, what version is the latest, and which file does what. To solve this problem, be very clear on your naming and file organization and which version the composite requires.

◆ **Passes require good render-farm management**. An efficient approach to rendering is critical when managing many separate passes. Frames need to be checked and each pass needs to be monitored for time. Also, be aware of when your renderer is generating passes: You don't want to accidentally regenerate passes and waste render time.

◆ **Passes need to be put back together correctly:** Perhaps the biggest drawback of rendering in passes is having to ensure that they are correctly reintegrated later. This takes knowledge of how things were put together in the first place as well as some basic compositing techniques. Without this knowledge, things can easily be put together incorrectly, resulting in an image that looks "wrong."

TIPS FOR SUCCESSFULLY USING RENDER PASSES:
✓ Stay organized
✓ Understand your scene
✓ Maintain good render practices
✓ Know how things are put together

18.2 PASS GENERATION

While many, many things can be separated out into passes, there are only two basic means of generating them. Passes may be generated individually, each in their own separate render, or they may be generated along with the calculations of another render. These methods of generation are discussed in this section along with guidelines on when to use each.

18.2.1 PRIMARY OUTPUTS/SEPARATE PASSES

Every render creates one *primary output*. This primary output is what we are used to seeing from our very first render. We render, and out comes an image or image sequence (Figure 18.2). We are all familiar with rendering primary outputs. We just don't usually refer to them as such. In this book, I will also refer to primary outputs as a *separate pass* to differentiate them from secondary outputs, discussed in Section 18.2.2, "Secondary Passes."

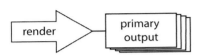

Figure 18.2 Every successful render creates a "primary output."

Separately rendered passes can be set up either by creating completely separate scene files or by using features within the 3D software to create different renders all within the one scene (such as Maya's render layers). Unless you run into problems, you should whenever possible keep all your passes within one scene to stay better organized and to be most efficient. For example, if the animation changes and all your passes are in one scene, you only have one scene to update, and you will not have to rebuild all of your passes.

Each new primary output can add significantly to the time of the render. Depending on your renderer, you may be able to send several primary passes to the render farm at one time, known as a *job*. Even when grouped into one job, each different primary pass is rendered one at a time, each a complete render adding to the total render time.

Primary outputs are suitable for use when certain objects are rendered in isolation from their fellows, have no or minimal light interactions ("light interactions" primarily being shadows, reflections, and indirect light), have cheated light interactions (such as mapped reflections), or have pre-calculated and reused lighting interactions (such as depth-mapped shadows and baked bounce-light calculations). Because each primary pass adds to the render time, each new primary pass should be given close scrutiny as to whether it is really needed. When in doubt, do without.

Render Visibility Attributes

When setting up a scene to render a primary pass, you will want to make use of *render visibility attributes*. These attributes, as their name suggests, control the visibility of the objects in the render. In CG land, you can do much more than make things visible or invisible. You can make them *partly* visible, so they show up in some ways but not in others (Figure 18.3). A bit like Dracula, who never had a reflection… For example, earlier chapters discussed turning off shadow casting on certain objects and making objects visible in only reflections or refractions.

Here is a list of the render attributes commonly controlled when setting up primary passes.

◆ Primary visibility: Controls whether the object is seen directly from the camera.

◆ Reflections: Controls whether the object shows up in reflections (ray tracing only).

◆ Refractions: Controls whether the object shows up in refractions (ray tracing only).

◆ Indirect light: Controls whether the object contributes bounced light (global illumination only).

◆ Shadows: Controls whether the object casts shadows; doesn't affect pre-calculated shadows.

Holdouts

Holdouts **are objects that cut out what is behind them, like a bite out of a cookie.** Holdouts are used when you want to render an object separately from another object that is in front of it, but this foreground object is actually rendered into the background layer. Holdouts are created by assigning a special material that will make the object black in color channels as well as the alpha channel. When setting up holdout objects, you don't want to hide them. You *want* them to render. You just want them to render perfectly black in all channels. If you hide them, nothing will hold out your layer. For examples of creating and using holdouts, see Section 18.3.1, "Beauty Passes."

TIP

Be sure to keep displacements on your holdout geometry.

18.2.2 SECONDARY OUTPUTS

The other way to generate passes is to render them as *secondary outputs*. Secondary outputs always render along with a primary output. Another name for secondary outputs is "arbitrary output variables," or AOVs for short. Because typing just three letters appeals to me, I will use the terms "secondary output" and "AOV" interchangeably throughout this book.

Secondary outputs do not add to the render time. This secondary output is *not* its own render, but piggybacks on the processing done in the primary render. While the primary output is being calculated, so is the secondary output. Any number of secondary outputs can be created at one time (Figure 18.4). For example, while the specular is being calculated in the main render, it is at the same time written out into a secondary output. Each AOV can be rendered into its own file, or it can be saved into the same file as the primary render if using the EXR image format. (EXR files can store more than three channels of information.)

Figure 18.3 From top to bottom: all render attributes on; primary visibility off for the leftmost vase; visible in reflections off for the leftmost vase; cast shadows off for the leftmost vase and glass bottle.

Secondary outputs work well with full global illumination. Because they are based on the data in the primary pass, the secondary passes all have the appropriate light interactions. Since a full global illumination render can take a very long time, being able to generate many AOVs along with it at no additional expense is a huge time-saver.

When using AOVs your choice of possible outputs is predetermined. This is both a benefit and a drawback. The benefit is that they are already set up, saving you time. As a drawback, however, you cannot easily create different kinds of AOVs. In some packages, you can get under the hood and create additional AOVs, but most often you will just be using the ones provided. Luckily, there is usually quite an impressive list from which to choose. However, if there isn't an an AOV provided for what you want to do, you can always set up your own separate primary pass.

Secondary passes are often created from the various shading and lighting components—specular separated from diffuse, reflection passes, etc. Other secondary passes are used, but shading component passes are common and make for a good example. Because secondary passes are essentially rendered "for free" (with no additional render cost), they are often rendered "just in case," as long as there is adequate disk space.

In some cases it may be difficult at first to tell what are secondary outputs and what are simply several primary outputs rendering as a group (Figure 18.5 and 18.6). The difference is critical to knowing how often you should be rendering these passes, however, so to render efficiently you really must find out. If reading the software documentation doesn't help, watch how it renders. If the renderer processes each pass independently (you see it process 0% to 100% for first one pass then the other), then these are separate primary renders. If it processes once and voilà, several outputs, then this is one primary pass with AOVs along for the ride.

SOFTWARE TIP

In Maya, "render layers" are separate primary renders. Mental Ray's "passes" are AOVs. In RenderMan, "passes" are separate primary passes, while "outputs" create secondary outputs.

Table 18.1 Comparison of Pass-Generation Methods

Generation Method	Means of Rendering	Render Time	How Often to Generate
Primary Pass	Each as a separate render.	Adds to render time.	Split out as-needed only.
Secondary Pass (AOV)	Along with a primary render and other AOVs.	No additional render time.	Split out "just in case" is wise.

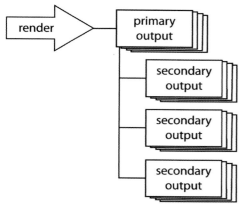

Figure 18.4 One primary output and several secondary outputs at the same time.

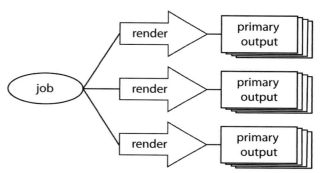

Figure 18.5 A job may contain several different primary renders.

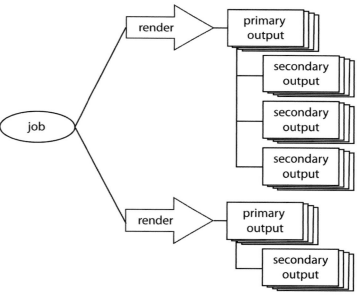

Figure 18.6 A job with two primary renders, each with different secondary outputs.

QUESTIONS TO ASK YOURSELF

When deciding if you should use a pass:

1. Is it going to give me control that I don't have in the 3D render and that I need?
2. Does a pass in the composite provide a better look?
3. Do I expect a lot of changes with this element?
4. Do I have a visual problem to solve that can be fixed with an additional pass in the composite?
5. Is there a means to do something in the composite that is significantly faster than if done in 3D, and is at equal or acceptable quality?
6. Is a pass the only efficient and effective way to do a certain thing?
7. Is the amount of time it takes to render commensurate with the need (for separate passes)?
8. Is this a separate render (a "primary output")? If so, split out only if you really need it.
9. Is this a secondary output? If so, then "just in case" is fine.
10. Does the render need to be a separate pass or can it be an AOV? Do not render as a separate pass something that you can generate as an AOV. To do so is unnecessary rendering.

18.3 COMMON PASSES

While just about anything you can imagine can be separated into a pass, this section describes the most commonly used passes. Additionally, this section tells when to use them, how to set them up (in the case of separate renders), and how to put them back together again.

18.3.1 BEAUTY PASSES

The most basic pass is known as a *beauty pass*. A beauty pass renders its subject in all of its glory—all of the lights and shading attributes are there; the render is complete for that subject. For example, rendering the character separate from its environment or characters separate from each other. Even pieces and parts of an object may be rendered separately, such as clothes or hair rendered separately from the character's body. Some literature refers to these kinds of renders as layers rather than passes, but the majority of professionals simply call them beauty passes.

When to Use Beauty Passes

There are several reasons why different elements may be separated out into different beauty passes. A big reason for splitting out beauty passes is so that if you need to adjust only one element, you can re-render just this one item and not everything, saving render time. For example, if a director wants to make changes to the hero character in your scene (and he is likely to want to make many changes) but there are no changes needed for the background, it then makes sense to split out the character and re-render it separately. Any character or element can be split out so that the look of it can be iterated independently without rendering the entire scene. In some cases, if the camera isn't moving, non-moving elements can be split out and only one frame rendered. This frame is then held in the composite for the desired length of time. For example, in Figure 18.7, splitting the render into two passes dramatically reduced render time from 26 hours to only 3 hours. When rendered all together, each of the 72 frames in this shot took 20 minutes, for a total of 26 hours. When the background was separated out, however, the resulting render time was 18 minutes for one frame of the background and only 2 minutes for each of the 72 frames of the character by itself, a mere 3 hours total.

Another reason to split out beauty passes is if the scene isn't able to render everything together because it's too big. The renderer simply cannot handle all the data and dies on you or hangs indefinitely. The first solution when you have such a problem is not to split out passes but to ruthlessly go through the scene file and optimize it by pruning unneeded geometry and lights and checking every possible setting. If the scene is well optimized, another solution is to spread the render of each frame out over multiple machines. The third option is to split it up into passes.

Rendering many different beauty passes used to be more common than it is now. In the past I have worked on shows where hair and even eyeballs of characters were separated out. This much splitting has become rare. The trend today is to keep more of the scene together and separate out only key elements, such as a hero character. This is especially true if rendering with full global illumination.

Figure 18.7 Two beauty passes, a foreground character and the background, combine to make a single image (scene from SCAD-Atlanta *Drag'N'Fly* short, lighting by Bianca Gee).

How to Split Out and Use Beauty Passes

The most straightforward way to set up a beauty pass is to simply to hide everything that you don't want to see in that pass. The simplest scenario (and I believe in starting simply) would be to place one object completely in front of another object. In this case hide the back object and just render the front object. Next, hide the front object and just render the back object. Voilà, two layers have been rendered out. These layers would be combined by compositing the front object *over* the back object, just as you place one layer over another in Photoshop. The transparency of the top image is indicated by its alpha channel (the fourth channel in an RGBA image). Black in A's alpha channel means the top layer is completely transparent, white means completely opaque, and gray means semi-transparent, like a layer mask in Photoshop. Simple, right? Indeed, it is. However, things are rarely that simple.

Things get a bit more complex if the object being rendered is not always in front of the objects being hidden. In this case, the objects in the front need to be made into *holdouts*. Any object that is a holdout must be included in the render and have a special holdout material applied, which renders black in all four channels (R, G, B, and A). Consider Figures 18.8 and 18.9. In these examples, the bag and skeleton are split into separate passes. In order for the bag to composite over the skeleton correctly, the arm of the skeleton must be held out from the bag. In Figure 18.9, the skeleton arm is included in the render of the bag but has a holdout material applied.

Figure 18.8 Without a holdout, the bag overlaps the skeleton's arm and fingers once composited—incorrect.

Figure 18.9 With a holdout, the bag has a hole in which the skeleton's arm shows through—correct.

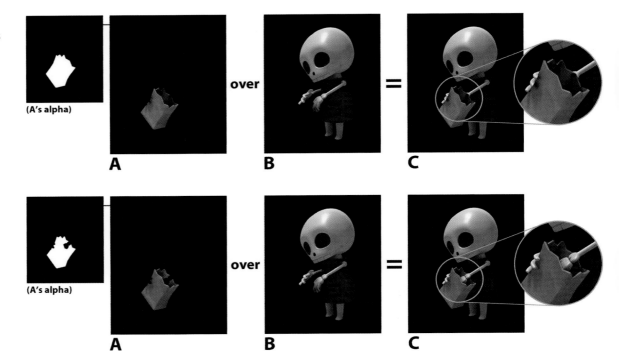

When using holdouts, you can combine the passes with either *over* or *add*. If an object in image A is held out by an object in image B, but B is not held out by anything, then A is composited *over* B as shown in Figure 18.9. On the other hand, if two objects are held out from each other (A is held out from B, and B is held out from A), then you will want to *add* the two in the composite rather than use *over*. Adding two layers is actually the most accurate, but it takes longer to render, as both objects must be included in each pass. Usually an over will suffice. In cases where your objects are heavily motion blurred, the more accurate add may be needed to avoid the bottom layer showing through around the edges of the top layer.

Light Interactions

An important consideration when separating beauty passes is how the elements interact. Often you cannot simply remove unwanted elements because you then lose the lighting interactions that would have come from them.

Lighting interactions to consider are shadows, reflections, refractions, occlusion, and indirect (bounced) light. For example, when an object casts a shadow on a ground plane, if you simply remove the object you will lose its shadow. This is going to be a problem when you go to composite your layers. To be accurate, each layer must have the correct lighting interactions. In our example, the background layer must keep the shadow even when the foreground object is hidden (compare Figures 18.10 and 18.11).

 **over**  =

Figure 18.10 A over B without the shadow included in B—incorrect.

 **over**  =

Figure 18.11 A over B with the shadow included in B—correct.

To keep lighting interactions, there are three possible solutions:

1. **Use pre-calculated data.** Many kinds of interactions can be pre-calculated and brought back into the 3D render, such as depth maps for shadows and point clouds for indirect light and occlusion. This not only solves the problem of light interactions, but saves on render time, too. When using pre-calculated data, unwanted objects can be completely removed from the pass.

2. **Turn primary visibility off.** Another option is to set up your render attributes so that hidden objects are only visible in the interactions. For example, the background render would still include the foreground object, but the foreground object's "primary visibility" would be turned off. This solution may work if you don't want to use pre-calculated data (for example, if you are using ray-traced shadows rather than depth-mapped shadows). However, this option renders more slowly than Solution #1 because all geometry is loaded into memory and calculated for each pass.

3. **Render out a pass of the interaction.** A third option is to render out a separate pass of the interaction and integrate it into the composite. For example, render a reflection pass or an indirect light pass. How to create these passes is discussed later in this section.

When rendering with global illumination, be especially careful of reflected light interactions. Since the render times for global illumination can be extremely long, many separate passes that include much complex geometry are generally to be avoided. Projects using point-based global illumination can pre-calculate the indirect light and save it into point clouds. Projects using ray-traced global illumination may optimize render time in other ways. Reflected light from hidden environment geometry may be cheated with an environment light mapped with an image of the virtual set, or complex geometry can be replaced with cards mapped with images. The cards will provide reflected light yet still render quickly (Figures 18.12 and 18.13).

Figure 18.12 A card similar to this one was used in Figure 18.13 to provide reflected light onto the arcs from complex ceiling geometry.

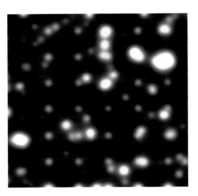

TIPS FOR GENERATING BEAUTY PASSES

- Use them primarily to speed up render time in the long run.
- Use render visibility attributes.
- Use holdouts.
- Account for shadows.
- Account for reflections and refractions.
- Account for indirect light.

Figure 18.13 Even though this scene from *2012* used global illumination, various beauty passes were still able to be split out. When rendering other passes, the complex ceiling geometry was replaced with a card similar to the one in Figure 18.12. (© 2009 Columbia Pictures Industries, Inc. All Rights Reserved. Courtesy of Columbia Pictures.)

18.3.2 Cast Shadow Passes

A cast shadow pass contains only a render of a cast shadow. This pass is then integrated in with other passes in the composite. Cast shadow passes should be used whenever it is difficult or impossible for your digital element to truly cast light onto other objects. Most often cast shadow passes are needed in visual effects shots so that digital elements can cast shadows onto live-action plates (Figure 18.14). In full CG shots, in which all geometry is present, the cast shadow is usually integrated into the render as part of the normal lighting calculation, and no composite pass is needed.

Generating Cast Shadow Passes

Here are the steps to create a cast shadow pass:

1. **Create match-move geometry.** If the shadow-receiving geometry doesn't already exist in the scene, then you will need to model it (or at least the portion of it receiving the shadow). Geometry that's in the 3D scene solely for the purpose of aiding in the matching of digital and live elements is known as *match-move geometry*. Match-move geometry needs to be highly accurate to the scale and proportion of the real geometry on the set; otherwise, the shadows and other effects will not properly line up (Figure 18.15).

2. **Make the shadow-casting geometry invisible to the camera.** You do not want to see the shadow-casting geometry; you only want to see its shadow. If the shadow type is a mapped shadow, then pre-calculate the shadow and then completely hide or delete the shadow-casting geometry. If the shadow is ray traced, then you will need to keep this geometry in the scene, but turn off primary visibility.

3. **Assign special materials.** To capture just the shadow, you will need special shaders assigned to both the light and the shadow-receiving material. The shadow-receiving geometry can be assigned a white lambert shader, with a diffuse coefficient of 1. Be sure to keep displacements on it, but bump isn't needed. The illumination from the light needs to be inverted so that it casts light only in the shadow areas. In many light shaders, this can be accomplished by making the light intensity 1, the light color black, and the shadow color white (Figure 18.16). You can render up to three cast shadows into one RGB file. To do so, just make each shadow a primary light color: red, green, or blue. Each of these channels can be extracted into the composite into its own cast shadow pass (Figures 18.17 and 18.18). The end result should be that the cast shadow appears as white or a primary light color, and the rest of the scene renders black.

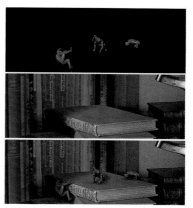

Figure 18.14 From top to bottom: the digital foreground element, the original live-action background, and the finished composite (lighting and compositing by Charles Trippe).

Figure 18.15 (Left) The books in this scene are the match-move geometry.

Figure 18.16 (Right) The completed cast shadow pass.

Figure 18.17 The final composite using the shadows in Figure 18.18.

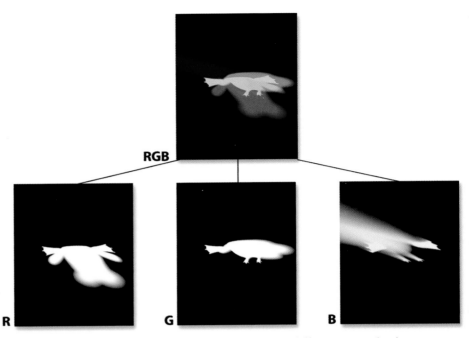

Figure 18.18 A cast shadow pass containing three different cast shadows.

Using Cast Shadow Passes

The cast shadow pass is typically used as a mask to color-correct the background in the area of the shadow. In the composite, the shadow can be faded or blurred as desired to best fit in with the plate. This approach gives the artist the most control over how the background is adjusted, while maintaining all the fine detail in the background.

Figure 18.19 The cast shadow pass can be used as a matte with which to color-correct the background plate, giving the most control.

18.3.3 Z-Depth Pass

A *z-depth pass* is a render that records how far objects are from the camera. It is called a "z-depth" pass because it indicates depth down the view of the camera. The axis that points down the view of the camera is the z-axis. A z-depth pass looks like a black-to-white (gray-scale) image. Typically, white means closer, while black means farther away, though this may be reversed in some applications. Only one channel is needed to store the data of the z-depth pass.

Z-depth passes are commonly used to create depth of field and/or add atmosphere in the composite. Depth of field can be created much, much faster in the composite. In production, therefore, depth of field is typically created using the z-depth pass and not rendered in-camera. Another very common use for the depth pass is to add atmosphere in the composite. A final use of z-depth passes is to determine the depth of different objects for the purpose of layering them in the composite.

How to Split Out Z-Depth Passes

Z-depth passes are typically created as AOVs. If needed, you can also create your own separate depth pass with special shaders that darken based on distance. This can be done by projecting a black-to-white ramp down the camera's y-axis, linking its position to the camera, and assigning this shader to everything in the scene. Be sure to keep displacement on for accurate results. Do not render with ray tracing or global illumination.

In all cases, carefully set the minimum and maximum distance to get a full range of values throughout the depth you see in the scene. Otherwise, you may not capture enough information, making the pass either harder to work with or prone to banding artifacts from too little data. To capture the most detail, depth passes are best if rendered into 16-bit or 32-bit floating-point formats.

TIP

If the renderer generates the depth pass based on the camera's clipping planes, be sure to set the clipping planes to just around your object for the best results.

If rendering several depth passes, be sure to keep the same min and max values for all renders.

Figure 18.20 The z-depth pass used for Figure 18.21.

Figure 18.21 Top: the original unadjusted render; bottom: a render using the z-depth to both defocus and apply atmosphere in the background (lighting by Ross Cantrell).

How to Use Z-Depth Passes

When creating depth of field in the composite, use the depth pass as a mask to determine where the blur is affecting (Figure 18.20). To accurately create defocus, you should use special compositing software that's designed to handle depth passes and defocus realistically (such as Nuke). Settings in some composite packages mimic real-world camera settings, such as focal length and aperture. This allows for the digital depth of field to perfectly match the depth of field from a real camera.

When creating atmosphere in the composite, use the depth pass as a transparency mask (an alpha channel) for a solid color. The depth mask can be color-corrected (gamma, brighten, or darken) to change the placement and look of the atmosphere. This atmosphere is then placed *over* the rest of the scene (Figure 18.21).

TIPS FOR GENERATING Z-DEPTH PASSES

- Use them to add depth of field or atmosphere in the comp.
- Make sure to set the min and max values the same for all z-depth passes.

18.3.4 ISOLATION MATTES

Isolation mattes **are renders that isolate certain elements** in a solid block of white or color (Figure 18.22). They are used, as the name suggests, to isolate certain objects in the composite. Isolation mattes, sometimes called *masks*, are particularly useful in combination with global-illumination renders and secondary passes. When rendering with global illumination, it's more common to keep objects together and render fewer separate passes, due to the long render times and many inter-reflections. However, it is often desirable to color-correct or adjust in some way specific elements in the composite. Isolation mattes help the artist to still easily access individual objects in the composite. (If an object is already rendered into its own pass, you do not need an isolation matte for it.) Isolation mattes are used very frequently.

To use an isolation mask, extract the channel with the data. Use the channel as a black-and-white mask to isolate the object in the composite for color correction or other manipulation (Figure 18.22).

Isolation mattes can be generated as AOVs or as separate passes. Setting up isolation mattes as separate renders is simple, and they render very quickly as the render needs no lights, ray tracing, or global illumination. To set up an isolation matte, place a constant shader on the object you wish to isolate. Delete any objects that don't appear in the render, and make any foreground objects that block the view into holdouts.

Each matte requires only one channel. Any number of isolation mattes can be rendered into a single EXR file. When rendering into a traditional 4-channel image, up to four isolation mattes can be rendered—one for each channel. To do so, make each material a different primary light color (red, green, blue), and each matte will appear only in the corresponding channel. Depending on the shaders you have, you can also have a final matte in the alpha. To do so, make the R, G, and B mattes black in the alpha and the A matte white in the alpha and black in the color channels (Figure 18.23).

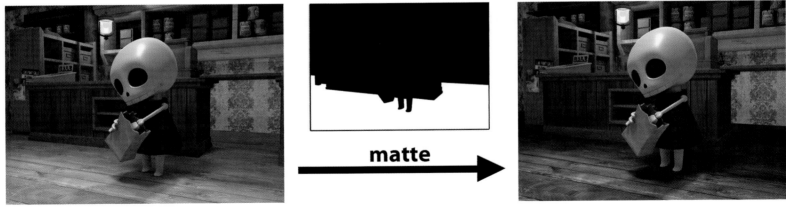

Figure 18.22 In this example, the floor matte was used to isolate and darken the floor only.

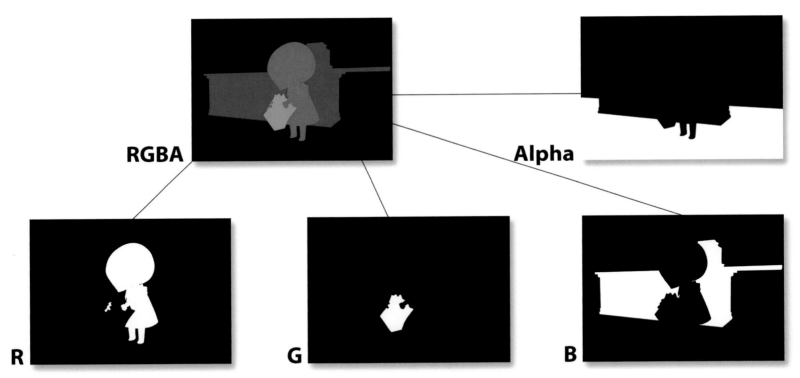

Figure 18.23 Example of four isolation mattes rendered into one image file, one matte per channel of RGBA.

18.3.5 SHADING COMPONENT PASSES

A *shading component* is a subset of the surface material calculation. Common shading component passes include specular, diffuse, reflection, incandescence, and subsurface scattering, to name but a very few (Figure 18.24). Essentially, any calculation done at the shading level can potentially be separated out.

Figure 18.24 Various shading component passes make up the final beauty pass (lower right).

Shading passes are used when a particular component needs extra treatment in the composite. For example, a specular pass may be used when the specular is very important and needs special attention to capture just the right look, as with a metallic or glassy main character. Other times a particular component has a problem that can be fixed in the composite with a pass. Occasionally a component pass is used to achieve an effect in the composite rather than the render. For example, both incandescent and specular passes may be used in the composite to create a glow effect.

How to Split Out Shading Component Passes

AOVs are the best and easiest way to split out shading component passes. If AOV capability is present, separating these passes out is quite common, regardless of whether they get used. Separate component passes can also be crafted by hand by setting up special materials, lights, or both. The basic principle when setting up separate component passes is to assign special materials to your objects that turn off all shading calculations except for the one you want to render. For example, an incandescent pass could turn off all lights and may not use global illumination, a specular pass doesn't need diffuse reflection, and so on. Carefully consider what your render needs for the most optimized render time.

In short,

◆ Turn off all other shading attributes.

◆ Turn off all lights and calculations not needed for the shading component.

◆ Hide unnecessary geometry.

How to Use Shading Component Passes

Understanding how to bring various shading components together requires understanding how they were put together in the first place. Most shading components get *added* together in the composite. Thus, if you have each shading component of a surface, adding them all together would be something like this:

> diffuse + specular + incandescence + subsurface-scattering + translucency + reflection + refraction

This is quite a lot going on if you were to add all of these things. However, few if any materials are going to have all of these things, at least not in equally large amounts. Take a close look at your material to determine what components are applicable.

If you have split out just a single component, it can be recombined with a render of everything but that component (Figure 18.25), like this:

> component pass + everything-but-component pass

Other times you may have a component pass and a beauty render with all shading components in it. Perhaps you created the pass with an AOV, and all your components didn't come together again as planned. Never fear, you can still use the pass. In this case, you will need to first *subtract* the component pass from the beauty render, then adjust the component as desired (darken it, colorize it, whatever you are needing to do), then *add* it back in for the final result, like this:

> (beauty—component pass) + modified component pass

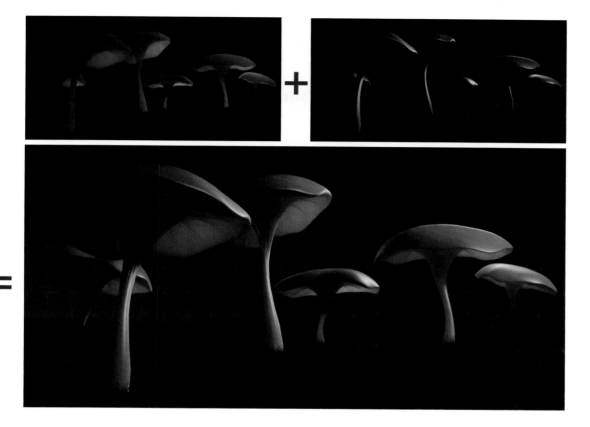

When you have various properties of the surface as different passes, you can exactly adjust what each surface looks like. If you have rendered out isolation mattes, you don't need to render each object separately in the shading passes, either; just use the isolation mattes to adjust the item of interest. Figure 18.26 is an example of different looks obtained just by working with the shading component passes and a matte pass.

Sometimes components get modified in other ways. For example, common practice is to use incandescence and sometimes specular passes to create bloom in the composite. To do this, just blur and color-correct the incandescent pass, then add to the beauty pass. Creating bloom (glow) in this manner has the advantage of being highly controllable by the artist and artifact-free (Figure 18.27).

Figure 18.26 Working only in the composite with shading components and isolation mattes, the mushroom image is greatly adjusted from the original render seen in Figure 18.25.

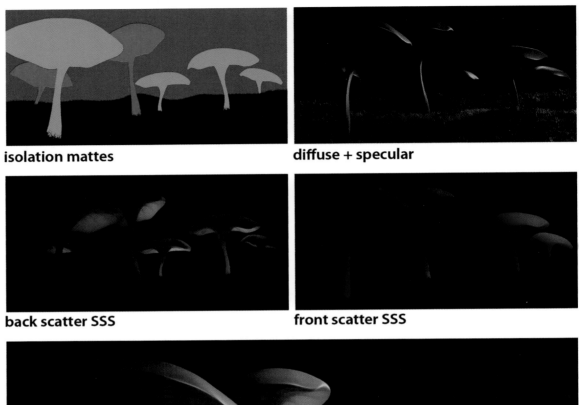

isolation mattes

diffuse + specular

back scatter SSS

front scatter SSS

composite = front scatter + back scatter + diffuse + specular

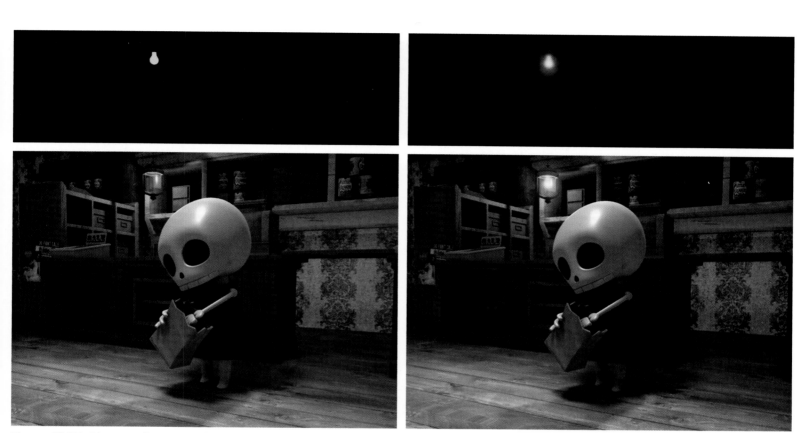

Figure 18.27 Glow can be created in the composite by blurring and colorizing an incandescent pass. Counterclockwise from top left: the original incandescence pass, a glow element created in the composite, the beauty pass with glow added, the beauty pass without glow added.

TIPS FOR GENERATING SHADING COMPONENT PASSES

- Use them when you need precise control over a shading component.
- Generate as AOVs whenever possible.
- Most shading components are added together.

18.3.6 Reflection Passes

Reflection passes are renders of only the reflection. Reflection passes have been around for a long time and can be used for a variety of reasons. Traditionally, reflection passes have been generated to save render time. If you are rendering primarily with scanline, then you can use a reflection pass in order to confine ray tracing to just this pass and thus keep render time down. Another use of the reflection pass is, as usual, for added control in the composite. In the composite you can fade, color-correct, or blur the reflection. Reflection passes are often needed in visual effects shots when the reflective object exists in the live-action plate. In these cases, a separate reflection pass is generated and then integrated into the plate in the composite (Figure 18.28), much like the cast-shadow pass.

Figure 18.28 A reflection pass added to the rest of the render in the composite.

How to Generate Reflection Passes

There are three ways to generate reflection passes. Which to use depends on how you are approaching your rendering in general and what you want the pass to do. Reflection passes can be generated as an AOV, as a separate render using ray tracing, or as a separate render using scanline rendering and reflection cameras. Generating AOVs is the preferred method if you are ray tracing and have AOV capability. Otherwise, you may set up a separate pass, as is described next.

To set up a separate ray-traced reflection pass, first decide what needs to be in the reflection. Make these objects "Visible in reflections" only, turning off primary visibility. Hide or remove all other objects not necessary to reflections or shadows. Make all foreground objects into holdouts. Don't hide or remove any lights, because you will need them all to correctly illuminate the reflected objects. If you are casting a digital reflection onto a live-action element, then you will need precisely modeled match-move geometry that represents the reflective live-action element.

Next modify the surface of the reflective object so that only the reflections show up and no other shading component is present. Turn diffuse to 0, and turn off incandescence and ambient light. Set reflectivity to 1 (you can fade the reflection in the composite). If your material has completely separate controls for specular and reflection, turn off specular for a pure reflection pass. If turning off the specular also turns off the reflection, make all lights nonspecular instead. In some cases combining specular and reflection passes is desired, as this is more physically accurate; in other cases, separating these passes is desired for added control. Finally, render using ray tracing.

TIP

If the reflection is not distinct, then you can assign special materials on the reflecting objects that are simplified and render faster. For example, if a furred creature has a dim reflection in a pond, you may get away with not rendering the fur in the reflection pass.

Reflections are sometimes cheated using special cameras called *reflection cameras*. These cameras render certain views with ordinary scanline rendering. The renders from the reflection cameras are then reincorporated back into the scene as reflections. Reflection cameras work well to cheat the reflection of planar objects, such as floors or flat mirrors. To set up a reflection camera, duplicate the render camera and then mirror or flip it around the reflecting planar surface (Figure 18.29). Due to the nature of reflection, the view from this duplicate camera will be the same as the reflection would appear to the render camera.

The view from the reflection camera is rendered using regular scanline rendering. When setting up a reflection pass using a reflection camera, be sure to turn off the primary visibility of the mirroring plane. Leave visible all the objects that are to appear in the reflection and all of the lights (Figure 18.30). In some cases the reflection is flipped and needs to be mirrored horizontally in the composite before being used. If portions of the reflection are behind the reflecting object itself, you can use a matte pass of the object to hold out the reflection (Figure 18.31).

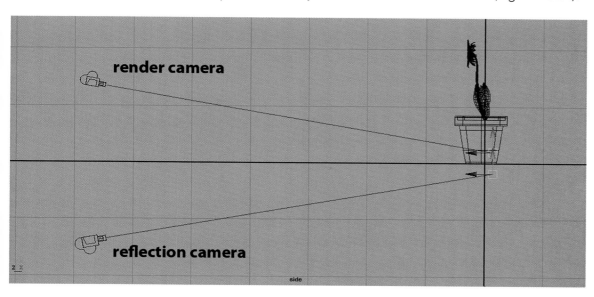

Figure 18.29 A side view of the scene used in Figure 18.30 showing how the reflection camera is mirrored around the reflecting plane.

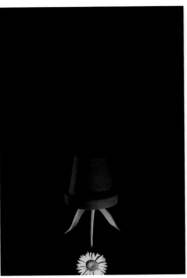

Figure 18.30 From left to right: the render from the reflection camera, the render from the main camera, a render of just the ground plane, and the final composited image.

Reflection cameras take a bit of setup. The choice to use them depends on how much ray tracing you are doing. For a project that needs realistic reflections but does not want ray tracing because of speed concerns, reflection cameras provide another option.

Using Reflection Passes

Like other shading component passes, reflection passes are typically added onto the rest of the scene. If the illumination is too bright from the reflections, they can be combined with a reflection occlusion pass to darken the reflective surface in just the areas where reflected objects appear (see Section 16.4, "Ambient and Reflection Occlusion"). Isolation mattes are used to isolate the reflection to just certain objects (Figure 18.31). Occasionally, a reflection pass may be projected back into the 3D scene using special shaders instead of integrating it in the composite, but this isn't very common.

> **TIPS FOR USING REFLECTION PASSES**
> - Generate them to speed up your render times, gain more control in the composite, or integrate with live action.
> - Use reflection cameras for planar reflections if you wish to avoid ray tracing.
> - Use AOV passes with isolation mattes if rendering with global illumination.

Figure 18.31 An example of using an isolation matte to cut out a reflection to just the desired element. From left to right, the original reflection pass (rendered from a reflection camera), an isolation matte of the countertop, the beauty pass with no counter reflection, and the final composite.

18.3.7 ILLUMINATION PASSES

Various passes can contain just a subset of the illumination calculation. These passes can be renders from particular lights or certain components of illumination, such as direct or indirect light (Figure 18.32).

Separating out lights can be useful in certain situations. If a particular light is problematic and needs to be constantly adjusted, requiring re-render, you may want to split it out so you can re-render just the one light. You can then adjust the color and intensity of light easily in the composite without re-rendering anything. Another situation in which you may want to separate out a light is if the light is animating—for example, flickering firelight or flashing streetlights. Since composites render much, much faster than the 3D scene, you will be able to iterate and achieve a satisfactory result much, much faster as well. On rare occasions, productions will follow a "lighting in the composite" approach, which means that every light is rendered out separately and then recombined in the composite as a standard workflow. When this is the case, the intensity and color of all of the lights are completely set in the comp.

How to Split Out Lights Passes

How you split out the illumination depends on what kind of illumination it is.

♦ **Separate lights:** When generating a pass for a single light, simply turn off all the unwanted lights. Leave all the surface materials the same as in a full beauty render. You might render the light with the same settings it has in a beauty render, or you could render the light at an intensity of 1 and a white color, then adjust both the color and intensity later in the composite. Advanced software and shading packages allow you to separate lights out as AOVs. When this is the case, the light pass has the same color and intensity as it does in the primary pass.

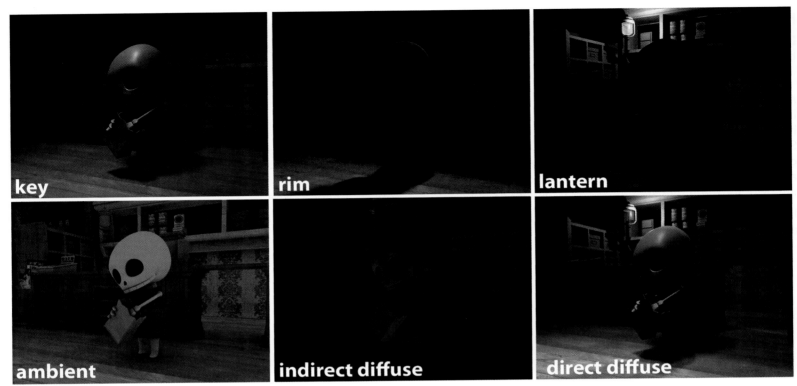

Figure 18.32 The illumination in the scene can be split into passes in a variety of ways.

- ◆ **Indirect light:** Another kind of light pass is the indirect light pass. This kind of pass is split out as an AOV. An indirect light pass can help to save on render time later. You would generate an indirect light AOV with the first render, so later iterations can calculate only direct light, integrating the indirect light in the comp using the pass. If your direct lighting isn't changing dramatically in color and position, this indirect pass will often work fine for later versions.

- ◆ **Direct light:** Direct light, like indirect light, is often separated out as an AOV in global-illumination renders.

- ◆ **Ambient light:** A special kind of illumination pass is the ambient light pass. While special in that ambient casts a different kind of light, and it is more commonly separated out, the ambient light pass is handled much like any other light pass. Ambient light is sometimes separated out from its occlusion shadow, and the ambient illumination and the occlusion are combined in the composite.

As usual, how you generate these passes influences how often you will split them out. If they are rendered out as AOVs, then often is fine. If you are setting up separate passes, then split them out rarely and only if a specific situation calls for it.

How to Use Lights Passes

Each light *adds* illumination to the scene. Thus all illumination passes are added together in the composite.

> light pass + other lights

Adjust the light pass before adding it to the rest of the comp. To reduce the intensity of a light pass in the comp, simply darken the pass by multiplying it by a value less than 1 (reduce its *brightness*). You can even turn the light "off" in the comp by reducing its brightness to 0. Similarly, to colorize a pass, you can multiply it with the desired hue. You can also desaturate, or adjust the gamma, or perform any other desired color correction (compare Figures 18.33 and 18.34). If you plan to animate a light in the composite, render the light on and at maximum intensity for the entire sequence, then animate its color and intensity in the composite.

If you have divided indirect and direct illumination, they are added together. If you also have ambient light, then the total of the three is all the illumination in the scene (Figure 18.35).

> indirect light + direct light + ambient light

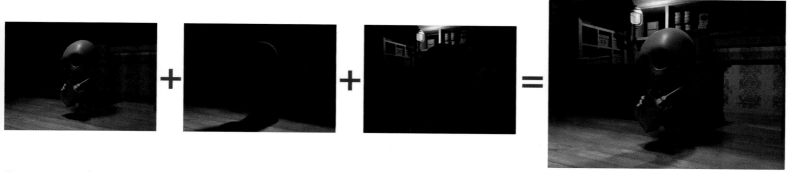

Figure 18.33 Three lights passes from the skeleton scene. From left to right: the key light, the rim light, the lantern light. Each light pass gets *added* in the composite to sum to the final image. (The scene is dark because the ambient pass isn't included.)

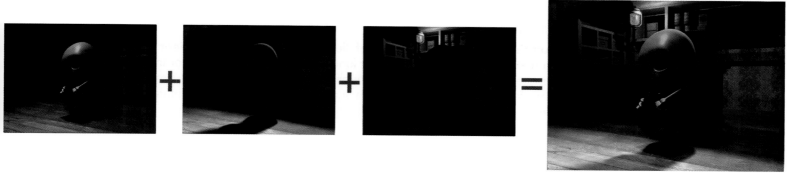

Figure 18.34 Each light pass can be color-corrected in the composite to change the look of the lighting without re-rendering.

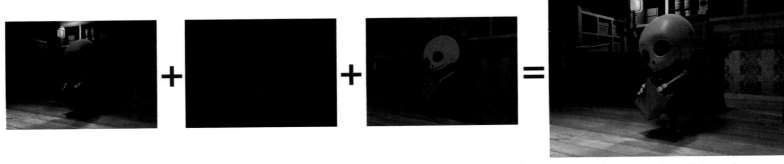

Figure 18.35 From left to right: direct light plus indirect light plus ambient with occlusion (if you have ambient) equals all light in the scene.

TIPS FOR GENERATING LIGHTS PASSES
- Generate them in order to fine-tune specific lights, if you wish to animate a light in the composite, or to pre-calculate some illumination like indirect diffuse.
- All illumination is added in the composite.
- If generating from an AOV, subtract the pass from the beauty, adjust the pass, then add it back.
- If generating as a separate pass, consider rendering the light white and at an intensity of 1, then setting color and intensity in the composite for maximum control.

18.3.8 EFFECTS PASSES

Effects are generally rendered separately and integrated at the compositing stage. Many effects may even be rendered in other packages, such as Houdini. Effects include particle and dynamic animations, such as smoke, rain, fire, snow, and so on. They may be as simple as a lighting effect, such as a fog light (Figure 18.36), or as complex as the rubble from a collapsing building. Complex effects are usually done by effects artists.

Figure 18.36 A fog light added onto a beauty pass.

18.4 LINEAR WORKFLOW

Linear workflow **is an approach to lighting and compositing that is physically accurate.** You may have heard of linear workflow but may still be a bit hazy on what it is or why it is important. Or perhaps the term is unfamiliar. Fully understanding linear workflow is an advanced topic. This section introduces linear workflow, explaining what it is and why it is important in a general way.

18.4.1 LOGARITHMIC COLOR SPACE

The average monitor has a gamma applied. *Gamma* is a kind of color correction in which the midpoints are raised or lowered, but black stays black and white stays white. A gamma of 1 does nothing; a gamma above 1 darkens the midpoint grays; a gamma lower than 1 brightens the midpoint grays (Figure 18.37). On most monitors this gamma is approximately 2.2. This gamma *darkens* the midpoint values of all of the images we see.

Figure 18.37 Different gamma corrections. From left to right: gamma of 2.2, gamma of 1 (no correction), gamma of .454 (which is 1/2.2).

The reason why you haven't noticed that your monitor is applying a gamma to everything is that all of the graphics created for display on the average monitor also have a gamma applied, in the equal and opposite direction. The gamma correction needed is 1/2.2, or .454, which *brightens* the midpoints of the image. When images that have been brightened are viewed on a monitor that is darkening everything, it all evens out, and the image looks correct (Figure 18.38).

A display device (such as your monitor) that has gamma applied is said to have a *logarithmic color space.* "Logarithmic" refers to the shape of the gamma curve. (It's something like a logarithmic curve, if you recall from high school science class.) "Color space" is a term that describes how the computer is interpreting the values in the digital image file into actual luminance values emitting from the display device. Likewise, images designed to be viewed in logarithmic color space are known as *logarithmic* (or just "log") images. Again, all this means is that the log image has a color correction applied to it—one that will adjust it so it looks right on the average monitor. Furthermore, as an artist working with a typical monitor, you have been creating images "by eye" and, until otherwise informed, have not

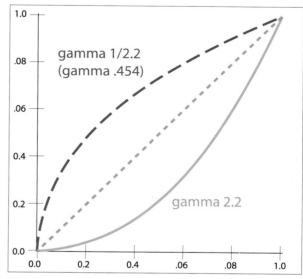

Figure 18.38 Graph of gamma curves.

noticed that things are displaying darker in the midpoint than they should. You also likely may not have noticed that the light in your 3D scenes was not behaving as it would in life.

18.4.2 WHY LINEAR?

Linear color space **describes a display that does not have a gamma applied.** Similarly, linear files are those that do not have a compensating gamma applied. Linear files will look correct in linear color space. If these files are viewed in log space, they will appear too dark. Similarly, log files viewed in a linear space will appear too bright.

In a logarithmic color space, luminance values will not behave as they do in life. This means that the lighting in your CG package will not match real-world lighting in significant ways. Also, when working with log files, the color correcting in your compositing package will not behave in an intuitive fashion, and it won't be mathematically correct. In short, logarithmic color space is not physically or mathematically accurate, while linear color space is. For this reason, most high-end productions light, render to, and composite in linear color space.

A *linear workflow* **means you are working in linear color space.** This means that your display needs to not have a gamma curve applied, and all the image files you work with also must not have a compensating color-correction gamma applied. How you put everything back into the right color space varies depending on the software you use and the workflow set up by the studio (or independent artist, as the case may be). To correct for the display device, some studios have a setting for the entire monitor to take it from log to linear color space. Other times, the monitor is left alone, and the viewer inside each software has a setting to display files in linear versus log space. When necessary, the files themselves are also converted (read: color corrected) to display properly in either log or linear color space.

When rendering, your 3D renders do not need to be color corrected to appear correctly in linear space—they have been rendering to linear color space all along. The fact that you have been rendering linear data that was then viewed in log space is why your lights haven't been behaving as they should, and you have been compensating by adjusting everything artistically. When you first switch over to rendering linear data and looking at it in a linear color space, your files may initially look "wrong" to you; they may look pasty and washed out. The files aren't wrong, you are just used to seeing them in a log color space. It is the log color space that's incorrect, actually. When working in linear space, the solution is *not* to color correct your renders to darken everything again—this just perpetuates the incorrect light behavior. The solution is to adjust your lights in the 3D scene and get used to working in a physically accurate environment.

TIP

When using a linear workflow, you must make sure all your texture files are also in linear space, or they will appear washed out. If these files were developed in log space, they will need color correction to appropriately darken them before being used in your linear workflow.

If you're working in a studio, they will tell you, "Set this display here, apply that conversion there," as needed. If you're setting up your own linear workflow, you will likely need to do a bit of research on where and how to set things. Depending on the software, these settings will vary. This may be a bit confusing and may require some searching and exploring on your part, but with diligence you will find the answers you need. Although it didn't provide directions for any particular software, I hope this section has given you a general knowledge about what is going on behind the scenes and why linear workflow is important.

18.4.3 BIT DEPTH

A topic related to color space is bit depth. The *bit depth* of a file determines how many possible values can be represented in each pixel of each channel. A 1-bit image, for example, can only display two possible values: black or white. Black or white in each channel can combine in various ways to give you eight possible colors. The default bit depth for most applications is to work with and output 8-bit files. Eight-bit files can store 256 possible shades of gray per pixel per channel, which translates to about 16 million different colors (Figure 18.39). In many cases, this range of values and color is plenty, but the human eye can perceive still more.

Figure 18.39 Different bit depths. From left to right: 1 bit, 4 bits, 8 bits.

256 possible values is not actually enough for us to perceive continuous tone. Due to how the human eye perceives luminance, we are very, very sensitive to value changes at the low end of the luminance scale. If you look carefully, you will see banding in the darkest areas of an 8-bit image. Bands appear as lines of flat color in areas that should have a smooth gradient. The lower the bit depth, the more apparent the banding (Figure 18.40). To see continuous tone in log space, you actually need 10 bits per channel. These bands become more obvious in linear color space, and for this reason linear files need an even higher bit depth.

To perceive continuous tone in linear color space, image files need at least 16 bits. Sixteen-bit gives you 65,536 possible shades of gray per channel, amounting to trillions of colors. Now that's more like it! Even though 16-bit linear files can store a full range of values and represent continuous tone, a common practice in professional studios is to render to 32-bit images. Thirty-two-bit images are high dynamic range and give you "extra" values that can be stored at the high end as super whites (values above 1) (see Section 9.3.2 for an introduction to HDRI). Thirty-two-bit is often referred to as *floating point* due to how it stores the luminance values.

In general, 8 or 10 bits is enough for most log images. Linear images need 16 bits, and 32 bits gives you extra and is reserved for high dynamic range imagery.

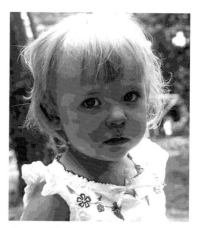

Figure 18.40 Banding can clearly be seen in the blue channel of this 4-bit image. Banding shows up any time there is not enough bit depth and will be most visible in the darkest regions of the image.

18.5 CHAPTER CONCLUSION

This chapter has covered many of the most common passes and the means for generating them. Even with these short descriptions, you may see how the number of passes can get to be quite high. Understanding how to correctly use the many passes requires a thorough knowledge of many areas, from compositing to lighting to shading, which is why rendering in passes is an advanced technique.

In the past, rendering 2D passes involved setting up separate renders for each pass. Since the introduction of secondary outputs and the increased use of global illumination and ray tracing, object-based beauty passes are fewer, and generating many AOVs from one primary render has become common. Because AOVs are split out from a render of everything, they maintain all the surface interaction created in global illumination. Even better, they don't add to render time. Since AOVs typically have the entire scene together, isolation mattes are essential to help isolate desired objects. The many AOVs generated along with a primary render may be split into their own files or saved into the additional channels of an EXR file.

When lighting and compositing, the most realistic and accurate approach is to use a linear workflow. While linear workflow may seem a bit confusing at first, all it really means is removing the built-in gamma on your display device and removing any compensating color-correction on your image files.

18.5.1 IMPORTANT POINTS

- Rendering in passes is an extremely common advanced technique.
- Most professionals use the term "pass" very broadly.
- Properly used passes will reduce render time and provide added control.
- Improperly used passes can increase render time and detract from the final look.
- Passes increase complexity.
- Each additional separate pass takes time to render and should only be used when needed.
- When creating separate passes, render attributes, materials, and lights need to be carefully set up.
- Consider interactions, such as holdouts and light interactions, when setting up separate passes.
- Secondary outputs don't add to render time and can be rendered "just in case."
- The fundamental pass is a beauty pass—an item rendered with all its shading and lighting.
- Z-depth passes are commonly used to provide depth of field and atmosphere in the composite.
- Shading components are often separated out as secondary outputs.
- Most separate shading components get added together.
- When rendering secondary passes, isolation mattes allow for individual objects to be isolated and adjusted.
- Several methods create reflection passes.

- Cheated reflections are common if keeping ray tracing to a minimum is desired.
- Each light can be independently adjusted in the composite if it's separated into passes as well.
- Linear workflow is a more realistic workflow used when lighting and compositing.
- Linear workflow removes the built-in gamma present on your average display device.
- Linear files are those that are designed to be seen on a display with no built-in gamma.
- Linear files need a higher bit depth to avoid banding.

18.5.2 Terms

composite	holdout	reflection pass
pass	cast shadow pass	reflection camera
render layer	match-move geometry	illumination pass
primary output	z-depth pass	color space
secondary output	isolation matte	gamma
arbitrary output variables (AOVs)	shading component	linear workflow
render visibility attributes	diffuse pass	logarithmic color space
primary visibility	specular pass	linear color space
beauty pass	incandescent pass	bit depth
	subsurface pass	banding

18.5.3 Exercises

1. If render visibility attributes are less familiar to you, I recommend setting up a simple scene with reflections, refractions, and shadows, then experimenting with turning render attributes on and off to see what they do. Try a few mapped shadows for good measure.

2. If you're newer to beauty passes (a.k.a. render layers), start simply: Set up a ball with its shadow on a ground plane. Render out two layers using a pre-calculated mapped shadow in one render and a ray-traced shadow in another.

3. If you are familiar with Photoshop, bring your passes in as layers and experiment with how they are combined. Layer your passes with the alpha channels loaded as the layer mask to imitate an "over." Use the "screen" blending mode to perform an "add." Then bring your passes into a compositing program and achieve the same results.

4. Split out all of the shading attributes of the subject in your 3D scene. Bring these passes into a compositing program and experiment with changing the appearance of the material in the composite. Next, try this with a variety of objects, using isolation mattes to make each object look different.

5. Create a reflection pass using the reflection camera technique.

6. Light a scene in the composite. Select a scene with a basic three-point light setup, then render each light into its own pass. Render all lights at an intensity of 1 and a white color; adjust the color and intensity in the composite. Next, animate one light in the composite.

Part V contains several interviews with people experienced in the computer animation and visual effects industries. The interviewees range from top executives within their companies to established freelance artists, to give you a wide variety of views, opinions, and insights. Subjects range from industry trends among the major players to what a day in the life of a digital lighting artist is like.

A big thanks to all the interviewees in the chapters for their time and input. It was a pleasure to interview each of you. To the reader, I hope you enjoy their voices of experience and gain some additional insight into the computer-generated imagery industry. And with that, dear reader, I leave you with my interviewees, and I bid you *adieu*, happy lighting, and a successful career.

PART V

INTERVIEWS
(WITH THE PROS)

"Not the fruit of experience, but experience itself, is the end."

—Walter Pater, 19th-Century English Essayist and Critic

Chapter 19
Interview with Rob Bredow, CTO, Sony Pictures Imageworks

Virginia: *A few years ago Sony made a move from rendering with RenderMan to using the Arnold, a path-traced renderer. Do you find that more ray tracing is a trend across all studios?*

Rob: Time will tell, but it looks like more and more studios are using very sophisticated ray tracers and global illumination renderers for more and more of their work. I believe that's driven by the level of complexity of the work that is required today. With even the best scanline or best REYES renderer in the world, there are many passes and a lot of intermediate data to manage. While it's certainly possible for someone to package that up in a clean method so that the user isn't encumbered by those extra passes, it's a very challenging job. In our workflow, the entire scene is recalculated every time you hit the render button, which means there are no intermediate caches. That has the advantage of an artist spending less time managing those intermediate passes and spending more time lighting in a more physically accurate environment. We've found that improves lighter efficiency and the quality of the work we're able to do, which is great news for our workflow and for our clients.

Virginia: *You mentioned that reducing the number of render passes was one of the advantages of ray-traced global illumination. What other advantages prompted Sony's decision to switch to a path-traced renderer like Arnold?*

Rob: The other reason is that it's a much better approximation of what happens in real life. Before we had algorithms designed to emulate the look of things we saw in real life. Now that we're able to leverage ray tracing more heavily throughout the rendering process, we're able to simulate real optical effects much more accurately, whether it's the way materials respond to the light or the way light bounces around the scene. That gives us more fidelity in the images.

Virginia: *With more of the burden of realism pushed onto the renderer, would you say that Sony is able to hire less experienced people?*

Rob: There's no question that you still need highly talented artists to make the kind of movies we make here at Sony Pictures Imageworks. The level of sophistication of the imagery is only going up. Nothing in the renderer would ever give us the ability to hire less talented artists. However, there is one thing that has changed: It used to take several years of specific experience learning how to use the toolset to make realistic-looking pictures. You had to know what all the tricks of the trade were; you had to know how to tweak your shadow maps; you had to know many things that weren't directly related to lighting but were related to using a particular renderer. Some of those steps are now completely eliminated in this new workflow. The good news is that a lighter with a strong artistic eye and a technical knowledge of how the pipeline works can make really compelling images without having to know some of the intermediate steps that were just technical hurdles. So I think that part has improved for artists.

Virginia: That's good news for talented lighters looking to get into the industry.

Rob: It really is about making a better paintbrush. If we're able to get the best lighters in the world to come in here and light our scenes, and they can adapt to our tools more easily because the tools are conceptually easier to understand or there are fewer immediate technical steps, then I think that's really good news for talented lighters. Instead of spending 60%–80% of their day dealing with technical minutiae, they're spending much more time working on the creative imagery.

Virginia: *Sony is one of the few film studios that makes both full CG animated features and visual effects features in a wide variety of styles. What would be the differences at Sony in the lighting approach for these two kinds of films? Would you say they are very similar or very different?*

Rob: Most of the building blocks between the two types of films, the animated films and the live-action films, are identical. The core tools for both pipelines are the same, but there are still some places where they diverge. If you look at a recent movie like *Arthur Christmas*, it has a very detailed and organic look, but no one would say a purely photorealistic look. Yet it was generated with roughly the same set of shaders we're using right now on the new *The Amazing Spider-Man* movie and *Men in Black 3*. So what that means is our shaders and our system have to be developed with enough flexibility to allow for much creative tuning. Our natural bias is to make things that approximate reality and then give people the controls on top of that to be able to meet the creative needs of an individual film. I would say the best analogy is, on a live-action movie that is shot with real light, and there's no opportunity to bend the physics of the way light works. Yet you still can have a dramatic range from a hyperrealistic to hyperstylized look. Our system can emulate that range and even a broader range because we have all the tricks available to us in our rendering and shading system.

Virginia: *So there is still the opportunity to make the look not as realistic.*

Rob: Absolutely.

Virginia: *Is most of this accomplished in the shaders?*

Rob: There are components of it that are in the shaders, but I would say the biggest tool in the arsenal is the creative choices that are made in how you decide to light. Whereas before I think most of the tricks were about faking the math to do something that was less photorealistic, now it's a matter of deciding how your lighting rig is set up and deciding how the light bounces around the room to get the certain look you're going for. That's not to say we don't do some mathematical tricks to get certain looks at times, for example, to get ice to look a certain way or take some shortcuts. We certainly do. But we take a lot fewer of those shortcuts than we did five years ago.

Virginia: *When I was there last, I remember a big concern was render time. How is the issue of render time being dealt with at Sony?*

Rob: Interestingly, the total amount of processor hours we spend on a show hasn't substantially increased as a result of changing from RenderMan as a primary renderer to a ray tracer as our primary renderer. When you see long renders of 6 hours to 12 hours a frame, that looks like a really painful process, which must require a lot more processors to get through. It was easy to forget, however, about all of the intermediate passes we had to generate before. For example, if a relatively simple scene had, say, 30 shadow maps in it, each one rendering relatively fast at 30 minutes a frame, the total render time added up. When we did our comparisons, they added up, per frame, to something quite comparable to the ray-traced final frame times, since with ray tracing we are not generating those intermediate passes.

We've worked very hard to make the ray tracer as fast as possible for our very complicated scenes. For a given complexity of a shot we actually end up with very close to the same total render time, and then we have the additional flexibility of being able to move a light at any moment and not have to do any re-rendering of intermediate passes.

Virginia: *You make a good point, considering all of the passes.*

Rob: Our historical processor usage is continuing along the same trend it always has, which is to say we are always providing more power to every artist in order to meet the needs of our shows, but we haven't seen a dramatic increase by changing from a REYES architecture renderer to a ray tracer. Intuitively everyone thinks the ray tracer is more expensive, but in that trade we got much more sophisticated imagery with fewer manual steps. Fortunately, computers are getting faster and our algorithms are getting better. The curve that shows how much processing we're allocating for each of our artists is continuing on the same trend. It's a steep curve; we're adding a lot of processing power for each of our artists to be able to do their work, but the curve didn't take a dramatic shift when we changed from REYES to ray tracing.

Virginia: *Is Arnold proprietary or is it a commercial product?*

Rob: Arnold is commercially developed software and it's sold by a company called Solid Angle that's owned by Marcos Fajardo. It is a commercial product, but we don't use the exact same commercial product; we have our own version of Arnold. A lot of our technology and innovation has made its way into Solid Angle's commercial product as well.

Virginia: *In recent years, Sony has released much of its proprietary technology as open source. What has motivated this change? What is the benefit for the studio?*

Rob: There's a real strategy behind our open-source effort because there is a cost to putting it out. Even though we have a very aggressive open-source program (we now have eight projects that we have released in the open source), most of our technology is still proprietary, meaning it's only able to be used within our building for our clients. But there is some technology that has more value to us if it is adopted as an industry standard, because then it's easy for us to use these technologies with third-party products and with other studios with whom we need to collaborate to get our work done.

In my opinion, that's the key thing in our industry that has changed in the last five years. Whereas we used to almost exclusively do shows in which we were the only vendor on the movie. Now, due to the post-production schedules, our clients desire to spread different kinds of work to different studios. The more normal thing now is to take a big part of the movie and collaborate with other studios to make sure our work is seamless with the other studios who are engaged on the project. For that we need good tools for collaboration, and that is one of the major reasons behind us starting our open-source efforts.

VIRGINIA: *Cooperation with other studios seems to be a key component.*

ROB: That's right. One of our open-source projects, Alembic, is actually a co-development between Industrial Light & Magic [ILM] and Sony Pictures Imageworks. Alembic is a baked geometry format that has announced support from all the major 3D application vendors. It's fantastic news for us because it means that a good production-proven geometry format will be making its way into third-party programs right away. It's also good news for the industry in general, because the kind of workflows that are useful at ILM and Imageworks can be very useful in shops that are doing dozens or hundreds of shots. Alembic technology is going to be in many of the third-party packages and available for free to anybody who wants to integrate it into their pipeline.

VIRGINIA: *In addition to more collaboration among studios, what would you say are the other notable changes in the industry as a whole in the recent years?*

ROB: The other big change that's related is there is more openness to share certain kinds of techniques between the major studios. Whereas before there were certain studios that participated at SIGGRAPH and showed some of their high-level work, now you see a higher degree of participation and you see it year round. You have ILM, Disney, Sony Imageworks, and even a couple of other players releasing code into the open source that are really building blocks or libraries that can power computer graphics for the next few years. Certainly there are some pretty exciting projects coming out of the big studios and some of the smaller studios that have participated in that. The collective focus of making the business of computer graphics and the pipeline of computer graphics more efficient across the whole industry is something we've seen develop significantly in the last five years.

Students and people building something from scratch can leverage off of some of the technology that's been developed over many years, as some of the best techniques available are available in the open source.

VIRGINIA: *How has Sony decided on which technologies to share?*

ROB: Each project has its own reasons behind why we think it's strategic to release it as open source. With Alembic, the primary motivation was to interchange work between studios and also interchange between applications. Our goal for Alembic, to put it simply, is to be the OpenEXR of the geometry world. Today, people still use OBJ files [Wavefront OBJ files] as an interchange format because it's a reliable format. But it's showing its age; it doesn't store everything we need to store today. Our goal for Alembic is to be a replacement for OBJs—just as reliable and simple, but a format that stores all of today's data in an efficient manner for interchangeability between applications, departments, or even between studios.

VIRGINIA: *Advanced lighters might be interested in Sony's Open Source Shading language. Would you tell us a bit more about that?*

Open Shading Language [OSL] is a programming language for writing shaders like RenderMan Shading Language. As compared to something like C, OSL is a simplified language that allows shader writers to do their shader development in a streamlined manner and not have to worry about memory management and compilation issues.

Virginia: *How does OSL compare to other shading languages, such as RenderMan Shading Language [RSL]?*

Rob: That's a good question. The biggest difference, of course, between RLS and OSL is that OSL is free and open source, and it can be integrated relatively easily into any renderer. Another difference is that we were inventing OSL at a time when ray tracing had become the primary way that our scenes were rendered. We wrote this language with that in mind. So we had the opportunity to make some big strategic decisions when authoring the language that allows us to continue to improve our renderer performance while allowing our shader writers to innovate visually on a stable platform.

It's a bit of a competitive environment out there. There are other shading languages, of course. RSL is production proven and has stood the test of time. There is also MetaSL, which is the proprietary system inside Mental Ray. So there are a few different movements out there in terms of where the future of shading might end up. As far as I know, OSL is the only open-source one that's completely free and unencumbered for people to leverage. I am optimistic that because of that, and if people think we've made the right choices in our implementation, that others might be inclined to take advantage of it.

Virginia: *What renderers will support the open-source shading language, OSL?*

Rob: That's to be determined. Our primary focus has been in supporting the other studios who are interested in integrating it into their in-house packages. When we announced OSL, Rhythm & Hues announced with us that they would be integrating it into their internal renderer. And there are other studios who have discussed integrating it into their internal renderer, but nothing else has been announced publicly. Presently the only renderer that I know of that uses OSL as its primary shading language is our internal renderer, our version of Arnold. Marcos will decide when and if he wants to integrate OSL into the commercial version of Arnold, which is something that he has indicated will be driven by customer demand. So it's to be determined when he would do that, but if multiple customers were to be very interested in that, it seems like it would be something that would make it onto his roadmap.

I'm optimistic that there will be commercial and perhaps freely available renderers that will leverage OSL soon. The reason we haven't seen that yet is because OSL is still in its infancy. Now that we're seeing Imageworks's first films deliver with OSL, I think you'll begin to see other studios seriously look at OSL for their renderers as well. The performance is really paying off for us.

Virginia: *Is OSL geared toward integration with larger studios or could it be integrated at smaller studios or universities?*

Rob: We support the adoption in both universities and small and large studios. OSL does not require an incredibly sophisticated production-tested renderer. Someone on the open shading language mailing list has already done a very simple open-source ray tracer as a test for OSL. You can imagine it would be useful not just as a training ground but also for continued research, because if you're working on a next-generation path-tracing renderer, it's unlikely that you are going to want to spend the time to develop a shading language for that renderer. Rather, you would really like to bolt some nice mature code into that. For research work and for training, OSL is an ideal candidate.

Virginia: *I've noticed the industry is becoming more global. Where it used to be primarily located in Los Angeles and northern California, we now see studios and branches of studios opening in other locations both within and outside of the United States. What do you think is motivating this change?*

Rob: Sony has offices in Culver City, which is our home base and where most of our research and look development happens, but we also have offices in Vancouver [Canada], Albuquerque [New Mexico], and in India. We had an office for a short time in Bristol [UK] when we were working with Aardman Animations on *Arthur Christmas*. Opening remote offices is more and more common over the past few years, and that's driven by many different factors. One of the biggest factors is the tax incentives. Because it's a very competitive business, if you're able to leverage a tax incentive in a particular location to land a particular job, then that can be the edge for getting a big film or not.

The other thing that factors in when we're looking at these locations is where the talent is. If we're not able to find a suitable level of talent that already is in the area or wants to relocate to that area, then that can be a challenge too.

Virginia: *Does Sony still hire Americans in their offices outside of the United States, or do they primarily hire citizens of that country?*

Rob: It's a combination of both, and it varies by each location. In each remote office we've opened, we've had people from Culver City go in and help start that facility. The percentage of people that have been transplants from Culver City has varied by each location, but a very important part of setting up the office efficiently is making sure we have people—who already understand the pipeline, the culture, and the level of quality that we bring to our films—go and seed that office, and get as much of a seamless extension of the company we've already built here [in Culver City] as possible. And, of course, we hire local talent as available. That's a big part of the plan.

Virginia: *What are the industry trends you see continuing into the future?*

Rob: The trend that excites me the most is the process of making the tools more and more artist-friendly. It's really fun to see an artist take the tools that we've developed now over the last almost 15 years here at Imageworks and use them in unexpected ways to create pictures that are beyond what we expected to come out of that toolset. I think we're really seeing that happen more and more, as we get more talent in and we get more challenging requests from clients on our shows. That's a pretty fun experience to be involved in. It's an interesting mix, of course, getting to work in this industry, because we have the technical and the artistic side by side, and it's fun to see them spur each other on.

Virginia: *Rob, thank you very much for your time and such an informative interview.*

Chapter 20
Interview with Mohit Kallianpur, Look and Lighting Director, Walt Disney Animation Studios

VIRGINIA: *Hello Mohit, thanks very much for the interview. Would you tell the readers a bit about what first got you into the full CG animation industry?*

MOHIT: I originally came from a programming background. During my master's program in computer science, I started taking some computer graphics classes, and I was hooked. After graduation I wanted to work at a company where I could utilize my computer graphics background to its fullest, and the film industry was the perfect choice because that industry was pushing the envelope of computer graphics at the time. Initially, I was thinking of doing visual effects or live action, but then I realized that I loved [full CG] animation because nothing in the image is outside of your control. You create every pixel of the image. You're not bound to the physical realities of the world, either; you can stylize it as much as you want.

VIRGINIA: *Would you tell us a bit about your job at Disney?*

MOHIT: Most recently I was the Director of Look and Lighting on *Tangled* and the *Tangled* short. The Director of Look and Lighting works closely with the Director and Art Director to realize the artistic vision of the film. I also make sure that the technical aspects of the pipeline are working in order to achieve the desired look.

VIRGINIA: *What was it like being the Director of Look and Lighting for* Tangled?

MOHIT: Being Director for Look and Lighting was a lot of responsibility, but it was very satisfying to be involved with the look of the movie from the start of production all the way until the end.

VIRGINIA: *Would you explain the relationship between lighting and look development?*

MOHIT: The look and lighting department are very closely intertwined because both contribute equally to the look of the final image on the screen. On *Tangled* we had environment teams and character teams, and in each team we had representation from all the relevant departments. For example, on a character team we had a modeler, an animator, a look artist, and a lighter. We built our characters and environments holistically from front to back. Ultimately, what the look department produces needs to be easily consumable when lighting the shots, and it's important to establish that early on.

VIRGINIA: *Does Disney have different artists for look and lighting?*

MOHIT: For the most part we have different artists for the tasks. Some artists can do both, however; they start in look and move into lighting as the production progresses. We certainly encourage and try to accommodate as much cross-departmental training as possible.

Virginia: *What kind of challenges did you face while working on* Tangled?

Mohit: We were on a very tight schedule. The challenge was to make a beautiful movie with a very high artistic bar within the time restraints given. There was also the challenge of establishing the look that the Directors and Art Directors wanted, and then overseeing a large group of people to execute that vision in a short amount of time. Additionally, there were technical challenges developing the rendering and shading pipeline, because we wrote those from scratch on *Tangled*.

Virginia: *What new lighting and shading techniques did you develop for* Tangled?

Mohit: One of the biggest developments of the movie was with the hair. Rapunzel has about 70 feet of hair, and it was a challenge for simulation and especially for lighting and rendering. The hair is like a character in itself, because Rapunzel uses it so much and it's in every shot. We wanted to make sure the hair looked absolutely beautiful. The hair shader we had prior to *Tangled* didn't give us everything we needed, so we hired a research assistant who specialized in the rendering of hair, and we completely rewrote our shader to be more physically based.

Virginia: Tangled *had a wonderful look. What were some of the notable inspirations for its visual style?*

Mohit: I divide the visual style of the film into three different categories: shape, texture, and color. The shape language of the movie was inspired by Disney classics, especially *Cinderella* and *Pinocchio*. In *Cinderella* they used repeated shapes and curves to harmonize the images. We used similar shapes in our environments for the same reason. For example, the inside of a bell-shape curve is used quite often. We also wanted a world that was very charming and comfortable, a world that people are attracted to. The world of *Pinocchio* gave us much of that inspiration. The scale of architecture is smaller, the buildings no taller than two or three floors. Things are low to the ground and chunkier. We also researched European architecture and were inspired by that.

As for texture, we wanted a look that was more realistic than stylized. It's not photoreal, but the details are more believable. We wanted wood to look like wood and stone to look like stone. When you look at an element you know what it is made of.

With the color we again went back to the Disney classics. We used a lot of saturated colors and pushed saturation especially in the darks. Shadow areas tend to look grayish, and we didn't want anything to go gray, especially on the human characters. We pushed saturation either in the lights or in the shadows but never both equally at the same time.

Virginia: *What was the visual approach with the lighting?*

Mohit: The lighting was also more believable than photoreal. We had some sequences where we had very theatrical lighting. Lighting was used to enhance the mood and direct the viewer's eye to where we wanted it, but it was always more in a believable sense. We also often used complementary colors such as warm light with cool shadows, or cool light with warm shadows.

Virginia: *What things did you take away from this experience?*

Mohit: One of the big things is the need to be flexible and nimble. No matter what production plan we came up with, a million things could go wrong, and they often did. It's essential to understand there's a lot of things outside of your control, and you can always be hit with something you won't expect. You need to be ready—never be surprised by anything.

Virginia: *If someone wanted to do exactly what you do now, what advice would you give them?*

Mohit: I believe no matter what your background is, if you work hard and persevere you can achieve your goal. I came into this job from a circular route. I started out in software back on *Dinosaur*. I wanted to get closer to the art, to the final image on the screen, though, so when an opportunity arose to do some lighting on that film, I took it. I worked hard and continued on with lighting and look, eventually becoming the Director of Look and Lighting on *Tangled*.

Virginia: *What qualities are important for a lighting artist to have?*

Mohit: From the lighting side, we have people in our lighting department who come from a lot of different backgrounds, but the three main things they all have are a passion for what they do, a good eye, and the ability to work very well on a team. Those three things will take you far.

Virginia: *What kind of education would you recommend to someone looking to get into digital lighting?*

Mohit: Having a background in art helps. There are many schools out there that have great fine arts or graphic design programs. I don't concentrate on certain tools or certain processes as much, though, because those are things we can teach. It's hard to teach someone how to light well because that comes from having that good eye. The artistic sensibility in terms of color and composition is what we look for. That can come from school or from being a good painter or photographer.

Virginia: *What has been your favorite project?*

Mohit: My most favorite project to work on so far has been *Tangled*. It was a lot of hard work, but putting out a great product that was well received has been very satisfying.

Virginia: *What do you think are the most notable changes in the animation industry in the past several years?*

Mohit: Animation production has become more global. Every major studio has smaller studios set up all across the globe, and every developing country is creating animation. The bottom line, however, is that we still need great stories with compelling characters to be successful, so that has remained the same.

As far as look and lighting goes, technology has progressed and keeps progressing so that we are able to do more and more in real time. This affects our production pipeline. We used to have a very linear pipeline: You would model something, do layout, animate it, and then you would light the shot. Now we're able to incorporate real-time preliminary lighting well before the final rendering stage, allowing us to get feedback from directors about the camera and lighting much earlier in the process.

Virginia: *Thank you, Mohit, for taking the time for our interview. It's been a pleasure to hear about your experiences as the Director of Look and Lighting at Disney.*

Chapter 21

Interview with Andrew Whitehurst, Visual Effects Supervisor, Double Negative

VIRGINIA: *Hello, Andrew. Firstly, would you tell us a bit about yourself?*

ANDREW: I am a VFX supervisor at Double Negative. My education background is in fine arts and filmmaking. I started out doing commercials, kids' TV series, and bits of graphic design. I worked on an animated feature for a year, then I went to DNEG [Double Negative Visual Effects]. The first visual effects project feature I worked on was *Tomb Raider 2*. After that I wanted to work on *Troy* so I went to Framestore. There I also worked on *Charlie and the Chocolate Factory*. About six years ago, I went back to DNEG and I've been there ever since. I've done several shows there as a Sequence Lead, CG Supervisor, and now as a Visual Effects Supervisor.

VIRGINIA: *What comes to your mind as the biggest changes in the past three or so years in terms of digital lighting technique for visual effects?*

ANDREW: Fundamentally, the big shift is toward a ray traced–based solution. In addition to more ray tracing and ray-traced global illumination, I think that lighting has become more sophisticated than it was, say, four years ago. Previously, we were using ambient occlusion and some kind of environment light to do our diffuse illumination as well as the reflection. Now we're still using IBL, but we are probably painting out the brightest light sources in the IBL map and then re-creating those at the appropriate distance in the scene using area lights so that we're getting a more realistic light falloff.

Shading models have also become more physically plausible than in the past. Being physically plausibile is not just purely a rendering issue, it's also a conceptual shift in the way look development is approached. Look development artists need to have a greater understanding of the physical properties of actual materials, rather than basically making it up and judging things by eye, which is what everyone used to do.

VIRGINIA: *Do you think working with IBL is less creative than traditional lighting techniques?*

ANDREW: No, I think you get to focus your creativity on the more artistically interesting things. Say, for example, you've got a racecar and you want to add dirt to it. The fun creative bit is then choosing where you're going to paint in that dirt. The creative part is not trying to work up what the actual specular response of the paint is.

I certainly think that lighting using physically plausible models gets you a more photographic image much more quickly. Actually, you should be spending more of your time doing the creative bits, such as where to add a highlight or kicker, rather than spending your time fighting a whole load of cludges just trying to get something to match with the plate, which is what shading and lighting used to be. So while there's a greater requirement for technical and physical knowledge, I think that means people are liberated to spend more time doing the fun stuff.

VIRGINIA: *When using IBL, how much of the lighting generally comes from the map?*

ANDREW: That's going to depend on the shot and the sequence. If you're lighting something like an environment, then probably most, if not all, of it is going to come from an IBL. If you are lighting a character, on the other hand, your IBL environment is your general lighting setup, but then probably 80% of the lighter's time is spent making things more creatively or aesthetically interesting. You're going to do the same thing that the DP [Director of Photography] would do on set. I've never yet been on set and watched a DP line up a close-up and say, "Yeah, the lighting is fine." They are always going to add in a couple of lights on the fly just to model everything a little bit better.

VIRGINIA: *Do you use much in the way of deep shadows or depth-map shadows?*

ANDREW: Deep shadows are still useful for volumetric rendering. Shadowing hair, for example, would probably still use deep shadow maps because it's a lot faster than ray tracing it. So for things that have a volume, there's still a place for deep shadow maps. Depth-mapped shadows are no longer used so predominantly.

VIRGINIA: *Weta Digital used depth-mapped shadows in the making of* Avatar. *What are your thoughts on this?*

ANDREW: I haven't worked at Weta, but I imagine that because Weta generally works on shows of utterly epic scope, rendering that amount of geometry using a purely ray traced–based approach would be nigh on impossible at this time. To enable the creation of these "whole world" type shows, using a lot of point cloud–based rendering and shadow maps makes a lot of sense from a render-efficiency standpoint. They also, I think, have a very aesthetically-led approach to lighting, which really bears fruit on the kind of projects that they do, like *Avatar* or *Lord of the Rings*, which have a particular look. Certainly you get a greater amount of artistic control by doing that [using more depth-mapped shadows], but I think if you're rendering something like *Transformers 3*, which is extremely photographic, full of hard material surfaces, and very based in a real, recognizable world environment, then you start to see the dividends of using a more physically based ray-tracing approach. Different studios, depending on the work they do, will make the appropriate decision on what rendering to use.

VIRGINIA: *What kinds of light types do you predominantly use?*

ANDREW: I only use area lights now.

VIRGINIA: *Do you use area lights for something like sunlight as well?*

ANDREW: For the sun I would use something that looks like a directional light, but really is a very small and bright area light. For example, if you have a 2K [about 2,000 pixels wide] lat-long IBL map, then the size of the sun would cover about 15–20 pixels, which is enough to give you a slightly blurred shadow and a certain kind of falloff, even without taking into account what the atmosphere is doing to it, especially when it is low in the sky. Rather than using a directional light, I would advocate using something that's actually a very tiny area light. It would have the correct color temperature to match the sun and it would just work out what the right size would be from the angle you've chosen to have it at. As far as the artist is concerned, it looks and smells exactly like a directional light, but under the hood it would be a very, very small area light.

VIRGINIA: *Do you use cards mapped with HDR images placed throughout the scene?*

ANDREW: Yes, and that's still a textured area light. It's a good approach because the end result speaks for itself—you just get better pictures. The light falls off correctly and matches the photographed plate better, and artists get to a finished look much quicker using this approach. There's nothing that makes a TD happier than if they get a final in three versions rather than ten.

VIRGINIA: *What would you say is the role of three-point lighting in IBL?*

ANDREW: Once you've got your IBL working and everything is sitting in the plate nicely, then you can think about the roles of the three main lights in three-point lighting, and see whether you need to add any extra lights to help make your subject look the best that it can. So, for example, if you've got an IBL that's really quite dull—say it was photographed on a very cloudy day—you might look at your character and they look rather flat. You might think well, it might be a broad area light, but I'm going to add some kind of key light to model the shape of the character, which is exactly what a DP might do. Or you could look at it and think the character is not really standing out from this background, so you might add a rim light behind him.

It's not thinking that three-point lighting is the only technique to use, but rather thinking of the role of each light in the three-point lighting system, and considering if those aesthetic requirements are being fulfilled by the IBL lighting. If not, consider adding additional lights to help it along a bit.

Art college gave me more than anything else the ability to look at things and break them down. What is the role of each light? Where are they positioned to do that role, and what emotional effect do they have? Being able to take something apart is useful because then you've got the component bits to create new and different shots. It's learning to look at things, and it's something you never stop doing.

VIRGINIA: *What are your thoughts on where the industry is headed?*

ANDREW: I believe it's going to carry along the path we are currently on of more physically realistic lighting and shading, which means that artists are going to work more like a director of photography and less like a painter. Having artists really understanding how a director of photography lights something on a set is going to be a lot more important simply because the rules of how light and surfaces behave are the same whether you are working in the virtual world or the real world.

I also think that balance is shifting more between 2D and 3D. It used to be the 3D artist would do the best that they could and put out an awful lot of passes that the compositor would then hit with a very large hammer so that it would behave itself in the plate. That's no longer really the case. The raw output from 3D is going to be a lot better. The dividing line between what work is done in 2D and what work is being done in 3D is certainly starting to blur. More 3D artists will do their own compositing, because there's a lot less work that has to be done to it. And equally, many 2D artists will actually be doing shots that previously would have required the 3D department, due to the new 2D compositing tools out there. Because you've got that mixing of roles, actually you will end up with a lot of people who will just be visual effects artists, and they will do both sides.

VIRGINIA: *What kinds of skills would you say are essential for someone looking to get into the industry?*

ANDREW: In terms of being a good TD, the core personality traits are being a good problem solver and having a good eye. Anything else you can learn. You have simple problem solving, such as finding out from the logs why your render is failing, to more complicated problem solving, such as when you've got a shot that no one knows how to do and you've got to figure it out.

VIRGINIA: *What advice would you give to people looking to get into the field?*

ANDREW: I would say that you need to be able to work well with others, that you need to be able to demonstrate that you have a good eye, and that you need to be able to demonstate that you can solve problems. If you can do that, you'll have a career, but it's a surprisingly small number of people who can do it. One of the reasons I tend to be very reluctant to prescribe a particular educational route to anyone is because I think those skills are not dependent upon any particular educational path. You've got them or you don't. You can nurture them in many different educational establishments.

My question to someone who wants to get into the field is, why do you want to work in visual effects? For me, I like to make pretty pictures. That's what I like to do. It doesn't bother me greatly whether it's the most difficult problem that we've ever tried to solve. I get a huge kick out of sitting in a cinema and looking at something on a screen and thinking, "That's really beautiful," and that's what I get out of visual effects. People get different things. A lot of people think, "Hollywood is really glamorous," but it really isn't. You know this because you've done it. For me, it's sitting in a dark hole in the ground in Soho for 12 hours a day.

VIRGINIA: *I believe our last question answered this, but what got you into the industry?*

ANDREW: Pretty much precisely that [the previous answer]. Even though I always did fine arts, I was the kind of kid who would take a clock apart to see how it worked. I got my first computer when I was 12 and I learned how to program it, and I really liked programming. That's something else I would always say to students, especially the more artistic students who tend to get sniffy about programming. I think programming is just as creative as lighting a shot; it's a different kind of creativity. When you talk to FX artists, especially ones using something like Houdini, you get a bit more of an understanding of what a creative endeavor it is. Because I was someone who was always painting and drawing, I knew I wanted to go to art college, but I equally enjoyed programming. I liked knowing how things worked technically. I've always had that kind of mind; I like fixing things and building things. Visual effects was the perfect outlet for both of those interests.

VIRGINIA: *I agree. The work is a mix of art and technical.*

ANDREW: There's a spectrum. On one end you've got someone who's entirely an artist like a matte painter, and at the other end you've got someone who perhaps works in R&D [research and development] and is really literally just interested in coding and creating code. Most everyone else is somewhere on that spectrum. I'm probably 60% artistic and 40% nerdy. The exciting part is getting the mixtures of different personalities and different kinds of minds, and sticking them in a room together and seeing what happens. You do need to have that mixture in some proportion to really get the most out of it.

I don't personally make a distinction between art and programming. I see them both as creative, and I prefer to use the word "creative" rather than using the words "artistic" or "technical." I think it's a willingness to keep learning. Certainly when I started I had to learn, but I enjoyed learning and I'm still learning today.

Virginia: *Is there anything else you'd like to add that we haven't covered?*

Andrew: I find it incredibly useful to have a very good working knowledge of art history, film history, and photography partially because it means you have a database of images in your head that you can draw upon when you have a particular creative problem to solve and also because it's the same creative language that everyone on set is using. For example, when I was a CG Supervisor, during the first meeting I had with a director of a new project, he said he wanted to have the feeling of German Romanticism for his movie's visual style. I asked, "You mean something like Caspar David Friedrich? I know some of his paintings. Is there a particular one you had in mind?" He said, "Yes, there's one with a big graveyard that's painted with a gray ochre palette...." Because I held that knowledge and because of the director's background, we could have a meaningful artistic conversation about what he wanted in the film without any concept art or reference to hand.

If you have a working knowledge of art history, it means that terms you use and the feedback you are going to get from the client will make much more sense. You may be asked, "Can you make this lighting a bit more Caravaggio?" and you'll understand they want it really contrasty. Art students or visual effects students wonder, why should I sit through art history if it's really boring? It's actually practically really useful as well as making you a better artist. If you're 18 years old, you have to take it on trust from somebody who's older and thinks that they know better, which I do [chuckles].

Virginia: *Thanks so much for your time; it's been a great interview.*

Chapter 22

Technical Director Interviews with Michael Kennedy and Quentin Frost

VIRGINIA: *Hi, Michael and Quentin. Would you mind starting by telling a bit about yourself and how long you've been working in the industry?*

MICHAEL: I've been working in computer graphics for about 18 years now. I started out working in the game industry, building 3D models for various game applications, and progressed to doing a bit of research and development for motion capture, then a bit of work for games again, and then finally made the jump over to movies probably about nine years ago. I've been bouncing around, doing a bit of everything. I'm currently working for the PlayStation Group, Sony Computer Entertainment Group. We're working on lighting in game cinematics for the impending release of *Uncharted 3*. I'm supervising the lighting on characters.

QUENTIN: I've been working in the industry since 1995. I started at Boss Film Studios, a truly amazing effects house, under the leadership of Richard Edlund. I've had the honor to work at every major studio here in southern California, including Disney, DreamWorks, Sony Imageworks, Rhythm & Hues, and Digital Domain. I've also worked for places that no longer exist here, Cinesite chief among them. I'll be going back to Rhythm & Hues in two weeks as a lead on *The Life of Pi*.

VIRGINIA: *What kind of training and education did you have before entering the field?*

MICHAEL: I have an BFA in graphic design from the University of Tennessee, but that has limited application in 3D. The thought process I learned was more important. When I lived in Tennessee, I think there was one SGI [Silicon Graphics] machine in the city, and I figured out who was running it and begged to get some time on it. I am mostly self taught.

QUENTIN: I have a BA in telecommunications from Ball State University, though at the time we didn't have a graphics department. We did get a new building that had traditional television studio equipment. And, in my final year, they got a very limited digital suite comprised of six Cubicomp machines and one SGI station. I did have a strong art background coming into college, though I did not pursue it while there. I should probably mention I had two years of computer programming experience during undergraduate work at Purdue University prior to Ball State and had programmed very simple games at home for fun. Looking back, had there been an active gaming industry at the time, I might have gone in that direction.

VIRGINIA: *What got you into the computer animation and effects industry?*

MICHAEL: It was really more of a couple of friends of mine. We were always screwing around with computers; one of them happened to get access to a copy of Electric Image on the Macintosh. That was the first real piece of software I had to tinker with and learn rendering. I started spending a lot time with that. It really clicked, and I was good at it. After a while I managed to get a job applying what I'd learned.

Quentin: Indiana doesn't have much connection to the film industry, so most of the exposure I had to film was from the magazine *Cinefex*, which was a very rare magazine to find at the time. The model work I saw in the pages was really fascinating to me. After I saw the first Indiana Jones film, *Raiders of the Lost Ark*, I decided that I wanted to work in film and managed to procure an unpaid internship at a TV station out [in California] at Lorimar. That went nowhere, but it did get me out here. From there I went and worked at a post house on the Universal Studios lot, initially working nights to get in the door. They started a 3D department, and I bugged them until they allowed me to work in that department. In a way I fell into our profession. I wasn't particularly focused at the time, but I did like working with computers and I do like art, and those two things fell into place.

Virginia: *What advice would you give to people looking to get into the industry?*

Michael: It's really just a matter of determination. If it's something you really enjoy doing, I think there's always a way, but it's a very concerted effort and it takes quite a bit of time to learn everything. If you don't have a natural talent for it, and it doesn't flow for you, then it might not necessarily be the thing you should be doing. I think a lot of people that end up being quite good at it are people who have a natural talent. It is something that is more discovered as opposed to something that is learned.

Quentin: I would recommend that you need a very good reel. You need to know what's out there and you need to develop a reel because you're really going to be judged based off what you can show them. I'd also recommend that they network, that they try and find contacts through people they know. You need to get a hold of someone whom you can talk to, whom you can directly contact.

I would also recommend that they take advantage of their institutions like SCAD, because I know they have a deal here with Sony to get interns some exposure. You certainly want to take advantage of that if you have a program like that in your college. I also want to make a point to tell anyone reading this not to be shy about what you want from your college placement office.

Virginia: *What kind of studies would you recommend?*

Michael: Photography is really helpful, and the traditional arts—sculpture and painting and drawing—come in quite handy if you're focused on the creative aspects of it. If you're more of a technical person and more interested in what's going on under the hood, then obviously a bit of computer science and math would be very helpful, along with trigonometry and geometry as well. I've run into a lot of people that have very diverse backgrounds, people who are philosophy majors, people who are math majors, people who are painting majors do this sort of thing, too. I feel it's a mindset as opposed to something that's learned.

Quentin: Well, certainly they need to have a technical background in the software that is used, like Maya, Houdini, and possibly any major compositing package. People that know additional 3D software have a greater chance of getting in. It's useful to be able to do some scripting, as that tends to get you more noticed. I think our field as a whole has become more technical as time has gone by. Having said that, an art background is still paramount. You need to have a good eye for composition and for lighting. This is an artistic job.

Virginia: *What kinds of skills do you think an artist entering the field needs?*

Michael: Able to spend a long time sitting in one place staring at a computer monitor! [laughs] The common [traits] you see in these people is that they are really focused people, very inquisitive, very technical minded, and very creative at the same time. You're bridging the two worlds of art and technology, and having a fair balance between the two is rather important. You have to be naturally curious by nature and have a desire to dig into things to figure out how they work. Also, something inherent with this line of work is being able to deal with the delayed gratification. Sometimes it can take quite a long time to finish something. You really have to enjoy the process. Obviously, you want beautiful stuff at the end, but you have to enjoy the entire process of creating the image and not just the finished image.

Quentin: Be a good communicator and a great listener. Be willing to ask for help when you don't know something and be willing to accept that you will never know it all. Learn about time management and about prioritizing your notes. Don't take yourself too seriously and love what you do. Be open to new ideas and new ways of doing things, because every studio will do things differently, and you have to adapt to their specific needs. I also agree with everything Michael said.

Virginia: *Do you think it is better to be a specialist or generalist?*

Michael: Initially it's a good idea to get an overall idea of the entire toolset. Granted that's a lot of learning and it takes quite a lot of time. But it lays down the foundation for understanding the overall concepts, before you decide on what you're really drawn to. Ultimately, it depends what your goal is. If you want to work on really super high-end stuff, there's no way you can be really awesome at everything. So you would need to focus on one area to specialize in, and really hone your craft. But if you're wanting to do work that's a little bit smaller scale and you're more suited to being a generalist, that's also equally valid; it's just a different focus.

Quentin: I don't think you should try to be a specialist, with perhaps an exception if you decide to become an effects artist, or one dealing with cloth or hair. But since every studio is going to have their own pipeline and controls, you could become really good at one proprietary software, only to have to set that knowledge aside when you find yourself at another studio. It's better to have a strong grasp of the underlying concepts and keep yourself flexible. The odds are you will not remain at one studio for your entire career.

Virginia: *What is a typical day like for you, in terms of your tasks and the hours?*

Michael: Oh my gosh, you show up to work and you get a big cup of coffee and check your email. Honestly, it comes down to applying steady pressure to small problems. So depending on what task you're doing, it can be accomplished quickly, like in a matter of hours, and other times something can take several weeks, if not months, to complete. Your days are based on the problems you're addressing. For example, the stuff I'm working on right now, lighting for a video game, I've been doing 10 to 15 shots a day. But with film the same amount of work could take six months. Shorter film shots can happen in the space of a week or less. If you're doing much larger and more technically complex work, then the timeline gets much longer. As for the hours, you can plan on at least a nine-hour day. Right now I'm doing 12 hours a day and working some Saturdays. I haven't had to do Sundays in a while, thankfully.

QUENTIN: The average day tends to run like this: You get in by 8 a.m. or 9 a.m., check your renders from the night before, and put those renders that finished overnight into a presentable form, addressing what notes you can. You will have some sort of rounds or dailies in the morning when people will review your work. Afterwards, you take those notes back to your desk and prioritize what you want to do first, what you can finish quickly and what needs to be sent back to rendering on the farm. In the afternoon you may have another review with your visual effects supervisor or director [depending on the show and how much they're trying to get done], so you'll have a chance to make a few more corrections. After that you'll get more notes, and you'll prioritize what you're going to have running in the queue overnight. You'll want to get those jobs going before you go, and set your composites up so that when you come in the next morning, you can take what's finished off the queue and drop it in the composite and repeat the process. And that's pretty much how it goes. Expect your day to range from 8–10 hours during the early stages of a production to 10–12, plus 8 hours on Saturdays (and rarely, Sundays) during the final few months before delivery.

VIRGINIA: *What was your favorite production and why?*

MICHAEL: From a creative standpoint, I really enjoyed working at Disney on *Tangled*. I believe it was the 50th animated feature that was released through Disney, and I got a chance to see a lot more of the traditional style that Disney works in. We were using new digital tools, but we were emulating a much older style, and so I got a chance to learn a lot of very interesting things from some really talented people. So I enjoyed that one a lot. From a technical standpoint, *Avatar* was probably my favorite one just from the scope and scale of what was accomplished.

VIRGINIA [TO MICHAEL]: *What was the lighting process like on* Avatar *versus* Tangled*?*

MICHAEL: Technically speaking, the work that was being done on *Avatar* was a bit more advanced but the basic process was not too dissimilar. At Weta they used spherical harmonics to get some very subtle shading on *Avatar*, but they were also baking out point clouds of indirect illumination at Disney. From a technical standpoint, many of the processes are very similar; it's really the scale of things and how you're steering it from an art-direction standpoint.

QUENTIN: I have three answers to this. From a creative standpoint, I loved working on *Harry Potter and the Sorcerer's Stone* because I was able to help develop the look of the troll [under Mark Lambert] and help kick off a fantastic series of films. As a father, I was able to give my daughter a form of immortality by getting her into one of the television screens in *Polar Express*, and as a pure artist, working on *Tangled*. Our color palette on that film was just perfect, the story solid, and the directors a joy to work with. It's nice to be part of something bigger than yourself.

VIRGINIA: *How do you stay competitive?*

MICHAEL: You get a lot more connections if you work at a lot of different places because you know a lot more people; it becomes a little of who you know and who you've worked for in the past. Honestly, we all know a lot of different sorts of things, but you're never going to be able to know it all. It's really knowing how to work effectively and how to accomplish things in as timely a fashion as possible. After you've worked at a few different places, the tools are all pretty much the same, but buttons are in different places and they're labeled differently. You also have to keep up on what things are developing and what directions are being taken with what tools.

QUENTIN: At this point in my career, I know a lot of people in a lot of different places, and they know me; they've worked with me. Because I'm constantly moving from one company to another, I get exposed to new pipelines and new ideas, so I stay current. So for me, it's not a problem because I'm established. Studios are going to train you on their proprietary software, which also helps. Every studio is going to have a new way of doing something, but the core concepts haven't changed since you and I started in this business; they're still the same concepts.

VIRGINIA: *How do you think the industry has changed in the past several years?*

MICHAEL: There is much more money pressure on things now, trying to get things done in a shorter amount of time. I think a lot of corners are being cut, unfortunately. The amount of time you have on a shot is drastically less than what we were able to spend three or four years ago. As an artist this can be frustrating because I don't feel like I have the time to develop things as well as I used to be able to.

QUENTIN: There's more long-term freelance and fewer staff positions. We've gone from developing and maintaining a skilled stable of artists to having far less stability for the studios and the artists. Competition for the cheapest labor and bids has really made this business much more fragmented than it once was. The opportunities are still there, mind you, but the days of wine and roses, so to speak, are long gone. On a technical note, we can get a lot more done with a lot less hassle, which is the only way these productions still get done on time and budget.

VIRGINIA: *What about developments in technique?*

MICHAEL: Most recently we've been getting illumination from maps instead of a direct light source specifically, so it's getting more technical in that regard. That's more for visual effects films. Sony has really pushed hard in that direction, and many other studios are following this direction as well. In some visual effects films, 80% of the shot lighting is already done just by dropping in the map and turning it up. Other films like *Avatar* and *Tangled* are using more direct illumination to allow for more art direction. In cases like that, we use maps to set the base lighting level, the bottom 10% or 20% of illumination.

QUENTIN: As far as live action goes, like *Smurfs*, everything tends to be headed toward image-based or global illumination, driven by an HDRI map. I think it's already there for the most part. You get so much wonderful lighting for free. You're also already starting from the same place for continuity between shot to shot. It's a lot more technical to set it up, but it gets you 80% of the way there. On fully animated films, I don't see as much change in techniques. The use of deep shadows and point clouds were the last major change I can recall off the top of my head, and that's been a while now.

VIRGINIA: *What are the most important things you've learned professionally?*

MICHAEL: Learning how to get along with many types of people. Learning how to be mentally flexible and open to developments and changes of things. And how to pack light for an airplane.

VIRGINIA: *And how to keep your sense of humor!*

QUENTIN: To keep an open mind, be willing to learn new ways to do things, and to be able to communicate clearly. I've already said you need to accept that you'll never know everything.

Everyone has something they can teach you, if you listen. And be willing to laugh often. We work way too hard not to find joy in our work.

MICHAEL: One other thing, the industry is very small even though it's all over the world; your reputation and how you work are of paramount importance.

QUENTIN: I have to repeat what Michael just said. Protect your reputation and be professional. Everybody talks to everybody in our profession—it really is a small community.

VIRGINIA: *Is there anything else you'd like to add that I haven't asked about?*

MICHAEL: Speaking in general, I feel very lucky to have worked on what I have and have had the chance to work with a lot of different people. Granted there's a lot of time and energy to pour into what we do, but it's pretty amazing to have the opportunity to create the stuff we do. There's room for diversity; you can be whoever you want to be and people will give you the space to do that. As long as you can create beautiful stuff and get the job done, that's all that matters.

QUENTIN: What we do is something really special. Films have the ability to inspire, entertain, and change people's lives in ways that so few other creative outlets can. It's important to remember that when you're in the digital trenches late at night while people with 9-to-5 jobs are having social lives or bonding with their families. Everybody sees your end product, so take pride in your work and in your co-workers. I've been blessed to work with some very smart and creative people. I guess I want to stress that we sacrifice a lot in this line of work, so it's important to take as much from the experience as you can.

VIRGINIA: *That's all the questions I have today. You've given the reader a great idea of what the industry is like and how to succeed. Thanks so much!*

Index

G

gamma color correction, explained, 459

gamma curves, graph of, 459

Geri's Game, refraction in, 325–326

global illumination, 30–33
  advantages, 32, 372–373
  algorithms, 371
  in animation, 371
  caustics, 31, 369
  disadvantages, 32, 372–373
  explained, 370
  fill lights, 265–266
  final gather algorithm, 374–376
  indirect light, 369
  learning curve, 384
  path-traced, 380–381
  photon mapping, 377–380
  point-based, 382–384
  processing speed, 371
  radiosity algorithm, 374
  render time, 372–373
  shot continuity, 372
  terminology, 370
  tips, 385
  in VFX production, 371

glows
  accomplishing, 362
  adding, 362, 365
  bloom-type, 363–364
  explained, 362
  methods for, 365
  ray tracing, 363
  scanline rendering, 363
  tips, 365
  visual characteristics, 365

gobos
  shaping light with, 338–339
  using with fog lights, 359

The Godfather
  hiding and revealing elements, 100
  underexposed shots in, 204–205

"golden hour," 83, 86

Green Lantern, path-traced global illumination, 381

H

The Hair Is Braided, analogous palette in, 107

hard light
  area lights, 218
  characteristics, 215–217
  creating digitally, 218–219
  diffuse terminator, 223
  directional lights, 218
  directionality, 215, 223
  effect on shape and texture, 223
  light types, 223
  mood, 215, 223
  parallel rays, 217
  physical properties, 223
  point lights, 218
  radial rays, 217
  ray direction, 223
  real-world examples, 223
  shadows, 223
  shape and texture, 215
  versus soft light, 219, 223
  sources of, 217–219
  specular highlight, 223
  spotlights, 218
  uses, 223

Harry Potter and the Deathly Hallows, lighting, 103

Harry Potter and the Prisoner of Azkaban, atmospheric depth in, 139–140

HDR reflection maps, using, 409

HDRI (high dynamic range images), 208–210
  rendering, 209
  sources of, 209
  super-whites, 209

high dynamic range images (HDRI), 208–210
  rendering, 209
  sources of, 209
  super-whites, 209

histograms, viewing for luminance, 203–204

HSL color model, 241–244
  hue, 241–242
  lightness, 243
  saturation, 242

HSV color model, 241–244
  hue, 241–242
  saturation, 242
  value, 243

hue
  adjustment of eye to, 229–230
  defined, 241–242

I

IBL (image-based lighting)
  advantages, 403
  blurring environment maps, 406
  color-correcting maps, 406
  combining with traditional lighting, 405
  disadvantages, 404–405
  environment maps, 401
  evaluating live-action plate, 418
  explained, 400–401
  maps used in, 402
  three-point lighting in, 477
  uses of, 401
  visual effects productions, 403–404
  working with, 475–476

W

wavelength, measurement of, 227
weather
    clear days, 87
    considering for lighting, 86–88
    fog, 87
    mist, 87
    overcast days, 87
    rain, 88
    smog, 87
    snow, 88
Welles, Orson
    Citizen Kane, 136
    Touch of Evil, 165
white balance
    camera lens filters, 233
    gel colors, 233
    setting, 232–233
white light, explained, 228
Whitehurst, Andrew, 475–479

Z

z-depth passes
    as AOVs, 443
    explained, 443
    splitting out, 443
    tips, 445
    uses, 443
    using, 445